A RESPONSE TO
ENSLAVEMENT

Peter A. Roberts

A **RESPONSE** TO **ENSLAVEMENT**
Playing Their Way to Virtue

The University of the West Indies Press
Jamaica • Barbados • Trinidad and Tobago

The University of the West Indies Press
7A Gibraltar Hall Road, Mona
Kingston 7, Jamaica
www.uwipress.com

© 2018 Peter A. Roberts
All rights reserved. Published 2018

A catalogue record of this book is available
from the National Library of Jamaica.

ISBN: 978-976-640-657-8 (print)
978-976-640-658-5 (Kindle)
978-976-640-659-2 (ePub)

Cover illustration: Slavery abolished by Great Britain medallion, 1834. Courtesy of the New York Public Library.

Cover and book design by Robert Harris.

Set in Scala 10/14.2 x 27

The University of the West Indies Press has no responsibility for the persistence or accuracy of URLs for external or third-party Internet websites referred to in this publication and does not guarantee that any content on such websites is, or will remain, accurate or appropriate.

Printed in the United States of America.

Contents

List of Illustrations / vi

Acknowledgements / vii

Note on Terminology / ix

Introduction: Two Questions, the Imagery of Happiness and a Hope / 1

1. Framing the Relationship between Play, Happiness and Honour / 9
2. Interpretations That Enhance and Diminish Play / 31
3. The Question of an Indigenous Template of Festivity / 47
4. Whites Promoting Play in the Colonial Beehive / 74
5. From Africa to the Caribbean: Singing and Dancing Marionettes / 111
6. Playing in Life and Death / 147
7. Dancing in the Street: Parties, Parades, Sets and Masquerades / 178
8. "Dancing with Soul in It" / 224
9. Singing to Survive and Jive / 263
10. Various Faces of Virtue and Honour / 308

References / 355

Index / 375

Illustrations

1. Haitian slaves valiantly fighting the French at Crête-à-Pierrot / 2
2. The Middle Temple Macaroni / 76
3. West India custom (creolizing) / 82
4. A Congo dancer with a band of musicians / 114
5. "Dancing the slaves" on board ship / 118
6. *Cruelty and Oppression Abroad* / 141
7. *New West India Dance* / 143
8. *Slave Emancipation; or John Bull Gulled out of Twenty Millions* / 144
9. First day of Yam Custom / 154
10. The English dance of death / 165
11. The City Benin (King of Benin parade) / 189
12. Fiesta of Our Lady of the Rosary / 191
13. The batuca of Sao Paulo / 226
14. *Calinda: Danse des Nègres en Amérique* / 233
15. *Negro Figuranti* / 248
16. Contests and Plays of the Negroes / 260
17. *Wouski* / 304
18. *Trudge and Wowski* / 305
19. Slavery abolished by Great Britain medallion / 309
20. *Negro Slavery* / 310
21. Jamaica, no problem / 310

Acknowledgements

A number of librarians were helpful, especially in the campus libraries (Cave Hill, Mona and St Augustine) of the University of the West Indies.

I am also grateful for being allowed to use the main library of the University of Central Florida (Orlando) and the library of the University of South Florida (Tampa).

Note on Terminology

There are a number of words which have become contentious or offensive when used to refer to people for various reasons. It is therefore necessary to account for the use of some words in this work:

1. *indigenous person/inhabitant* is used to refer to the people who were living in the Americas before the advent of Europeans in 1492. *Indian* is not used in this book to refer to these people, except when it occurs in a citation. Other alternatives (for example, native American, First American, neo-American) are not favoured in this work.
2. *black* is used to refer to African-derived people, especially as a contrast to the term *white*, meaning European and European-derived people.
3. *negro* is used to capture the terminology of a specific era; it may or may not be capitalized according to the context.
4. *slave* is used when other alternatives are clumsy or would be semantically inaccurate. Note that *enslaved person* is semantically accurate only in reference to Africans, not to those who were born in the Americas (that is, creoles) as slaves.

Introduction
Two Questions, the Imagery of Happiness and a Hope

PLAY TODAY IS "BIG BUSINESS". IT BRINGS FAME AND FORTUNE, whether from major periodic activities like the Olympic Games and the World Cup or from annual activities like carnivals or from the everyday entertainment industry. Entertainment generates billions of dollars and provides a livelihood for millions of people across the world. In the Caribbean, entertainment, through tourism, has long replaced sugar and other raw materials as the mainstay of the economy in most countries. Two hundred years ago play was considered frivolous or marginal, not a proper way to earn a living; today that is no longer so – play is seen as virtuous. It is seen and promoted as a way to show off one's culture, to represent one's country, to prove oneself.

Historically, proving oneself was associated more with fighting than with playing, although both are fundamentally competitive human activities that are not always distinguishable. For example, puberty rituals in modern and traditional societies have blended the two. Yet when one's dignity, safety or life is at stake, fighting is seen as the honourable way to respond. In the case of a community of people or a society, when there is a reality or threat of extreme dominance, internally or externally, fighting or war is seen as the honourable way to defend oneself. Still, the question that invariably recurs in the face of threats to life, limb, liberty and dignity is: Is fighting the only virtuous way to respond to extreme dominance?

Though the Bible is contradictory on this matter, Western law and morals are guided by its two recommendations – an "eye for an eye" in the Old Testament (Leviticus 24:19–21) and "turning the other cheek" in the New Testament

Figure 1. Haitian slaves valiantly fighting the French at Crête-à-Pierrot, by Auguste Raffet. In M. de Norvins, *Histoire de Napoleon* (Brussels: Société typographique belge, Wahlen et compagnie, 1839), between pages 236 and 237.

(Matthew 5:38–40). The nineteenth-century Anglican ethic in Mrs Alexander's hymn "All Things Bright and Beautiful" is to be acquiescent, because the hierarchical order of things is ordained by God:

> The rich man in his castle,
> The poor man at his gate,
> God made them high and lowly,
> And ordered their estate.

Christopher Boehm, in his 1993 paper "Egalitarian Behavior and Reverse Dominance Hierarchy", identifies through a survey of societies across the world four "mechanisms" through which egalitarian behaviour is achieved – public opinion, criticism and ridicule, disobedience, and extreme sanctions (for example, assassination). In other words, the response to extreme dominance is to remove it.

This book presupposes a combination of Alexander's ethic and a weak form of Boehm's "mechanisms" as the response of the people in the Caribbean islands (excluding Haiti) to slavery, a response powered by play and visibly expressed in an image of happiness. The question it addresses is: Did that image of happiness indeed reflect happiness, and, if so, was such happiness without virtue, dishonourable and a mask for weakness in the face of extreme dominance or was it virtuous and honourable, providing a viable model to follow? Bear in mind that in the last quarter of the eighteenth century, whites in the thirteen North American colonies had fought for their honour, and enslaved blacks in Haiti had done the same, whereas neither whites nor enslaved blacks in the Caribbean islands (except for Haiti) fought steadfastly for theirs; they played instead.

In answering the latter question, this book has tried to distinguish, in the historical record, between genuine happiness and cultural assumptions. Then and now, writers have often gone beyond making straightforward assertions and resorted to familiar comparisons and metaphors to portray happiness. For example, in temperate cultures, happiness is often associated with ecology (that is, the brightness/colourfulness of nature) as well as with lively activities, dancing and singing being the main ones. However, metaphorical representation is not always universally applicable, for symbols can be contradictory and, as to dancing and singing, they are media for expressing all degrees and types of emotion, not just happiness.

The bluebird is recognized as a symbol of happiness in parts of the United States. That in those places a brightly coloured bird signals the return of spring and happiness implies that happiness is seasonal for people of temperate climates. A logical inference from this is that happiness is perpetual for people of tropical climates with colourful vegetation. Thus, European writers may well have been inclined to believe that people in the Caribbean would "naturally" be happy.

Another problem with the bluebird's association with happiness is that a "bright" colour does not always signal happiness. In English, the colour blue is used to represent sadness (as in "singing the blues") as well as extreme anger. Consequently, for the Caribbean context, one can reasonably reject the bluebird as a symbol and substitute the blackbird – the latter is more familiar to the Caribbean and more generally to areas where enslaved blacks were and the adjective "black" applies to both the bird and the people. The problem is that although black people have been associated with happiness, the colour black has never been.

Note, however, that the two birds were connected by the American singer Florence Mills in her signature song and biggest hit "I'm a Little Blackbird Looking for a Bluebird":

> Never had no happiness
> Never felt no-one's caress
> Just a lonesome bit of humanity,
> Born on a Friday I guess
> Blue as anyone can be
> Clouds are all I ever see
> If the sun forgets no one
> Why don't it shine for me
> *Chorus*
> I'm a little blackbird looking for a bluebird too
> You know little blackbirds get a little lonesome too and blue
> I've been all over from East to West
> In search of someone to feather my nest
> Why don't I find one the same as you do
> The answer must be that I am a hoo-doo
> (Clarke and Turk 1924, 2–4)

It is interesting how she plays on the meaning of the word "blue" when it applies to her and when it applies to the man she wants. It is clear that for Florence Mills the bluebird is a "sugar daddy" (probably a white man from the northeastern United States) who will make her happy.

Florence Mills was the daughter of former slaves, who was honoured by the island of Grenada by having her portrait put on a postage stamp to celebrate "the birth of the silver screen". In her day (1920s) she was called the "Queen of Happiness", and because of her untimely death at a young age she did not get to be the headliner, as she was slated to be, in the show *Blackbirds of 1928*. This Broadway show publicly established African American entertainers, principally singers, as blackbirds, probably seen as happy ones. Enslaved blacks in the Americas had previously been compared to songbirds by Paul Laurence Dunbar (1913) in 1899 in his poem "Sympathy", which influenced Maya Angelou's "Caged Bird" in 1983.

No doubt the most famous blackbird of all was the polymath Ziryab. Chapter 8 of John Gill's book *Andalucía* is titled "The Blackbird of Baghdad: Ali Ibn-Nafi and the Invention of Rock'n'Roll". Gill says:

> It is simply too irresistible . . . not to identify . . . Abu i-Hasan "Ali ibn-Nafi" (789–857) as perhaps the iconic intellectual figure of Islamic Córdoba. [He was] nicknamed Ziryab, blackbird in Arabic . . . *pajaro negro* (blackbird) in Spanish. . . . He was probably Persian Kurdish, although others argue he was a liberated African slave, which would lend itself to the legend that his nickname "Blackbird" came from the colour of his skin as much as his musical ability. . . . Ziryab turned Córdoba into a centre of musical excellence . . . Ziryab is credited with the invention of a school nowadays known as "Andalucían classical music", an African-based "early music" form. (2009, 81–82)

Ziryab, therefore, in spite of the mythical nature of much of the evidence, can be said, almost like a national epic figure, to have single-handedly established the blackbird as a symbol of virtuosity in the arts and especially in music in the medieval Islamic world.

Whereas, in discussions of happiness/sadness, there is now this familiar connection between blackbirds, birds "singing" and enslaved blacks and their descendants in the Americas, there is no such connection between birds flying, dancing and Africans and their descendants in the Americas. Other than the belief in the transmigration of souls back to Africa, which could be associated with flying, the only other well-known image of black people flying is modern – African American versions, including Bob Marley's reinterpretation, of Albert Brumley's song "I'll Fly Away" ("One bright morning when my work is over / Man will fly away home"). However, neither one of these specifically links flying to dancing.

There is today a "flying" image of the principal dancer of the American Ballet Theatre, African American Misty Copeland, deriving from her performance in Stravinsky's ballet *Firebird* in which she is pictured flying like a "firebird", which is also the title of her first book. The firebird, however, is a mythical feature of Russian culture and has little association with American or African cultures other than in the metaphorical sense of a distant, difficult, exotic goal to reach, which is partly expressed in the everyday phrase "flying high".

"Flying high" and "having your feet on the ground" are two mutually exclusive images of living life. Whether it is in relation to Caribbean people now or in the net of slavery two to three hundred years ago, observers have had the same views about which of the two modes is virtuous and should be followed. Usually, those who think that moving away from "having your feet on the ground" is embarking on a vacuous path are vociferous in their condemnation. It is only when "flying high" is validated, as in the case of Misty Copeland, that most people concede that dreams and aspirations should not be stymied with "logical" practicality. The chapter headings in this book refer to the era of slavery, but they are equally applicable to the Caribbean today as they systematically analyse the courage/cowardice and happiness/survival dilemmas provoked by play.

Colonial Caribbean societies were unusual in that they started as dependencies, with gender imbalances and with the majority of the populations being the property of or under the control of an ethnic minority. The fundamental problem in accurately visualizing the early colonies is that one has to interpret virtually everything through the words and images of the ethnic minority. At a time when there was a dearth of information but where new accounts sought to be comprehensive, cursory remarks in earlier accounts were often repeated with modifications or amplification to make them seem current. Also, there is no way of verifying the prominence or lack of prominence of any cultural characteristic – it could have been factual or illusory. There was no objectivity either in what caught the attention of one eyewitness as opposed to another or in what the person chose to write down, and there is no way of recovering omissions.

Primary or eyewitness writers had to find words to describe items that were unfamiliar to them. Even if they managed to discover the local word for an item, that in itself did not provide an explanation or picture of the item for the reader. They then resorted to comparisons with things presumed to be familiar to the reader and/or to define by explanation of structure, construction, function, use or by reference to authority. To complicate matters, historians, who sometimes depended on word-of-mouth reports, converted such items into their own image of them. This practice is apparent when early European illustrations of people and things unfamiliar to them at the time are compared with reality. "Borrowings" and omissions from the works of predecessors as well as translations across languages complicated matters even further.

The value given to eyewitness accounts as opposed to third-party accounts was not always of great importance to publishers, although there were differences between writers according to their training and intent. Moreover, the historical movement from ignorance to knowledge was not uniform across European countries or writers. There was violent disagreement among eyewitnesses from the very beginning, as was the case when Bartolomé de las Casas said of his Spanish compatriot Fernández de Oviedo: "Oviedo can say nothing big or small because he was not capable either of seeing or understanding" (2011, 29).¹ Las Casas was of the view that understanding a people required being able to converse with them in their language, and this Oviedo could not do.

The French writers were mostly missionary-type priests who became immersed in the local culture. However, even among the French writers, competitiveness led to harsh words, as was the case when Labat summarily dismissed De Rochefort's work, saying: "Minister Rochefort, who never saw the islands of America except through the eyes of others . . . since he copied Father Du Tertre, but he completely spoilt his narrative by descriptions totally removed from the truth, in attempting to make things more pleasant and to hide his thievery" (Labat 1722, 1:xi–xii).

In the case of the British, those who were writing were mostly secular plantation types or people connected to the political and military administration of the colony or casual visitors who did not stay long enough to acquire a penetrating knowledge of the colonial culture. Some of these, like Trelawney Wentworth and James Phillippo, could be charged with the same "crimes" as Oviedo and De Rochefort in that they, without acknowledging it, included in their accounts with modifications and embellishments information that they copied from earlier writers.

In his introduction to the writings of Jean Barbot on West Africa, Paul Hair says: "The attractiveness of Barbot's printed account . . . has in no small part lain in its illustrations" (Hair, Jones and Law 1992, 1:xlvi). He goes on: "As he [Barbot] put it . . . : 'my pencil has made some amends for the defects of my pen'" (1:li). However, since historical and social accounts were not dominated by illustrations, paradoxically, the few illustrations assumed greater importance as representations of reality and because they had memory value. Visions of colonial life were complemented by the works of those who drew or painted and produced their own versions of reality according to their political or religious intent or the likes and dislikes of patrons.

African slavery was the economic foundation upon which twentieth-century Europe was built and attempts to dismantle it were met with fiery opposition from many quarters, including several in Britain. Satire and caricature were used to bolster arguments on both sides and they became increasingly strident as the realization of the costs of dismantling slavery became more apparent. However, the problem with eighteenth- and nineteenth-century British visual

---

1. Unless otherwise indicated, all translations are by the author.

satire dealing with slavery was that it increased the skewed images of life in the colonies and especially the image of the enslaved. Consider, in contrast, Auguste Raffet's visual presentation of the battle at Crête-à-Pierrot during the Haitian Revolution (see figure 1). Even though Raffet was a nationalistic Frenchman, his portrayal did not show a simplistic ridicule of black effort, for he foregrounds the Haitian soldiers as they overpower the French forces. It is by reproducing and commenting on such historical visual images that this book demonstrates the ways in which visual artists were like soldiers on one side or another of a cause.

In today's world, with the universal availability of the Internet and the explosion of social media, there are limitless possibilities of skewing visions of different people, practices and beliefs in the pursuit of power. Practices and beliefs are being given diametrically opposed valuations within and across cultures with the emphasis on converting souls to one's point of view, whether that be political, racial, religious or moral, by constructing attractive arguments. The struggle between honour (warrior) and happiness (non-warrior) will intensify because migration from former colonies or poor countries to First World countries will increase. Yet the same Internet and social media, by facilitating fluidity, creativity, interchange and transfer of a variety of ideas across the world among peers, will eventually break down negative territoriality at all levels in all countries. "Outside the box" music, dance and artistic entertainment generally will play an even greater role in facilitating the pursuit of happiness across the world than today and historically, especially in the lives of young people. Hopefully, in spite of the duplicity of imagery, the study of older colonial situations will help to lessen the problems of contemporary "colonisation in reverse" (Bennett 1966, 179–80).

1. Framing the Relationship between Play, Happiness and Honour

> In no country in the world are there stronger or more unequivocal indications of happiness and enjoyment than in the West Indies. Their song is the song of joy; their dance is the dance of hilarity and delight. All they wish for, all that they can enjoy, is in their actual possession.
> —Resident 1828, 234

IN THE EPIGRAPH ABOVE, THE WRITER LINKS happiness and enjoyment to song and dance, which, as he indirectly points out, are available to all human beings. If one moves beyond the writer's primary objective (to argue that since their happiness is complete, these slaves in the West Indies lack nothing), it is clear that in the writer's mind the "song of joy" and the "dance of hilarity and delight" were unique in these people. It is easy now to dismiss this anonymous writer's image of enslaved Africans as a political posture driven by the need to justify injustice, but the fact is that the same idea was elaborated sixty years later (that is, after emancipation) by the (in)famous James Froude (1888, 43–44), who became the Regius Professor of History at Oxford University:

> In no part of the globe is there any peasantry whose every want is so completely satisfied as her Majesty's black subjects in these West Indian islands. They have no aspirations to make them restless. They have no guilt upon their consciences. They have no food for the picking up. Clothes they need not, and lodging in such a climate need not be elaborate. They have perfect liberty, and are safe from dangers, to which if left to themselves they would be exposed. . . . In their own country they would have remained slaves to more warlike races. In the West Indies their fathers underwent a bondage of a century or two, lighter at its worst than the easiest form of it in Africa; their descendants in return have nothing now to do save to laugh and sing and enjoy existence. Their quarrels, if they have any, begin

and end in words. If happiness is the be all and end all of life, and those who have most of it have most completely attained the object of their being, the "nigger" who now basks among the ruins of the West Indian plantations is the supremest specimen of present humanity.

Even if one were to remove all the racism from these statements, the fact remains that both writers were singling out West Indians as extraordinary on the basis of their experience. One therefore has to account for this "positive" image of West Indians by asking not what caused these writers to come to this conclusion but, more importantly, what was the real significance of their assertion. Is it that they were really implying that perfect happiness, touted as the most positive human state, was actually only for simpletons and carefree people and that more important and serious people pursued greater goals?

If we take the answer to the question to be "yes", then it means that for these writers the world was essentially hierarchical and closed, with rulers and subjects who respectively operated by different philosophies. In that world, happiness was a vague, changeable state open to all, whereas honour was noble, long-lasting, measurable and achieved only by the superior. In that world, race was integrally worked into the construction of social hierarchy to guarantee caste-like social systems. Accordingly, in the Americas, African slavery was justified on the basis of "natural" dominance of white over black and Africans were seen as having ignoble codes and philosophies.

Not even emancipation could alter this construction. Evidence of this is simply but ironically made clear in J.W. Orderson's 1832 play, *The Fair Barbadian and Faithful Black*. In the last scene of the play, Judge Errington tells his "confidential black servant" Hampshire, as he gives him his freedom: "no society can exist without subordination". The judge also says to Hampshire: "And now, Hampshire, that you are free, by the liberal spirit of our laws you are possessed of all the rights and privileges of a British subject, equally with myself." Hampshire's response to this is especially poignant and ironic (not that this is what Orderson intended): "(With amazement, examining his hands and opening his bosom.) 'Hey! – I like you? Massa, you making you fun! – I tan [am] like you? Ha, ha!'" (1835, 34). Clearly there was no social equality and never would be between freed servant and former master and they both knew that. The social codes and philosophies that ruled their lives would continue as before.

In that colonial world of rulers and subjects, the guiding illusion for the judge/planter was honour. The importance of honour in the European mind is exemplified in the famous act 3, scene 2 of Shakespeare's *Julius Caesar* in which the word "honour/able" occurs fifteen times. The importance of honour is still proclaimed generally today even though, as Roberto Unger (2014, 44) points out, "this heroic and martial ethic was associated with a particular class or caste – the rulers or fighters". On the other hand, the guiding illusion for those formerly enslaved was happiness and, in the case of the Caribbean, the quest for happiness has been strenuously pursued in play.

Though today, no extreme "happy" statements are being used to characterize people in the Caribbean, there is no question that the small island states of the Caribbean are a special zone of achievement in music, dance, sport and literature – they have produced world-class performers far out of relation to their small size (for example, Bob Marley, Rihanna, Usain Bolt and Nobel laureate Derek Walcott). So, one may argue that there is a connection between the extreme nineteenth-century assertions of happiness and intellectual and behavioural goals in the Caribbean today, and that by looking at the early colonial history of this special, small geographical zone, one can better explain the relationship between play, the image of happiness and honour.

Notwithstanding the absence today of extreme "happy" statements about Caribbean people, in various parts of the world, the Caribbean, like Hawaii, spontaneously conjures up images of fun, pleasure and relaxation because it is made up of tropical islands. But beyond this tourist imagery of islands, there is also the case that the Caribbean expands far beyond its shores, for its music, dancing and performances have been spread to affect people worldwide.

During the twentieth century, the bigger, Spanish-speaking islands especially became famous internationally for music and dance – Cuba for the rumba, the Dominican Republic for the meringue and Puerto Rico for the salsa.[1] The French and French-influenced islands also gave the world the béguine, and even more recently zouk and kadans became popular in parts of Europe. The music of the English-speaking Caribbean became popular internationally from about the middle of the twentieth century and has remained so into the twenty-first century. Today, calypso and reggae music[2] immediately call to mind the West Indies generally, and the limbo dance has been a happy experience of many tourists

---

1. There is an ongoing debate as to whether salsa is Puerto Rican, Cuban or trans-Caribbean.

2. The terms "calypso" and "reggae" are meant to include predecessors and/or derivatives in each case.

over the years. The academic norm has been to study suffering (which is often associated with honour) rather than happiness, but today, when no one is exempt from the threat of unpredictable violence, it is imperative to examine images of happiness to see what models of living they provide and for whom.

Even a cursory analysis of calypso and reggae music will show that they were not simply tourism products; they are rooted in the history of the islands. In the case of calypso music, it was the time of the Second World War and the agency of US servicemen that were initially important in the spread of the music. Subsequently, it was the migration of West Indians to some of the major cities of the world that led to the international popularization of Jamaican music and dance. Added to the social and political factors that account for its spread, the music in itself captivated many other people of different cultures across Europe, Africa and Asia.

Caribbean music is rooted in the New World experience and is fed from different sources, a major one being carnival. Though carnival established itself initially as a Christian festival in Europe, its most prominent manifestations today are in the Americas – Brazil, Colombia, New Orleans and Trinidad – and they all prominently feature the African-derived part of the population in each case. Remarkably enough also, migrants from the English-speaking Caribbean islands are responsible for the transfer and development of huge "carnival" celebrations in New York, Toronto, London and other major international cities. These carnival celebrations have spread with migration because for many migrants, "playing mas" is psychologically indispensable and represents for them, whether at home or abroad, an annual renewal of the spark of life.

Two significant, summary statements on the development and widespread influence of Caribbean music complement this introduction – one straightforward and prosaic, by Kenneth Bilby (1985, 181–82) and the other steeped in poetic imagery, by Édouard Glissant (1990, 275–76):

> During this [twentieth] century . . . the Caribbean region has become a major exporter of culture. The material products exported in previous centuries have more recently been joined by a succession of musical forms, born and bred in the Caribbean. Not only Europe, but much of the rest of the world as well, has developed a steadily growing appetite for the indigenous musical creations of Caribbean peoples. This process has unfolded gradually, one wave of musical exportation following another, and practically every major linguistic sub-region of the Caribbean (hispanophone, francophone, and anglophone) has been rep-

resented. Afro-Cuban and Dominican music, Haitian meringue, and Trinidad calypso have all had international success. More recently, Jamaican reggae has had the widest, and perhaps the most significant, impact of any Caribbean form to date.

Night in the cabins gave birth to this other enormous silence from which music, inescapable, a murmur at first, finally burst out into this long shout – a music of reserved spirituality through which the body suddenly expresses itself. Monotonous chants, syncopated, broken by prohibitions, set free by the entire thrust of bodies, produced their language from one end of this world to the other. These musical expressions born of silence: Negro spirituals and blues, persisting in towns and growing cities; jazz, *biguines*, and calypsos, bursting into barrios and shantytowns; salsas and reggaes, assembled everything blunt and direct, painfully stifled, and patiently differed into this varied speech. This was the cry of the Plantation, transfigured into the speech of the world.

This book represents a contrast to, not a contradiction of, the customary treatments of the emergence of Caribbean festivity, treatments that usually feature the pain and struggle of the people, as in Glissant above. In this book, the emergence of Caribbean festivity with its image of happiness is used as a test case for the role of play in situations of extreme dominance.

Several national epics or founding myths have some combination of a sojourn, a journey and battles to overcome foes as the necessary experience for the birth of a nation. Two classic examples are *The Aeneid*, which tells of the founding of Rome and thus the Roman Empire, and the books of Genesis and Exodus in the Bible, which tell of the birth of the nation of Israel. National epics are celebratory and are used to bolster national pride and identity. For African descendants across the Americas there is no national epic, principally because, except for the Empire of Haiti (1804), there has been no African/black nation that could be said to have come into being in the Americas. Nevertheless, there is no shortage of works celebrating the struggles and deeds of African Americans. In national epics, there is some characteristic in the emergence of the people that is seen to identify them and this is also the case for African Americans. This book sees play as such a characteristic.

This book is an exploration of the experience of enslaved people, considered lowest on the human scale, to see how they were able to rise above their subjection and to project an image of well-being and happiness without material wealth, armaments, scientific technology or anything external to themselves.

This is a case in which dispossession and brusque removal of sub-Saharan Africans from their homes did not allow them to take their material accompaniments of music, dance and other implements of festivity to their new homes across the Atlantic. Also, because there was an enforced shift from native language to colonial language and because a considerable percentage of captives were young and not fully experienced in their own cultures, they had no complete store of ancestral material to call upon. In our analysis of the role of play and the development of the image of happiness, we show the resources human minds invoked, imagined and fashioned, in the face of various limitations, deprivations and negative beliefs, in a situation which initially was one of exile in a new, though not adverse, environment.

The Acquiescent Slave

Robert Morris (1984, 39–40), in a paper given on the occasion of the one hundred and fiftieth anniversary of emancipation in the British West Indies, posed what seems to be a simple question: "Why did the black slaves, over the extended period of slavery, remain in a position of economic, political and social dependence on the whites who were a numerical minority?" He then uses the words of Karl Watson (1979, 92–93), supported by those of Monica Schuler to answer the question: "In giving a general assessment of the reaction of enslaved people in Barbados to their situations, one must note the functional importance of compliance. It was on the basis of acceptance of the status quo that the system functioned. 'The whole slave system began as a coercive one, but developed into a system of consent.'"[3] Morris complements his view of the compliance of the slaves with the words, "it would appear to me that the unspectacular, uneasily chronicled reality of day-to-day work on the plantation by thousands of slaves, patiently learning the masters' language, forming family relations, tilling the soil, studying the masters' foibles and weaknesses, were as much preparation for freedom, as actual open rebellion or resistance, the impact of which was likely to be, especially within the context of the time, costly and ephemeral" (1984, 37).

---

3. The inserted citation is from a University of the West Indies seminar paper, "Slave Resistance and Rebellion in the Caribbean during the Eighteenth Century", by Monica Schuler.

Acquiescence was not glorious, but the fact is that it was the reality for the majority of enslaved persons in the British West Indies. It is only in French Saint Domingue that slavery was removed by the enslaved against the wishes of their rulers.

Extreme dominance in the form of slavery has been a part of human societies all over the world from time immemorial. The Old Testament of the Christian Bible gives guidance on slavery and trading in slaves in the book of Leviticus (25:44–46). It is only probably from the twentieth century that slavery has been seen across the world as contrary to natural justice and as something to be removed.

Some geographical situations in the Americas facilitated escape from slavery in the form of maroonage, but many did not, especially those in the smaller Caribbean islands. Moreover, escaping from slavery was not just a matter of getting away from or removing the slave master, but escaping from the slave society and all the neighbouring ones. In Jamaica, where maroons fought to maintain their independence, they agreed not to help enslaved Africans to escape from the English colony in Jamaica. Even in the case of Haiti, though those enslaved won their freedom internally, they were confronted externally by a cordon of white enemies who were bent on suffocating them.

But it is not only the widespread existence of extreme dominance that explains enslaved Africans accepting enslavement, but also the dangers of trying to escape. The many and varied forms of punishment used were illustrated in broadsides and identified in evidence presented to the British Parliament by abolitionists in the 1790s, and other methods of punishment were also illustrated in Bridgens (1837), for example. One broadside (figure 8, 1793) shows "a slave at work cruelly accoutered – with a head frame and mouth piece to prevent his eating – with boots and spurs round his legs, and a half hundred weight chained to his body to prevent his absconding". This iconic image of punishment is powerful evidence showing why acquiescence was general.

Yet it was not physically menacing deterrents principally that caused the enslaved to carry out their daily work; it was the system of rivalry and reward that bolstered the hierarchical structure of slavery. The divide-and-rule policy was strengthened by the fostering of animosities and competitiveness that worked both ways (rebellion and acquiescence), but maintaining ascendancy over social inferiors was a powerful spur for preservation of the status quo. Some plots to revolt were revealed by those who favoured their own position (for example, house slaves) in the social hierarchy and some rebellions were not fully supported. One of the factors that precipitated the revolution in Saint Domingue was the attempt on the part of the administration to reduce people of colour to the level of common slaves by preventing them from wearing clothes like whites and behaving like whites. If they had been allowed to, probably the status quo would have prevailed.

The basic divisions of the enslaved part of the population were house slaves, tradesmen and field slaves, with the latter separated into gangs at different levels of achievement. Attempts were made daily in all these divisions to win the favour of the master or mistress to improve occupational status or gain privilege – promotion to head of group, promotion to a higher group, making a sex case to get special consideration or be relieved of some chore. In his comments on the slave plantation, Orlando Patterson ([1967] 1973, 65) argues that assignment of status to slaves had little to do with the qualities of the slaves themselves, but "was merely a reflection of the attitudes and estimation of the masters". Patterson gives the following interpretation of what he calls "the personality structure of the slave", based principally on the many comments made by white observers: "Quashee may be said to have existed on three levels. First, as a stereotyped conception held by whites of their slaves; secondly, as a response on the part of the slave to this stereotype; and thirdly, as a psychological function of the real life situation of the slave. All three levels of Quashee's existence were closely related and mutually reinforced each other" (178).

This interplay of levels shows the extent to which the enslaved person was a player/actor as well as a product of play. One can also use this interpretation to characterize the image of happiness the enslaved person portrayed. It is obvious that one could pick out some of their experiences and label them as happy while identifying others as not. That, however, is not going to resolve the fairly normal "happy" appearance of the enslaved, which could have been masking pain and suffering or expressing genuine happiness. The mysterious expression that is a characteristic of the Mona Lisa (slightly smiling lips plus sad eyes) has made it intriguing and famous; probably the slaves' image of happiness can be thought of in the same way.

Another factor that contributed to and reflected the acquiescence of enslaved Africans was naming. In the television series *Roots*, renaming of Africans was dramatized as a contentious issue (that is, the name change from Kunta Kinte to Toby), but generally the naming of slaves was not, and in the case of creole babies, it was routine for the master to see and name his new property. While in many cases there was nothing remarkable about the names beyond the fact that they stamped the person as a slave, in other cases accounts highlighted the comic contrast between the grand name given and the lowly person so named, as in the following:

> The names given to the Negroes are the prettiest you can imagine. All the histories and romances, ancient and modern, have been ransacked for names; and I do not think there is a name in Shakespeare's, or any body else's plays, that does not belong to a Negro: some are very *a propos*, others not at all so. I have seen the haughty Cleopatra descend to wash dishes, and the mighty thunderer of Olympus rubbing down horses. There are Romeos the fathers of Juliets, and Juliets the mothers of Romeos. Augustus Caesar cleans shoes, and works at a pestle and mortar; and old Adonis is an excellent hand at making up medicines of all kinds. The chaste Lucretia has lost so much of her Roman virtue, that Tarquin, or any one else is welcome to her. Othello is a waiter at a tavern, and Hamlet – (what a falling off was there!) – was whipped through the town lately for robbing a henroost. (Anon. Irish 1776, 43–44)

Slave masters gave their slaves famous European names in order to remove Africanness from them, but they chose names that were different from the normal ones of their own children to maintain the distinction between white and black. In these cases, whether or not the slaves were aware of the apparent incongruity of their famous European names, they became the subject of fun for visitors. The names thus diminished them further psychologically and magnified their image as comic characters.

There are two other constituents of the slave's personality structure that need to be mentioned explicitly – the curse of blackness and slavery, and the benefits of prison. The curse of blackness and slavery is often referred to as "the curse of Ham" and David Goldenberg, in his book of the same name, explains how, in spite of the fact that there is no such curse in the Bible, it might have come into being (2003, 169–70). Goldenberg also points out that 'the curse of Ham' is not restricted to Judaeo-Christian contexts but is also "very widespread in Islamic sources" (170). Since "the curse of Ham" is prominent in the Christian tradition and since enslaved people in the Americas came to be a part of that tradition, they themselves came to be besieged by this "curse" and to accept it to some extent as part of the "divine mandate". Together with the colour hierarchy (white on top and black at the bottom), which came to be a part of it, it was difficult for some slaves not to accept the nadir position of humanity.

The "benefits" of prison life are that prisoners get food, clothing and shelter without having to worry about where they are coming from. Slaves were seen to be in the same position, but to have the additional advantage that they were totally in control of their free time during which they could sing, dance and enjoy themselves to their heart's content. What better life could one hope for. Although it is unlikely that any slave would have preferred these "benefits" to freedom, some slaves may have wondered how they would make a living and survive, if free, and whether they could have had a truly independent life, free of the abuses and dominance of whites. These considerations could have led them to question the advantages of freedom in their context, just as many in the small states of the Caribbean during the 1950s and 1960s had doubts about the advantages of political independence. It is this questioning of self that would have made for a more cautious slave, tending more towards acquiescence.

The slave's personality was also shaped by self-preservation strategies forged from the experiences of everyday life which contrast with that of Tony, a ringleader in a failed rebellion in Barbados in 1675. His uncompromising stance even after capture caused his white captors to say: "We shall see you fry bravely by and by. To this taunt Tony, with bravado, replies: If you roast me today, you cannot roast me tomorrow" (*Great Newes* 1676). Tony is burned alive in front of his peers and so dies honourably, but dies. So, slaves would have asked themselves: What was the worth of such bravado/honour? Dying honourably meant that Tony was in the morally superior position, but after several failed revolts, the slaves surely realized that a less confrontational strategy was needed for them to survive and thrive.

Creation of an Enhanced Alternative Reality

The thesis of this book is that the enslaved created an enhanced alternative reality for themselves in circumstances of cognitive deprivation. They were excluded from using their brains, as normal human beings do, to make a living and nurture a family. Moreover, across the entire slave population, perhaps the majority suffered from inadequate sleep and chronic stress, and almost all children were illiterate, had a poor learning environment and no formal schooling. The cumulative effect of these factors on the slaves would have had to be extremely significant, for there seems to be general agreement on the following:

- All areas of the brain should work for its full development
- Adequate sleep allows the brain to reorganize and restore itself.
- Chronic stress affects learning and memory.
- Literacy facilitates cognitive development.
- Early cognitive development is aided by a rich learning environment.
- Formal schooling seems to help verbal logical reasoning (for example, deduction) and abstract reasoning.

Furthermore, while it is difficult to assess the effect of physical abuse (for example, constant corporal punishment) and exposure to trauma on the young children and their early addition to the workforce, it is quite clear that these too could have affected their cognitive development. Factors such as warmth, stimulation and family cohesion are even more difficult to assess, but it is also clear that in the case of the children these would have been far less than optimal. All these negative factors could have led to a compensatory right-brain dominance in the slaves.

The idea of an alternative reality is, as will be seen, the function of play, but in normal circumstances it is usually thought of as subordinate or marginal. Play is given a central role in human evolution by many scholars. In the case of the slaves in the Caribbean, a number of factors contributed to the creation of an enhanced alternative reality. The expression of some forms of play is associated with youth more so than maturity and old age, and most of the Africans brought to the Caribbean were teenagers or just a little older. The tendency to physical play was therefore typical and strong among them. Second, play is what the enslaved were allowed to do by their owners, with only occasional repression. Third, play is what they could make most use of for their own aesthetic and spiritual development partly because they could utilize the memories of their traditional culture in developing play in the Caribbean.

Furthermore, in a world in which slavery was not an unfamiliar reality and in a situation in which whites dispensed favours to suit their own interests, play provided the impetus to keep the slaves together and moving forward with comparatively little destructive violence to themselves and their masters. This operated because there was a certain balance (ratio) between whites, browns/coloureds, creole slaves and African slaves in the population. The ratio between whites and slaves was established by law from the early years, though it was gradually disregarded in favour of increasing the number of slaves to maximize profits. The fundamental problem in Haiti was that the administration lost control of the colony by creating (through greed) an untenable ratio between Africans, who were not born into slavery; creole slaves, who might have been easier to control; a relatively big number of aspiring coloureds; and a small number of intransigeant whites over a relatively big island with regional differences and a mother country in the throes of enlightenment. No other colony, not even Jamaica, provided this combination of factors to give a general slave rebellion a realistic hope of succeeding. As a result, slaves generally opted for acquiescence and play. So, play must be seen as an option that flourishes when the dominated do not perceive a good opportunity for complete reversal. When whites in the colonies consistently said that the slaves looked happy, it was because they had chosen the option of play.

In the early days of slavery in the Americas, the slaves pursued their own varieties of play, but as they got caught up in the hierarchical value system of slavery, the masters' varieties (the rituals, dress and celebrations of European religions, military exercises, mummery and sports) became more significant. As part of this "entrapment", the desire to best the master at his own games became entrenched in their psyche, gradually dispelling the notion that play was non-serious or frivolous. The strong inclination to best the master is best exemplified by the superlative importance West Indians attached to the game of cricket in the second half of the twentieth century, at a time when most of the islands were moving to political independence. The game of cricket could be rivalled only by carnival, another creature of Europe, which has now surpassed cricket in importance.

The term *play* has featured in several philosophical and cultural studies and here requires some explanation. *Play* is the creation of the non-real, essentially as fun/pleasure. Of course, participants may differ about the fun in the activity, but in many cases there is general agreement. The activity in itself cannot be defined as play: it is how the participant perceives the activity that is the defining factor. Play is not restricted to humans.

Play is essentially fun/pleasure (an element of happiness) and can be experienced through dance and music, among other things. Since the perception of fun/pleasure is critical in the definition of play, it means that its intent can be variable – it can be light-hearted or serious and it can be ambiguous. As was the case with the gladiators in the Roman Colosseum, play could routinely result in death. The same is the case for bullfighting, where play routinely results in the death of the bull and, occasionally, the matador. In addition to the example of these "blood sports", where death becomes the ultimate pleasure in play, the basic dilemma of play is captured in the Golden Age Spanish work *La vida es sueño* by Calderón de la Barca ([1635] 1831), which removes or questions the distinction between reality and fantasy. A (black) man kisses a (white) woman on a movie set. Is it a real kiss? In other words, the interpretation of play or non-play takes place in the brain of the participants as well as the spectators and the "spirit of the game" may not be the same for all parties.

Play, in the case of the slaves, was an alternative choice to violence, but play is not a form of negative escapism from the harshness of life, like alcohol, drugs and, some would say, religion. Play is a part of human beings (and other animals). The way human beings perceive has an element of interpretation in it that is fed by by both memory and imagination. It is this way of perceiving that allows for play, and allows play to be suppressed or expanded in the brain/mind. Play also has within itself an element of beauty that causes play to be able to increase or decrease according to experience. In other words, the perceptual element of play, which is universal, is actualized and expressed according to cultural and individual preferences.

As a variant of the Cartesian *cogito, ergo sum*, "I think, therefore I am", one can make the assertion "I feel or sense, therefore I am (a human being)". Thus, using the etymology of the word *aesthetics* as a starting point, one can argue that what makes one human is that one has a sense of beauty or, in other words, there is in every normal human being an innate sentient facility that satisfies itself through the senses. Of course, one has to address the question whether this "innate sentient facility" is essentially subjective in itself or is fashioned either by individual cultures or by higher order internal (brain) factors. So, is the common English saying "Beauty is in the eye of the beholder" basically sound, or is there a broader (accepted) notion of beauty within cultures, or is there a universality in notions of beauty across all human beings?

Innateness of an ability in itself suggests a formulation, as is the case with language, that there is a core of universality across all human beings which has a periphery that is modified by variation in experience. This means that those who dwell together and have been doing so for generations will have high levels of uniformity in their notions of beauty and that these notions of beauty may differ from those of people who dwell elsewhere. It also means that societies with high levels of migration (in and out) will peripherally have varying notions of beauty. Additionally, those societies that undergo sudden and massive immigration will show differences in both notions of beauty and in the ways in which the different groups accommodate conflicting notions of beauty. Therefore, opting for play and the levels of happiness that result from it will vary according to perceptions of beauty.

A relevant point one to consider here is a claimed ethnic distinction in the United States between "functional" and "aesthetic" music. In his book on the history of African American music in the United States, LeRoi Jones (Amiri Baraka) ([1963] 2002, 28–29) makes the following claim: "African music . . . was a purely *functional* music. . . . *Serious* Western music, except for early religious music, has been strictly an *art* music." One has to wonder what is meant by "purely functional" as a contrast to *"art* music". In other words, the distinction between functional and "non-functional" not only seems baseless, but one could argue, more specifically, that *"serious* Western music", in the form of orchestral music, reflects a kind of social cohesion, training and governance that demonstrates how the individual should function in a well-organized and well-governed society. As such, there could be nothing more functional than that. However, the more serious problem with the distinction is that it contains a suggestion that "purely functional" music is not concerned with aesthetics while art music is. This clearly is not so because it is obvious that music cannot be separated from art, as it cannot be separated from play.

Play and Art in Evolution

Another area in which considerations of function and value arise is when play is assessed as an element of human evolution. In the foreword to his book *Homo Ludens*, Johan Huizinga argues that "civilization arises and unfolds in and as play", but he does not seek to give an evolutionary account of play. He starts by summing up the many ways in which writers have tried to explain the *biological* function of play:

> By some the origin and fundamentals of play have been described as a discharge of superabundant vital energy, by others as the satisfaction of some "imitative instinct", or again as simply a "need" for relaxation. According to one theory play constitutes a training of the young creature for the serious work that life will demand later on. According to another it serves as an exercise in restraint needful to the individual. Some find the principle of play in an innate urge to exercise a certain faculty, or in the desire to dominate or compete. Yet others regard it as an "abreaction" – an outlet for harmful impulses, as the necessary restorer of energy

wasted by one-sided activity, as "wish-fulfilment", as a fiction designed to keep up the feeling of personal value, etc. ([1949] 1980, 2)

Huizinga's central idea is that "it is precisely this fun-element that characterizes the essence of play" (3) and his intention is to treat play as a "special form of activity, as a 'significant form', as a social function". He proclaims his general thesis, that play is central to the development of civilized life, by saying: "Now in myth and ritual the great instinctive forces of civilized life have their origin: law and order, commerce and profit, craft and art, poetry, wisdom and science. All are rooted in the primaeval soil of play" (5).

In her book *Homo Aestheticus*, Ellen Dissanayake, in direct contrast to Huizinga, is centrally concerned with the evolution and biological function of art in humans. For her, art is closely allied and similar to play. She mentions the idea that "there might not be immediate survival benefits associated with play", but she makes the point that "individuals who play, and thereby learn practical and social skills, survive better than individuals who are not inclined to play or who are deprived of play and therefore lack practice with these essential things" (1995, 44).

For her, the *core* of art is that it is "extra-ordinary" and "special". She argues that "humans everywhere, in a manner that is unlike that of other animals, differentiate between an order, realm, mood, or state of being that is mundane, ordinary, or 'natural', and one that is unusual, extraordinary, or 'supernatural'" (49).

> I suggest that the standard and unexceptional animal inclination to differentiate ordinary from extra-ordinary, to recognize specialness, would have been developing over tens of thousands of years . . . At some point in their evolution, humans began deliberately to set out to *make things special* or extra-ordinary. . . .
>
> Making special emphasizes the idea that the arts, biologically endowed predispositions, have been physically, sensuously, and emotionally satisfying and pleasurable to humans. . . . Before they were ever consciously used to make things special, the satisfaction of rhythm, novelty, order, pattern, color, bodily movement, and moving in synchrony with others were fundamental animal pleasures, essential ingredients of life. Using these bodily pleasurable elements to make ceremonies special – elaborating and shaping them – the arts, and art, were born. (51–60)

Dissanayake does not directly recognize Huizinga in the formulation of her theory, but it is interesting to note that Huizinga highlights "fun" as central, whereas Dissanayake highlights "pleasure". In addition, note Huizinga's words: "We find play present everywhere as a well-defined quality of action which is different from 'ordinary' life as well as Play as a special form of activity . . . that is our subject" (emphasis added). Clearly, these similarities establish a fundamental link between the two theses. Furthermore, the idea that play and art are extra-ordinary and special, in the sense of an alternative to the ordinary and the mundane, is virtually the same idea that Huizinga expresses in the statement "Behind every abstract expression there lie the boldest of metaphors, and every metaphor is a play upon words. Thus in giving expression to life man creates a second poetic world alongside the world of nature" ([1949] 1980, 4).

Since consciousness is located in the present, non-human animals' only concern is with the present: they have little or no concern with the past or the future or anything else (the non-real), even though they distinguish between real and non-real in play. Dissanayake argues that, in the case of humans, concern with the non-real was qualitatively affected by the development of higher-level cognitive skills and that humans consciously began to use art to mark or embellish the non-real, what she calls the extra-ordinary or special. She concedes that embellishment is not restricted to humans: "There is a reason for embellishment in other species – notably, songbirds, who elaborate their songs much more than is necessary simply to advertise their presence or individuality" (1995, 52). However, the idea of consciously "making special" (artification) is, for which she later proposes two "ultimate adaptive functions", that is, artification would "(i) alleviate the deleterious effects of the stress response and (ii) instill collective emotions such as trust and belongingness" (2014, 53–54).

Eugen Fink's *Play* versus Blaise Pascal's *Divertissement*

Eugen Fink followed in the footsteps of Johan Huizinga in stressing the primary importance of play in human existence. In his article "The Oasis of Happiness: Toward an Ontology of Play", Fink argued that play should not be conceived of as an antithesis of work, seriousness and reality, but "as an essential element of man's ontological makeup". He takes issue with the "commonsense" view of play, which he sets out as follows:

> It is said that the purpose of man's life is to strive arduously for knowledge, for excellence and virtue, for fame and honor, for power and prosperity. Play, on the other hand, is supposed to function as occasional interruption, as a pause. . . . According to this conception play seems to occupy a legitimate, if limited, place in the rhythm of human life. . . . Play is thought of more or less as frivolous and pleasurable nonsense, as a carefree sojourn in the airy realm of phantasy and sheer potentialities, as an escape from unyielding reality to a dream-utopia. (Fink, Saine and Saine 1968, 19)

His argument is that that vision of play is fundamentally wrong; he contends that "the great philosophies have always recognized the eminent essentiality of play" (25).

Clearly, Fink interprets striving arduously for knowledge, excellence, virtue, fame, honour, power and prosperity as a quest for happiness, but about this quest he says: "It is one of the profound paradoxes of human existence that in our never-ending pursuit of happiness we never attain it, and that strictly speaking no man can be reckoned to be happy before his death." In contrast to this "curious futurism of human life", Fink presents as his main point the idea that "play resembles an oasis of happiness that we happen upon in the desert of our Tantalus-like seeking and pursuit of happiness" (20–21). In other words, in the unending striving and struggle that is life, play repetitively facilitates happiness along the way.

Fink's conception of *play* is a response, direct or indirect, to Blaise Pascal's seventeenth-century concept of *divertissement*. Pascal argues that "all the unhappiness of men arises from one single fact, that they cannot stay quietly in their own chamber", and this is because of "the natural poverty of our feeble and mortal condition, so miserable that nothing can comfort us when we think of it closely" (1958, 39). Pascal contends that men are subject to two contrasting instincts: "They have a secret instinct which impels them to seek amusement and occupation abroad, and which arises from the sense of their constant unhappiness. They have another secret instinct, a remnant of the greatness of our original nature, which teaches them that happiness in reality consists only in rest, and not in stir" (41).

He goes on to support his argument showing men's preference for the pursuit of happiness through divertissement (a word which in Pascal's days would have been taken to mean "distraction" more so than its modern meaning "amusement/fun") because they really believe that "without amusement there is no joy; with amusement there is no sadness" (42). So, while Pascal sees divertissement (and he uses dancing as an example) as a reaction to human malaise caused by a consciousness of the futility of life and the inevitability of death, Fink sees play as a facility naturally provided to counteract the struggle and repetitively create happiness. The question then is whether play is the solution provided by nature itself or whether play is self-delusion and there is a higher solution, as in Pascal's belief in the power of Christianity.

In the case of slaves, one may argue that if one is deprived even of those things that free people have, play will assume a bigger and more pervasive role in one's life. It seems reasonable to believe that in cases of poverty and subordination – that is, where the pursuit of knowledge, excellence, fame, honour, prosperity and power is beyond one's reality – happiness will be sought in the oasis that play repetitively facilitates. In fact, this kind of happiness seems more real than the "normal" futuristic happiness that Fink speaks of and does not have the Christian birfurcation into living and post-life heaven. It is not odd, therefore, that many writers regarded the slaves in the Caribbean as happy and that Resident and Froude could make their extreme assertions (given at the beginning of the chapter) about their happiness.

Another of Fink's points that is relevant to slaves is that because the human being is in control of his own imagination, "play is an eminent manifestation of human freedom" (Fink, Saine and Saine 1968, 25). In other words, the imagination in play is a freedom that cannot be taken away from any human being and it can be (and often is) used to construct alternative worlds where all things are possible.

The fact that the old English saying "All work and no play, makes Iack a dull boy" (Howell 1659, 12) is well known means that it is general knowledge that play is of fundamental importance; but even if one recognizes the increased value of play in harsh circumstances, one still has to consider the primordial role of play highlighted in the controversy explicitly articulated by Pascal and Fink – is there virtue in play?

Play as Imagination and Creativity

The Colombian Gabriel García Márquez said in his Nobel lecture (1982): "Poets and beggars, musicians and prophets, warriors and scoundrels, all creatures of that unbridled reality, we have had to ask but little of imagination, for our crucial problem has been a lack of conventional means to render our lives believable. This, my friends, is the crux of our solitude." In effect, Márquez presents the people of Latin America as almost the complete opposite of the happy picture of the slaves presented at the start of this chapter. It is a mournful picture that results from endless wars, political upheavals and probably lack of respect from Europe and America. However, Márquez went on to end his speech by saying: "Faced with this awesome reality that must have seemed a mere utopia through all of human time, we, the inventors of tales, who will believe anything, feel entitled to believe that it is not yet too late to engage in the creation of the opposite utopia." In this formulation, Márquez thus associates happiness with utopia, with the imaginary and thus with play.

Significantly, with reference to the Caribbean and the imaginary, Márquez, in an interview with the journalist Plinio Mendoza, says: "The Caribbean is a distinctive world whose first work of magical literature was *The Diary of Christopher Columbus*, a book which tells of fabulous plants and mythological societies. The history of the Caribbean is full of magic – a magic brought by black slaves from Africa" (Mendoza and Márquez 1982, 52). It is not surprising, therefore, that where Márquez sees the people of Latin America in the past as "the races condemned to one hundred years of solitude", many of the colonial writers were of the same opinion as Resident that the people of the Caribbean, that is, the Africans and their descendants were happy. It is therefore important to come to appreciate, following Márquez's formulation, how Caribbean people who also lacked "conventional means to render [their] lives believable" could create a strong image of being able to enjoy themselves. Thus, people in the Caribbean not only may have had an unusual capacity to create happiness through the imaginary (for example, play), but also may have used media such as music and dance to bolster it as well as the spirit to spark it into being. It is probably this last element that makes the difference between solitude and happiness.

No Honour for Eunuchs and Servile Play as Dishonour

In his article "Honor, Eunuchs, and the Postcolonial Subject", Leonard Harris (1997, 256) baldly states: "Eunuchs, as individuals and as a category, cannot receive the exalted regard of honor." He goes on: "No slave, eunuch, serf, or peasant was ever honoured as slave, eunuch, serf, or peasant. When members of such groups attained honourable regard it necessarily had to be a function of behaviour or attributes which made them exemplary as 'above' their lowly station" (258). This is because "honor is a good that can be held just in case one is a member of a group that is susceptible to honor" (256). Bearing in mind the extreme assertions of happiness made by Resident and Froude about West Indians as well as the idea that honour is not applicable to persons of lowly station, one would have to conclude that happiness and honour are mutually exclusive – the one applicable to the lowly and the other to the mighty.

In his comprehensive book on slavery, *Slavery and Social Death*, Orlando Patterson (1982, 78) makes a strong case for "death before dishonour" in the following statement: "The idea that a person's honor is more valuable than his life, and that to prefer life to honor betrays a degraded mind, comes close to being a genuinely universal belief." Patterson's argument is consistent with Epicurean doctrine, which states: "It is not possible to live pleasantly without living wisely, honorably, and justly. Nor can one live wisely, honorably, and justly without living pleasantly. But those who for any reason do not live wisely, honorably, and justly cannot possibly live pleasantly" (Cassius Amicus 2011). But there is disagreement about what constitutes dishonour, since many believe that dishonour results not from what is done to you but from what you do. This is based on Mattthew 15:11, "Not that which goeth into the mouth defileth a man: but that which commeth out of the mouth, this defileth a man." So, it would be doubly tragic for people to be overpowered and then to have no alternative but suicide. An indigenous group in Grenada whose "heroic" jump to death is associated with the place name Sauteurs is said to be an example of this kind of honourable suicide.

Belittlement, Cowardice, Courage and Virtue

Roberto Unger's view of the human condition bears some resemblance to Pascal's when he says (2014, 24), "the ordinary experience of life, although punctuated by moments of joy . . . is one of blockage and humiliation". It also recalls Fink's characterization of human existence as having a "curious futurism" in which "no man can be reckoned to be happy before his death" (Fink, Saine and Saine 1968, 20). Unger uses "blockage and humiliation" as a synonym for belittlement.

Unger comments on belittlement not just from the point of view of what is done to the individual but also from the point of view of the individual's response to it: "Cowardice is belittlement. The acceptance of belittlement negates a defining goal of the spiritual transformation for which the religion of the future speaks." The opposite of cowardice is courage, and Unger argues that "we become freer and greater by standing up to the structures of society, of thought, and of character and by refusing, in our relations to others, to settle for the middle distance" (2014, 375–76). He however cautions against the old-fashioned idea of courage ("martial valor") and proposes instead *"agape* and mindfulness of others"* (376). Unger's proposed solution to the human condition – coming to terms with "the relentless confrontation with death, groundlessness, and insatiability" (191) – is conceived as the religion of the future in which paradoxically we become "more human by becoming more Godlike". This is done through self-transformation. So, he proposes that just as "we should seek in our institutions and practices that they facilitate their own revision", so we should do similarly in our moral lives: "The hardening of a character denies each of the attributes of life: its qualities of surfeit, fecundity, and spontaneity. . . . The solution . . . is to form a character distinguished by its openness to experience and by its readiness to change" (367–68). What is therefore central to Unger's "religion of the future" is the dynamic, self-revising nature of institutions and characters.

Though Unger's philosophy does not specifically address play and any possible role that it might have in his religion, he does speak of imagination in different ways, first by identifying an important element of our humanity as "an appreciation of what we most want from one another: to be imagined and accepted for what we are and might become" (370–71). Then, more generally, he recognizes the powerful role it has and argues that its limits are subject to the organization of society and culture: "The relative power of this anti-machine, which we call the imagination, is not shaped solely by physical features of the brain, such as its plasticity. It depends, also and even chiefly, on the organization of society and culture. This organization may widen or narrow the space for the workings of the imagination, and afford it or deny it equipment" (109).

This book has imagination as a basic element of play and it sees play as a force creating an enhanced alternative reality which, by facilitating the dynamic and self-revising nature of characters and institutions, improves human status and value in real life.

For enslaved Africans in the Caribbean and their descendants, play has not been an academic construct. From the early years of the colonies the slaves chose or resorted to the word "play" to describe activities in their spare time. Today, in most Caribbean countries, there is some sort of carnival in which participants "play mas". In most cases "playing mas" is a nationally recognized and government-supported activity because it is seen as culturally important for various reasons. There is no shortage of theorizing about carnival generally, but in the Caribbean there is still a need to delink play from a happy, carefree image and evaluate it more closely in terms of the ideas enunciated by Huizinga, Fink and others, as with the ideas of cowardice and dishonour enunciated by Unger, Patterson and Harris, among others, and with its capacity for change.

2. Interpretations That Enhance and Diminish Play

> For when mothers want their restless children to go to sleep they do not employ rest, but, on the contrary, motion – rocking them in their arms; nor do they give them silence, but they sing to them and lap them in sweet strains.
> —Plato 2009, book 7

TWO MAJOR EXPRESSIONS OF PLAY ARE MUSIC AND DANCE, and these have been the subject of speculation and theorizing, from time immemorial, in terms of both their biological and cultural functions. In the epigraph above, motion and singing are given a primordial universal function by Plato in *The Laws* (2009, book 7) when he focuses on the way they affect infants. He then goes on to explain: "the motion coming from without gets the better of the terrible and violent one, and produces a peace and calm in the soul, and quiets the restless palpitation of the heart . . . sending the children to sleep". Here Plato presents good motion and singing as being able to overturn bad motion and noise for the human infant. Essentially, the idea here is that inaction (rest and silence) has no power, only action (motion and singing); paradoxically, however, inaction allows restoration to take place. Since the circular relationship between action and inaction is perpetual, singing and dance are indispensable in that they bring about balance in human beings.

When Plato goes on to speak of the education of the young, he outlines and then amplifies a grand cultural thesis about the role of music and dance (2009, book 7). In relation to music specifically, Plato argues that music, through rhythm, plays a powerful role in the aesthetic formation of the older child in that it can make one graceful, beautiful, noble and good (2006, 91). This cultural ideal would have been espoused as appropriate for the education of their children, especially by those in the nobility or those who wanted to be. It certainly featured in the formation of the virtues of "Renaissance man".

The practice of sub-classifying art into high and low or folk art is based on notions of sophistication and technological development that are inextricably tied to social class. This aesthetic valuation derives from classical Greek thought which sees high art as the province of the educated (that is, for the educated and by the educated) and folk art the province of the uneducated, even if this latter is varied to mean uneducated in that specific area of art. Nowhere is this socially contrastive ranking of music and dance more expressly set out and related to education than in Plato:

> The fairest music is that which delights the best and the best educated. (2009, book 2)

> Such motion may be in general called dancing, and is of two kinds: one of the nobler figures, imitating the honourable, the other of the more ignoble figures, imitating the mean. (Book 7)

> I must distinguish the dancing about which there is any doubt, from that about which there is doubt. Which is the doubtful kind, and how are the two to be distinguished? There are dances of the Bacchic sort . . . all this sort of dancing cannot be rightly defined as having either a peaceful or a warlike character, or indeed as having any meaning whatever and may, I think, be most truly described as . . . not suited for a city at all. (Book 7)

The contrast reeks of social snobbery, for it banishes the music and dance of the uneducated and strongly recommends that only the music of the educated should be considered worthwhile.

Another way in which social bias is seen is in reference to the manner in which different people express themselves, especially in the idea that spontaneity in the show of emotion should be curbed. Again it is in Plato that hierarchy is seen in demonstrative behaviour and dancing (book 7) – Plato puts dancing in a subordinate relation to singing and suggests that dancing emerged from an inability to control pleasurable emotions when trying to communicate. Then, even within dancing itself, there is a further hierarchy in which "nobler" dances are those in which the dancer is in more control and "disorderly" dances the opposite.

When an influential treatise like Plato's associates cowardice with spontaneous, demonstrative behaviour ("if he be a coward, and has no training or self-control, he makes greater and more violent movements, and in general when he is speaking or singing he is not altogether able to keep his body still") and courage with repression of spontaneity ("if he be more orderly and has learned courage from discipline he waves less"), it tarnishes spontaneity in such a way as to preserve hierarchy not only (in social class) within societies but also across cultures and ethnicities. In some societies there has never been any such view of spontaneous "violent" movements. In any case, one has to consider what is seen as prowess in dance in different societies as well as the message or intent of the dancer and how this is best achieved. Indeed, if dancing is considered to be a powerful form of non-verbal communication, there can be no universal evaluation of dance or singing that could sensibly banish what is natural or spontaneous. Of course, one of the powerful reasons for repression of spontaneous, pronounced movements in dancing is sex related. Such movements are in varying contexts associated with "lascivious" behaviour and frowned on by those in authority.

Another far-reaching principle espoused by Plato is the primacy of the established order. He specifically illustrates this in *The Republic* (2006, 117) by saying that singers should not deviate from forms and structures that are approved. If this recommendation is generalized across the arts, it would mean that there would be little artistic innovation of worth and that artists would have to master what is already set out. This principle, of course, essentially frowns on and squashes individuality. Within the Plato principle is embedded the idea that discipline is of paramount importance and discipline can only be achieved by practising what is prescribed. It automatically relegates public festivity to the level of the rabble.

In contrast to Plato's pre-Christian conception of music and dance, a God-inspired explanation of music uniting Heaven and Earth comes from St Isidore of Seville (AD 560–636), one of the most respected scholars of his day. He said: "And without music there can be no perfect knowledge, for there is nothing without it. For even the universe itself is said to have been put together with a certain harmony of sounds, and the very heavens revolve under the guidance of harmony" (Brehaut 1912, 137). The idea of harmony here is a higher-level version of Plato's (2009, book 7) idea that motion and singing bring "peace and calm in the soul". In other words, while Plato sees it at the level of the human being, St Isidore extends it beyond the Earth to the Universe. St Isidore's view is not different from the concept of "music of the spheres", which means that music and dance are considered to be beyond man and mortality and are seen as limitless in space and time in the same way that some people consider the mind/soul (psyche) element of human beings to be so. The idea of music and dance transporting human beings beyond this world is therefore quite normal, for both music and dancing are used as media through which certain cultures access their deities and, as is pointed out by Gallini (1770, 13): "The Hebrews, after the example of the Egyptians, accompanied all their religious ceremonies with songs and dances." Igor Stravinsky, almost two hundred years later, expresses the idea in his own way at the end of his *Poétique musicale* (1970, 187): "And that is how music comes to reveal itself as a form of communion with our fellow man – and with the Supreme Being." When song and dance are major components in a people's belief system, they invariably assume a high status.

Music and Dance as Creatures of Behavioural or Innate Systems

Louis de Cahusac (1706–1759), in his explanation of the origin of music and dance, perpetuates the Christian ethic of St Isidore, but, over and above that, he saw early humans as having sensations and emotions which were expressed through movement and vocalizations. These he considered to be the crude beginnings of dance and music respectively. In human beings, the vocalizations were gradually refined until they became music, which then helped to develop the natural movements of the body into dance:

> Man had feelings from the moment he first breathed and the sounds of his voice, the play in his facial features, the movements of his body were merely the expressions of what he felt. There is naturally in the voice sounds of pleasure, sadness, anger, tenderness, affliction and joy; similarly, there are in the movements of the face and body physical expressions of all these feelings. The former are the original sources of singing and the latter of dance.
>
> There is to be found the universal language understood by all nations and even by animals, because it precedes all conventions and is native to all beings that live on Earth. These inarticulate sounds were a kind of singing, and (if one may say so) natural music, developing little by little, painted in an unequivocal, though crude, manner all the different situations of the soul. These were preceded and followed on the exterior by gestures relative to these diverse situations. The body was peaceful or disturbed; the eyes were glowing or getting dim; the face was ruddy or pale; the arms opened or closed, stretched to the heavens or fell back to earth; the feet made slow steps or fast ones; in short, the whole body responded through postures, attitudes, leaps and shakings to sounds whose movements the soul painted. So, singing, which is the very first expression of feeling made

a second one develop, which was in man, and this expression was called dance. (1754, 13–15)

Thus, Cahusac posits a pre-existing universal language common to all beings and manifested in sounds and gestures, which evolve into singing and dance.

As to the original function of music and dance, Cahusac went on to say (19): "It is therefore very probable that men first celebrated in song the benefits God gave and danced, although no doubt very badly, to express their respect and gratitude. Sacred dancing is the most ancient of the dances and the source from which spring all the others." Thus, for Cahusac, the giving back to the Creator was the natural response of human beings. What this meant, therefore, was that religion was the point of departure for all other forms of music and dance.

A modern scientific theory that can be interpreted as a very sophisticated variant of Cahusac's idea about the origin and development of music (and language and dance), without any religious interjection, comes from Colwyn Trevarthen, psychologist at the University of Edinburgh. The fundamental idea in Trevarthen's intersubjectivity can be stated in broad terms as "social precedes individual", and in this is embedded the argument that music, dance and language are derived forms of a social capacity that infants are born with; that is, humans are born wired with a need to communicate with other humans. Trevarthen (1999, 415–19) makes his argument in the following:

> A different conception of human consciousness . . . perceives interpersonal awareness, cooperative action in society, and cultural learning as manifestations of innate motives for sympathy in purposes, interests, and feeling – that is, the human mind is equipped with needs for dialogic, intermental engagement with other similar minds (Jopling 1993).
>
> The vocal exchanges between a mother and a young infant are found to have measurable parameters of "communicative musicality": a rhythmic "pulse", changing "quality or expressive intensity of pitch and tone, and capacity to entrain attention and purposeful imagination in "narrative' sequences of many seconds (Malloch 1999), out of which all elaborated forms of human companionship in action and experience are constituted. . . .
>
> The evidence that infants learn by emotional referencing to evaluate experiences through attunement with motives of familiar companions, for whom they have, and from whom they receive, affectionate regard, proves that it is the sense of individuality in society that is the derived state of mind, developed in contrast to more fundamental intersubjective needs and obligations.

Thus, for both Cahusac and Trevarthen, music and dance are evolved manifestations of interaction in a predetermined system of communication or system of engagement. The idea that vocal exchanges between a mother and a young infant have "communicative musicality" speaks to the centrality of music in human behaviour and establishes it as a "basis of human companionship", thus the book on that theme spearheaded by Stephen Malloch and Colwyn Trevarthen (2009). So, music is not an appendage; it is the source of social bonding, a formative source of society.

Music and Dance as Indexes in Popular Culture

The most appealing and persuasive European argument used to account for differences between societies and peoples was ecological determinism. What was interesting in its most noteworthy application to the Caribbean in the eighteenth century to account for dance there is that it was put forward by a Caribbean-born person. M.L.E Moreau de Saint-Méry was born in Martinique and achieved high political status in his own day and more general renown historically because of his writings. His short work on dance was different from his other major descriptive works because it sought not only to be informative about dances in the Caribbean but also to account for prominence and difference in dance across the world in a theoretical way.

Dancing was one of those features that was constantly highlighted in descriptions of the various Caribbean countries. It was so prominent in the public mind that when Moreau de Saint-Méry wrote his thesis on it in 1789, his main objectives were to explain it as a human phenomenon generally and to explain its prominence in the Caribbean specifically. He considered it first in terms of its origin and explained it as a basic expression of the human soul, one which spontaneously developed into joyous group communion (1796, 1–2). Then, to account for variation across human societies, his main argument was that the prominence of dance in a society was dependent on three factors:

1. climate – ranging from cold snowy to hot tropical
2. economic occupation – ranging from hunter-gatherer or warrior to farmer
3. developmental and social level – ranging from busy and uniform to free and stylish

Moreau de Saint-Méry's generalizations and examples have a common-sense appeal that is enticing, but whether factual information from a range of societies would actually support his claims is doubtful. At the time, because of lack of available evidence to the contrary, his claims seemed reasonable. What is quite clear in any case is that it was his knowledge and preference for America that was driving his theory: "since America is the principal object of my research, it is easy for me to find proof there of the theory I am advancing" (1796, 15)

Moreau de Saint-Méry made a straightforward comparison of the climatic zones to show that dance would have been differentially favoured in each one, and ends by presenting the Caribbean as the optimal climate (19, 37). However, even if there is some reason to agree with Moreau de Saint-Méry that extreme cold and snow discourage activities like dancing, the idea that heat and ardour for dancing, and heat and passion are factually linked is doubtful. In fact, as will be seen, many Europeans in the tropics had difficulty coming to terms with dancing as a practical activity there.

Referring again to temperate climates, Moreau de Saint-Méry (1796, 11) indirectly argues that it is really only spring that can be imagined to have a natural connection with dancing. However, whether the suggested natural connection between spring and dancing is demonstrable is again doubtful. When Moreau de Saint-Méry's argument adds factors of lifestyle and livelihood to climate, it becomes more convincing, but this is because there was a more general argument which linked the stages in human food gathering/production methods (hunter-gatherer, shepherd, farmer and so on) to increase in wealth and sophistication. A later nineteenth-century expression of this argument dealing with pre-Christian times and favouring the farmer was presented by the Egyptologist John Gardner Wilkinson (1841, 4). Later in the nineteenth century Charles Darwin (1871, ch. 5) used virtually the same argument to account for progress in human societies.

What Moreau de Saint-Méry did was to apply the same kind of argument to dance and to argue (1796, 11–19) that the farmer was the one most favoured by circumstances to be the best dancer. Yet in Moreau de Saint-Méry's mind there must have been a distinction, in relation to the slave societies of the Americas, between a person who actually works the land (who clearly did not have as much free time as he suggests) and a person who owns a farm and has slaves to do the work. It is this latter who better fits his argument.

In any case, Moreau de Saint-Méry then moved from stages in human economic evolution to an intriguing proposal about using dance as a barometer to measure levels of civilization. In his formulation, just as the different stages of food gathering/production could be put on a scale of progress, the same could be done for different dances. Accordingly, to support his argument, he first identified the circle dance as the most primitive of dances: "the circle dance [which] is evidently the original dance, since it is really a rural dance. ... In the circle dance each person is tied to the circle, each person sees all the others, and the chain formed by human arms becomes the regulator of the movements of the dancers" (1796, 3). He then moved to what he considered civilized dances with an explanation of how such dances could be considered more sophisticated:

> Dance among civilised people is subject, as are almost all other parts of their customs, to caprices of fashion, whilst simple or savage people, if I can use a word that pride uses in relation to them, preserve dance practically invariable. Since a greater sum of ideas offers more combinations, variety of all types can only be attributed to a more perfect people; and perhaps dances of diverse peoples could serve as a kind of graduated scale to identify their level of civilisation. (8–9)

In short, he was tying imagination and creativity to economic evolution and simplicity to uniformity. The fact is there is no universal proof for any of these two links.

In summary then, Moreau de Saint-Méry, having started out with the idea that dance was at first an outburst of joy, concludes by arguing that dance can be used as an indicator of level of civilization. Bear in mind from the start that Moreau de Saint-Méry's intention was to put sophisticated creoles like himself in the superior position by arguing that a tropical, agricultural people not burdened by daily chores had to be the best at dance. Yet his argument, though self-serving, was revolutionary in that it put creoles at the top of the scale of human progress.

During the course of his thesis, Moreau de Saint-Méry identified differences in the national character of three of the colonizing nations in the Caribbean in the following way: "you can find among them nuances of national character, in that the English colonist dances less than the French colonist and the Spanish colonist more than the English" (1796, 37). The implication here is that these national characters would have been formed by ecological factors and furthermore that, if set out on a hierarchical scale, the English would be the least civilized of the three. This argument assumes not only that these national characters are fairly fixed but also reveal themselves clearly through passion for dance, frequency of dances, variety in dances and types of dances.

Jean-Baptiste Thibault de Chanvalon (1763, 55) declared that "the pleasures of a nation always carry the imprint of its character" and Joseph Strutt ([1801] 1903, xv) asserted that "in order to form a just estimation of the character of any particular people, it is absolutely necessary to investigate the Sports and Pastimes most generally prevalent among them. . . . When we follow them into their retirements, where no disguise is necessary, we are most likely to see them in their true state, and may best judge of their natural dispositions." A basic assumption in these statements is that national "character" and "true state" reveal themselves more clearly when one is relaxed rather than when one is tense. However, there is a contrasting argument that it is only when people are under stress that one can see their true self and character. Notwithstanding the fact that these two arguments contradict each other, in the case of enslaved Africans in the Caribbean, it would seem as if one has no problem, for they were under constant pressure and they were singing and dancing, so presumably their "true state" and "character" must have been transparent in the one way or the other. Moreover, since the slaves, and creoles generally, could be said to have had few political or military exploits of significance from which their "character" could be assessed, it is their pleasures and pastimes that become the main focus of attention.

Strutt's documentation of the sports and pastimes of the people of England was meant to show the English in a positive light. However, because Strutt depended on reports which were from different sources and at times varied according to social class, there are contradictions in the information he presents. In addition, because Strutt's research covers centuries and is inconsistent, there is an inherent difficulty in making general claims. In contrast to what the French creole writer Moreau de Saint-Méry suggests about the English in comparing them with the French and the Spanish, Strutt, in a number of both general and detailed statements, suggests the opposite by presenting the English as a much more fun-loving people. Thus, Strutt's exuberant vision of the English, just like Moreau de Saint-Méry's grand vision of creoles, demonstrates a tendency towards self-serving arguments.

Bertrand Russell, the Nobel laureate and philosopher, uses "dancing in the streets" as a context for the expression of joy when he said: "At every moment of life the civilized man is hedged about by restrictions of impulse: if he happens to feel cheerful he must not sing or dance in the street." He then went on to say: "All this makes zest more difficult to retain, for the continual restraint tends to produce weariness and boredom." However, Russell does believe in restraint. He specifically says: "a civilized society is impossible without a very considerable degree of restraint upon spontaneous impulse, since spontaneous impulse will only produce the simplest forms of social co-operation". Russell has no qualms about identifying certain cultures as "savage" and their music as "barbaric" when he consolidates his point about the need for restraint: "When the tribe is going to war the tom-tom rouses military ardour, and herd excitement inspires each individual to the necessary activity. Modern enterprises cannot be managed in this way" (1930, 171). Perhaps it is because he was an upper-class Englishman born in the Victorian era that Russell could not move away from preaching "restraint", "the golden mean", "moderation" and "balance" even as he said that "the most universal and distinctive mark of happy men is zest" (158).

Clearly, levels of civilization feature prominently in Russell's scheme of things and even though in the following statement he is referring to birth of children, his point can be generalized to refer to culture: "The most civilized are the most sterile; the least civilized are the most fertile; and between the two there is a continual gradation. . . . And as soon as the immigrants acquire the civilization of the country of their adoption they in turn will become comparatively sterile" (194). In other words, Russell sees (Western) civilization as a sterilizing process.

One of Russell's many advisories to the common man in his quest for happiness that is relevant here principally because of its wording is: "In emancipation from the fears that beset the slave of circumstance he will experience a profound joy, and through all the vicissitudes of his outward life he will remain in the depths of his being a happy man" (226). Whereas "the slave of circumstance" in this case refers to an ordinary person reacting predictably to and feeling trapped by everyday stresses and responsibilities, Russell's choice of words links it to slaves and emancipation and to Marcus Garvey's ([1938] 1990, 791) words "we are going to emancipate ourselves from mental slavery", made popular by Bob Marley in his "Redemption Song". Russell's words can therefore be interpreted to mean that if slaves free their minds from their constant and immediate fears of bondage, they will experience joy and be happy.

Touting the Medical and Societal Benefits of Music and Dance

In more modern times, speculations about music and dance have not changed fundamentally. One significant advantage that modern writers have in discussing the functions of music and dance is that there are today many detailed results of brain studies which have been obtained through the use of sophisticated technology. One of the many writers showing the benefits of such research is Oliver Sacks, whose thesis on music and the brain sets out some current and relevant ideas about links between music and dance. The special worth of this work for our purposes is that in it Sacks, a physician and researcher, summarizes the statements of several modern thinkers.

As to the functions of music, one that Sacks highlights in the work of his contemporaries is one that is typically related to language. He says: "Anthony Storr [1992] . . . stresses that in all societies, a primary function of music is collective and communal, to bring and bind people together." He explains his argument by saying: "The binding is accomplished by rhythm – not only heard but internalized, identically, in all who are present. Rhythm turns listeners into participants, makes listening active and motoric, and synchronizes the brains and the minds . . . of all who participate" (2008, 266). He summarizes the encompassing nature of rhythm by saying: "rhythm binds together the individual nervous systems of a human community" (269).

Sacks spends the major part of his book illustrating the role of music in the treatment of disorders. One observation he makes is that "it is clear that music, above all else, can kick start a damaged or inhibited motor system into action again" (257). He gives examples of music causing limbs, which previously felt like inanimate objects after some accident, to work or react. Sacks also demonstrates with many anecdotes (324 et seq.) how music functions as a tool to counteract loss of feeling and depression when people are mourning the loss of relatives.

In another influential twenty-first-century work on music and the mind, edited by Irène Deliège and Jane Davidson, writers discuss the transformative role of music. Richard Parncutt and Angelika Dorfer, speaking on the role of music in cultural integration, argue that since "self-esteem tends to be weakened by migration" (2011, 384), "the music of one's cultural group can function as a strong reminder of that culture, triggering nostalgic feelings and in that way strengthening cultural identity" (404). Eric Clarke is more comprehensive in his claims, saying: "musicking is overwhelmingly an extraordinary human asset, even if it brings with it the potential to turn that asset to repressive or destructive purposes" (2011, 23–24). He also says that musicking has the following benefits – "cognitive, social, aesthetic, cultural diversity, creative, economic, political, personal development, educational and therapeutic" (22n4). He goes on to say: "diverse research strands all point to the crucial role that musicking plays in people's lives, to its transformational capacity, and to the insights that it can afford" (24).

Although Barbara Ehrenreich's claims are not always supported by evidence, her prejudices are not always concealed and her statements may have inconsistencies, her 2007 book *Dancing in the Streets: A History of Collective Joy* is, as she herself says, in a minority of books that deal with joy through dancing, music and play. In addition, it is substantial enough to provide us with at least two conclusions that can be used to examine the image of happiness in the Caribbean.

In her sweeping historical (and pre-historical) account of "dancing in the streets", Ehrenreich deplores the traditional white European higher-class male attitude to public group expression of joy in dancing and related activities. There is in her thesis a basic antagonism between civilized, restrained (European) behaviour (in which she sees a systematic repression of natural joy) and the natural expression of joy (which Europeans deemed to be "savage" behaviour). She notes in the early part of her argument that "when the phenomenon of collective ecstasy entered the colonialist European mind, it was stained with feelings of hostility, contempt, and fear. Group ecstasy was something 'others' experienced – savages or lower-class Europeans" (2007, 9). Her avowed mission then is "to speak seriously of the largely ignored and perhaps incommunicable thrill of the group deliberately united in joy and exultation" (16).

Ehrenreich tries to discount European prejudices against group expression of joy, not to do an analysis of dancing and music to see if, how and when they are an expression of joy. She takes it as self-evident that what she labels generally as "dancing in the streets" is an expression of joy and because she thinks that it is natural and applicable to all societies, she starts by looking at the roots of it in human society. In her first chapter, "The Archaic Roots of Ecstasy", her conclusion is that the evolutionary function of dance was for defence and preservation of the species: "Anthropologists tend to agree that the evolutionary function of dance was to enable – or encourage – humans to live in groups larger than small bands of closely related individuals" (23). Although Ehrenreich labels the function as "evolutionary", presumably it would have remained dormant as long as societies had a critical mass, but could have surfaced in cases where migration (forced or free) caused splintering to a level dangerous for survival. In such cases, it would be the unconscious fear of disappearance that would provoke the need for critical social solidarity, which would eventuate through joyous outbursts in dancing. The idea of dance as a factor in society building is relevant to the colonies in the Caribbean some of which started with an almost *tabula rasa* situation as well as to the indigenous communities, some of which were small and nomadic.

Ehrenreich presents evidence for a second conclusion (which is relevant here): despite the common modern perception that restraint has always been the fundamental characteristic of European worship, dancing was an integral part of church experience in Europe: "Priests danced; women danced; whole congregations joined in. Despite the efforts of the Church hierarchy, Christianity remained, to a certain extent, a danced religion" (77). She also shows that, in spite of the nebulous distinction anthropologists make between "ritual" (as religious) and "festivity" (as pagan), the historical connection between the two is abundantly clear in the church's historical relationship with carnival. For her, therefore, there was a strong connection between joy, dance, music, play and religious practice. Note that all this is consistent with Cahusac's (1754) view that dance was originally sacred and that all other dances emerged from this source. However, the puritanical forces in the Protestant churches that have championed restraint (which was seen as a virtue from Plato's time) have virtually removed joy from religious expression. It is the increasing influence of the church and specifically Protestant churches that is relevant to the expression of happiness in the Caribbean colonies, especially among the masses of the population before and after emancipation.

Other Factors Affecting the Popularity of Music and Dance in a Society

Several writers today caution about the exaggerated claims (from Plato up to today) made for the transformational power of music by drawing attention to the fact that music does not play a major role in the lives of some people, either on an individual level or because it is not a major part of their culture. Yet we see in these influential writers the ways in which music and dance are said to be transformative in aesthetics, education and morality (Plato); knowledge and harmony (St Isidore of Seville); religion (Cahusac); sex (Darwin); communication, community and healing (Sacks et al.); and cultural integration (Parncutt and Dorfer). The suspicion that immediately arises is that these formulations do not hold true across all cultures.

One of the most common reasons for a society not to have a great amount of singing and especially dancing as a prominent pastime or art form is if that society has a dominant religion that regards popular play, especially singing and more so dancing, as ungodly. In these cases, dancing is often seen to be sexually perverse and societal reactions to it vary to the extreme. Some Christian denominations forbid any kind of mixed (man with woman) dancing and in these cases all positive references to dancing in the Bible are narrowly interpreted to mean separate-sex dancing. In some Muslim societies, music and dancing are interpreted to be strictly forbidden by the Koran. An interesting variation of religious restriction is narrowing of use, and Coptic society in Egypt may be a case in point. Parncutt and Dorfer report a female Copt interviewee in a research project as saying: "our music is very difficult, rhythmically etc. – it is only for prayer. It helps you meditate. Austria is a land of music and I think they would just find our music boring" (2011, 404).

Ballet is a European form of dance that tells a story or communicates with an audience, often without the use of normal speech. Despite the fact that it is not acceptable in some societies because the costumes and movements accentuate details of the human body, some form of ballet is popular in many societies across the world. We can borrow the word "ballet" and use it in a more generic sense (dance + play) with the emphasis on mime/acting and argue that ballet became popular as a form of non-verbal communication in difficult situations of communication.

In other words, ballet has been used to convey meaning in a multicultural setting in a way that is easier and more appealing than words to reach across linguistic barriers and intellectual levels. It does not matter that the meaning being conveyed in such situations is not as detailed as that carried in verbal communication. In this formulation, ballet, or meaning-filled dancing, goes beyond (Darwin's) conveying sexual messages (not excluding it), and can be seen as an easy, artistic way of communicating and creating social solidarity. It was popular, although not necessarily in a totally non-verbal form, in preliterate as well as early colonial societies and could have remained popular up to today as a publicly permissible, indirect way of communicating and competing with new people and superiors, for example.

A time and situation that may have fostered a significant amount of music and dancing in a society is what can be called a "frontier" context, engendering a "frontier" mentality. In the era of conquest and colonization, colonies had a significant percentage of adventurers on land and at sea, exiles, fortune hunters and people who eschewed the sedentary and safe life back home. They regarded themselves as being at the border of the known and the unknown, the familiar and the new, confronting it with courage and excitement. The relationship between colony and mother country was fraught with animosity partly because those on the frontier were often regarded by those in Europe as peripheral, uncultured and tainted with barbarity. The many words written by academics in the postcolonial period about the relationship between Caliban and Prospero in Shakespeare's *The Tempest* attest to the perceived importance of this conflict. In response to the supercilious attitude of the mother country and not confident enough to claim the extent and level of "culture" of the mother country, colonials over the years tried to outdo their European "superiors" in those areas in which they saw themselves as having expertise. Popular dancing and singing, areas in which all classes of colonial societies benefited from intercultural fertilization, may thus have become areas of pride and prominence for them.

A frontier mentality can be said to have been characteristic of colonial societies across the Americas, which, in their embryonic stages, were crude, with the people being primarily visceral in their everyday concerns. A good example of this would have been Hispaniola in the heyday of buccaneers and pirates. These were restricted-choice societies with few people who were educated or interested in education and few who had sophistication in fine arts or technology. One could argue that in such societies, carousing with music and dancing was the most popular pastime and that, as these societies developed, this pastime remained prominent.

When the rhetorical question is asked in Psalm 137 "How can we sing the Lord's song in a strange land?", the implication is that the situation of exile and oppression is incompatible with singing the Lord's song and singing songs of joy for one's captors. Thus, songs of joy are associated with positive situations within a context of freedom, with a possible corollary that enslaved people singing songs of joy, and especially for their captors, would be psychologically abnormal and would be suffering from some kind of dissociative disorder. One could also conclude from the question that if indeed "slaves" are singing songs of joy in their everyday life, then their situation could not be dismal and oppressive for them.

However, the assumption in the question may be misleading because on face value it suggests that singing in itself is an emotion rather than it being a medium through which different and often contrasting emotions may be expressed. In other words, singing (and the same may be said of dancing) may express feelings of sadness or joy or anything in between. The fundamental suggestion in the rhetorical question – that is, that the emotional situation of slavery should discourage songs of joy or belief – conflicts with the thesis in this book.

3. The Question of an Indigenous Template for Festivity

> The Savages of these islands are the most content, the happiest, the least depraved, the most sociable, the least deformed, and the least troubled by sicknesses of all the nations in the world.
> —Du Tertre 1667, 357

THE FIRST MODEL THE EUROPEANS USED FOR living even in the smaller islands was the indigenous people, for they knew the sources of food, the lie of the land and the weather. Even in the case of Barbados, for instance, which had no indigenous communities living there at the time the English arrived in the first half of the seventeenth century, South Americans, as well as natives of neighbouring islands (Ligon [1657] 1970, 54), were brought to help with the start of an English colony. In St Kitts, there were early reports of Europeans marrying indigenous people (Maurile de S. Michel 1652, 78). In Dominica and St Vincent especially, indigenous societies remained a help to the Europeans until the end of the eighteenth century. Across the smaller islands, there were early reports of European servants and Africans fleeing from European settlements to join indigenous communities. In St Vincent, the rise of the Black Caribs as a cultural phenomenon was the result of the flight and abduction of enslaved Africans from European colonies into indigenous communities.

In the epigraph to this chapter, Du Tertre presented a picture of the indigenous people living an idyllic life before the advent of the Europeans. Then, writing about Puerto Rico more than a hundred years later, Fray Iñigo Abbad y Lasierra ([1788] 1966, 185) had no doubt that the indigenous people had had widespread influence over the colonists there. What may have seemed a logical consequence to Abbad y Lasierra requires close scrutiny in order to fathom the extent to which the indigenous people really did shape colonial life by providing the template for festivity.

Though it is difficult today to think of the islands without the kinds of political affiliation they came to have as a result of their colonial history, this is precisely how they have to be seen when one considers the everyday life and culture of the indigenous people at the beginning of the colonial period. In a situation where the islands were not the titled possessions of anyone and were close together, a maritime lifestyle was central to the existence of the majority of the people and it was maritime mobility that engendered similarity in culture and philosophy of life across the islands.

In the early Spanish image of the indigenous inhabitants of the smaller Caribbean islands as fierce and man-eating, there was little said about their festivities. It was only the French, in the middle of the seventeenth century, who made any concerted attempt to study their way of life and record it. In the early historical records, writers made generalizations based on evidence mostly from the bigger islands. For instance, when Las Casas spoke of "the Indians of this island and indeed of all of the Indies" (1957, 196), there is no guarantee that he had actual information other than from Hispaniola to substantiate the breadth of the claim he was going to make. The same was true when Oviedo spoke of "this way of singing in this and other islands and even in a great part of the continent" (1959, 117:114), but he did refer to eyewitness experience in 1515 (117:114) to support his comparisons. In addition, he did point out that there were language differences (118:116).

As to Jamaica (called Santiago at the time), Oviedo claimed that this island was similar to the neighbouring ones in its flora, culture and language. He went on to say: "As to the rites and ceremonies of the people of the island of Santiago I have nothing more to say because, as I have said before, these people have the same customs and ways as the people of Haiti and Cuba" (1959, 118:116). Assumption of basic similarity in culture is also implicit in the even wider comparison of terms made by José de Acosta late in the sixteenth century: "In Peru these dances are commonly called *Taquí*; in other provinces of the Indies they are called *Areytos*; in Mexico they are called *Mitotes*" ([1590] 1894, 226).

Overall, the early narratives about the various ethnic groups are not consistent in their comments about uniformity or lack of uniformity in culture and even those written in the eighteenth century in most cases tend to be either too general or too narrow in their scope. A typical kind of general comment is that by Prévost d'Exiles (1746, 15:488): "The marriages, funerals, dances and festivals of the Caribs are not so different from those among the majority of other Indians to warrant specific comments." While this conclusion may seem to be based on extensive evidence, it is more than likely an attempt to gloss over ignorance and absence of information.

Yet even if some islands were big enough to have both hinterland and coastal cultures, there still must have been significant similarity and overall dominance in coastal cultures throughout the archipelago to validate use of evidence from some islands to speculate about all. In any case, because Jamaica and Trinidad are at opposite ends of the island chain and both were Spanish colonies that became English, it does not make sense in our analysis to group the festivities of the indigenous people across the islands according to the colonial divide but rather to be aware of possible differences in culture determined by size of land mass – that is, big versus small islands.

AREITOS IN THE SPANISH COLONIES

The earliest information about the music of the indigenous people, in Hispaniola, comes from Fray Ramón Pané's 1498 account,[1] which Martyr later referred to as "a book written by one *Ramonus* an Heremite, whom *Colonus* hadde left with certayne kinges of the Ilande to instruct them in the Christian faith" (Anghiera 1628, 50). Without giving a name for the songs he refers to, Pané (1999, 20) said: "they have their laws gathered in ancient songs, by which they govern themselves, as do the Moors by their scripture". According to Pané, then, the primacy of these "ancient songs" was that they were functional – they were used to govern the people.

The function of the songs is emphasized in 1516 by Martyr who, by his own admission (Anghiera 1628, 50), repeated (51–52) Pané's observations. He also gave a further explanation of the preservation and ordering of the culture of the people: "They [*boitios*] give themselves chiefly to two things: As generally,

---

1. It is important to note what Donald Thompson (1993, 183) says: "Unfortunately, we have the Pané document only at third hand and seen through several layers of translation and interpretation. First, Pané was a Catalán and his report was written in Castilian, not his principal language. In addition he was a well-intentioned but rather simple-minded man, according to Padre Las Casas, who claimed that much of what Pané wrote was of little substance. Furthermore, while some of Pané's reporting was from first-hand observation, much of it repeated what he was told by tribal leaders in a language he may not have fully understood."

to learne the originall and successe of thinges, and particularly, to rehearse the noble factes of their graundfathers, great graundfathers, and auncestours, as well in peace as in warre. These two things they have of old time composed in certayne meeters and ballettes [songs with words meant to accompany dancing] in their language" (132). However, Martyr changed Pané's moral or religious focus to one of songs as historical records and prophecy: "In their ballets left them of their auncestours, they have prophecies of the comming of our menne into their countrey. these they sing with mourning, and as it were with groning, bewayle the losse of their libertie & servitude" (132–33).

From a sixteenth-century European point of view, there was a natural curiosity about "new" people in a "new" world and their history. As a result, there was an early preoccupation among writers with trying to explain them to curious readers. Songs and history coalesced and it was Oviedo who in 1535 amplified the explanation of the songs now referred to as *areitos* as a historical record in lieu of books. Bearing in mind Las Casas's rejection of Oviedo's account of the indigenous people, it is clear that Oviedo presumed that non-literate people were as interested in a historical record as literate people and that the difference was how the record was achieved.

The first time Oviedo mentioned areitos (that is, in his 1526 *Sumario*), his explanation of them was narrower and functional, closer to what Martyr said: "and for this and to make up for memory and the absence of writing, they therefore make their children learn and know in a choral way why, because of the way in which the dead died, they [their bodies] could not be placed there, and this is what they sing in their songs, which they call areitos" ([1526] 1996, 131). However, he was so intrigued by the areitos as historical record that in his fuller 1535 work he expanded his explanation to show the combination of methods by which this was achieved.

The kind of "poet" called *boitio*, of whom Martyr spoke, was not unique to Hispaniola and indeed formed part of the tradition of Europe as well as Africa. There are at least two interpretations of the widespread occurrence of such a tradition: either it was a case of writers projecting a concept from their own experience onto others or it was a universal kind of development in which glorification of the dead becomes ancestor worship which turns into deification of ancestors. In this process, there may be no distinction between historical fact and the supernatural. The historical record becomes the foundation of the culture and at the same time embodies the beliefs of the people and their concepts of the future and afterlife. In the case of the indigenous inhabitants of the islands, Pané no doubt came closer to an understanding of their cultural practices than Oviedo, who limited himself too much to the idea of the areito as a song of historical documentation.

As to what precise "artistic" activity the word *areito* was used by the three early writers to refer to, Pané (1498) spoke of songs accompanied by a musical instrument, Martyr (1628) spoke of *ballettes* (dancing songs) and Oviedo (1535) used the phrase *bailar cantando* (singing while dancing). By using the term *ballettes*, Hackluyt (Martyr's English translator) gave a sense of the areito as an activity including song, dance and musical accompaniment. Oviedo (1959, 117:114) noted, however, that the areito could be performed with or without musical accompaniment. Oviedo thus presents the areito as a variable combination of reciting, singing, dancing and drumming. Even though Pané did not mention dancing, Martyr, Oviedo and all subsequent accounts treated dancing as an integral element in the meaning of the word.

The use of the term *areito* was not restricted to ritualistic and rehearsed song and dance, but was also used for singing and dancing in casual and small groups, according to Oviedo (1959, 117:115). The areito could also be considered as having sexual ramifications, seeing that in some cases there were young female participants. This idea comes through in the reported comments about an areito which Anacaona, the wife of the cacique, put on for Governor Ovando: "More than three hundred maidens took part in the dance, all of whom were her servants, and all marriageable" (117:114).

Early in his account Martyr mentioned other types of areitos: "They have also songs and ballettes of love, and other of Lamentations and mourning, some also to encourage them to the warres" (Anghiera 1628, 132). Later in his account, another significant type of areito reported by Martyr is a praise song which was part of a ceremony of offering (Anghiera 1989, 644) linked to a stage in the agrarian cycle. The reciting of deeds of ancestors was an integral part of this celebration as an appreciation of the past before praying for a good future.

The areito was also mentioned in the testimony of a Puerto Rican woman who was held captive in Dominica towards the end of the sixteenth century. This very early "eyewitness" evidence of practices among the indigenous inhabitants of the smaller islands comes from Luisa Navarrete, "black skinned ... free ... and Spanish-speaking" (Hulme and Whitehead 1992, 39), who was captured by indigenous Dominicans and spent four years in captivity in Dominica. This reported use of the word *areito* by a native of one of the bigger islands supports an argument that the word was really a catch-all term used to refer to almost any type of entertainment activity. Indeed, in a twentieth-century comment on the meaning of the word *areito*, Pedro Henríquez Ureña (1938, 112) says that it was not just a popular song but "a compendium of all the choreographic, musical and poetic art of the Antilleans".

Débauches in the French Colonies

More than a hundred years after the Spanish settled in the bigger islands, the French and the English began to colonize the smaller ones. The French priests were an integral part of colonization efforts and provided most of the first-hand information about indigenous culture there. There was not a considerable amount of re-presentation of cultural information from Spanish sources in the French accounts. Almost immediately, the Spanish image of fierce cannibals began to recede, especially since some French servants were reported to have run away from the French settlements to live among the indigenous people.

The colonizing efforts of the French and English in the smaller islands in the first half of the seventeenth century brought them into direct contact, and often conflict, with the indigenous people. Many on both sides lost their lives in the clashes but, at the same time, coexistence and regular trading in goods increased substantially. John Nicholl's (1607) account mentioned a Master Tench "singing of Catches with the Carrebyes" and a Master Alexander "jesting and playing arme in arme with the two Carrebyes" in 1605 in St Lucia.

By the middle of the seventeenth century, the increasing success of French colonization led the French writers Du Puis ([1652] 1972, 234) and De Rochefort (1658, 454) to present a more pleasant image of the indigenous inhabitants in their day-to-day activities. Labat (1931, 2:114) repeated more or less the same information as part of the daily routine of the indigenous people at the end of the seventeenth century: "After they have eaten . . . some return to their hammock, others squat around the fire on their haunches . . . and they remain whole hours in this position and in silence as if they are in profound meditation or they whistle with their mouth or a kind of flute or pipe and always the same tune."

In 1652, Mathias Du Puis, who spent six or seven years (1644–50) in Guadeloupe, gave one of the earliest descriptions of the get-togethers, which he called *débauches* (revels). Immediately following Du Puis's work came Du Tertre's – the first edition in 1654 and the second, expanded edition in 1667. In between Du Tertre's two editions came the work of De Rochefort (1658), which paralleled much of what was in Du Puis's work and Du Tertre's first edition. De Rochefort, without first-hand knowledge of the islands, assembled a fair amount of information about the music and dancing of the indigenous inhabitants in the middle of the seventeenth century. He commented on the topics of their songs, their dancing, dress, food and drink, and the occasions for their festivities. In addition to these works, there appeared another one at the same time by Paul Boyer (1654), which contained information on the Galibi, and another by Pelleprat (1655). Probably the most significant feature of all these French accounts was the high amount of "borrowing" or plagiarism which they exhibited.

In his account, Du Puis used the word *débauches*. Two years later, Du Tertre (1654, 427) used the same word and so did De Rochefort (1658, 456) four years after him. Du Puis ([1652] 1972, 205) identified drunkenness as the central element in the festivities, and went on to comment: "They do not believe that drunkenness is a crime, but just entertainment. Consequently, the women drink just as hard as the men." This centrality of drunkenness was repeated by Du Tertre a little later (1654, 426–47). At the end of the century, Labat (1931, 2:115) reiterated the same point and even went on to put these revels into a context of evil. As to the reasons Du Puis, Du Tertre and De Rochefort gave for the festivities and the frequency of them, there were only minor differences between them. Du Puis's were: (1) when they intend to wage war; (2) when their first-born children are male; (3) when their children's hair is cut for the first time; (4) when they have reached the age to be able to endure the stress of war; (5) when they want to start a new garden; (6) when they put in the sea a canoe that has been in the mountains ([1652] 1972, 205).

Du Tertre included "when men are cut with agouti teeth; after their women have given birth; when children's hair is cut for the first time; . . . when they want to . . . make a new dwelling" (1667, 386). De Rochefort added, "when they return from their expeditions, whether they were successful or not . . . when they are cured of some illness" (1658, 456). While the words of Du Puis and Du Tertre were very similar, those of De Rochefort had some embellishments but, overall, it was like a single account with several editions.

In sharp contrast to all these works which highlighted *débauches* and the accompanying activities, an earlier work, by Guillaume Coppier, was quite different. It did speak of a *vin* as a major activity before going off to war, but almost paradoxically there is no mention of drinking or drunkenness. In fact, reference to idols, wooden statues and divinities gives this event a religious undertone. In addition, the alternative word given for *vin* and the activities involved is *caramémo*, which must have been an indigenous reinterpretation of (Spanish) *cuaresma*/(French) *carême*, "Lent". Coppier (1645, 61) introduced his description of the activity by saying: "Before they set out, they have a *vin*, which consists of ceremonies like the following which they call their *Caramémo*, which lasts two months."

It is with the same religious vision that Bernard Picart, a few decades later in his voluminous work on the religions of the world, used information from the early French writers to depict the "ceremonies" of the Caribes verbally and pictorially (1735, 116–17). Not much in Picart's verbal description or his pictorial representation inspires confidence in the accuracy of the supposed activity. In his illustration, instead of a carbet (a hut), the room in which the activity takes place resembles the inside of a tall, Aztec-like, stone building and his words – "each one foams at the mouth and shakes like a demon" – sound like a typical European view of the supernatural practices of "others". His depiction of the funeral ceremony and dance among inhabitants of the Gulf of Paria also features a round dance and offerings of food at the grave, but instead of the indoor burial the verbal description identifies, his illustration shows an outdoor burial by the sea.

Benigne Bresson in Grenada, reporting the consequences of a French attack from Martinique on natives of St Vincent in 1654, said: "they spread the alarm everywhere and from there to St Vincent. They also had an assembly and had a drinking party at which they made a resolution to vent their anger on us [in Grenada]" (Roget 1975, 102). What Labat (1931, 2:115) reported at the end of the century was not much different from what the previous French priests had earlier said. Around the same time also, Le Breton ([1702?] 1998, 31) reported as follows: "Nor do they have a surer way of manifesting their joy at the arrival of friends than that of inviting the largest number of people to drink together." In short, for the French, the most salient feature of indigenous parties over the last half of the seventeenth century was revelry with drunkenness.

As to the activities that took place during the assemblies, the similarity in the accounts of Du Puis and Du Tertre especially and the difference from Coppier are again striking. Coppier gives the context for the performance as outdoors, on the sea shore and, unlike the others, the performance has 'religious' associations: "they kneel on one knee facing the sun, utter horrible shouts at it as well as horrible howls which would make the hair on the most timid stand up" (1645, 67). On the other hand, Du Puis ([1652] 1972, 203–4) and Du Tertre (1667, 386–87) give the context as indoor and the performance as nothing but secular. In the latter descriptions, besides drinking, two elements seemed to be familiar occurrences – music and dancing on the one hand and a bird masquerade on the other. Yet at the end of the century, Le Breton did not mention any dancing or music at the assemblies he saw. In other words, differences in purpose, differences across groups and changes over time make it difficult to come to comprehensive conclusions about the assemblies.

In the observations about festivities in the small islands generally, there is little detailed description of dancing or singing: the French writers did not highlight music or dancing during the assemblies. There is no specific mention of deaths of chiefs or important people in which their great deeds are celebrated in areitos, as was said to be the practice in the bigger islands. It is only towards the end of the seventeenth century that one gets a report of a kind of celebratory expression of past military exploits from Le Breton ([1702?] 1998, 31): "On the occasion of this most copious binge . . . I heard with my own ears each one of the elders recount, in proportion to the number of years he had lived, his brilliant exploits." Since these were speeches that elders were making about themselves, there is no certainty that when they died, their speeches would have become songs celebrating dead heroes.

As to the manner of singing at a funeral for a common individual, Du Puis's comment was: "When a Savage dies violently or naturally . . . they all together intone a weeping song: one doesn't know whether they are crying while singing or singing while crying" ([1652] 1972, 246). At the end of the century, Gautier du Tronchoy (1709, 91) said that there were only minimal festivities associated with burials. He did however also say: "all the women standing around the hole sigh and sing mournfully and send such moving shouts towards the heavens that one cannot help but be moved" (215).

As to the kinds of dancing that took place in the assemblies, Du Puis and others almost exclusively used Raymond Breton's information from Dominica. What Du Puis highlighted was the amount of body movement and energy involved: "They assume a thousand different positions, and dance in a barbarous fashion, which is tiring rather than entertaining" ([1652] 1972, 204). Du Tertre repeated the same words exactly (1667, 387) and added a few of his own.

This was a case of men dancing together in twos apparently in file and causing laughter by their antics. Ogilby's English version (1671, 358) added little that was new.

When both Du Puis and Du Tertre said the dancing in the masquerade "tires rather than entertains", one gets the impression that it was vigorous, extended and done to a fast beat. Significantly, this contrasts with comments later made by Chanvalon, who said that these festivities were almost mournful. Most likely this was just one type of music played at the assemblies. It seems reasonable to assume that incitement to go to war, for example, would have required "inciting" music, whereas buffoonery would have required another type.

In contrast to the picture of "a thousand different positions" and buffoonery, De Rochefort described some dances as beautiful, well arranged and performed as part of solemn ceremonies (1658, 454). However, this description had no details to support it. More generally, though De Rochefort used the same source (Breton) for his information as Du Tertre, the dancing he described seemed less robust and more sophisticated, but one has to bear in mind that Labat saw De Rochefort as a thief who wanted to make his account more pleasant.

Du Puis noted a fundamental difference between dances when he said in reference to dancing that was prompted by an eclipse of the moon: "This dance is different in principle from those performed when they get drunk, because the former comes out of superstition and the latter out of merriment" ([1652] 1972, 223). No details of the differences are given, however. Sieur de la Borde (1674, 38) also made a distinction between dances when he said: "They dance more sedately and with a more sombre air at their funerals." Du Tertre (1667, 388) himself made a comment about women dancing: "The women also dance in a circle, holding one hand on their head and the other on their hip, and without jumping or walking, they move their feet and though they exert a lot of effort, they move forward very little."

Further evidence of sex differentiation, in both posture and formation, comes from La Borde (1674, 38) a few years later. La Borde characterized the women's dances as more decent and modest, presumably because while dancing they did not reveal their genitals and they covered their breasts part of the time. Whether this was critical to their intent, however, is not immediately obvious. Yet one is left with the impression of a people who were playful and light-hearted in their dances. This is further confirmed by the way they ended their dances, by hugging and embracing each other.

Overall, the fact that no comprehensive, detailed picture of singing and dancing at assemblies survives indicates either that they were not spectacular, not easily observed or of little direct interest to Europeans. In comparison with the descriptions of areitos in the bigger islands, the absence of detailed description of dancing and singing in the smaller islands is quite striking. While it is easy to blame the historical record for lacunae, it may well be that absence of cohesive forces like dancing and singing was a reliable indicator of societies that were socially and politically more fluid.

The Bird Masquerade

The use of coloured feathers on the forehead and body, plant material as nose and lip decoration, rings of shells or metals on the ears and arms, and dyes (for example, roucou) as means of general body colouring was widespread and common among the various indigenous groups in the islands. The first known book written in English (printed in 1511) contains an "eyewitness" description of the indigenous inhabitants of the islands using feathers as body decoration: "But the men and women have on theyr heed/necke/Armes/knees/and fete all with feders bounden for there bewtyness and fayreness" (Arber 1885, xxvii).

Over and above this universal practice, the use of feathers stuck to the body together with exaggerated dancing seemed to point to something organized and meaningful. It also seemed to be more than the "buffoon spectacle" suggested by Du Tertre or a simple descent into drunkenness. Boyer thought that the use of feathers and such like was the typical fancy dress of unsophisticated people. Du Puis interpreted it as a portrayal of a cock, which also suggests simple and innocent amusement. De Rochefort regarded it more sympathetically, but still as part of the people's attempt to appear at their best. He did not highlight any element of buffoonery in their performances: he saw them as orderly and part of "solemn feasts". De Rochefort had everyone dressed up and painted up for the occasion and wearing their feather headdress, thus displaying themselves at their best. There was definitely an element of sexual display in De Rochefort's description, with the idea that the more attractive the plumage displayed by the males, the more the females would be impressed. At the end of the century Gautier du Tronchoy (1709, 91) highlighted only a crown of feathers as part of the costume. However, around the same time, in a detailed eyewitness account that also highlighted a crown of feathers, Le Breton ([1702?] 1998, 31) depicted what seemed to be a different purpose for the bird masquerade: "They smear their bodies all over with different colours to show they are warriors, and to frighten the enemy."

The bird masquerade is more explicitly reported as a sex, courtship and marriage display in the seventeenth century for a group in Brazil by Souchu de Rennefort (1688), whose description and wording bear a striking similarity to Boyer's. In the first half of the eighteenth century, Gumilla described it for Venezuela as part of the way the "Mapuyes" celebrated their weddings. Benoit (1839) described it in some detail for nineteenth-century Suriname as a dance for young people. The masks and decorations on the body which Benoit mentions relate to features given by Du Tertre and De Rochefort. Benoit's verbal description of this dance makes it seem quite different from what Du Tertre, De Rochefort and Le Breton described.

Even though the indigenous bird masquerade in the Caribbean was far removed from Mexico, it is interesting to note the association of birds with divinities there. Huitzilopochtli, the Aztec sun and war god, was portrayed as a hummingbird – in the Tovar Codex, he wears a hummingbird helmet with a plumage of quetzal feathers behind. It is possible, then, that the Caribbean bird masquerade with the feathered headdress could have had a higher symbolic value than a "bird masquerade" suggests.

Much of what seventeenth-century French writers presented as the customs of the people of the smaller islands echoes Jean De Léry's sixteenth-century account of Brazil. There is little doubt, for instance, that the following passage from De Léry (1578, 114) was seen by Du Puis, Du Tertre and De Rochefort: "having rubbed themselves with a certain gum which they have specifically for that, they cover, feather and bedeck their bodies, arms and legs, so much so that they appear to have a soft feather covering like recently hatched pigeons or other birds". De Léry (146) created the idea that the decoration with feathers was part of a post-battle celebration in which prisoners were eaten. His words inspired the 1606 engraving on a map of Brazil by Jodocus Hondius, which has males wearing feathers, drinking and playing music.

Ironically, however, the cannibalistic ritual said to be one reason for the Tupi festivities in Brazil is not mentioned by Du Puis, Du Tertre or De Rochefort. Evidently, by the 1650s, claims of cannibalism in the smaller islands could not be substantiated and in fact by the end of the century were being emphatically rejected by Labat (1931, 2:116). Indeed, as the indigenous people of the smaller islands began to decline in the face of the increase of Europeans, the image of the once ferocious cannibal began to be converted into one of innocent and even entertaining savage (see Le Breton [1702?] 1998, 31).

Whether it was the dazzling plumage of tropical birds that caused the indigenous people to imitate them in their courtship displays or it was the more menacing aspect of birds of prey that they chose to adopt as part of their festivities, the bird masquerade was central, constant and deep-seated in their psyche. It appears in descriptions of groups over a wide geographical area in North and South America and the Caribbean islands. Yet one could argue that dressing up for parties has always been typical of human societies, and also that bird costumes are part of the imagination of all human beings and thus a bird masquerade in later Caribbean culture does not have to have an indigenous origin.

Varying Interpretations of Indigenous Differences

After the seventeenth century, the period of early colonization in the smaller islands, little was said about indigenous parties as the people were gradually pushed back from the fertile lands and then dispossessed totally. They no longer had freedom at sea or on land and became peoples under siege. Their culture changed, in St Vincent especially, when escaping Africans joined their societies and gradually began to supplant them in numbers and power. By the end of the eighteenth century, the indigenous people no longer had vibrant societies separate and apart from those who had begun to invade their lands from three hundred years earlier. The image of fierce, hostile cannibals which European writers had painted to rationalize their intent to dispossess them of their lands disappeared in the latter part of the seventeenth century to be replaced by the picture of indolence which had become the accepted truth about indigenous groups in the bigger islands. To this was added the element of general drunkenness.

This now "pathetic" picture of the once "fierce and hostile" Carib emerges from Chanvalon, a white creole, whose views exuded all the prejudices of the day. Chanvalon (1763, 55) amplified his picture of a listless people when he said, in reference to their dances: "So they do a round dance which is so solemn and serious that the body takes no greater part in it than the soul. Moreover, this dance has a rhythm which is determined by the slow beat of a monotonous and lugubrious chant, which escapes from their mouths almost inaudibly."

Continuing this negative picture towards the end of the century was Isert (1793, 337), who presented the indigenous people as remnants of their former selves and as melancholy and sombre. This view contrasts with the carousing and drunkenness described in the seventeenth century and, in the eyes of the writer, seemed to reflect a defeated and demoralized people. The kind of pathos which was at the heart of Chanvalon's and Isert's descriptions came to be exaggerated in the decades following and in fact came to refuel the "noble savage" concept which had been there from very early in the French and English accounts (see Hulme and Whitehead [1992, 1], for a comment on Samuel Purchas's [(1625) 1905] use of the term "wilde majesty").

However, because of this general resurgent view of the "Indian" as an innocent victim of European colonization, eighteenth-century descriptions of indigenous groups in the Caribbean islands were probably being fitted into the more general ones which characterized indigenous groups from temperate zones. Moreau de Saint-Méry (1796, 18) argued, for instance, that "the dancing of all uncivilized people between twenty and fifty degrees latitude is always sad and monotonous". He went on to exemplify his idea by saying that an indigenous dance in St Vincent was dull (62). He even accounted for the general exacerbation of this dullness by pointing to the Europeans' introduction of alcohol to the indigenous inhabitants (19). Moreau de Saint-Méry's statements contained two implicit claims: first, that drunkenness among the indigenous people was the deliberate and malicious work of Europeans; and second, that alcohol had caused the pace of dancing among the indigenous people to decrease. It is not easy to substantiate either one of these claims.

Apparent differences in dance between indigenous groups in the seventeenth century, on the one hand, and those of the eighteenth, on the other, may have been caused by an increase in descriptions of indigenous peoples across the Americas and subsequent indiscriminate comparisons of them. In other words, while the early (French) writers on the smaller islands followed the lead of their predecessors in South America (Brazil, principally), the later writers may have been overly influenced by descriptions of groups in North America.

Spanish evidence from the area of Venezuela and Trinidad suggests a maintenance of traditional cultural characteristics. For example, Gumilla's (1741, 65) description of Caribs and other groups preserves the image of the flute-playing sometime-warrior going about his daily business – in other words, a cultural identity with music-making as prominent in daily life. In addition, Gumilla's description of special occasions, especially weddings (65–66), shows little of the negativity featured by Isert. Yet the extent to which Gumilla's description represented practices in Trinidad itself and other nearby islands is not easy to ascertain. Nevertheless, evidence of constant movement across maritime space and the widespread occurrence of the bird masquerade suggest similarity in cultural practices across groups.

Another general reason for what was presented as a difference in energy among the indigenous people in the smaller islands, a difference that is introduced as a difference in time (seventeenth versus eighteenth century) and circumstance (free versus defeated people), could in reality have been a difference in the events that eyewitnesses actually experienced and recorded in the eighteenth century. In other words, what is interpreted as part and parcel of the change of vision as the indigenous inhabitants accepted their subjugation – from a vision of male fierceness to one of mournful acquiescence and docility – could have been descriptions of different dances. Nevertheless, the "loss of energy" picture was most likely an accurate reflection of a people under siege and a receding culture.

Life-cycle ritual displays (around birth, puberty, marriage, death) generally give a good indication of religiosity and celebration in a community, but in comparing activities associated with marriage and death across indigenous groups in the islands and northeastern South America, one is confronted with contradictions which seem to point to abnormality in practice or inaccuracy in reporting. First, there is no mention of marriage in the lists of events celebrated given by Du Tertre and De Rochefort for the smaller French islands. Du Puis ([1652] 1972, 190) leaves no doubt about the matter when he said: "They do not observe any ceremonies in their marriages." Lack of recognition of marriage is also noted by La Borde (1674, 35) two decades later: "For marriages they do not have big ceremonies."

In contrast to this absence in the small islands, Boyer's (1654, 279–80) account about groups in the Guianas presents marriage as an event that was fully celebrated: "Their marriages are formed only by the union of their wills and by touching hands and by calling all their relatives and friends to come for seven or eight days to rejoice with them. There they dance to songs and get drunk like owls." He then went on to make a generalization about big occasions, as if marriage celebration was one of them. There is also a similarity in description and wording given by Souchu de Rennefort (1688) referring to preparations for marriage in Brazil.

Overall, according to the reports, celebration of marriage in Hispaniola, the Guianas and Brazil stands in sharp contrast to absence of celebration in the smaller Caribbean islands. What is contradictory in this contrast is that the Caribs of the Guianas, whom Boyer spoke of, not only were related historically to the Island Caribs but also continued to be in contact with them at least up to the seventeenth century. Thus, one would expect some similarity in customs.

The contrast in marriage celebrations is paralleled by a contradictory similarity in funeral "celebrations". Some items of decoration and "dress" (for example, roucou, feathers of various colours, pendants around the neck) mentioned by Boyer in relation to marriages also appear in accounts of funerals. In fact, Boyer's description of the celebration of marriage (on the mainland) is similar to La Borde's (1674, 37) description of a funeral (in the smaller islands). Indeed, La Borde compared festive celebrations with funerals and drew attention to similarities in dancing: "The dances which are marks of rejoicing are also, for these people, signs of mourning and sadness" (38).

If it is true that marriage was not a significant institution among the Island Caribs, it may have been because of the oft-referred-to, uneven historical relationship between men and women in which the women had been originally spoils of war captured from among different ethnic groups. Indeed, it seems logical that in a peculiar "society" in which wives were captives, dance would have had no matrimonial function and that such a society would celebrate the death of famous warriors but not marriage.

What's in a Name? *Areitos, Vins* or *Ouicou?*

In looking at comparable "parties" across the islands, it could be argued that whereas the Spanish developed a word which highlighted song and performance, French priests used a word which focused on drinking and drunken behaviour. Interestingly enough, the Frenchman Coppier, who was not a priest and did not focus on drinking, used a Christian term (*caramémo*).

The Spanish record from early highlighted the element of drink and drunkenness, for Oviedo's characterization of areitos in the bigger islands more than a century before French accounts of the smaller islands was that they were events in which no one was left sober and standing at the end. French priests, starting with Du Puis, a Dominican friar assigned to Guadeloupe, also identified the festivities of the indigenous inhabitants with drunkenness, but it was Du Tertre (1654, 426) who almost immediately thereafter gave a name for the festivities, a name that was the same as the alcoholic beverage they drank – "ouycou". A few years later, De Rochefort (1658, 456) made exactly the same claim. Both of them even went further and stated that after the indigenous people came into contact with the French they changed the name of their festivity to a French name – "vin" (Du Tertre 1654, 426; De Rochefort 1658, 456). The change in the name of the drink has to be interpreted as one example of a more general policy of change in vocabulary and language which the indigenous people adopted to facilitate communication with the respective European colonizers.

Whether overlap in cultural practices was extensive or not, the similarity across French accounts compounded the matter. This is evident, for example, in Froger's (1698, 170) account, which made the following observation about an indigenous group in South America: "They have amongst themselves several fêtes where they are invited from one carbet to another. They decorate themselves with crowns and belts of feathers and spend the day doing round dances and having feasts where they get drunk on a very strong drink called ouicou." This transfer of a number of cultural features (*carbet*, drunkenness, crowns of feathers, *oüicou*) from the Caribbean islands to South America shows clearly the problem that the practice of copying among French writers presents for accurate documentation.

As to the word *areito* used in the Spanish islands, a relationship which is central to its origin but passes virtually unnoticed is that between *areito* and *aria*. The similarity between *areito* and *aria* is self-evident and is not coincidental. Up until the sixteenth century the word *aria* and its cognates in European languages, including English *air*, as a musical term meant a piece that could be sung; it was not a technical term. From the sixteenth century onward, *aria*, like other Italian words, came to acquire specialized meaning in opera. The word *areito*, which Martyr introduced in 1516, has a hispanicized ending (*ito/-to/o*). The rest of the word is far too close to the Greek and Latin *aer*, the widespread Romance derivatives *aria* (Italian) with its diminutive *arietta*, *aire* (Spanish), *air* (French) and *air* (borrowed into English). The coincidence of a sung piece in Romance languages being the same word as a sung piece in a language of the indigenous people of Hispaniola seems remote, especially when the writer whose work it seems to have first occurred in (Martyr) was Italian. It is significant that when Martyr was repeating information from Pané, in the

First Decade, he gave no name for the songs of the indigenous people, but it is when he was later elaborating on them in the *Third Decade* that he said: "These rymes or ballettes, they call *Areitos*" (Anghiera 1628, 132).[2]

There is no mention by French writers of the word *areito* and judging from Breton's dictionary of the Carib language, there was no root word resembling *areito* in that language. To justify the term *areito* as indigenous, one would have to argue that it emerged within the bigger islands after indigenous communities were established there and after the events in question became fixed, definable and more elaborate.

Pedro Henríquez Ureña states categorically, without supporting evidence, that *areito* is "an authentic word from the Tainos of Santo Domingo". The problem is that, in spite of his reference to Martyr's alternate form *areiti*, the word does not have a typical Taino structure. Henríquez Ureña even repeats what Las Casas specifies about the pronunciation – "their dances and rejoicings, which they call areítos, with a long i" (1938, 111). What this means is that the word is even more Spanish-like in its structure, with the typical Spanish ending *-ito*. Bachiller y Morales (1833), in a treatise on language and traditions in Cuba, repeats two proposed explanations of *areito*, neither of which is satisfactory and it is not clear whether they were intended to be. Both proposals indicate that the word is not easily and satisfactorily explained as an indigenous word.

The origin of the word *areito* as American becomes even more suspect when Oviedo, in 1535, compared the areito with singing dances in Etruria and Rome (1959, 117:113). This comparison with early opera-like performances means that there was an awareness of the similarity between the two and, furthermore, Martyr's use of the word *ballettes/ballets* adds substance to the idea that one is dealing with a loanword. Even the fact that it was a word that the Spaniards are said to have taken with them to Mexico and Central America indicates that there was some preference for the word among them. It would seem, judging from the time of emergence of the areito and aria as features of performance, that there was influence in both directions – *aria* on *areito* and the reverse – in the evolution of the words.

In summary, then, the term *areito* was a facile way for early Europeans to

---

2. Donald Thompson's scepticism about an authentic indigenous source for the term *areíto* is clear in the following words: "the practice which was later to be given the name areíto by other writers"; "the *areíto*, so designated by Las Casas and other writers" (1993, 184).

refer to the variety of indigenous cultural activities – songs, dances and festive events. It is not just accidental that Pané, the person on whose work cultural claims made by subsequent writers were generally based, did not use the term and thus, one would have to assume, had not heard it. Since it was ingenuously adopted by Spanish writers, it is not surprising that French writers were not attracted to it. Consequently, the contrast in usage between French and Spanish writers created a spurious distinction between the entertainment activities in the bigger islands and the smaller ones.

Carousing in the Old World and the New

Probably the most widespread, negative generalization about the indigenous people of the Americas is that they loved strong drink and would drink until they were drunk. In various early accounts in the seventeenth century, drunkenness was said to characterize their festive behaviour. Oviedo's description of the areito (1959, 117:115) as an event ending with no one standing is one of the earliest instances of this generalization. By the end of the eighteenth century, this view had become the accepted one for indigenous people across the Caribbean islands, judging from Chanvalon's (1763, 50) statement that "they passionately love strong drink" as well as Abbad y Lasierra's ([1788] 1966, 185) reference to "their affection for strong drink and spirits". Though the presentation of "other" people in a negative light was typical in the European colonial thrust, it is difficult either to discredit or verify general claims of continual, excessive drunkenness among the indigenous people. Remember, however, that Las Casas dismissed Oviedo's account as fictional and that that is where the drunken image of the indigenous people started.

From early, in the French accounts, writers intimated that there was an interdependence of drinking and dancing. Pre- and post-war festivities were the major examples given. De Léry (1578, 146) said that the Tupi in Brazil, during their caouïn-ing, were "singing, whistling, encouraging and exhorting each other to behave valiantly and to take prisoners when they go to war". Around the mid-seventeenth century among the Galibi in the Guianas, drinking with dancing was identified as primarily either preparation for fights and battles or as celebration after such events. In the former, the activities were portrayed as occasions during which prospective warriors whipped themselves up into a state of frenzy to go off to attack their enemy without fear: "they will often have assemblies to surprise you, as they often do against other savages, when they will sometimes spend eight days or three weeks making 'wines' in order to incite themselves to do better" (Boyer 1654, 277).

Drinking with dancing was given as characteristic of indigenous groups across the islands and in South America, but it was not exclusive to them, for the same kind of behaviour was given as characteristic of white *boucaniers* in Hispaniola and Tortuga in the first half of the seventeenth century. Samuel Hazard, in his historical account of this group, not only gave a pictorial illustration of "merry-making", which included music and dancing (1873, 74), but also said the following: "Their principal vice was drunkenness, which they brought about by imbibing pure brandy, drinking it as freely as the Spaniards did water. Sometimes they bought together a pipe of wine, and staving in the head of it, they never ceased to drink until the wine was exhausted and their money spent" (73). Were the identical behaviours of the indigenous people and the white *boucaniers*, some of whom had arrived in Hispaniola and Tortuga from the smaller islands, independently caused or did the one influence the other?

In early reports of the bigger islands and the smaller ones (for example, Oviedo and Breton respectively), drunkenness was reported as totally and solely the doing of the indigenous people themselves, which suggests that it was they who set the pattern for those came into their communities. However, in other cases, Europeans were said to have introduced alcohol to indigenous groups as part of merry-making. Following is an instance of the latter in St Lucia in 1605 involving a band of Europeans (would-be colonists for Guiana) who were stranded and joined in entertainment with the people of the island: "But Maister Tench . . . did show himselfe so extraordinarie pleasant, that hee fell a singing of Catches with the Carrebyes, and caused them to drinke carouses of Agua vitae and water" (Nicholl 1607). The citation thus gives an early example of Europeans offering alcohol to the indigenous people and the latter seemingly having a great liking for it to make themselves merry.

Yet it is difficult to attribute blame (or credit) for what is often regarded as the dissolute lifestyle in the early European colonies in the Caribbean. Perhaps it may simply be that among non-literate people involved in fairly mobile or nomadic occupations (hunters and warriors), there was nothing else to do to make the interim periods between tasks enjoyable and entertaining or to counterbalance the harshness and dangers of these tasks.

The practice of having a music and singing activity end in total drunkenness is presented in the historical record as a cultural aberration, as if it were unfamiliar to Europeans. However, recorded cultural practices from Ancient Egypt, Greek mythology and other European literature indicate otherwise. Notions about festivities and drinking in Ancient Egypt were formulated based on comments like the following 2200 BC inscription at the Temple of Dendera: "The mouth of a perfectly contented man is filled with beer." Evidence from other inscriptions and images also suggests that drinking was seen as a way of facilitating access to deities and that in the worship of the goddess Hathor, worshippers got drunk on beer. In Greek mythology, Bacchus was the god of wine, merrymaking and joy. In 1623, just a few years before the French colonial writers were penning their accounts, Guido Reni painted *Drinking Bacchus*, in which the god in the form of a child is leaning against a barrel of wine, drinking wine and urinating at the same time. It is unlikely that this kind of image of Bacchus and his association with merrymaking did not inform depictions of the indigenous inhabitants.

Even if seventeenth-century French colonial writers were unaware of drinking practices in Ancient Egypt, it is unlikely that they were unaware of their own cleric and countryman, François Rabelais, whose many statements on drinking are notorious; for example: "I drink eternally. This is to me an eternity of drinking, and drinking of eternity. Let us sing, let us drink, and tune up our roundelays. . . . Drink always and you shall never die" (1890, 29) and "Come, therefore, blades, to this divine liquor and celestial juice, swill it over heartily and spare not! It is a decoction of nectar and ambrosia" (32).

That Rabelais was aware of the Caribbean islands is clear because he mentions (178) the "Cannibal Islands" as a source of "ingots of gold" for his "Thelemites". Whether he had read the reports of the prodigious drinking of the indigenous people, in Oviedo's account for example, is not known. Whether it was Rabelais who was influenced by the reports from the islands and consequently featured drinking in his work or whether his work influenced other French priests who subsequently highlighted and exaggerated indigenous drinking, or whether the one was unrelated to the other, is impossible to know. In any case, excessive drinking and festivity cannot be seen to have been determined by race, class or social status.

Did the Indigenous People Leave Any Imprint of Festivity?

Samuel Wilson (1997, 207) sets out his approach to indigenous legacy by saying: "I particularly want to avoid what might be called the 'contributions' mode of analysis, which identifies modern cultural elements as hold-overs from centuries past." Here the intention is to answer the question about legacy by looking at a general philosophy of life that governed the deeds of the indigenous people as well as at specific practices that were common to them. Of course, the degree and nature of their interaction with Africans, Europeans and creoles are most critical in any discussion of legacy.

As far as a general philosophy of life is concerned, the shock of the European invasion, which resulted in the rapid decimation and psychological decline of the indigenous populations across the islands, meant that whatever philosophy of life they had before the coming of the Europeans was not able to stoutly sustain them and provide a powerful model for the succeeding European colonies. Yet in the bigger islands, writers claimed that the *dolce farniente* lifestyle of Spanish creoles was adopted from the indigenous people. Whether this was so or not, it is difficult to sustain the same argument for creoles in the smaller islands, even though they were said to exhibit the same lifestyle, because the extent of their contact with the indigenous people was limited and also because the indigenous people in the smaller islands were not as agricultural and sedentary as those in the bigger islands. In other words, what is seen today as a *dolce farniente* lifestyle across the Caribbean is a naive generalization – such a lifestyle cannot be "credited" to the indigenous people.

A general philosophy of life among the indigenous people would have to be broken down into various elements – for example, their attitudes to work and acquisition of wealth; to the land, nature and the supernatural; and to music, dance, masquerade and festivity. It is only the last group of activities that had any chance of influence within the framework of European colonization, dominated as it was by acquisition of wealth through agriculture, territoriality and a monolithic religion (with variants). Even the "leisure" activities had little chance of influence because, among the indigenous people as normal societies, they were tied to specific cultural activities (identified in detail by European writers) and these cultural activities had little social relevance to European colonizers and their African workers. In other words, there were few overlapping contexts of festivity during the slavery period and therefore little influence.

However, there were certain specific features of festivity among the indigenous people that were later noted in the English and French colonies. The first among these was that the indigenous people danced a lot and were proficient at it. Martyr was one of the first writers (in 1516) to make a general statement about dancing among the inhabitants of the islands and then to give an explanation of it: "They exercise themselves much in dauncing, wherein they are very active, and of greater agilitie then our men, by reason they give themselves to nothing so much" (Anghiera 1628, 132). Las Casas, to some extent, supported part of Martyr's comment about the love of dancing in a general statement about all the islands (1957, 196). The idea was repeated by De Rochefort, who expanded it into a general statement about "barbarous peoples" (1658, 454). Thus, it came to be generally accepted that the inhabitants of the islands danced a lot. Some of the notable features of dancing the historical record speaks of are "antics" and "postures", some of which were sexual; it also speaks of mimicry. These elements were subsequently repeated for the slaves in West Indian colonial society and, eventually, the observation and explanation came to be applied generally to all creoles.

This sameness did not result from transfer from the indigenous people to others in the colonies; it was mostly the result of a European undifferentiated vision of "others". Critical factors in transfer would have been the nature and degree of interaction between ethnic groups, but the fact is that the indigenous people were consistently presented as being socially and psychologically apart in the Caribbean colonies and, in spite of the general statements about their love of dancing, the French record does not support this in the smaller islands.

The second feature in the early record is that a "call-and-response" technique was a fundamental method of memorizing used in the historical areito. It was essentially a technique which involved imitation in singing and dancing simultaneously. The social significance of this technique is the solidarity it would engender and the collective joy that it would generate. Call-and-response is regarded as a distinctive singing technique of African descendants in the Americas. It is true that in their case the "response" is not a direct imitation of the "call", but it seems reasonable to argue that a conventional group behaviour characterizes both and that there could have been some influence from one on the other. In any case, the interactive nature of the technique highlights the primacy of group behaviour in these cultural practices.

The third feature in the early record is the long duration of festivities. It is clear that there was a difference between Europeans and the people they encountered in the Americas in the way that they regarded time, especially leisure time. There was the general European view that natives of the tropics, because of propitious weather and the bounty of the land, were not driven to make use of all available time to secure "food" or "goods" and so spent a lot of time in idleness. Presumably it was this mindset that led European writers to repeatedly comment on the length of time events of entertainment lasted and the amount of energy that was expended. It is not that there was necessarily any influence of the indigenous inhabitants on Europeans or Africans in the matter of the use of time; it is that all people living in the tropics were regarded in the same way, as spending a lot of time in leisure.

In the seventeenth century, French writers paid scant attention to preceding Spanish accounts and generally preferred to describe the cultural features of the people in "their" islands within a French tradition and, as a result, their perception of the level of earlier Spanish and Portuguese influence on the indigenous inhabitants was not always acute. So, linguistic and other cultural features that the indigenous people had adopted and adapted from the Spanish and Portuguese were at times not recognized and were treated as "Carib" or "Indian". In short, singlemindedness in the French historical record contributed to uneven development in knowledge and understanding and masks the legacy of the indigenous people in the area of entertainment in the smaller islands.

Furthermore, in spite of the strong testimonial to Raymond Breton's knowledge of groups in Dominica and Guadeloupe, what French writers wrote about their customs were selections from, additions to and updatings of what previous French writers, especially De Léry, had said about indigenous people especially in Brazil and the Guianas. On close examination of the development of French involvement in the New World, it is clear that the picture of indigenous culture that developed was formulated according to the movement of the French from Brazil through the Guianas and into the smaller islands. In these descriptions, mostly by missionary priests following in their own traditions, there was a practical dependence on the experience and ideas of predecessors for survival and success in the business of conversion.

A perusal of four documents from the pre-sugar period of early colonization and before does not give any reason to believe that music and dancing were prominent just before and at the time of the first colonization of the smaller islands by the French and English. The illustrations in the book *Histoire naturelle des Indes* ([1996], actually a sixteenth-century, presumably French, pictorial depiction of various places in the Caribbean) do not indicate that music and dancing figured prominently in the everyday activities of the people. Only one of the forty-three illustrations in the second half of the book (which deals with ways and customs) depicts music making. Even in this case the focus in the illustration is not on music – it shows men walking around a house playing music (while a woman gives birth inside). One other illustration shows a woman tinkling a bell, but this was not really to produce music.

John Nicholl's 1607 *An Houre Glasse of Indian Newes*, which describes the first English attempt at settlement in the smaller islands (in St Lucia), has just passing reference to any kind of entertainment. Guillaume Coppier's *Histoire et Voyage des Indes Occidentales*, the first part of which was based principally on the author's three-year stay in St Kitts in the 1640s, has a single reference to dancing and singing, without any fanfare. *L'histoire de l'isle de Grenade en Amérique: 1649–1659*, said to be the work of Benigne Bresson, documents the interaction between the French and the indigenous people in Grenada over a ten-year period; it does not contain any references to music and dancing. It seems logical, then, to conclude that if music and dancing were prominent, they would have featured more in these documents.

It could be that there really were few festivities to be commented on among the indigenous groups in the smaller islands because their loose political structure did not allow for or promote inter-group cohesion and solidarity. One could argue that since dance and music are indicative of solidarity within ethnic groups, the paucity of it in the written record reflected reality. Thus, even when the indigenous inhabitants had special expeditions (for example, war), they had to rely not on bonds that had been fostered by daily cultural communion but on a more temporary excitement to action whipped up by dancing and alcohol. In other words, one could argue that they were more of a hunter-gatherer people not bound together by music and dancing on a daily basis, and had no generally festive image of themselves.

A feature of one of the smaller Caribbean islands (St Vincent) that definitely speaks to the matter of cross-cultural influence was the presence of Black Caribs among the indigenous people there. These Black Caribs were regarded at the time as a cultural phenomenon in that they were physically West African and culturally Island Carib. Their rise and decline coincided with the Europeans' changing level of interest in the island: they grew and prospered while the Europeans disregarded the island, but were banished to Central America at the end of the eighteenth century when the British became more interested in the fertile lands in St Vincent. While they were regarded by l'Abbé Raynal (1777 4:383) as being "doubly Savage" (that is, Carib and African), there is no general image of them as lovers of singing and dancing.

From the initial encounters, exotic pictorial images of "Indians" dominated European imagination and images of the people in the smaller Caribbean islands were the first lurid ones. These islands were first referred to as the "Cannibal" Islands. This name changed to variants of "Caribbee" Islands and then the name "Caribbean" was used to refer to the sea around the islands. As the name "Caribbean" extended geographically, the cannibal image that had first brought the area to prominence receded. As the lurid image of the Caribs declined in import in the colonial situations, the image of a vanquished foe took the place of the image of a bloodthirsty warrior before that image also receded.

However, the idea of the vanquished foe might have had a more critical influence than it at first seems. In 1834, Trelawney Wentworth described a pantomime put on in St Johns, Antigua, called *Harlequin Planter*, which was essentially a comic history of European colonization. In the pantomime, the original conception of the indigenous people had changed remarkably (1834, 2:171) – the indigenous people were given a happier image, one which presented them as a people dancing joyfully in harmony with nature before they were undermined by European territoriality. This image, a far cry from that of the bloodthirsty cannibals that the Spaniards had created, was much nearer to the French image created by Du Tertre in the words glossed at the head of this chapter and could be characterized as festive.

In European imagery, the indigenous people were presented as happy before the advent of Europeans, then resisting dishonourably (being cannibals), and then being decimated or wiped out (being technologically and intellectually backward). Thus, even though in reality they were mostly unsuspecting victims of their diseased adversaries, they were converted into either a happy/noble memory, an example of honourable suicide, or remained a morose vanquished foe. In short, there is no iconic image of them as a dancing or festive people.

A general psychological question that arises from this characterization is: To what extent would the cultural features of a pre-modern, different and conquered civilization be adopted as models in a new, developing civilization? The consistent use of the word *sauvage* by the French historically as a label for the indigenous people suggests that, in the French mind at least, the answer to the question is "very little".

A further question that arises is: Would an enslaved people (Africans) have been open to cultural influence from another subordinated people (the indigenous inhabitants)? The evidence from St Vincent supports a positive answer, but opinion from Barbados, where a slave, probably typically, associated Caribs with crabs ("Me neder Chrab, nor Creole, Massa! – me troo Barbadian born" [Pinckard 1806, 1:133]), suggests the contrary. Through the period from 1834 to 1950, it cannot be said that the indigenous people and their heritage were held in high regard by any sector of the population in Dominica or St Vincent. Finally, illustrations of the indigenous people enjoying themselves (and they may not all be accurate representations) are not convincing evidence of a strong, contextually relevant festive influence in those islands that became typical sugar plantation colonies.

4. Whites Promoting Play in the Colonial Beehive

> Before I take leave of the Caribbee, or windward Islands, I must observe to you, that there are not a set of more sociable happy mortals in the world than the inhabitants of those islands.
> —[Anon. Irish] 1776, 26

IN HER 1995 ARTICLE "THE BEEHIVE AS A MODEL FOR COLONIAL DESIGN", Karen Kupperman discusses the social and economic ways in which the beehive was promoted as a model for success in the early English colonies in the Americas. This was in the first half of the seventeenth century when colonies were seen as replicas of England, with a predominantly English workforce. Kupperman (1995, 287) makes the point that it took some time to realize that economic success had to be linked to the expectation that one would enjoy the fruits of one's labour. However, in the Caribbean, with the change to sugar production and the consequent dramatic dependence on slave labour, the idea of benefiting from one's labour did not apply any longer – the belief that took hold was that profits from an economic venture belong rightfully and exclusively to those who take the risk. Accordingly, the French writer Pierre Saintard (1756, 232) asserted that "a colony does not exist for itself: it exists for the nation that founded it". Twenty years later, the thirteen British possessions in North America declared their independence from Great Britain because they believed that they did not exist for Great Britain but for themselves. No such revolution took place in the English islands.

O'Shaughnessy (2000) puts forward the simple argument that there was a sharp difference in British America between whites in the islands and those on the mainland – the former were never attached to the islands as home whereas the latter never had any other concept of home other than America, where they were born. Consequently, the former never supported the latter in their rejection of the mother country but instead preferred to remain closely tied to Britain. The fact is, however, that Europeans who came to the Caribbean colonies were from different ethnic groups and social levels, they had different reasons for migration, and they had different attitudes to work and play according to whether they were administrative, military, entrepreneurial or contracted. Some in Barbados in the early years were political exiles who perforce had to see the colony as home; many in Jamaica were indeed fortune hunters who saw themselves returning to England with wealth. In general, over time, the colonists developed contradictory sentiments and their creole children even more so, principally because of their upbringing in slave societies and the image of exoticism that they acquired.

Although the beehive model fitted British North America more so than the English islands, it surfaced in a description by Peter Marsden (1788, 36), who said: "All the time the negroes are busy with the crop, they make so much noise in singing that they may be heard a great way off; and from this circumstance, added to their dusky hue, they have no small resemblance, in the eye of a stranger, to a swarm of bees." The beehive image becomes more dramatic here because it is amplified by sound. It is the noise of the bees (the singing of the "negroes") that really is the most powerful element in the perceptual experience of the swarm of bees, and it is this repeatedly noted experience in the historical literature that sustains the beehive model, which can be expanded to include the slaves at play.

There are other problems with the beehive model when it is applied to the Caribbean. First, the total activity of the beehive conflicts with the image of debauchery and dissipation among whites; second, the love of dancing, which was said to be characteristic of whites, conflicts with the industry of the bee. Yet there are elements of the beehive that make it a useful model for the slave colony. The noise of the bees as a reflection of work is, as Marsden shows, relatable to the singing of the "negroes", and the dances of honey bees are comparable in terms of communication to the dancing on the plantation. Furthermore, the hierarchy of the bees (queen, drones and workers) is also comparable to the social hierarchy on the plantation as well as the interdependence of the different bees for overall success. Moreover, domesticated beehives are traditional agricultural ventures set up for economic gain and are thus comparable to Caribbean plantations owned and run by whites as businesses.

The behaviour of West Indian whites in the colonies must not be equated

Figure 2. The Middle Temple Macaroni, "In short, I am a West Indian". *The Macaroni Scavoir Vivre* and *Theatrical Magazine*, July 1773, facing page 504. Courtesy of the British Museum.

with their behaviour in Britain. Many West Indian whites in Britain were parvenus who publicly displayed recently gotten wealth without the requisite social decorum. As a result, they were lampooned by British playwrights and artists. The best known fictional characters were Sir Peter Pepperpot in Samuel Foote's *The Patron* and Belcour in Richard Cumberland's *The West Indian*. In relation to the latter, an image appeared in the *Macaroni Scavoir Vivre and Theatrical Magazine* in July 1773 with Belcour's words: "(I am an idle, dissipated, unthinking fellow, not worth your notice:) in short, I am a West Indian" (act 3, scene 3). This image of the white West Indian or *Creolian* in Britain as a macaroni (a dandy with an extravagant hairstyle/wig, clothes and affected mannerisms) made him a part of the British social scene because no such character, especially with a sword, was described in the islands. In fact, there was a regular complaint in the West Indies that when children of whites went to Britain for education or refinement, they changed in that direction and became spoiled.

Generally, the English colonists who came to the small islands from the first half of the seventeenth century onward were not fashionable, sensitive or artistic. Drinking was their most common social activity – it did not require any training and expertise. In the fledgling colonies, when there was not yet a lot of leisure time for or commitment to the arts, even music and singing were marginal preoccupations at that time. Ligon ([1657] 1970, 107) gave an impression of this mindset and the lack of appreciation of music on the part of some early colonists/planters in Barbados when he said:

> And though I found at Barbadoes some who had musical minds; yet, I found others, whose souls were so fixt upon, and so riveted to the earth, and the profits that arise out of it, as their souls were lifted no higher; and those men think, and have been heard to say, that three whip-sawes, going all at once in a Frame or Pit, is the best and sweetest musick that can enter their ears; and to hear a Cow of their own low, or an Assinigo bray, no sound can please them better.

In the port areas it was different, for there there were gatherings of whites (administrative, military and merchant marine people) who were not permanently resident and who wanted to enjoy themselves. For those whites in Barbados who were interested in music and singing, importation of music and musicians from England (that is, extension of English traditions) was their vision, according to Ligon (107). There is no evidence that this dream of imported, resident, professional musicians was ever realized in Barbados or any other colony.

As far as dancing was concerned, one of the major constraints was seen to be the weather, more specifically the temperature. Ligon, in suggesting what dances could be done, specified "some kinds of Dances, but none of those that are laborious, as high and loftie Capers, with Turnes above ground; these are too violent for hot Countries" (105–6). This negative view of dancing in the tropics was still being expressed as a matter of course a hundred and fifty years later when John Stewart (1808, 178) remarked: "It is, however, rather a painful sight often to see, in a hot room, where even the sedentary spectator pants for the refreshing air, a groupe of charming well-dressed young women *sweltering* through the fatigue of a long country dance." However, this negative reaction to vigorous dancing was more typical of the English than of the French and Spanish. Indeed, the English through the colonial period established a cultural distinction between themselves and others by invoking a refined sensitivity to climate.

A Scarcity of White Folk Culture in the Historical Record

At several points in his book *The Outline of History* ([1920] 1951), H.G. Wells makes summary statements about the evolution of European music across the centuries. His information about Europe is to some extent applicable to colonial situations, especially those of the nineteenth century, for "song and pianoforte pieces for the refined home" as well as "dance music for the social gathering" (1030) also became a part of the English colonies in the Caribbean. What is significant about Wells's summaries, however, is that they have the same prejudice as those of the early writers on the colonies in that they create the impression that there was little in the way of music and entertainment among lower-class whites. It is this kind of prejudice that resulted in a signal absence of written information on the white working classes in the colonies.

St Kitts and Barbados, each of which the English used to dominate neighbouring islands, initially were intended to be replicas of England demographically, with white indentured servants as the working class, but the successful expansion into sugar production in the 1650s caused this model to vanish and whites to become the minority group in West Indian populations. Yet if the second quarter of the seventeenth century provided the social base for St Kitts and Barbados, then the role of whites of all classes would have been critical.

Only odd comments give an idea of features that came from lower-class European whites in the West Indies. For instance, Moreton (1790, 156), in describing Jamaican slave activities, resorted to a comparison with the "vulgar peasantry" in Ireland to make his point. On the other hand, Long (1774, 2:422) referred to the Scottish, although what he said apparently equally applied to the Irish. Although few similar comments are made about the English, Tobin (1785, 96) does refer in a derogatory manner to "the dismal scrapings, and aukward caperings of an English May-day, or a country wake".

The account of an anonymous Irishman who stopped at some of the Leeward Islands on his way to Jamaica highlights significant influence of the Irish in St Croix, which was officially Danish at the time but was dominated by Irish residents. Even more significant is the same writer's mention of one of the earliest traditions of a St Patrick's Day parade in the Americas, in the island of Montserrat: "St Patrick's day, and his wife's day, are kept here with greater solemnity than in any other place. The taylors are closely employed for months before the day, in making superb green clothes for the principal gentlemen of the island, all of whom walk in grand procession on Patrick's day" ([Anon. Irish] 1776, 15).

This gives a better indication of the cultural transfers from the British Isles that would have influenced the population as it developed in this island and others. In the case of the St Patrick's Day parade, not only is it evident that whites walking in parade provided a model for slave parades but also that a specific colour (in this case green) was being used uniformly as an ethnic symbol.

From the beginning, military and professional people, administrators, plantation owners and managers, adventurers, tourists, and other Europeans moved from one colony to another for various reasons. Consequently, all the Caribbean colonies, except for Barbados, had significant mixtures of Spanish, French, British and other Europeans. In the case of Jamaica, for instance, in its early years as a colony it had a Spanish culture; in its late years as an English slave colony, it was a refuge for whites from neighbouring, revolutionary Saint Domingue as well as a holding place for French prisoners captured in the everlasting war between the French and the English. Then, in the years after the Haitian Revolution, the French language and French culture became a noticeable element in urban areas of Jamaica.

In a diary entry for 28 October 1803, Lady Nugent (Wright 2002, 180), wife of the governor of Jamaica, commented on "a party of French people", military men and their wives from St Domingue, who attended one of her many dances:

"In the evening, eight or ten more French gentlemen came . . . and we had a dance. I got up a French country dance for Madame Fressinet, but the exhibition was so extraordinary, that I almost repented my civility; for her clothes were very thin and she kicked about, and looked as if she had no covering at all." As can be seen from Lady Nugent's remarks, their behaviour so differed from that of the English upper class that they attracted negative comments. Yet, overall, reactions to the French presence in Jamaica were ambivalent. For example, Stewart (1808, 176) was more sympathetic when he pointed out some of the positive consequences of the Haitian Revolution on Jamaica.

In the case of the other islands, migration from the French islands resulted in increased fusion of music, singing and dancing. It was probably Trinidad that received the most emigrants from the French world in the early nineteenth century, but French culture was already an integral component of the culture of other islands (for example, Dominica, St Lucia, Grenada), which over the colonial period had been French possessions on one or more occasions. In the case of Trinidad, which was a Spanish colony up almost to the nineteenth century, its closeness to the South American mainland guaranteed continued Spanish influence after it became British. Consequently, Spanish music and dancing were basic ingredients in their culture.

As will be seen, the dearth of white folk culture in the historical record has led to speculation that certain European "plays" that the slaves performed came not from direct observation of them but through church activities, church literature or literature provided by priests. This kind of explanation has come right down to account for practices in the twentieth century: "Thus we have direct confirmation from a performer that the St Kitts and Nevis Mummies originally drew their text from a book" (Millington and James 2011, 67). Nevertheless, it would be unwise to discount more regular forms of transfer of folk culture from earlier centuries in the Leeward Islands, where the Irish were well represented.

In 1640 the population of Barbados (approximately thirty thousand) was more than 90 per cent white and, in spite of the decrease of the white indentured servants in the second half of the seventeenth century, whites were still about 25 per cent in 1700. It is therefore reasonable to assume that many English holiday sports and pastimes were transferred to Barbados in the first hundred years of its colonial history and that these radiated across the English islands. Gradually, because of the perceived inappropriateness of white physical exertion in public, except in relation to military exercises and one or two games, white entertainment became more indoor.

Happiness at the Frontier: "Creolizing", Secularity, Excess and Refinement

Despite the fact that foreigners held sway administratively right through the colonial period, creoles became dominant culturally and, because of the inevitable animosity between locals and foreigners, it took time for foreigners to be accepted into local communities. The constant negative comments made about creoles by visitors did not help this process. Probably the easiest way to understand the difference in mentality between creoles and foreigners who came to live in the Caribbean is in the concept of "creolizing". If "creolized" signalled acceptance by creoles, creolizing was symbolic of the exact opposite – creolizing was a behaviour that foreigners indulged in, believing that they were behaving like creoles, and it revealed a patronizing and basically insulting attitude to creoles. It is hardly likely that creoles used the word among themselves – it would have been tantamount to accepting the designation "indolent" with which historically Europeans branded them. It was a branding that derived from a perception of their total dependence on slaves to execute their every whim and fancy, operating, as far as work was concerned, like drones in the beehive.

The practice was explained thus: "Creolizing is an easy and elegant mode of lounging in a warm climate; so called, because much in fashion among ladies of the West Indies: that is, reclining back in one arm-chair, with their feet upon another, and sometimes upon the table" (Wright 2002, 117n1). While creolizing was presented as an "elegant mode of lounging", British caricaturists at the turn of the century used it to denigrate white colonial habits and reinforce the image of them as indolent and dissipated. The word has much in common connotatively with the modern word "laid-back" and is probably not distinct from it historically and in terms of the people to whom it is applied. Ironically, though the word suggests inaction, people to whom it is applied are seen as fun-loving, given to partying and always ready to enjoy life.

It is not surprising, then, that whites in the West Indies were not seen to be under the heavy influence of the church. Indeed, the dearth of comment about church music corroborates the view that early colonial societies in the Caribbean were generally irreligious. An anonymous Irish visitor to Jamaica in 1776, after noting that "there is but one church in Kingston" (31), went on to observe that "'tis very seldom the church is more than half full" (32). About thirty years later, John Stewart, also in Jamaica, said: "all those in the planting line (indeed all those in the interior, of whatever description) seldom or never

Figure 3. West India custom (creolizing). Richard Hawkins, Quizem, *Sketches of West Indian Life*, 1810–14. Courtesy of the National Library of Jamaica.

attend any religious institution. . . . Sunday here is a day like any other" (1808, 205) and "with a few exceptions, the congregations in the churches consist of usually a few white ladies, and a respectable proportion of free people of colour and blacks" (1823, 182).

The first of the early comments about church music was made by Labat (1742, 7:428) in one of the French islands: "the principal cantor in the Jesuit Church . . . could sing very well and had a perfectly beautiful voice, but . . . was so proud and arrogant that when it came to rubrics, singing and ceremonies, he thought he knew more about them than a director of a seminary". Another comment, about a church organ in Barbados, occurred in Prévost d'Exiles's

(1746, 15:602) work (probably from Labat): "Its church is the normal size of English cathedrals; the organ singularly beautiful; the bell-tower majestic; and no less worthy of praise, a beautiful carillon of seven bells, which is seen as a modern work of art." Another compliment came from a visitor to Jamaica: "the organ which is a very fine one, is richly ornamented, and the organist is reckoned to be as good a performer as Stanley, or any other" ([Anon. Irish] 1776, 31). Another one was made about the organist at the church in St Johns, Antigua, by Luffman (1789, 120) Again, an "excellent" organ is referred to by Sir William Young when he visited Grenada in 1792 (Edwards 1801, 3:297). In contrast to these generally positive comments from across the islands, in Spanish Town in Jamaica the organist at the parish church incurred the wrath of the vestry for damaging the organ and was suspended (Wright 2002, 14–15n1). In all, these few incidental remarks suggest that church music in the colonies was of minor significance among the white population at large and that whatever zeal developed for it elsewhere in the society did not come from them.

Military bands were another source of music in the colonies, but were principally intended for ceremonial occasions rather than for any real military purpose and in that capacity usually evoked admiration. Though such ceremonial performances became popular in the colonies, military bands, in reality, did most of their work for social occasions, serenading the top brass in the military and performing at concerts, dramatic presentations and balls. In comparison, music for the concert hall was more sophisticated or exclusive and was restricted to those who saw themselves as cultured or artistic and performances often involved visiting musicians. In short, the relatively small percentage of whites in slave colonies limited the demand for white musical performances.

From the early colonial, frontier situation in which women were at a premium, balls became a socially sanctioned marketplace for the acquisition of women for sex and marriage, even if it was not a straightforward matter of young women being brought forward and put on display for men to select. It was not that this reality was only in the minds and expectations of men, for as Mrs Carmichael (1833, 2:22) said: "To young ladies arrived in a new colony, a ball is a great affair." It is at balls that they would come to the attention of all who mattered; it is here that they would be assessed and put in place in society. For women, it was their opportunity to make a mark and establish whatever credentials they had.

Special balls were put on when royalty visited, as was the case when Prince

William Henry went to various islands in 1786. Commenting on his visit to Barbados, Poyer (1808, 576) said: "The short time which the prince remained in Barbadoes was the season of mirth and festivity. Besides the balls and entertainment given by Governor Parry in honour of his illustrious guest, his royal highness was sumptuously entertained by the legislature." No doubt his presence in other islands evoked similar responses. Besides such rare high-society balls, there were more ordinary causes for celebrations, for example, welcomes and farewells for colonial administrators, plantation owners visiting their plantations, new regiments arriving and old ones leaving; colonial events (such as coronations and the monarch's birthday); church holidays; ethnic holidays; and births and weddings.

In spite of these various reports of festivity, in an overall assessment of social life in Jamaica at the beginning of the nineteenth century, Stewart (1808, 180) said: "The inhabitant of the town, as well as the country . . . is liable to the dull uniformity of a perpetual unvaried sameness of life and objects." One would have to accept, from a Jamaican resident of over twenty years, that monotony was the reality for many whites. Yet, since this reality contrasts sharply with the social life depicted in Lady Nugent's diary, it suggests that there must have been sharp differences in the experiences of whites according to personality and geographical location.

It may be that in order to counterbalance boredom, the shortness and precariousness of life, and, for foreigners, the sense of limitation in the colonies, vigorous entertainment and display came to be the overwhelming feature of social life for many whites. In this situation, performing at balls and dressing in the latest European fashions helped to dispel the spectre of a crude and barren frontier life and create an illusion of being modern and up-to-date.

Dancing was an integral part of the social life of colonial administrators and the military, especially the officers. Thus, urban balls were dominated by people in military uniforms. It became even more so during Lady Nugent's stint in Jamaica (1801–5) when she instituted a regular schedule of dances as a result of her personal experience and conviction that there was "a sad want of local matter, or, indeed, any subject for conversation" with local whites (Wright 2002, 14).

There is no question that Lady Nugent preferred dancing as a way of getting through her social evenings. This is clear from her words: "so, after answering many questions about how I liked the country, &c. and being thoroughly examined by the eyes of them all, I sent for fiddlers, and we had a very merry dance till 11 o'clock, and before 12 they all took their leave. I mean in future not to attempt anything like a conversazione, but to have Friday dances" (14). In fact, she quite liked dancing as a response to pressure. She used it as a way to calm her social group in the face of possible insurrection in the aftermath of the Haitian Revolution: "I thought it was best to set them all dancing, and this kept up their spirits till 11 o'clock" (237). She used it as a way to get over a bad experience: "she flattered me so much, that I was quite sick, and glad to dance off my ill humour in the evening" (15). It was only when she was pregnant and after she had the children that she complained that dancing was tiring. Yet three years later she was still enjoying her dances, for on 6 January 1804 she wrote: "we had a very gay dance, till 11 o'clock. Then, as this is to be my last party this season, another hour was asked for, and the evening ended most merrily. How glad I am!" (191). It was therapy for her.

Before and after the Nugents were in Jamaica there was little change in the popularity of dances and balls. Stewart (1808, 177–78) noted that "Monthly assemblies in the different parishes are a source of some amusement here, particularly to the females, who, as before observed, are very fond of dancing. These are continued throughout the year." Monk Lewis ([1834] 1969, 139) noted that "there was a great dinner and ball for the whole county given today [25 January 1816] at Montego Bay". One can well imagine the social significance of this county dinner and ball.

It was the kind of formal, official ball at King's House in Spanish Town which in about 1801 provided material for Ensign A. James, a soldier based there, to produce his caricature *A Grand Jamaica Ball!*. The caricature reproduced the "Great Saloon" at King's House fairly accurately and one would assume that the high-stepping dances featured were genuine, even if a little exaggerated. The sheer variety of activities presented, the various groupings, the servants, the musicians, the onlookers meant that the "grand ball" was not an event to miss. The force of James's caricature was that the ball was dominated by creoles and that the whole affair was pretentious.

Based on his experiences as part of a military family in Barbados, St Vincent and Grenada in the late 1820s, Frederic Bayley (1830, 466) was prepared to bet, with all confidence, that "a young and lovely creole would dance in one evening as many galopades, and half as many mazourkas, as the most experienced of our *"debutantes"* would accomplish in a whole season". Part of the reason for this was that balls went on until morning, as Bayley (467) explained: "The clock had actually struck five; the loud report of the morning-gun had burst upon the ears of the fair assembly at Government House before they could find resolution enough to leave the merry dance, and proceed towards 'home, sweet home'."

In St Vincent, where previously, after dining, men would play cards among themselves, leaving the ladies to their own devices, according to Carmichael (1833, 1:40–41), social activities became more integrated and men "improved". Yet moderation in size of activity was the order of the day at the beginning of the nineteenth century because of the huge cost of putting on a ball and the difficulty travelling. Carmichael (41–42) went on to say: "Small evening parties, which created little or no expense . . . now became common. . . . These parties usually met about eight in the evening, and broke up before, or at eleven, at farthest."

In the islands that came under French influence, balls were also a main feature of high society. Adolphe Granier de Cassagnac (1842, 1:115) made the comment that "dancing is a virtual malady for Creoles" and, with some exaggeration, left no doubt about the intensity of creole dancing, as if it was all-consuming. Following is his "description" of a planter's ball, which allowed for much greater self-expression among less sophisticated types:

> When a planter fancies having a ball. If the decision to have the ball is made at eleven o'clock, six negroes are sent to deliver the invitations at midday, and at 7 p.m. the huge gallery and the unending salon is packed with women, silk, lace and flowers. . . . When a Creole spends a night at a ball, when you look at all her clothes, she does not have on her a thread of silk or linen that is not crumpled, twisted, broken and is good for anything. Ten out of twelve have lost their shoes and leave the hall barefooted. (1:115)

In summary, then, white colonial society chose to have balls as their major form of entertainment. The splendour of balls contrasted with the sordidness of everyday life in a slave society. Balls allowed whites to display their superiority over those under them without overt force, as if all was well and working smoothly. Dancing and drinking no doubt attenuated some of the rage and fear that interaction with "savages" occasioned. Balls were used to put ladies on display, and this gave an appearance of genteelness to the society. Balls required decorum and grace, which created an atmosphere of sophistication. In short, balls constituted a counterpoint to the drudgery of frontier life and the violence of slavery.

In Europe, formal dancing was an integral part of the social life of the upper classes, who had ample free time to hold their balls, especially in the colder months of the year. Participation in high society demanded refinement in certain skills, and competence in dancing was one of them. The relevant music and dancing were formal, requiring instruction. It was this kind of upper-class music and dancing that provided the model for the ruling classes in the colonies.

In the first half of the eighteenth century, Charles Leslie (1740, 37) spoke of boys in Jamaica going to dancing school as a priority: "After a little Knowledge of reading, he goes to the Dancing-school." About two decades later, as an alternative to the wastefulness of sending young men to England for schooling, Long (1774, 2:254) proposed that, in addition to practical subjects, music and dancing should be taught locally: "The pupils might likewise be taught music, dancing, fencing, and the military manual exercise, to qualify them better for a course of life which requires agility and strength of body, and occasionally the use of arms." Long's recommended school syllabus for young men clearly retained elements of Plato's ideal in its linking of dance to military readiness. Although Long saw the education of girls differently, he believed that they also needed competence in music and dancing (2:250).

James Phillippo (1843, 121) for his part, some decades later, saw female creoles' addiction to dancing as a result of the lack of education: "The females, excluded from the advantages of a liberal education, became addicted to pleasures, such as horse-races, dances, and convivial entertainments, thus acquiring habits which could not fail to operate unfavourably on their domestic circumstances and general character." Phillippo was a Baptist missionary who clearly did not approve of the "immoral" pleasures that he listed. His argument was no more than a variation of the view that lack of education caused the white woman on the plantation to sink to the level of the slaves and adopt their social and linguistic habits. This in turn was but one feature in the more general view that the institution of slavery caused degradation in whites. The fact is, however, that colonial whites, enjoying a life of privilege, could not easily see any advantages in a liberal education.

The reality of the influence of the slaves on whites was most evident in the upbringing of children. In a situation where most white children were brought up by nannies, it was inevitable that the nannies shaped their behaviour and culture. Even Lady Nugent seemed happy to have her Jamaican-born children come under the influence of nurses: "This evening, nurse sung again to the children, who had their usual dance, and went to bed happy, dear little innocent souls" (Wright 2002, 227). Mrs Carmichael (1833, 1:188), as the wife of a plantation owner in St Vincent, observed how nannies tended to their charges: "I have seen a negro nurse quite proud of her little charges, – teaching them to make a curtsy, and answer politely; and she always keeps them good humoured, by dancing and singing to them." Such "lessons" in dancing and singing produced white creoles who were culturally different from their European parents.

It is not surprising that, because of early informal training by nannies, later mingling with slaves at dances and the general milieu in which they were raised, creole whites were thought to be better at dancing than Europeans. Yet Edwards (1793–94, 2:10) saw this superiority not as the result of training and experience but as the result of inborn physical difference: "All of them [white creoles], however, are distinguished for the freedom and suppleness of their joints; which enable them to move with great ease and agility, as well as gracefulness, in dancing." Edwards's argument was of course tied to the reputed power of warm climates on physical evolution as a part of a general theory of ecological determinism.

Breen, writing after emancipation, was more glowing in his tribute to white creole dancing, but part of the reason for his praise was that he was reacting to what he saw and noted elsewhere as shallowness in European and especially French behaviour. Breen's (1844, 190) comparative assessment of creole dancing as "a chastened and rational exercise not infringing any of the decencies of life" prominently positioned it in the same way that Moreau de Saint-Méry had done half a century earlier. In addition, his view of French dancing echoed Lady Nugent's attitude in her unflattering description of Madame Fressinet. What is most noticeable, however, is that Breen, like most others, conceived of creole dancing in terms of gender, projecting the female as the heart and soul of dancing. In this way, creole dancing was an extension of the image of the beautiful creole woman, associated especially with the French(-influenced) islands.

Generally across the various European colonies, it was put forward as a fact that creoles were indolent, a condition brought about by the absolute dependence on slaves to perform even the slightest of tasks (for example, picking up a pin that fell or threading a needle). It was with this image of the indolent creole in mind that Chanvalon (1763, 38), referring to Martinique principally, commented on the presumed relationship between indolence, lack of education and dancing: "Only dancing can overcome this indolence, at any age and despite the heat of the climate. This exercise never seems to tire them. One would believe that it is the liveliest of their pleasures or the only one that affects them."

There was therefore no difference between French and English writers in the accepted wisdom that lack of motivation and the climate made the pursuit of education too strenuous for creoles, but that when it came to dancing that was a different matter. Some fifty years after Chanvalon's observation, Bayley (1830, 236–37) made the same point:

> If you pay a morning visit to a fair West Indian, you may find her reclining upon a sofa, indulging in that luxury of ease which the intolerable heat of a tropic climate appears to encourage and require. She may seem lovely and beautiful, but she will still be languid and oppressed: follow her to the ball room, "elle a changé tout cela;" the countenance which, in the morning, looked lovely in its languor, in the evening looks more than lovely in its smiles. She is lively and animated – and hour passes upon hour, and quadrille follows quadrille, and the morning dawns, and the dance continues unabated, and the fair Creole is neither tired nor fatigued.

Captain Alexander (1833, 1:160) closely repeated much of what Bayley said. Of course, constant admiration and praise reinforced creoles' belief in their own superiority as well as in the importance of and the necessity for excellent dancing and music. In turn, through the acculturation process, it was easy for slaves to do the same – to put music and dancing on a pedestal, whether or not they had any ancestral inclination to do so.

Moulding Caribbean Variants of European Genres: The Ball

From early the ball took pride of place as the event of formality in the colonies mostly because it allowed for pomp and ceremony. One gets a sense of this from the *Barbados Gazette* of 1 March 1734 and of the naive tussle between excited anticipation and respect for convention on the occasion of a ball celebrating "her Majesty's birthday" (*Caribbeana* [1741] 1978, 31). The presence of important dignitaries resident in the colony, acquisition of the latest styles from Europe and execution of the latest dances from London created an event of the highest sophistication and inspiration for those who attended. The planning and management of balls were critical to their success and seemed to have acquired a set structure in the nineteenth century. Bernard Senior (1835, 66) gave some idea of the management of balls when he said: "At a *race ball*, the stewards of the races officiate as stewards of the ball. At the military balls, a field officer, two or three captains, and the like proportion of subalterns, generally are nominated. At the subscription assemblies, the resident gentlemen take it by turns to perform the duties of the evening."

By the end of the eighteenth century a certain protocol had emerged at official balls. Lady Nugent set out what happened in her case, as wife of the governor of Jamaica – a number of entries in her diary show what behaviour was expected of the governor and wife at the ball (Wright 2002, 81). That they were expected to socialize with all the guests rather than to stay close together is clear. She was expected to dance with as many gentlemen as possible "to please both civil and military, Army and Navy" (41). That she was expected to grace the whole assembly with her presence is also clear (90). The ball therefore was a social as well as a political forum for interaction. It preserved social rank, but it also provided opportunities, through the dancing, for liaisons and exchange of confidences.

Remarking on the participants at an official ball at Government House in St Vincent "to celebrate the arrival of the new regiment, and, also, as a farewell entertainment to the officers of the old", Bayley (1830, 236) said: "There were more ladies at that assembly than I had ever seen before, or have ever seen since at any party in St Vincent. The red coats were also pretty numerous, and the gentlemen of the colony were not backward in their attendance." In his generally favourable portrayal of balls in the smaller English colonies, Bayley concluded that "from the ball room lassitude is expelled, and 'ennui' dares not intrude itself into the fairy circle of so many charms and graces" (236). For the specific ball at Government House, which he described in detail, Bayley said that there were three bands present to play the music (240) and that "a few songs succeeded his Excellency's toast; after which the party resumed their dancing, and the morning gun had fired before the conclusion of the entertainment" (241).

More generally, there was a difference, according to Bayley, between metropolitan and colonial preferences in dances:

> This practice of dancing quadrilles after opening the ball with a country-dance, appears to prevail throughout the West Indies; and in the Island of Grenada they seldom even vary the figure, dancing the "Lancers" only occasionally instead of the regular set; and if the fashionable galopade, and still more fashionable mazourka, ever find their way to the tropics, I must question their power of being able to expel the modern quadrille, or even the ancient country-dance. (463)

This shows quite clearly that the colonies were not just mimics of the mother country, but selected and stuck with dances that suited their own tastes, either because of their liveliness or the kind of interaction they involved. It could also be that the non-whites in the colonies had a preference for certain dances (the quadrille and country-dance) and that whites in the colonies conformed to this preference because by this time (early nineteenth century) a certain cultural identity had already established itself across the social classes.

The Concert

About a hundred years after the founding of the Barbados colony, a thriving cultural scene among whites was being reported in the *Barbados Gazette* (16 August 1732): "Here, each attempt to please, has found Success; The Dance, the Concert, and the Courtly Dress" (*Caribbeana* 1741, 37). Apparently this drive towards social refinement continued over the years as part of the urban social scene, judging from advertisements in local newspapers, such as the following in the *Barbados Mercury* (6 October 1770, 4): "On Tuesday the 30th of October will be performed, at the British Coffee House, a concert of vocal and instrumental music. . . . N.B. Proper music will be provided for country dances as soon as the concert is over." The concert was the most refined, purely musical activity for the ruling class in the West Indies and it is one that had a consistent measure of appeal for some throughout the slavery period. The concert required trained musicians and singers and, theoretically, a knowledgeable audience. It thus created an aura of intellectual sophistication which no doubt appealed to those who were and those who wanted to appear refined in their taste as well as to those who wanted to remain connected to Europe. Yet this advertisement's highlighting of "proper music" for dancing after the concert was clearly intended to get an audience by encouraging those who were more interested in dancing to attend.

In Jamaica there was the same practice of having a ball after a concert and about this marrying of two events Richardson Wright (1937, 291) made the snide comment that "it was as though the audience was being subjected to nursery discipline – you simply had to eat your meat and potatoes before you could have dessert". Wright also quoted the Jamaican *Daily Advertiser* of 8 May 1790 as bemoaning the fact that "it is somewhat astonishing that in this town, which can boast more Musical People than almost any other place of its size and population, there should be only four Public Concerts in twelve months" (286).

At the beginning of the nineteenth century a remark from Stewart (1808,

176) made it seem that concerts would have foundered were it not for colonists fleeing Haiti: "In Kingston there are occasionally tolerable concerts, the principal performers in which are French emigrants from St Domingo." Stewart's remark pointed to the fact that the upper class in pre-revolutionary Saint Domingue had reached an unparalleled level of musical sophistication which Jamaica was now benefiting from. Nevertheless, concerts never became popular and were not well attended, not least of all because in the urban setting they depended on the patronage of military and naval people, and, as Wright (1937, 286) remarked: "How, I ask, could you expect hairy-chested and tatooed sailors to sit through a piano duet by a lady amateur?"

In Trinidad in the early 1820s, Carmichael (1833, 2:74) commented favourably on the proficiency of Trinidad-trained singers, thus testifying to the store that was put on music education in the colonies, especially for women. Parallel with voice training was practice on the pianoforte, which was a favourite instrument in concerts. A casual comment by Carmichael gave some idea of the importance of the pianoforte to her when she arrived at her residence in Trinidad after moving from St Vincent: "I was glad to find my piano forte in safety, after a drive of fourteen miles in a cart" (2:118). The concert, with its trained voices and specialized instruments, may not have been attractive to the general population, but it was still important as an index of social and intellectual refinement.

The Serenade

The term "serenade" is used here to mean a casual musical event, which was not sharply defined in its format: sometimes it was a musical get-together among friends for their own enjoyment and at other times it was an informal performance intended for someone special. In contrast to concerts and balls, serenades were often impromptu. In many cases, they were interactive, often involving dancing.

Lady Nugent recorded different types of serenade in her journal. There was one specially put on for her and her husband with minimal participation on their part: "but General N. left those that remained to enjoy their bottle, and he and I retired to our own apartment, but not to rest, for the garrison gave us a grand serenade, and the house was a scene of dancing, singing, and merriment almost the whole night" (Wright 2002, 13). There was another less formal affair involving sets of women singing for her and her husband when they went visiting in St Ann: "Immediately, sets of singing women sent me word of their approach. They danced, and sung several songs; some made in honour of General N. and some of me, till we were heartily tired of them" (80). In the absence of any information to the contrary, one has to assume that the performers in this case were white women who were accustomed to singing in groups. If this was the case, then singing must have been an appropriate way for white women to welcome and regale important visitors, but no information is given about the nature of and reason for these *sets*.

Another serenade in Jamaica is mentioned by Cynric Williams (1826, 9): it was an informal get-together involving singing and dancing on the occasion of the visit of an acquaintance. The variety of features in the event was impressive, but in terms of sophistication it may have been different from what took place at concerts because the emphasis was more on enjoyment than refinement. Yet another serenade, an impromptu get-together involving a combination of religious and military persons, is recorded by Waller (1820, 65) while he was in Grenada: "Some very beautiful pieces were performed in a masterly manner, and so inexhaustible were their resources of amusement, that we did not think of separating till past midnight. The Sicilian Evening Hymn to the Virgin was then sung, (*O sanctissima, O purissima, &c.*) after which we retired." Here again the piano-forte was the instrument of choice, which in itself stamped the event as characteristic of a higher social level. Again, the overriding feeling coming from the participants was one of enjoyment and appreciation.

Serenades were musical experiences in a context of cultured informality and would have illustrated a kind of entertainment which inspired camaraderie and demonstrated hospitality. A guest or visitor would have formed a very positive view of a host after a successful serenade. In all cases, the prominent involvement of ladies shaped the serenade, giving it a measure of refinement and decorum. The serenade, though it was not a formal event, featured "proper" music, singing and dancing, and consequently it was symbolic of what sophisticated and educated whites in the colonies aspired towards in their cultured social activities.

The Rural Feast

Probably the most romantic, artistic and influential description of what was called a "rural feast" was done in 1767 by John Singleton. He also referred to it as "the Indian barbecue" and "the rural banquet". It was essentially an excursion into the countryside to a beautiful spot or the seaside where a group of acquaintances enjoyed a day of food and music. Singleton (1767, 19–31) dedicated almost two hundred lines of verse to a description of this event, which took place in a rural part of Barbados. This was an event of leisure, with no set format. Singleton's adjectives "soft" and "nimble", describing the music and the dancing respectively, create a feeling of delicacy in the event, as if it were for only "refined" persons. It obviously went back for its inspiration to words like those of Rabelais (1890, 82–83):

> Nevertheless Ponocrates, to divert him from this vehement intension of the spirits, thought fit, once a month, upon some fair and clear day to go out of the city betimes in the morning . . . and there spend all the day long in making merry, drinking healths, playing, singing, dancing, tumbling in some fair meadow . . . for in the said meadows they usually repeated certain pleasant verses of Virgil's agriculture, of Hesiod, and of Politian's husbandry; would set abroach some witty Latin epigrams, then immediately turned them into roundelays and songs for dancing in the French language.

Thus, Renaissance culture was being admirably exhibited in Barbados, according to Singleton.

Later in the century, the name that seemed to become more popular in the West Indies for this kind of event was "maroon party". References to maroon parties in the eighteenth century indicate that they were a well-known activity among whites. In Barbados in 1796, Pinckard and his hosts went on a "marooning party" (Pinckard 1806, 1:327) and then after a good night's sleep were "prepared for another marooning day" (1:356). Resident, in Dominica, observed that "marooning parties" were in some cases a continuation or extension of a ball: "the ladies often, instead of retiring to rest after a ball, only change their dresses, and proceed into the country on *marooning parties*, as they are called; that is, parties of pleasure, hastily resolved on, and immediately carried into effect. They generally resort to the woods, or a river's side. At the first of these parties I attended, the dancing did not terminate till four o'clock in the morning" (1828, 83–84).

Another informative account of a maroon party comes from Lanaghan (1844, 2:313), who related the maroon party in Antigua to the *fête champêtre* or (European) rural feast. She went on:

> groups of beautiful girls and gallant youths, stayed matrons, and gentlemen of riper years, assemble together, with full purpose to enjoy the passing hours. Some

sweet spot, generally near the sea-side, is chosen for the day's resort . . . and although no "Weippert's band" is in attendance, the sound of the lively violin, or soft-breathing flute, often floats across the blue waters, and mingles with the murmur of the playful wavelets.

The West Indian islands were ideally suited to this kind of excursion to rural bliss and the lifestyle of local whites, serviced continually by slaves, went hand in glove with it. It was also popular with visitors, as the references from Singleton and Pinckard attest. Day also in both St Vincent and Trinidad in the 1840s mentioned these outings (1852, 1:82, 86).

An English parallel for this kind of activity is given by Strutt as part of May Day and other celebrations ([1801] 1903, 277). Continental Europe had its own version of the "rural feast", which acquired the French label *fête champêtre*, with echoes of Rabelais (1890, 28): "After dinner they all went out in a hurl to the grove of the willows, where, on the green grass, to the sound of the merry flutes and pleasant bag-pipes, they danced so gallantly, that it was a sweet and heavenly sport to see them so frolic." This in turn was directly related to the southern European or Italian concept *dolce farniente*, which came to be used repeatedly, by extension, to describe the "indolent" lifestyle in the Spanish Caribbean islands. The *dolce far niente* image (in Europe) was illustrated in a painting by Frans Winterhalter in 1836, which Ormond and Blackett-Ord (1987, 9) described as "ostensibly a scene of the siesta hour during the grape picking season, it is, in reality, a peasant version of the *fête champêtre*, in which the figures abandon themselves to the pleasures of the senses".

It is probable that maroon parties from early were the context in which some May Day and other holiday activities (for example, Maypole dancing) took place and that it was from these that the slaves learned them. Bear in mind that although the West Indian descriptions tried to convey an aura of upper-class sophistication, most of the whites who would have been involved were not from an upper-class background and so the sports they would have enjoyed would have been popular sports.

Fashioning Holiday Fun: From "Saturnalia" to Carnival

For whites in the colonies, Christmas and Easter were festive occasions that evoked cheerful ancestral traditions, some of which were historically connected to the pagan festivities of the Greeks and Romans. One Christmas tradition deriving from the pagan festivities of the Romans was what was called the Saturnalia. In his article on the Feast of Fools, Herbert Thurston (1909, 132) quotes John Beleth, a twelfth-century liturgical writer, who said: "it was customary of old among the pagans that during this month [December] slaves and serving maids should have a sort of liberty given them, and should be put upon an equality with their masters, in celebrating a common festivity". Some writings on the Caribbean mentioned the Saturnalia by name, while others made indirect references to the tradition, but in all cases they expressed surprise about its occurrence in the Caribbean.

The reality of the matter is not as puzzling as it may at first appear because the Saturnalian practices of the Romans persisted throughout Europe over the centuries in Christmas celebrations, but with changes in name. In England, one expression of them was "the Lord of Misrule". Strutt ([1801] 1903, 268–69), referring to the close of the sixteenth century, gives a detailed description of this English practice and, in accounting for the source of it, he supported the argument that "all these whimsical transpositions of dignity are derived from the ancient Saturnalia . . . when the masters waited upon their servants" (271). It is possible that these "vulgar" practices became a part of the early West Indian colonies when white indentured servants were the mass of the workforce, in which case it was they (not enslaved Africans) who were adopting the dress and behaviour of their superiors. Alternatively or additionally, since these practices had over time formed the basis for masquerades among the higher social classes in England, it could have been the higher classes who brought them to the colonies.

Terry Castle (1986, 11) supports the historical connection between the Roman Saturnalia and the "classic" features of masquerades and also provides pertinent information on inversion in these eighteenth-century English masquerades: "Contemporary accounts inevitably focus on the antithetical surprises generated by the masquerade crowd: duchesses dressed as milkmaids, footmen as Persian kings . . . noblemen as ancient bawds, young ladies of the court as 'trowser'd' hussars" (5). In other words, since both the upper and lower classes in England had these Saturnalian traditions, it would have been strange if they did not become a part of white colonial festivity.

Some features of masquerades made them very appealing in the colonies. First, as Castle says: "the eighteenth-century public masquerade, like the earlier holiday revel, was an eminently unscripted, unstaged event" (19–20). Second, the timing of them in England fitted into the plantation schedule in the colonies, for as Castle noted: "Indoor masquerades took place in the carnival months, October through February, and clustered around Christmas and New Year's" (21).

The great era of masquerades in England was in the eighteenth century, but Wright provides evidence that even before that masquerades were popular among the upper class in Jamaica. Henry Egleton, clerk of the council, wrote on 6 November 1681: "The Governor entertained all the principal gentlemen and officers with a very sumptuous dinner; and in the evening the Governor's lady, being waited upon by all the gentlewomen of quality, gave them a very fine treat, and afterwards entertained them at a ball, composed of a suitable number of masqueraders, very curiously habited" (quoted in Wright 1937, 6–7). The occasion for the masquerade ball was the king's birthday celebration, a major occasion, as was the case with coronations and jubilees, for masquerades in Britain and its colonies. The fact that these were state events shows that masquerading in the colonies was not necessarily tied to the Christian calendar.

An old form of English drama which also could have had some influence in the West Indies is the masque. There is a similarity between explanations of the masque and the following carnival incident in Grenada described by Bayley (1830, 479–80):

> The good catholics, however, account it a duty to put on masks, and therewith to enter the houses of the worthy people of Georgetown, and to amuse them with such behaviour as best beseemeth the characters they sustain . . . On the evening in question, the family of Mrs. — were sitting socially, as was their wont, around the tea table, when suddenly the window opened, and two ruffians, armed cap-a-pie, in the guise of banditti, entered the room, and presented their pistols at the heads of the ladies. *Le bruit de ce terrible moment reste encore dans mes oreilles*; the screams, like ladies' screams, were deep, deafening, and delightful; so the gentlemen thought it right to interpose, then the ladies became more faint, and the ruffians more furious; at length four, Oh, marvellous achievement! contrived to conquer two, and the banditti were expelled "vi et armis," the ladies were restored to their senses, and the scream was converted into a laugh.

In effect, disguising, breaking into a party, the joining of performers and audience in a dance and wearing elaborate costumes – all part of carnival in Grenada – were features of the masque. It is therefore likely that "mas" in the modern West Indian phrase "playing mas" is historically related to the English genre "masque", even though Caribbean carnivals have a strong Roman Catholic influence.

Notwithstanding the Roman Catholic/carnival link in the Caribbean, the fact is that the features or activities associated with carnival have never been exclusively pre-Lenten seeing that there has historically been transfer of features from pagan to Christian and across Christian feasts. The fundamental link between agricultural rites and religious rites meant that variation in dates was normal to correspond to the seasonal variations (for example, spring and winter) of different geographical areas. If the link between masque, which had no specific relation to a season, and carnival (pre-Lenten) is valid, the juxtaposition of "play" and "mas" in the colonial West Indies brings together different colonial and religious traditions and points to a more complex development of carnival in the English colonies of the West Indies.

Indeed, carnival in Grenada was celebrated in a different and very "innocent manner" (Bayley 1830, 480) in the 1820s in Grenada and involved almost exclusively indoor activities. About the incident cited above, Bayley said: "This was the commencement of the carnival, and the two first masks had made their *entrée* rather roughly and their exit with as little ceremony." He then went on to describe the rest of the carnival as follows:

> Four ladies, richly dressed and masked, though without supporting any particular characters, danced a quadrille with the gentlemen, with much spirit, and played some very pretty airs on the piano. After giving their partners each "One kiss at parting" they left the room, and were succeeded by a masked group of negro boys and girls, who danced for a while, after the chimney-sweepers on the first of May, and then very cooly helping themselves to some wine and cake, departed with many a profound bow to the company. (480)

Carnival in Grenada, as witnessed by Bayley, was a very unspectacular affair, involving possible masque as well as May Day elements. The emphasis was clearly on wearing masks and costumes and on entertaining small, private gatherings indoors. This kind of carnival did not seem to be significantly different from that which Borde (1883, 269) described for Trinidad during the Spanish regime. This Spanish variant or season of carnival, lasting from Christmas to Ash Wednesday, complemented the *dolce far niente* lifestyle associated with the Spanish.

In the case of Dominica, Resident (1828, 82) saw Christmas festivities as following both French and English models: "In the French islands, and those which have been originally settled by the French, these holidays are further enlivened ... by the merry groups of morrice dancers, or masqueraders, who go from house to house in the evenings, dancing waltzes, &c. ... As in England, small bands of music go from house to house, and street to street, enlivening the scene, and making their Christmas collection." This is a rare mention of whites in the colonies indulging in traditional European outdoor entertainment activities. Even so, it is clear that it was the secular or "pagan" aspects of the Christian "holy" days that whites in the colonies were attracted to and that their happiness was only marginally, if at all, religious. In other words, right from the beginning in the colonial setting, it was the element of fun, playing with hidden or imagined identities that was most evident in Christmas celebrations.

European Dramatic Performances Struggling to Survive

Plays in the European tradition are of various types but the informal, mobile type with itinerant players or "strollers" has always been popular. Short scenes of variable fixity and form are popular for many reasons – they allow for more extemporizing, the actors can perform them outside of a fixed context or as they move about, and there is more audience participation. The term "play" has been called into question in discussions of British folk performances by Alex Helm (1981, 6), who dismisses it as inappropriate as a characterization of what mummers did: "The use of the word 'Play' [as in Mummers' Plays] is misleading. ... If the word 'Play' could be discarded in this context and either 'Ritual', 'Ceremony' or 'Act' replace it, then the way is clear for a better understanding of what the Mummers are about." The problem with this suggestion is that it is a modern attempt to revise an older word usage, for in the eighteenth century the term "play" did not in any core sense mean only stage plays.

European-type dramatic performances were a constant reality from the earliest days of English colonization in Jamaica. Wright shows the relative popularity of the theatre and performances of various types in Jamaica from 1682 to 1838, roughly the period of slavery. He provides evidence from "Mr. Francis Hanson's Account of the Island and Government of Jamaica ... in or about the year 1682" of plays being put on only a couple decades after the English took over the island (1937, 6). Yet Stewart (1808, 176) at the end of the eighteenth century complained that "there are no theatrical exhibitions in this island". He conceded that a theatre group had come to Jamaica from North America because of the hostilities associated with the American war of independence but had returned when those hostilities subsided. Stewart clearly discounted local performances and the French theatre that was dominating the Jamaican stage at the time.

At the beginning of the eighteenth century, Oldmixon (1708, 2:127) mentioned a group whom he called "Poppet Strowlers" in Barbados: "There was once a Company of Poppet Strowlers in this island; they came from England, and set up their Fairy Drama at the Bridge, where, for the Novelty of the Matter, they found a good Market; From thence they went to the Leeward Islands, and thence home." In the *Barbados Gazette* of 18 March 1731, the editor notes: "about three Years ago, some Gentlemen were pleased to act several Plays for the Diversion of themselves and their Friends, but more especially of the Ladies of this place. I shall therefore only observe, that, after they had given General Satisfaction in *Tragedy*, they were at length persuaded likewise to attempt a Comedy" (*Caribbeana* [1741] 1978, 1:19).

Towards the end of the eighteenth century, Luffman (1789, 120) enthusiastically described the beginnings of a theatre in Antigua, making the customary comparisons with England. A close look at the choice of pieces shows a selection of both contemporary and classic ones, with a preference for the comic as opposed to the tragic: "The Orphan, King Henry the Fourth, West-Indian, Lethe, and Lying Valet, are among those already played, and King Lear. The Fair Penitent, Jane Shore, and several farces are getting in readiness" (155). No doubt, for Luffman this was a labour of love, which most likely declined as soon as he left.

From the end of the eighteenth century through until the time of emancipation there was also repeated mention of plays and theatres in Guadeloupe (Isert 1793, 326–27), Jamaica (*Authentic History* 1810, 8), Antigua (Wentworth 1834, 2:177) and St Lucia (Breen 1844, 270), giving the impression that dramatic performances continued to be generally appealing. It was virtually impossible for any of the islands to have sustained a theatre and a company of actors over a long period of time. Plays needed actors, audiences and financial support and no island had a critical mass of people to provide these on a consistent basis. Although they may have been enthusiastically received, plays were sporadic and even rare in some islands.

The Fair Barbadian and Faithful Black; or, a Cure for the Gout: A Comedy in Three Acts, written by a white Barbadian, J.W. Orderson, was first performed in Barbados in 1832. There is no word about how it was received. It presented a "faithful black" in Barbados playing a significant and influential role. The black was not a tragic figure, precisely because the writer intended to put a positive spin on the character's experience. Singing and dancing are openly used to signal the happiness and contentedness of the slaves and the play ends, inevitably, with the freed slave singing and dancing. Orderson's intention in writing the play was to contradict what he regarded as abolitionist propaganda. Jerome Handler (1991, 41) notes: "The play, set in Barbados in the 1830s, has eight main characters: seven white, including the central character of a wealthy planter, and Hampshire, the planter's 'confidential black servant' who also has a prominent role. The cast includes blacks playing plantation slaves, some of whom have small speaking parts." Orderson's play was unusual because by the end of the first quarter of the nineteenth century, the popularity of pantomime was almost universal across the region.

Wentworth's (1834, 2:171–77) lengthy description of a performance in Antigua testifies to this popularity. The subject matter was a comic portrayal of the history of the region. Apparently, by this time, in spite of the general acrimony in arguments about emancipation, all parties could sit back and laugh at themselves. The comic and action-oriented elements of farce made it appealing to all levels of society, but the very dominance of farce in itself indicated that other genres had difficulty drawing audiences. It is those dramatic performances that were, as Strutt ([1801] 1903, 141) says, "relished by the vulgar" that continued to be popular in the West Indies.

Another type of unsophisticated drama which was part of the European experience of coming to the Caribbean was a ritual which took place at sea. Religious, ceremonial and mumming elements were all part of this activity that was repeatedly referred to and described by writers from the sixteenth century onward. In the passage from Europe to West Africa and from Europe to the Caribbean, ships crossed the line of the Tropic of Cancer. What probably started out as a superstitious practice by European sailors to protect themselves from the "fire" of the tropics developed into a farcical ritual in which all those crossing the line for the first time had to go through an initiation ceremony or had to pay in some way to get out of it.

The popularity of the crossing the line ceremony meant that all Europeans in the Caribbean went through the experience or knew about it. It was described by Coppier (1645, 47–48), Gautier du Tronchoy (1709), Barbot (1752; Hair, Jones and Law 1992, 2:755) and Pinckard (1806, 1:206–7). Cruikshank pictorially represented it in 1817 showing a full cast of characters in costume (*Sons of Neptune*

Shaving a Landsman), Bridgens in 1837 (*Crossing the Tropic*), and so did Ruhière in 1838 (*Baptême sous la ligne*).

In European consciousness, crossing from the temperate zone into the tropics originally marked a change from normalcy to an inferno, as if one were descending into the fires of hell. In reality, it was not only the increase in temperature that was a problem for some Europeans but also the prospect of experiencing a hurricane while crossing the Atlantic Ocean. Though the original protective ritual of passage in time declined in seriousness, it still required all to participate. There were several variants of it over the centuries and across nationalities. Thus the European's crossing over, as it came to be symbolically marked by a farcical ceremony, ironically provided a funny and happy introduction to the Caribbean. The fact that it did not apply to Africans probably ensured that it did not become a feature of the dramatic lore of the Caribbean.

Dancing over the Racial Divide

The institutions and practices that whites established in the colonies were for their own security, well-being and amusement. Cheap, enforced labour was intended to provide wealth and comfort, and a rigid colour bar within a scale of hierarchy was intended to preserve privilege and the enjoyment of wealth for a few. Wright (1937, 284) quoted a newspaper advertisement for a performance in Jamaica in February 1790 as saying: "Only white persons will be admitted to the above performance. Tomorrow he intends exhibiting to persons of colour." However, audiences at white events were not in every case exclusively white: it was normal for non-whites to attend variety shows and dramatic pieces. In Jamaica, Nugent noted that at "Mr. Cussan's exhibition", which was in part a comic show, "the audience were of all colours and descriptions: blacks, browns, Jews, and whites" (Wright 2002, 147–48). Wentworth (1834, 2:177), who attended a pantomime in Antigua in the 1820s, noted that "the audience [was] white, yellow, and black, freemen and slaves". In any case, racial hierarchy was most meaningful and satisfying when it was physically demonstrated – that is, where separate spaces, behaviours and privilege were designated at social events according to colour.

Economics and social mores controlled the behaviour of whites, but unofficial understandings put no limits on the privileges of white men – they indulged their fantasies and pursued their own sexual interests to their heart's content. What the racial barriers did was to restrict the freedom of white women – there were no reports of white women participating in non-white dances. Even when Lady Nugent decided to dance with "an old negro man", it was shocking to the creole ladies present (Wright 2002, 156).

A statement of racial exclusion is made by Marly (1828, 288) in a description of the Christmas celebrations of specific groups of slaves when he speaks of "a negro ball, at which, however, no white person is allowed to be present". Other evidence shows, on the contrary, that slave dances did not exclude whites. Dickson (1789, 92), whether naively or not, noted the openness of slave festivities: "If a well dressed white man wish to enter the circle, the cry is, 'Tand a by, let Massa come forward!' when they immediately make a way for him, respectfully bowing or court'sying as he passes." White men would hardly have felt free to "come forward" if it was taboo for them to do so. Yet the fact that Marly's reference was to an indoor event whereas Dickson's was to an outdoor one may be critical in that indoor events would have been by definition restrictive.

The typical kind of white man who frequented the social gatherings of the slaves was from among the lower-level whites who worked as bookkeepers, for instance, on the plantation. The writer who called himself "Marly" was one of these white men who moved easily between higher-level whites and the slave population, having direct everyday dealings of various types with the latter. In his description of the crop-over ball, Marly presented a picture of white men enjoying the best of both worlds, black and white. The female slaves were always on the dance floor and, according to Marly, changed from one partner to another with no indication of unease, cheerfully (or so it seemed) allowing for the lack of skill among some of their white dancing partners. In other words, privilege reduced the element of competition for all white men and reduced the pressure on them to excel.

It was the fortune-seeking adventurer "Johnny Newcome" who became the butt of jokes among British caricaturists. This character represented those white men who, from the time they arrived in the colony, had no problem crossing racial lines and doing whatever was necessary for sex, enjoyment and fortune. It was this character who to a great extent shaped the British image of white life in the West Indies at the turn of the century, an image of rampant immorality that did not help the position of the colonists as the abolition debates increased in intensity.

The visual satire suggested that Johnny Newcome could operate in a more formal, indoor, urban setting (where *Johnny Capers a la Samboise to the Tune of*

Morgan Rattle-her, by W. Holland [1800]) or outdoors/in the plantation setting (which shows *Johnny Dancing with Rosa – the Planter's Beautiful Daughter*, by W. Elmes [1812]; and also *Johnny's Reception by Merry Jonkanoo at Negro Ball*, by W. Elmes [1812]). He was comfortable whether surrounded by slaves amusing themselves or when they were only playing musical instruments. He could woo the planter's daughter, mulattos or black slave women. This "Johnny Newcome" image complemented that of the parvenu for the British public.

A white creole male who fancied himself when it came to knowing the slaves and being able to interact musically with them was Samuel Mathews of St Kitts. Mathews, on the one hand, could be considered a white musical rebel or, on the other, a white man with a strong attraction to "otherness", in the same way that white men were attracted to indigenous women and slave women. It may not be just coincidence that a repeated topic of his songs was the triangular relationship between female slave, white man and male slave.

Naturally, in a colonial situation in which the English language and European culture were dominant, "plays" (both the literate, dramatic type as well as the more informal activities within the folk tradition) were a constant influence on slave performances. Bearing in mind that slaves were always in attendance to serve their masters and mistresses when they went out in public, it can be construed that the influence of European dramatic performances on the slaves was constant from the earliest days of English colonization. Indeed, there is evidence within the first hundred years of English colonization of different types of European plays that would have been witnessed by slaves and, according to the colonial value system, would have caused the slaves to develop a taste for them.

The symbiotic relationship between master and slave meant that in a very simple sense there was no white event at which only whites were present. Even in cases of exclusion, there was the image of "the slave behind the door", which recognized the fact that slaves were always surreptitiously observing. Slaves were constant attendants on whites; they were used to play music at dances and to provide entertainment, especially on plantations where whites were not numerous enough to entertain themselves. Thomas Rolph (1836, 21) speaks of being invited by a plantation owner to a dance put on by his slaves on the occasion of his daughter's birthday. The more lavish the event, the greater the number of slaves present. Though some slave owners were more "indulgent" to their slaves than others, the racial divide was always evident. It is only when it came to dancing and sexual entertainment that the racial divide went into eclipse – that is, except for white women and non-white men.

"More Education in the Heels Than in the Head"

Mulattos were, by force of circumstance, pretentious – that is, they pretended to be what they were not (white), for they were not seen as having any uniform historical lineage (like Africans, Europeans or indigenous people). They had no secure role and position in the economic order of colonial slave societies; free mulattos were the only group that had to use their wits to earn a living – whites had slaves working for them and slaves did not work to support themselves. In short, mulattos found themselves having to create an image for themselves outside those of whites and blacks.

In the last quarter of the eighteenth century, Agostino Brunias painted the West Indian mulatto woman as mostly a free, good-looking, well-dressed female strutting about buying or selling goods. The painting titled *Two Caribbean Women Returning from Market* is a good example; it shows the mulatto woman walking ahead of her slave who is carrying the produce on her head. Other Brunias paintings associating the mulatto woman with trade are *Linen Market, Dominica*; *A West Indian Flower Girl and Two other Free Women of Colour*; *West Indian Creole Woman with Her Black Servant*; *A Linen Market with a Linen Stall and Vegetable Seller in the West Indies*; *Barbados Mulatto Girl*; and *Market Day, Roseau, Dominica*. It is as if, for Brunias, a certain kind of domestic trade was completely dominated by the mulatto woman.

In the social sphere, several writers complemented this picture of the mulatto woman, describing her as a belle in society strutting her stuff on the dance floor, or operating as a dance entrepreneur, facilitating and selling (sexual) services. The work that mulattos did was circumscribed by contemporary social values (that is, no field labour) and by their in-between position in society (that is, work separate from but not independent of white and black). Yet mulatto women can be said to have been a part of white society, because of their role as housekeepers and concubines of white men, as madams of establishments catering to white men and because of their link to their white fathers.

Mulatto women were the result of white-black sexual encounters, but they also seemed to become the preferred racial type in the sexual fantasies of white men. From the earliest years of the West Indian colonies, white society was said to be being corrupted by white men's desire for and cohabiting with non-white women, especially mulattos. However, the image of the mulatto woman, in relation to the white man, varied considerably but in a sense simply perpetuated that image of woman in relation to man that goes back to Eve's role in the "fall" of Adam.

In the English colonies, there was no overwhelming preoccupation in the historical record with "brown" women. Note, for example, that in Brunias's paintings of mulatto women, the islands that were English for most of their history do not feature prominently. Note also that Brunias's island of choice for the mulatto woman was Dominica, an island that had a strong French cultural history.

In the Spanish colonies, on the other hand, the *mulata* was an object of hostility and abuse. A typical example of the negative image of the mulatto woman is presented in one of the many cigarette-box pictures making fun of blacks and mulattos in Cuba at the end of the nineteenth century. The caption of one such picture is "El palomo y la gabilana" (the dove and the hawk) and it encapsulates the idea of the mulatto woman (beautiful and finely dressed) as a vulture preying on innocent white men. In other words, the tables had turned and the white man was now presented as the weak, the prey.

The image of the mulatto woman as a hawker and a hawk gives the impression that such a person was proactive and not led by others. However, in the historical literature a constantly repeated view was that mulattos were imitative. Accordingly, "coloureds" were invariably being described as striving to be white and adopting the habits and practices of whites, as is evident in the following from Beckford (1790, 389) in late eighteenth-century Jamaica: "The mulattoes likewise at this season [Christmas] have their public balls, and vie with each other in the splendour of their appearance: and it will hardly be credited how very expensive their dress and ornaments are, and what pains they take to disfigure themselves with powder and with other unbecoming imitations of the European dress."

In 1823, though he was more positive in his reactions to mulattos in Jamaica in their execution of European dances, Williams (1826, 63) still showed them as imitative: "The dancers, male and female, acquitted themselves famously well, and performed country-dances and quadrilles quite as well, if not better, than I had ever seen at a country ball in England." In reference to Barbados, Alexander (1833, 1:159–60) made the same kind of favourable comparison with things "at home". However, in spite of the element of imitation, these comments give the impression that mulattos used Europeans as their models and not local whites and also that they were very knowledgeable about the fashions of Europeans.

Just after emancipation, the aspirations of educated coloured people were seen by Lloyd (1839, 49) as justified, but being frustrated by unreasonable whites who insisted on the traditional racial barriers. Such aspirations, however, were later scoffed at by Day (1852, 1:91), speaking about St Vincent in the 1840s. Having scoffed at their music, Day (1:48–49) complemented his picture of the "ludicrous" mulatto with an equally derisive attitude towards their dancing, even though the event (one in Barbados) was not one of sophistication.

In the West Indies, dancing and the music that accompanied it became essentially creolized, which meant that despite the attempts of writers to dismiss mulattos as imitative, they had elements that distinguished them from Europeans, from Africans and also from the indigenous inhabitants. In fact, the very passion which writers spoke about was probably the result of the kind of creativity that a new situation allowed for. In terms of artistry, it allowed mulattos to feel that they were on the one hand bringing life and "soul" to European music and dancing, and on the other "refinement" to African expression. Moreton (1790, 128) saw dancing as more important for them than basic education: "In towns, Mongrels are commonly taught to read and write, when their parents can afford it; and every one gets more education in the heels than in the head, (for, like the white Creoles, they are amazing fond of dancing)." Moreton's concept of "education in the heels", though derisive, succinctly captures the priority accorded to practically beneficial proficiencies by coloured women.

Colonial societies were controlled by white men, who generally viewed mulatto women as available opportunities for sex and unofficial relationships. Mulatto women had little option but to work within the box they found themselves in. Coloured women generally, then, might have seen no better option for a satisfactory life than to court white men and, in order to do this successfully, they thought they had to highlight their uniqueness but at the same time be proficient in whiteness. Mulatto children had little choice but to try to obtain favours from their white fathers, who were in a better position to assist them financially than their mothers.

Mulatto men, in contrast, had no access to white women. There was a fundamental difference between the lives and expectations of mulatto men and those of mulatto women. In fact, little is said about the men, who found themselves at a grave disadvantage, not even being able to compete for their own women on an equal basis with white men. According to Marsden (1788, 7): "The brown men are never received into the company of white people, who scarce condescend to speak to them; but, on the contrary, are very free with the females, who are remarkably quick and lively." This exclusion of "brown men" from white society seemed to have been especially so in Jamaica. The perceived practice for the "browns" therefore was as expressed in the words of Lewis ([1834] 1969, 172): "the females generally preferring to live with white men, and the brown men having thus no other resource than black women".

Thus, while entertainment among slaves and among whites was reported in both cases as intra-class/race, entertainment by mulattos/coloureds was reported predominantly as interracial and sex-/liaison-oriented. Entertainment within the mulatto/coloured group not only seemed to be non-existent but probably could have been considered dysfunctional. Yet there is a rare example of it mentioned by Lewis (171) in Falmouth, Jamaica: "On our return from dinner at Mr. Dewer's, we discovered a ball of brown ladies and gentlemen opposite to the inn. No whites nor blacks were permitted to attend this assembly."

Mulatto balls, otherwise called "quality" or "dignity" balls, became a structured context for professional white men (for example, lawyers, merchants, clerks, doctors, soldiers, sailors) to meet women. Such balls took place in an urban context and this is where coloured women used the system to do well for themselves as hostesses. Marsden (1788, 7) remarked that "some of them [brown people] have large property, and carry on an inferior kind of trade, especially the women, keep lodging-houses and taverns". Marsden also noted that "with these [brown women] they [white men] hold a dancing assembly, which is generally much more crowded than the first assembly composed of Creole white ladies of the best families in the island, who in general are very haughty" (8).

The following extracts give some details of the workings and dynamics of balls held by coloured women, the first two from Jamaica in the last quarter of the eighteenth century and the second relating to the smaller islands in the decade before emancipation:

> I went once out of curiosity to a Mulatto ball, where I met several gentlemen of my acquaintance; the women were all either Mulattoes, or Blacks; every gentleman pays a dollar, and the mistress of the house has an elegant entertainment provided, which generally costs more than the amount of the collection produces; but so they have their diversion of dancing, and make new acquaintances, they desire no more . . . It is not very advantageous to a man's character to frequent those balls often, as the white ladies are jealous of having their prerogatives and dominion invaded by those tawny-visag'd and sable filles de joie. (Anon Irish 1776, 45–46)

> When one of them makes a ball, as they frequently do on Saturday nights, she invites a number of her female acquaintance, also, such merchants and clerks as

will honour her on the occasion, (none of her own coloured men are admitted); she engages a bands of music, and prepares an elegant supper, with sweetmeats, wines, &c. &c. for which each gentleman pays three or four dollars: lawyers, merchants and clerks, &c. frequent such assemblies, and promiscuously meet and jostle each other: I have spent many merry nights at such balls. (Moreton 1790, 128)

They have very frequent public balls, to which many of the white unmarried gentlemen go by invitation; but the ticket is paid for by the visitor. They keep up their dances until daybreak, the scene of gaiety being either the hotel or some other public room in the colonial town. (Carmichael 1833, 1:76)

The mulatto ball, which was a feature across the islands, speaks to the important role of the "dance hall" as a venue for procuring illicit sex and liaisons in colonial society, especially in the last part of the eighteenth century and the beginning of the nineteenth. Through this facility dancing became a critical part of a kind of private enterprise in which "brown women" were the brokers.

The use of the word "quality" or "dignity" to describe these events basically was intended to distinguish them from what the lower level of society (the slaves) did and to situate them at the same social level as white balls. It therefore revealed something of the mulatto self-concept and belief that such events were to be associated with dignity. Moreton's characterization of these events, on the other hand, was far removed from any notion of dignity and left no doubt about their venality from the viewpoint of white men, who were given the following advice: "and when the ball or rigadoon is over, escort her to your house or lodging, and taste all the wanton and warm endearments she can yield before morning" (1790, 129). Moreton also did not attribute any dignity to some mulatto women's understanding of the purpose of the balls:

Females use every art to set themselves off to the best advantage, to make themselves pleasing and engaging companions for white men; and when one of them is disbanded by the man who had her in keeping, (or as they say, she had in keeping) she plumps up her breasts like an innocent virgin, or wanton bashful bride, visits balls and plays, and stroles about until she is picked up by somebody else. (125)

In other words, Moreton reduced mulatto balls to crass opportunism – there was no consideration for the mulatto's insecure position in colonial slave society and no acknowledgement of the sense of precariousness that must have attended that kind of existence.

Several coloured hostesses in towns became famous and influential through their catering to visitors and locals. Names such as Rachel Pringle, Susan Ostrehan, Mary Bella Green, Susy Austin (Barbados) and Mary Moore (St Vincent) form a colourful part of the historical record. Pierre M'Callum (1805, 146) claimed that Governor Picton got to know "the sentiments of the inhabitants generally" of Trinidad through Rosetta Smith, who managed to "bribe almost all the kept ladies in the colony to reveal the secrets of their paramours".

There is no question that from the eighteenth century, coloured women exerted considerable influence at high levels throughout the Caribbean (Spanish, French, English and other). Creole high society, with its balls and other cultural events, foregrounded women: creole women, coloured and white, were highlighted for their dancing and, in the Spanish and French Caribbean especially, for their beauty. Portraits of some of these women have become a part of promoted Caribbean heritage. While it is impossible to specify the overall effect these women, especially the coloured ones, had on the direction Caribbean societies took, it seems reasonable to argue that they maximized their influence in the direction of economic stability and humanistic interests rather than militaristic ones. They were central to Caribbean colonial values – the coloured ones not necessarily being seen as dignified and virtuous but, for their own survival and growth, as a manipulative force in Caribbean colonial entertainment.

5. From Africa to the Caribbean
Singing and Dancing Marionettes

So, everything is an occasion to make the Negroes dance: national holidays, religious holidays, visits by the President, by the General, by every important person, by the departure of the army, by the entrance of the army, everything is a pretext for the official outpouring of public joy.
—Price 1900, 426

IT SEEMS REASONABLE TO ASSUME THAT THE WORDS of Psalm 137 are a poignant and apt expression of the psychological conflict experienced by African slaves brought to the Americas, as had been the case for the Zionists of old:

For there they that led us captive required of us songs,
And they that wasted us required of us mirth, saying
Sing us one of the songs of Zion.

The rhetorical question that was then posed stands out in considerations of slavery wherever it takes place: "How shall we sing the Lord's song in a strange land?" In answer to this question and with specific reference to Africans in the Americas, the French priest Jean-Baptiste Du Tertre (1654, 476) cynically said: "They make every land their homeland, provided they find food and drink there." He went on to say elsewhere: "they quite often sing, dance and amuse themselves better than their masters do and those who give them orders" (1667, 526). What Du Tertre believed was that there was no cause for Europeans to distress themselves about enslavement of Africans because as long as Africans had their bellies full they would be happy, wherever they were. They would sing and dance because it was a part of their genetic makeup.

For Moreau de Saint-Méry, another French writer, Africans who were brought to the Caribbean islands would have liked dancing and would have wanted to dance because they were from the tropics – the warm, bright climate dictated it. On the other hand, Hannibal Price, a Haitian diplomat and writer, proposed a different reason for their love of dancing and singing – he spoke of a "dancing policy" in Haiti, captured in the maxim "the more the Negroes dance, the quieter they are" (1900, 426). Price said that this maxim had started with the old French colonists (before the revolution) and had come right down to his time, for it was still being used by certain politicians for their own gain. Price expressed the view that "dancing was one of the keenest passions of the frivolous colonists of St Domingue. From the great house this passion passed into the slave yards the more quickly because the whites encouraged the development of it by all means in their power" (425–26). In short, Price regarded the love of dancing as cultural trait that emerged among the white population of St Domingue first and was foisted on the black slaves by their white rulers.

So, which one was the slaves' love of dancing – genetic (as Du Tertre said), environmental (according to Moreau de Saint-Méry) or political (using Price's argument)? First of all, it needs to be said that just as a genetically programmed festive African is a baseless notion, so too is the contrary idea that Africans were empty bottles that others filled. Starting with the fact that play is at the centre of human life but enhanced or diminished by preferences in individual cultures, chapter 3 showed the sociopolitical strictures on the survival of indigenous influence and chapter 4 showed the structural influence of European culture on the development of festivity in the colonies. To further answer the question, one now has to look at the contribution of West African cultural expressions of play in the development of festivity.

What Performance Features Did Africans Bring with Them?

The direct connection between Africa and the Caribbean was a reality not only for some "armchair" historians but also deceptively for those giving eyewitness accounts. This was especially so with writers who were associated with the trade in Africans and made the trip from Africa to the Caribbean. For them, the most obvious fact was that the individuals who were put on the ships in Africa were the same individuals who got off them in the Caribbean. So, what they did in Africa was the same as what they did on board the ship and that was the same as what they would do in the Caribbean. The essential weakness in this line of thinking is that social conditions and relationships changed when the Africans were removed from their homes, for in the transfer of Africans to the New World there were many new people, social structures and experiences that affected the context of, reasons for and functions of music, singing and dancing.

The earliest statements made about Africans were generalizations and what later writers said were substantially repetitions of these generalizations. In most European accounts of West Africa, there was one section on music, singing and dancing and the comments in this section were applied to all the people who were encountered, with little discrimination between them. Consequently, the direct transfer of comments from African contexts presents major difficulties for an accurate assessment of cultural practices in the Caribbean. Nevertheless, after looking at comments on African dancing and music made by Europeans who journeyed to West Africa on slave ships in the seventeenth century (namely, Marees [1602] 1987, 171–72; Jobson 1623, 105–6, 107; Villault 1670, 207–9; Dapper 1686, 327; Cavazzi 1687, 168; Phillips 1732, 223; Barbot in Hair, Jones and Law 1992, 2:395, 563), the following statements can be identified as significant in themselves or as themes carried forward and repeated in accounts of life in the Caribbean:

- men and women loved dancing, especially women
- men and women dressed themselves up to go dancing
- dancing took place every evening before going to bed
- dancing took place on Sunday and at festivals
- there was a yearly dancing festival lasting eight days at Abramboe on the Gold Coast
- dancing started in the evening at sunset
- dancing continued all night until the musicians were tired
- dancing continued day and night
- the dancers performed while dancing
- Congo dances were extremely immodest
- the dances were tiring and caused the dancers to lose time from work
- the dancers paid the musician after each dance
- women danced around a corpse while it was being prepared for burial
- there were schools for dancing and for musicians
- musicians were an ornament of status and were used even during the slaving process

Figure 4. A Congo dancer with a band of musicians. Giovanni Cavazzi, *Istorica descrizione de'tre' regni Congo, Matamba, et Angola: sitvati nell'Etiopia inferiore occidentale e delle missioni apostoliche esercitateui da religiosi Capuccini* (Bologna: Giacomo Monti, 1687), book 1, 167.

Overall, music and dancing among West Africans are seen to be not irregular, spontaneous outbursts but a constituent part of their social and political structure. This substantially refutes Price's idea that music and dancing were uncommon customs foisted upon Africans by whites as part of their enslavement in the Caribbean, as a means of controlling them. In fact, the critical notions about slave dancing in the Caribbean that came to dominate European reports were those in Giovanni Cavazzi's observation – that is, it was well loved, lewd, long-lasting and dissipating. Ironically, Cavazzi's pictorial illustrations (as in figure 4) do not support these notions.

One feature of the historical literature that raises eyebrows, however, is the similarity between comments made about Africans in Africa and comments made about the indigenous people of the Caribbean. While there is nothing unusual about similarities in culture in diverse and unconnected areas, in the case of French colonial writers, as already pointed out in reference to their documentation of the customs of the indigenous inhabitants, there is a lack of distinction in their transfer of cultural features from one ethnic group to another. So, when comments in relation to West Africa by Dapper (1686) about preparation of a dead body for a funeral (washing, shaving and painting it red) show some similarity to Boyer's (1654, 280) and La Borde's (1674, 37) comments about natives in the Americas, there is no certainty that these are on both sides independent and valid observations. Clearly, the more frequent indiscriminate comments were, the more unreliable the literature would be. In fact, one could argue therefore that European writers were, through plagiarist and eclectic practices, opting for a certain image of Africans and that this image was not really as widespread as it was represented to be.

Evidence that could be presented to support Price's position is that only the kinds of music and dancing that would have been supportive of the system of slavery would have been encouraged and that those that were inimical to the system would have disappeared. It is therefore not surprising that one comment about music among West Africans that is not made much of in analyses of survivals in the New World is the one which Jobson and Dapper made – that it was a mark of status among important people, who on social occasions had a singer to recount in song their greatness and, when they were travelling, they had a band going before them to, as it were, announce their importance. It is thus ironic that in this case where there was a cultural parallel between West Africans and the indigenous inhabitants of the islands, the genre did not continue and in fact had no chance of doing so in the context of slavery. The parallel was between the griot in the West African context who recounted the exploits of forefathers and the *boitios* who performed in the areitos of the indigenous inhabitants. The glorification of ancestors which this tradition was about would have been in absolute conflict with the hierarchical colonial value system. What appealed more to the European imagination and was therefore popularized in the historical literature was the kind of light-hearted dancing and singing that converted the African into a pleasant marionette.

Did Entertainment Figure in Captives' Lives in the Factories?

Methods of procuring slaves from West Africa varied according to the size of the economic enterprise – that is, whether the ships were linked to large companies or were small undertakings. Big slaving companies (for example, the Royal African Company) had established connections along the west coast of

Africa which facilitated the collection and delivery of captives, whereas smaller undertakings involved ships that had to scour along the coast acquiring captives in an ad hoc manner. One consequence of this, as it affected the experiences of those captured and enslaved, was that some captives were delivered directly to boats which went from place to place and set off for the Americas when they were full; other ships, on the other hand, collected captives from trading houses or "factories" that stored them until the ships came to collect them. The initial experience of enslavement of the latter was thus somewhat different from the former in that the latter gave the captured Africans a preview of slave life while they were still in West Africa.

There is little information on life in the West African forts among the Africans who were to be transported across the Atlantic. Barbot (Hair, Jones and Law 1992, 2:392) described that part of the fort at Cape Coast Castle on the Gold Coast where the captives were housed as follows: "The most noteworthy item is the slave-house, which lies below ground. It consists of large vaulted cellars, divided into several apartments which can easily hold a thousand slaves." This method of housing the captive Africans before transport was much like the conditions on the slave ship, where they were put down into the hold below the deck in the same way. It is possible that bringing them up and making them dance could have been part of their daily routine to keep them in good shape for purchase and transport, but it would be mere speculation to try to identify the general effect of such a possibility. It seems reasonable to assume, however, that whatever "entertainment" there was for the captives, it would have been totally African or without much significant European cultural input, even though the forts were like small European enclaves. On the other hand, the prevailing view about exercise for captives in the forts could have been nothing but work on the agricultural plots to produce food for the Europeans and others who lived at the fort.

While there is no evidence of the captives dancing in the forts, there is evidence presented (Phillips 1732, 201, 202) of women dancing for men and visitors as a part of the slaving or procurement process involving fort personnel. Evidently, women were used to entertain European slavers as a part of business dealings on the west coast of Africa, but there is no information about whether the captives witnessed or had any knowledge of this.

"Dancing and Singing the Slaves" to Preserve Their Health

> The above account of shackling, messing, dancing, and singing the slaves, is allowed by all the evidences.
> —*Abstract of the Evidence* 1792, 33

The epigraph to this section, taken from a British House of Commons committee report, was most likely the source of what came to be a well-known term, "dancing the slaves", but, as can be seen, the term "singing the slaves" was used in exactly the same novel way to convey the idea of coercion. The fact is that even if the latter practice was less prevalent, both were known to be used, the one as physical therapy and the other as psychological.

After their capture, the greatest life-changing event for West Africans was the passage across the Atlantic, which could take as long as seven weeks. Dancing was done during the middle passage principally to provide exercise for the captives, who were being transported in cramped conditions. No doubt European slavers thought of dancing and, to a lesser degree, singing as a perfect solution to the problem of physical and psychological deterioration. They believed that their captured Africans would derive pleasure from them or at least they would be distracted from their pain and fears, for there seemed to be a belief that if Africans were not kept amused and moving, they could remain still and will themselves to death (Mannix and Cowley [1962] 1976, 120). In addition, slave ship captains and crew experienced pleasure, notwithstanding that it was often sadistic, from making or seeing Africans dance.

As to the captives, it would seem that dancing, as part of middle passage survival, etched a critical mark on the "shipmate" bond that the majority of them who came to the Americas attested to. It was also the case that the actual experience of having to dance, often in chains and while weak, and keeping their balance on a rocking boat daily for a number of weeks must have inured them to subservience and toughened those who survived for their life of enslavement.

Some of the earliest information provided on "dancing" on board ship comes from the voyage of the slave ship *Hannibal* on its way from the Guinea Coast to Barbados. Thomas Phillips (1732, 230), commander of the ship, noted in the journal entry for May 1694: "We often at sea in the evenings would let the slaves come up into the sun to air themselves, and make them jump and dance for an hour or two to our bag-pipes, harp, and fiddle, by which exercise to preserve

118   A RESPONSE TO ENSLAVEMENT

Figure 5. "Dancing the slaves" on board ship, by T. Ruhière. In *France maritime*, edited by Amédée Gréhan (Paris: Postel, 1837), 3: between pages 178 and 179.

them in health." Phillips's emphasis was on exercise for the protection of his investment: there was no expression of opinion that the Africans enjoyed what they were doing. In any case, it could hardly have been a case of the captives freely expressing themselves, because they had absolutely no control over their movements, bound on board ship as they were.

However, the way that dancing on board ship was reported in other contemporary accounts gave the impression that a merry time was had by all. For instance, one Barbot account (Hair, Jones and Law 1992, 2:780) said the following:

> Towards the evening they diverted themselves on the deck, as they thought fit, some conversing together, others dancing, singing, and sporting after their manner, which pleased them highly, and often made us pastime; especially the female sex, who being apart from the males, on the quarter-deck, and many of them young sprightly maidens, full of jolity and good humour, afforded us abundance of recreation; as did several little fine boys, which we mostly kept to attend on us about ship.

Even though some journals deliberately tried to put the best face on a dirty business, it could hardly be the case that Barbot's "positive" version was a total fabrication. What gives it some credibility is that the dancing of the females provided amusement and titillation for the crew. It seems unlikely that if the females were being beaten while dancing, it would have been reported in this manner.

Another later middle passage example giving the same positive image of dancing on board ship comes from Christian Hoffmann, assistant to the captain of the Danish-Norwegian slave ship *Fredensborg*, who recorded in the captain's journal on the way from the Guinea Coast to St Croix in 1768: "Thursday 28 April: The female slaves enjoyed dancing their 'Negro Dances' on the quarterdeck" (Svalesen 2000, 108). No doubt there were some captives who got some solace from being able to dance and sing during the passage, but this small reprieve for the Africans was heavily counterbalanced by the horrible below-deck experience. In addition, even when they were on deck, the fear of mutiny, an ever-present threat, must have been apparent in the attitude of the crew and must have tempered whatever levity was possible.

Another version of the captives dancing and singing on board ship which is more muted in its attitude is one cited by Hugh Thomas (1997, 419) as having been given by a French captain: "Both sexes were indeed 'encouraged to sing and dance as much as possible', the captain of a French vessel declared; ' . . . Slaves who danced well might be given a small ration of eau de vie, as well as a little piece of meat or a biscuit. This gave them something to look forward to.'" The factor of encouragement or enticement by a promised reward again gives credibility to this version, even though it was reported in this way primarily to make slavers seem humane.

Just about the time the slave trade was abolished in 1807, Captain Hugh Crow (1830, 147), in keeping with his view of himself as a benevolent slave trader, made the following positive comment about treatment of captives on board ship: "Pipes and tobacco were then supplied to the men, and beads and other articles were distributed amongst the women to amuse them, after which they were permitted to dance and run about on deck to keep them in good spirits." This is in keeping with Barbot's account about a hundred years before and with the view held by many involved in slaving and slavery that captives were well treated.

These citations are testimony of Europeans' belief that dancing, singing and amusement were part of the very being of Africans, especially the women. Barbot went as far as to prescribe it as a way to keep them from revolting during the middle passage: "Above all, make them plenty of friendly gestures (*caresses*), and often jest with them and make them play various games, giving them freedom to sing and dance, especially the women" (Hair, Jones and Law, 1992, 2:775). Barbot's advice suggests that the lascivious intent of European sailors came to shape the identity of the slaves' culture. No doubt the delight of the crew could have fostered a spirit of exhibitionism and could have encouraged some women to seek their favour for their own protection or gain. On the other hand, the historical record suggests that one captured female who resisted the demands to dance ended up dead. In 1792 John Kimber, the captain of a slave ship, was tried for causing the death of a female captive during the middle passage because she refused to dance naked. Kimber was acquitted, but the evidence given by the witness was graphically illustrated (I. Cruikshank, *Captain Kimber's Treatment of a Young Negro Girl*, 1792), which suggests that it was believed to be the truth. The image of captives enjoying dancing on board ship during the crossing contrasts sharply with the illustration by T. Ruhière in 1837 (see figure 5) where dancing is presented as an exercise the captives were being forced to carry out under the constant menace of the whip. In addition to Ruhière's graphic illustration, there are also the following verses supporting the notion of "dancing the slaves":

> At the savage Captain's beck,
> Now like brutes they make us prance
> Smack the cat about the Deck
> And in scorn they bid us dance
> (More 1795, 5)

These verses were of course a part of the anti-/abolitionist rhetoric that came to dominate British politics towards the end of the eighteenth century up until abolition. Here Hannah More purports to give a captive African's viewpoint, a strategy increasingly adopted by the abolitionists.

Another example of evidence from an abolitionist viewpoint is given by Falconbridge, who reported in 1788: "Exercise being deemed necessary for the preservation of their health, they are sometimes obliged to dance, when the weather will permit their coming on deck. *If they go about it reluctantly, or do not move with agility*, they are flogged; a person standing by them all the time with a cat-o'-nine-tails in his hand for that purpose" (Fyfe 2000, 209; emphasis added). The same abolitionist viewpoint comes through strongly and repeatedly in the evidence given before the House of Commons committee which in 1790 sat to hear testimony from those who were directly involved in the trafficking of Africans:

> After meals they are made *to jump in their irons*. This is called *dancing* by the slave-dealers. *In every ship* he has been desired *to flog such as would not jump*. He had generally a cat of nine tails in his hand among the women, and the chief mate, he believes, another among the men. (*Abstract of the Evidence* 1791, 33)
>
> The necessity of exercise for health is the reason given for compelling the slaves to dance in the above manner. (34n)
>
> Even those who had the flux, scurvy, and such oedematous swellings in their legs as made it painful to them to move at all, were compelled to dance by the cat. (34)

More of the same evidence from the minutes to the House of Commons committee is provided by Mannix and Cowley ([1962] 1976, 114): "After the morning meal came a joyless ceremony called 'dancing the slaves'. 'Those who were in irons,' says Dr. Thomas Trotter, surgeon of the Brookes in 1783, 'were ordered to stand up and make what motions they could, leaving a passage for such as were out of irons to dance around the deck.'" Years later, Thomas Clarkson (1839, 304), in his post-emancipation documentation of the abolition of the slave trade, reported that, contrary to the anti-abolitionist claim that "when upon deck they made merry and amused themselves with dancing", the reality was that "after meals they jumped in their irons for exercise. This was so necessary for their health, that they were whipped if they refused to do it; and this jumping had been termed dancing" (305).

In spite of the fact that the House of Commons minutes made it seem as if dancing the slaves happened on every middle passage voyage, it is only a few slavers' logs that actually refer to or provide documentary evidence of the practice.

The complementary activity of "singing the slaves" was not extensively reported. One instance of it is given by Falconbridge, who reported in 1788: "The poor wretches are frequently compelled to sing also; but when they do so, their songs are generally, as may be naturally expected, melancholy lamentations of their exile from their native country" (Fyfe 2000, 209–10). Note that in *An Abstract of the Evidence* (1791, 34) these remarks are presented as the words of Ecroide Claxton: "He [Claxton] says also that on board his ship they sometimes *sung*, but not for their amusement. The captain ordered them to sing, and they *sung songs of sorrow*. The subject of these songs were their *wretched situation, and the idea of never returning home*. He recollects their very words upon these occasions."

Of course, the assertion that the songs were "melancholy lamentations of their exile from their native country or songs of sorrow" was strong emotional testimony used to argue for abolition of the trade, but the truth of it is questionable. It could hardly be that sad songs were the kind that the crew was ordering captives to sing and it does not seem likely that they would risk the possibility of incurring more punishment by making understandable complaints in song. Furthermore, it seems unlikely that a European at the time was familiar with or could understand the words of African songs.

The view put forward by Barbot and others that Africans were able to freely dance and sing during their time of greatest mental pain and physical distress clearly distorted the psychological profile of Africans and dehumanized them. Some European slavers, because they had no alternative plan for improving health, must have deluded themselves that entertainment, enforced or not, was a pleasant medication to overcome depression and physical deterioration. As to the captives themselves, it is reasonable to assume that some of them who were subjected to this enforced "medication" on board ship or even witnessed it developed an aversion to dancing and singing.

Heralding Their Arrival and Displaying Their Readiness

In some islands up to today, when boats come back in with their catch of fish, sellers collect the fish and proceed into the neighbourhoods announcing fish for sale by blowing a conch shell or horn and calling out "fish". When the slave ships came into port in the Caribbean, it was the captured Africans who had to announce themselves for sale by singing loudly and lustily and by displaying themselves in dance or marching. So, the merchandise announced itself.

Slaves, especially plantation slaves, had to do strenuous physical work over their active lifetime. Buyers of captured Africans had to have some way of determining their soundness and readiness when they arrived in the West Indies and were put up for sale. Over time, buyers came up with various ways of doing this, but one way which the seller thought he could use to demonstrate soundness and readiness was by displaying the captives singing and dancing, which presumably demonstrated physical soundness and psychological readiness. The Africans, for their part, having just been traumatized continuously for weeks and ignorant of their impending fate, knew that they had to obey whatever instructions they were given. There is no record of the reactions of individual captives and there is no observation about the success or failure of this index of soundness. The practice lasted up until the final years of the trade.

James Aytoun, a young British soldier who did a three-year stint in Dominica in the 1780s, remembered the following about the slaves' arrival in port: "The shipmasters had to have the slaves on deck at certain times during the day and it was said, obliged them to sing a yo-yo-yo but whether by compulsion or voluntary I know not, but it is certain they yo-yo'd in concert, so that we could hear them more than a mile." What Aytoun highlights is not only that they sang "in concert" on deck but also that when they came ashore, they walked "in Indian file . . . following one another like geese" (1984, 21). In other words, the whole performance was orchestrated.

William Young (1801, 268) provides a credible picture of captured Africans' arrival in St Vincent in 1791 which in particular gives an idea of the practice of dancing the slaves on deck. He shows first that "every thing was prepared for our visit, as the least observing eye might have discovered" and that the captives were instructed what they had to do before the buyers arrived. From Young's subsequent comment, it is clear that he, as a buyer, found the dancing disgusting and that he was under no illusion that the Africans were dancing because they were happy:

> In particular I was disgusted with a general jumping or dancing of the negroes on the deck, which some, and perhaps many of them, did voluntarily, but some under force or controul; for I saw a sailor, more than once, catch those rudely by the arm who had ceased dancing, and by gesture menace them to repeat their motion, to clap their hands, and shout their song of *Yah! Yah!* Which I understood to mean "Friends". (1801, 268)

In fact, Young insisted that the dancing be stopped and then concluded that, despite the enforced dancing, all the captives, except one who was perhaps ill, "were even cheerful for the most part, and all anxious to go ashore" (268–69) since they had already been informed by Vincentian slaves who had been allowed to visit them on board about what to expect in St Vincent.

Contrasting with Young's conviction about enforced dancing and his negative reaction to it is a view appearing in a work published at the end of the first decade of the nineteenth century in which there is a naively positive or misleading presentation of the newly arrived captives' preparation for viewing and their dancing (*Authentic History* 1810, 25–26). The passages, like much of the rest of the work, are actually copied directly from Stedman's account of Suriname in the 1770s, but the work purports to be about the British West Indian islands, making reference to them by name. Apparently, the dressing up for dancing which Africans did in their own contexts had now been transformed into presentation for show and sale. The writer then goes on to describe the subsequent stages in the procedure: "After this operation, one part of them is sent ashore for sale, decorated with pieces of cotton, arm-bands, beads, and other ornaments, being all the captain's property; while the others spend the day in dancing, hallooing, and clapping hands on board the vessel, almost forgetful of their companions, who walk along the waterside and through the streets, where every planter selects out the number of which he stands in need" (26). The writer thus gives the impression that the captives who remained temporarily on board ship were oblivious of their own pending fate and were so happy to see land presumably that they just had to dance and sing. Dancing had therefore become an expression of their joy rather than a factor in their display for sale.

Pinckard, about ten years before the end of the trade in the British islands, showed that he realized that there was a difference between the intent of the traders and how the captives really might have felt during the pre-sale activities. Yet he speaks of the Africans' parading on shore as contributing to their health and amusement:

> Often we observe the captains parading the streets, accompanied by parties of their prime slaves – apparently with the intention of exhibiting them to the eye of the public, in sound state and good condition. This contributes, at the same time, to the health and amusement of these poor beings, who seem delighted at feeling their feet on shore, and, in due obedience to their captain, dance and frolic as they go along, either in real, or in well dissembled contentment and happiness. (1806, 1:326–27)

From Pinckard's words one has to infer that the captain had preselected his best captives and was parading them to give the public an impression of the quality of his "merchandise" overall. This preview therefore was an advertisement for an upcoming sale.

In contrast to Pinckard's suggestion that the newly arrived Africans danced because they were "delighted at feeling their feet on shore" is the observation made two decades earlier that capture and enslavement had a deep traumatic effect on them for years:

That new negroes, although they seem cheerful upon their arrival in the colonies, are apparently heavy in body and mind, is an observation that cannot be easily refuted.*

*The African negroes when first imported seem not to have any moral feelings, the tenderness of sentiment, or weight of thought. They are unfeeling in the plenitude of power, and savage in the cold revenge of spilling blood. They look upon sudden or violent death in others with apathy, and will bear the approaches of their own, not only without dread, but with indifference. It is amazing to see how little they interest themselves in the common occurrences of life, they do not foresee the want of means, are careless of what may happen, and thoughtless of what they have; in short their characters for many years after their arrival can hardly be defined by the most perspicuous eye of those by whom they are governed, so that for what we know they may be happy when silent, or dangerous when sullen. The characters of creole negroes are widely different, and in many instances may serve as a faithful contrast. (Beckford 1788, 88)

While other writers speculated about the difference between the slaves obeying orders to dance and their real feelings about dancing, Beckford had no doubt in his mind about it and he went further and converted the enslaved African into a dangerously deceptive being quite different from the creole slave. However, Beckford's contrast of the demeanour of the enslaved African and that of the creole slave was really driven by the contemporary belief that enslaved Africans were more apt to be rebellious and took some time to fit in. What is more significant is that the dancing and singing which the ship's captain forced the captives to do during the passage and on arrival for practical, economic reasons was for the captured Africans themselves a preview of one aspect of slave life and the start of the seasoning process.

Evangelists' Reaction to a Perceived "Dancing Policy"

The slaves' dancing and singing were repeatedly mentioned within the framework of a Christian contrast between work and rest, in the sense that after a hard week's work when Christians thought that Sunday should be a day of rest, the slaves were said to indulge in vigorous and prolonged dancing. Ligon ([1657] 1970, 50) identified dancing among the slaves in Barbados as a once-a-week, half-day, Sunday activity. However, he also described dancing as an activity that sometimes could go on for the entire day. Blome's (1672, 86) version a decade or so later was much the same. Leslie (1740, 310), almost a century after Ligon, also identified Sunday afternoon as the time for dancing among the slaves in Jamaica.

For the slaves, Sunday was their day off, the day of the week that the field slaves did not have to work for the master. The problem, however, was that dancing on Sunday was offensive to those who thought that the Lord's day should be kept holy as well as to those who thought that the slaves should be Christian. This view emerges quite clearly in Daniel Defoe's *The Family Instructor* (1718, 2:304) in which a young slave from Barbados who was taken to England is questioned about his lack of knowledge of God and, in response to the question "Do they [the slaves] work on Sabbath Days too?", explained, "No, they sing, they dance, they sleep the Sunday."

An increasingly powerful force in colonial society that not only wanted to curb the slaves' dancing but eliminate it altogether was the missionaries. Their real intention was to rid the slaves of their "savage" African characteristics. It was during the period when slavery was under consistent attack that "constant frolic" among the slaves was more pointedly called into question and the idea that dancing was an activity forced upon them became more prominent. The idea was also typical among abolitionists, who believed they could see behind the mask of merriment and blamed slave owners for what they considered to be bad habits among the slaves. An example of this view, which incidentally supported the one later espoused by Hannibal Price, is given by an observer who called himself the "Negro's Friend" (1830, 6): "I was informed, that the managers of these poor creatures are rather diligent in procuring noisy amusements for them, and exciting them to a love of dancing, for the sake of encouraging and pleasing them."

On the other hand, most of the colonists, who were not abolitionists or missionaries, were convinced that the slaves loved dancing of their own accord and that they were being dissuaded from it by zealous types (Barclay 1826, 10–11; Carmichael 1833, 1:229–30, 293–94; Wentworth 1834, 2:229–30; Lloyd 1839, 58, 59). There was therefore a fundamental difference between the missionary and the colonist. In time, there also came to be a difference of opinion among the slaves themselves about the morality of dancing. Waddell (1863, 115) gave an example of the strength of conviction of some of his church members and the consequences thereof: "They were taunted as my fools, because they declined to receive the customary bottle of rum, and were even denied the usual sugar, because they would not attend the 'busha house' dance."

The decrease in dancing and singing, which was brought about by Christian missionaries, made the slaves more "civilized" for those who saw the kinds of dancing and singing which the slaves did as the perpetuation of African behaviour. It was one of the clear indices of the adoption of European ideals and values imposed on colonial societies. However, the extent to which evangelists managed over the years to change the Sunday activities of the slaves varied. By the second decade of the nineteenth century, Carmichael (1833, 1:290) noted only a slight change in St Vincent. As Carmichael conceded, change was difficult to effect because the slaves had come to believe that Sunday was their day by right.

However, in the late slave period, the Christian missionaries achieved what many pieces of legislation over the whole slave period had failed to do. From early, the idea of letting the slaves dance and sing to make themselves happy had been counterbalanced by the knowledge that large gatherings of slaves could lead to plots and rebellions. As a result of this knowledge, prohibition of such activities came to be a regular feature of law making in slave colonies. In contrast to evangelization, such measures had only a minimal, short-term effect on the culture of the slaves. The difference between the legislators and the missionaries was that the former had their own safety in mind whereas the latter ostensibly had the welfare of the slaves in mind.

Endless Dancing, Fears of Rebellion and Changing Attitudes

It was an unchallenged view among European writers that Caribbean slaves had a natural and strong predilection for dancing; Labat (1931, 2:51) was one of the first to say so: "Dance is their favourite passion; I don't think there is a people in the world who is more attached to it than they are." There was no accompanying claim that dancing was induced by drugs or alcohol, even though rum was regularly given to the slaves as a form of medicine or stimulant.

In the early years of the new colonies in the smaller islands, when the numbers of enslaved Africans were small and there were not many of the same ethnic group living together, apparently they were less active, judging from a comment by Bouton (1640, 101): "they are extremely idle and spend the time sleeping and chatting". With the change to sugar cultivation and the consequent increase in the numbers of slaves and the consolidation of plantation slave society, an active lifestyle then came to be presented as the norm.

A characterization of the slaves' dancing that was probably adopted from descriptions of Africans in Africa but was also similar to characterizations of entertainment among the indigenous inhabitants of the Caribbean was that it stretched over long periods, night and day. In trying to show the slaves' passion for dancing, writers highlighted its duration and it was not long before a picture was created of slaves dancing throughout their free time. Du Tertre (1667, 527), from early in the slave period, claimed that some slaves danced from Sunday afternoon until it was time for work on Monday morning. Labat (1931, 2:51), referring to the end of the seventeenth century, not only extended the starting-point to Saturday night but also gave the impression that the slaves had an almost uncontrollable urge to go to dances: "When the masters do not allow them to dance in the yard, they travel three or four leagues, after they finish work at midnight on Saturday at the sugar factory, to get to some place where they know a dance is taking place."

Towards the end of the eighteenth century, Stedman's ([1794] 1806, 2:229) account, because it was written in English and was about a colony that had been English (Suriname), consolidated the notion of continuous dancing: "So indefatigable are they at this diversion, that I have known the drums continue beating without intermission from six o'clock on Saturday night till the sun made its appearance on the Monday morning; thus had passed six-and-thirty hours in dancing, cheering, hallooing, and clapping of hands." At the time, the picture of non-stop dancing among the slaves – from Saturday night to Monday morning – was reinforced by (Moreton 1790, 155) in Jamaica and Pinckard in Barbados (1806, 1:263–64). A little later in Jamaica, Stewart (1808, 261–62) repeated the same idea. Thus, the slave came to be represented as a being who danced nonstop for thirty-six hours.

However, some years later De La Beche (1825, 40–41) was a little more realistic and believable in his explanation when he pointed out that there was a break between morning and evening: "the dance . . . commences about eight o'clock in the evening, and . . . continues to daybreak with scarcely any intermission. . . . The dance is discontinued at day-break in the morning. . . . The dance recommences the second evening, but does not continue through the night." The idea of non-stop dancing assumed that there was no contextual difference between dancing done during the daytime and dancing at night. Indeed, the impression was created by Carmichael (1833, 1:293) that a fundamental reason for this was that heat did not affect the slaves. This was a familiar claim and just a version of the more general European conviction about tropical heat and its debilitating effect on whites, as opposed to its lack of effect on blacks and creoles.

While, on the one hand, the constant noise (music) and activity were a source of annoyance to whites on some plantations (for example, Thomas Thistlewood in eighteenth-century Jamaica repeatedly beat his slaves and broke up their instruments), on the other hand, it was reassuring to others in that they knew where their slaves were and what they were doing, and as long as they were using up their energy entertaining themselves, they were no threat to the whites. In this sense, the slaves' entertaining themselves inspired a feeling of comfort and security. There might even have been a feeling of pride among slave owners who came to believe that they were responsible for providing and fostering a milieu for the enjoyment and contentment of their slaves and even for their artistic expertise. This was very much so in the last years of slavery when there was a strong intent on the part of anti-abolitionist plantation owners to show that the slaves were happy and contented.

However, the picture of continuous dancing must be seen within the context of one abiding and contradictory reality – whites' belief that it was at gatherings of slaves that plots were hatched. A look at laws passed during the period of slavery shows that up until emancipation local houses of assembly in trying to reduce the possibility of revolts not only banned certain instruments but also set time limits on dances, as, for example, in the following law passed in Jamaica in 1826:

> That no person having charge of slaves shall permit nightly meetings, beating of drums, or other such music, blowing of horns or shells, or such like, under pain of six months imprisonment... Nevertheless, this is not to prevent any owner, or other person in charge of slaves, from allowing those belonging to the plantation or estate to divert themselves, but they must not use warlike instruments; and in such cases the amusement must terminate by twelve o'clock at night. (Senior 1835, 149–50)

The stipulation about the finishing time for activities meant that thirty-six-hour dancing, if it had indeed ever been a reality, could no longer be. As was said, however, such legal stipulations were not as definitive as they appeared to be because not all masters sought to make sure that they were adhered to, not least of all because they thought that dancing was a sign of happiness.

Du Tertre's opinion of enslaved Africans in the Caribbean was that "they are no less joyful being enslaved than if they were perfectly free" (1667, 2:526) and, quite significantly, there were no reports that dancing and singing among the former slaves changed dramatically in frequency or intensity after emancipation. The change that was noticeable was European attitudes: they now highlighted the bad economic consequences of prolonged dancing, where before emancipation they seemed to have believed more in the psychological benefits.

Breen (1844, 190), speaking of St Lucia where the French had had a major influence, resigned himself to the continued influence of festivity on the "lower orders", but he pointed out both the positive and negative effects of it:

> Amongst the lower orders the dance exercises a still greater influence. Not satisfied with aping those above them in finery and dress, the Negroes carry their love of dancing to the most extravagant pitch – much too extravagant perhaps for their means. True, the evil has its bright side in the encouragement of trade and the promotion of a spirit of emulation and industry amongst the labouring classes; but it must greatly impair their physical energies, if it does not ultimately mar their independence.

However, he could not help taking a stab at the French, whom he thought, as Price did, were responsible for promoting "artificial enjoyment" among their slaves.

Breen's comments about the pros and cons of frequent festivity and the intractable nature of it ("it is not to be put down either by preaching or persecution" [1844, 190]) were essentially highlighting the need for a change which, for him, had to go along with emancipation: free people had to be responsible; they could no longer be "carefree". However, his hope that they would remain simple and innocent ("preserve their primæval character of innocence and simplicity" [191]) seemed incompatible with this perceived change in status and also with "their independence".

Day (1852, 2:87–88), in his customary way, presented a purely negative vision of festivity in the post-slavery period. His vision was ironic. The image of the happiness was all that was needed during the period of slavery, as is evident in the words of Marsden (1788, 33), who was actually anti-slavery, in the heyday of the plantation system in Jamaica: "When the holidays are over, without the least appearance of fatigue from their extraordinary exertions night and day, they chearfully return to their work." Now, when Europeans were no longer responsible for their welfare, the behaviour of former slaves had become a fundamental weakness and a cause of loss in economic productivity.

The Image of the Slave as a Natural Dancer and Singer

The two opposing views of the musical ability of the slaves were that they had no sense of music or that they were naturally gifted. The first view was expressed in the early years when the slaves were deprived of well-made musical instruments. It was also common throughout the slave period in the minds of writers who disliked the slaves or disagreed with any and all favourable comments made about them, as for example Bryan Edwards (1793–94, 2:86):

> An opinion prevails in Europe that they possess organs peculiarly adapted to the science of music; but this I believe is an ill-founded idea. In vocal harmony they display neither variety nor compass. Nature seems in this respect to have dealt more penuriously by them than towards the rest of the human race. As practical musicians, some of them, by greater labour and careful instruction, become sufficiently expert to bear an underpart in a public concert; but I do not recollect ever to have seen or heard of a Negro who could truly be called a fine performer on any capital instrument. In general they prefer a loud and long-continued noise to the finest harmony, and frequently consume the whole night *in beating on a board with a stick*.

Edwards was judging the slaves according to their ability to play European instruments, but even in this he appeared to concede that his view was not the prevailing one in Europe.

The second ("natural gift") view of the slaves' ability became common as Europeans became accustomed to the slaves' music and dancing. It was consistent with the picture of the happy slave and thus became an established and generally accepted view, as the following citations attest:

> The organs of Negroes are uniquely fashioned for music. (Chanvalon 1763, 66)

> I saw seven to eight hundred Negroes accompanying a wedding to the sound of a song; they jumped in the air and landed back on the ground all at the same time; their movement was precise and so universal that the sound of their landing was just one single sound. (Chanvalon 1763, 66)

> The absence of clothes revealing all their muscles, one sees that there is no part of their body that is not affected by this rhythm and that does not express it. (Chanvalon 1763, 66)

> They have good ears for music. (Long 1774, 2:423)

but mirth, festivity, music, and dancing, engross no small portion of their leisure: they have an ear for music, and a graceful activity in dancing. (Tobin 1785, 96)

The negroes are famous for the justness of their ear (*Short Journey* 1790, 1:90–91)

I have often been surprised to observe how infinitely more the negro appears to be affected by music and by dancing, than the white children in Jamaica. (Beckford 1790, 1:391)

They are extremely fond of music and dancing; they have good ears, and preserve the most perfect tune and time. (Beckford 1790, 2:387)
Their style of dancing is by no means ungraceful. (Beckford 1790, 2:388)

Mr. L—— and myself both impartially allowed the negroes, young men and girls, to dance better in step, in grace, and correctness of figure, than our fashionable, or indeed any couples at any ball in England; taking that ball generally, there is no one negro dances ill. (Young 1801, 283)

Both the singers and dancers shew the exactest precision as to time and measure. (Stewart 1808, 261)

But the fact is that the negroes are a singing race. And they not only sing at their feasts and dances, but at their work. There is scarcely an occurrence that attracts particular attention which they will not turn into a song. (Dallas 1823, 145)

I must not, however, charge the slaves with a crime of which, if we except their young ones, they are seldom guilty, namely that of producing inharmonious and nonaccordant sounds; on the contrary, they have, generally a good ear for music, they sing or whistle with wonderful correctness any tune they may have heard, they dance in excellent time, and are altogether very intelligent persons in any thing connected to music. (Bayley 1830, 437)

The extreme accuracy with which they preserve the time in the dance . . . (Rolph 1836, 32)

Negros have great aptness in singing, and all join in, whether they know the words or not. (Lloyd 1839, 46–47)

Europeans tried to account for expertise among the slaves by identifying the notion of "natural gift" (that is, instinct), which fundamentally meant that they did not have to concede acquisition of skill through practice or reason.

It is true that there is mention of the slaves starting to dance from the time they were small children, which would logically suggest acquisition of expertise over a period of time. For instance, in the early colonies in the small islands

Du Tertre (1667, 527) mentioned the integral involvement of the children: "but what is astonishing in these children is that they are not any more bored in these pastimes than their elders, so that they sing and dance until sleep overpowers them". However, one gets the impression that, for Du Tertre, the children were only doing what came naturally to them and that there was no difference between child and adult in their natural expression. It is only almost two hundred years later in reference to Jamaica that there is explicit mention of the children watching and learning, but the overall picture of the scene is virtually the same as that given by Du Tertre (Hosack 1876, 29):

> Even the little children dance apart
> In the safe corners, looking at their feet,
> In mute attention, to acquire the art –

In this scenario, dancing and singing among the Africans and their descendants would be skills activated from small which became second nature and were perpetuated from generation to generation. Thus, the slaves' expertise would have nothing to do with normal intellectual capacity.

Wentworth was quite explicit about the relationship between the slaves' dancing expertise and intellect. He set out his argument in two parts basically – first, "negroes" had an uncontrollable attraction to music and, second, they could execute music with expertise because they were low-level humans:

> If a quadrille bring up the rear of the evening, the number of visitors in the vicinity of the dwelling inevitably increases, and a novice might conjecture that dancing had become epidemic, and that the whole black multitude on the estate, men, women, and children, had been inoculated for it by a *tarantula*. The sound of music seems to affect all ranks, grades, or distinctions among them. . . .
> It is indeed, a striking characteristic even among savages of every region, as well as among those who may be advanced grades nearer to civilized life, and it seems to argue that the organ of sounds becomes repressed as the mind expands, to adapt itself to the various occupations which a refined state of society imposes upon it. It is certain that a love of music is by no means so universal in that state, as it is known to be among a barbarous people; and few instances, we believe, can be adduced among the most eminent musical composers, of their possessing any remarkable superiority of intellect. (Wentworth 1834, 1:283–84)

What is remarkable in Wentworth's logic ("the organ of sounds becomes repressed as the mind expands") is that he takes it to the extreme to even discredit great European musicians as having no "remarkable superiority of intellect" because, like the slaves, they had an aptitude for music.

For Wentworth, then, the happy Negro playing, singing and dancing was to be explained as typical of a being of low intellect. Bridgens in 1837 was of the same mind, for he said: "Such boisterous mirth is characteristic of this light-hearted race, one of whose chief resources, in the absence of more intellectual pleasures, it was, doubtless, intended to be." For them, and presumably for many Europeans, it was the flip side of the fundamental image of the black, uncivilized and unintelligent African seen to be at the lowest rung of humanity – a playful ape. It was just another face of the same idea that music, singing and dancing constituted a force that kept the unsuspecting and unintelligent slaves under control and made them innocuous marionettes.

The "Happy Slave" in Anti-Abolition and Reparation Arguments

How did the image of the happy slave in the West Indies come to supersede all the other images of the black slave in the Americas? There was the fundamental image of the black, uncivilized, unintelligent and ugly African seen to be at the lowest rung of humanity and not far removed from the ape. There was a long history in the Americas of the image of the brutal and rebellious slave, culminating in the spectre of the Haitian in the early nineteenth century. There was the image of the brutalized and disfigured slave together with all the implements of brutality. And there was the image of the singing, dancing, carefree slave. Why did this last image flourish in the face of the other powerful, negative stereotypes?

First of all, even if the horrors of slavery were rendered invisible and the simplistic connection between food, clothing, shelter and happiness were disregarded, there must have been something in the eyes, on the faces, in the voices and in the behaviour of the slaves to cause whites to believe that they were happy. It must have been something of this order to cause Beckford (1790, 2:394) to say: "The amusements of the negroes betray a contentment and independency of mind, which I have not often beheld in other people." Lady Nugent really seemed to believe what she said when she wrote in her diary: "Give the servants an entertainment in the evening, and a dollar each. Poor creatures, they seemed the happiest of the happy, dancing and singing almost the whole night" (Wright 2002, 98). One thing that is certain is that the image of the happy slave was inseparable from music, dancing and frolic. Also, the belief that the slaves were carefree meant that Europeans saw them as not having to provide food, clothing and shelter for themselves and that, as such, their mind was free from "the various occupations which a refined state of society imposes upon it" (Wentworth 1834, 1:283).

Probably the strongest statement using song and dance as a measure of happiness was made by Resident (1828, 234) during the period leading up to emancipation: "In no country in the world are there stronger or more unequivocal indications of happiness and enjoyment than in the West Indies. Their song is the song of joy; their dance is the dance of hilarity and delight."

It encapsulates several of the notions of pro-slavery Europeans and creoles, who, from the earliest days, saw their views as factual and based on lived experience in the West Indies.

A fundamental and widespread belief among whites and others which has come right down to today is that European civilization improved Africans and one way that this was illustrated in the historical literature was to contrast the dumb, emaciated, newly arrived African with the bright, singing and dancing slave. An early example occurs in a long poem titled "The field negroe, or the effect of civilization" written in 1783 by a person calling himself "A Native of the West Indies". The following verses from the poem capture the "effect of civilization":

> Poor Arthur was the wretch's name,
> And Guinea gave him breath;
> While he to sad Antigua came,
>   To meet, he fear'd, his death. . . .
> And now the rank *baba*[1] he throws
>   From off his polish'd limbs,
> And every day he nicer grows,
>   Improving in his whims. . . .
> And now we daily hear him sing,
>   The merriest and the best:
> He seems, he moves another thing,
>   And portly rears his crest.
> (Native 1783, 8, 15, 16)

---

1. *Baba* = an inferior kind of clothing.

This conviction was so strong among creole whites that their "civilization" of the African had brought him happiness that to challenge it by saying that the slaves were not happy was an affront to colonial society.

James Grainger's intention in his poem was to exhort masters to allow the slaves to express themselves freely so that their happiness and contentment would shine through. He did this by portraying them singing and dancing almost in a bucolic and romantic European tradition:

> On festal days; or when their work is done;
> Permit thy slaves to lead the choral dance,
> To the wild banshaw's[2] melancholy sound.
> Responsive to the sound, head feet and frame
> Move aukwardly harmonious; hand in hand
> Now lock'd, the gay troop circularly wheels,
> And frisks and capers with intemperate joy.
> Halts the vast circle, all clap hands and sing;
> While those distinguish'd for their heels and air,
> Bound in the center, and fantastic twine.
> Meanwhile some stripling, from the choral ring,
> Trips forth; and, not ungallantly, bestows
> On her who nimblest hath the greensward beat,
> And whose flush'd beauties have inthrall'd his soul,
> A silver token of his fond applause.
> Anon they form in ranks; nor inexpert
> A thousand tuneful intricacies weave,
> Shaking their sable limbs; and oft a kiss
> Steal from their partners; who, with neck reclin'd,
> And semblant scorn, resent the ravish'd bliss.
> (Grainger 1764, 157–58)

The tone of Grainger's work, in a celebrated literary genre, was laudatory and did not reek of the usual image of wild, savage Africa. For instance, in the line "A thousand tuneful intricacies weave", Grainger essentially equated the dance with the steps and sequences of European dances. Grainger's exhortation to slave masters to let their slaves reach that state of bliss through dancing and singing presumed a salutary and curative power in those activities.

---

2. *Banshaw* = banjo.

The image of the happy slave was in the majority of cases put forward and promoted in response to criticism of the degradation and violence of slavery. In 1785, James Tobin, who regarded himself as a "Friend to the West India colonies and their inhabitants", made a stout defence of slavery in the face of a sharp attack by the English priest James Ramsay, who had criticized creoles after he returned home after being stationed in the Leeward Islands for a few years. Tobin (1785, 98) used Brunias's positive pictorial representation of the slaves as a response to Ramsay's criticisms since he regarded Brunias's representations as those of an objective eyewitness: "To the mere European reader I beg leave to recommend an inspection of a set of prints, etched by Brunias, an Italian painter, from drawings made by himself on the spot, representing the negro dancings, cudgellings, &c. &c. of the different islands; which are drawn with much exactness and strong character." For Tobin, Brunias's depiction showed the slaves as "plump, active, and merry figures". Bear in mind, however, that Brunias had been commissioned to produce images of the slaves which of course would have been rejected if they had been unfavourable in the eyes of his patron.

The need to create or put forward the image of the happy slave increased as the abolition debates escalated. Writers took up one position or the other in the debate and their descriptions and comments reflected their bias. Pinckard was one of those who saw the slaves as happy and carefree and he said so repeatedly (1806, 1:289, 290, 368). Barclay was another one and he cited the following song to support the vision of the carefree slave playing his "bonja" and singing:[3]

> What are the joys of white man here?
> What are his pleasures? say;
> Me want no joys, no ill me fear,
> But on my bonja play.
>
> Me sing all day, me sleep all night,
> Me hab no care, my heart is light;
> Me tink not what to-morrow bring,
> Me happy, so me sing.

---

3. Barclay was mistaken in his belief that "The Bonja Song" was written by R. Dallas. The name at the end is given as Charlotte, who was probably Dallas's sister.

> But white man's joys are not like mine,
> Dho' he look smart and gay;
> He proud, he jealous, haughty, fine,
> While I my bonja play.
>
> He sleep all day, he wake all night,
> He full of care, his heart no light;
> He great deal want, he little get,
> He sorry, so he fret.
>
> Me envy not dhe white man dhen,
> Me poor but me is gay;
> Me glad at heart, me happy when
> Me on my bonja play.
>
> Me sing all day; me sleep all night,
> Me hab no care, my heart is light;
> Me tink not what to-morrow bring,
> Me happy, so me sing.
> (Dallas 1823, 144, quoted in Barclay 1826, 213n)

The acrimonious debates about the condition of the slaves, the abolition of the slave trade and the movement towards emancipation had made little difference apparently to Barclay, who found the image of the happy slave produced in "The Bonja Song" to be still apt twenty years later.

The strongest "exponent" of the idea of the happy slave was Monk Lewis. Whether it was a matter of self-deception, self-interest or just plain stupidity, Lewis recounted a picture of bliss among the slaves on one of his plantations. He made the comment: "For myself, it appears to me almost worth surrendering the luxuries and pleasures of Great Britain, for the single pleasure of being surrounded with beings who are always laughing and singing" ([1834] 1969, 101). He thought that he could bring about a state of happiness among displaced slaves if he were to "distribute a little money, and allow a couple of play-days for dancing" (366). He even suggested that "in defiance of Sunday the negroes had the irreverence to be gay and happy" (126). Such a conviction was an integral component in the systematic rebuttal of claims made by "the African Institution" and other pro-emancipation forces in Britain.

One of those white creoles who was still challenging the negative picture of slavery on the eve of emancipation with the image of the happy slave was

M.J. Chapman (1833, 72), a Barbadian, who made his case in the following lines:

> How beautiful the night! how sweetly fall
> Its shadows! 'tis the negro festival.
> To the sound of flutes and drums they dancing come.
> Not sweeter nor more musical the hum
> Of falling waters to the drowsy ear,
> Than those far sounds the wings of Zephyr bear.
> ....
> Lovers in pairs go dancing o'er the green,
> While Bacchus cheers them with his honest mien.
> Here may be seen the dance of Libya,
> While honoured bands their native music play, –
> The deep-toned banjoe, to their ears divine,
> The noisy cymbal and the tambourine.

Part of this passage was also used by Cruikshank (1835) to accompany his engravings.

There were some descriptions which were not explicitly produced to support the image of the happy slave, but by sheer ingenuousness were probably more convincing. A description of this type, one which was oft repeated with many geographical variants, was given by Carmichael (1833, 2:286–87): "Sitting outside their doors, in the fine nights of a tropical climate, – cooking, and eating their suppers, telling stories, and singing songs, is also a common negro recreation." This was the most reassuring, quaint and believable image of the slave, and because it seemed on face value to have no political agenda, it was the most convincing. Of course, Carmichael was more forthright in her support of the happy slave image when she spent a whole chapter ("Conversations with native Africans", 1:299–332) getting African-born slaves to say that they were happier in St Vincent than they had been in Africa.

After emancipation, the image of the happy, carefree Negro continued because, as Day (1852, 2:87) argued in reference to Trinidad: "They, however, need not care, as their food is so easily obtained, and their houses involve neither rent nor taxes. Play is all they want, and as little work as possible is done." The only islands Day excepted were St Vincent and St Kitts (2:109, 212). The Protestant ethic that had become a noticeable part of these islands had presumably in Day's opinion created a more serious and acceptable person.

From early, the English developed an image of the islands that featured music and dancing prominently. The expectations of English visitors and the fulfilment of such expectations were quite evident in the following comments made by Thomas St Clair (1834, 377):

> I found Barbadoes a cheerful residence during my stay upon it, and every evening was put in mind of that old song:
> Come, let us dance and sing,
> While Barbadoes bells do ring;
> Quashi scrapes the fiddle-string,
> And Venus plays the lute.

The same verses, which were taken from George Colman's 1787 opera *Inkle and Yarico*, were also quoted by Wentworth (1834, 2:278) and also appeared partially in an illustration (*The Jollification*) by Robert Cruikshank showing slaves partying.

Two ideas linked together gained strength publicly in England from the last quarter of the eighteenth century, when motions were first brought to the British Parliament for the abolition of the slave trade, up to the time of emancipation. These ideas were that the slaves in the West Indies were happy and that they were better off than comparable workers in Britain. They were first presented together by Tobin (1785, 98), when he referred to Brunias's paintings of the slaves in the West Indies: "Let him [the European reader] compare these plump, active, and merry figures, with the emaciated, squalid, and heart-broken inhabitants of the distant English villages."

However, it could have been the more influential account of Stedman which brought these ideas to the notice of anti-abolitionists. Stedman's intention, expressed in the words "But to proceed with my description of a happy slave" (Price and Price 1992, 278), was to counterbalance, in his own account, the picture he painted of atrocities suffered by some slaves with what he saw as a more wholesome life enjoyed by others. Stedman's image of happy slaves was thus part of an overall account that was thought to be helpful to the abolitionist cause. Yet it contained the following comment that came to be distorted and generalized by anti-abolitionists: "Then if we draw the comparison between this class of people [happy negro slaves], and the numberless wretched objects that disgrace the streets of *Europe*, we can assuredly not call these Africans who fall under the above description – *unhappy*" ([1794] 1806, 2:300).

In 1792, a few weeks after Wilberforce first introduced a bill to abolish the slave trade, William Holland published a pair of satirical prints titled *Justice*

Figure 6. *Cruelty and Oppression Abroad.* Richard Newton/William Holland, 1792. Courtesy of the John Carter Brown Library (Luna: 64-101).

and Humanity at Home and *Cruelty and Oppression Abroad*. The latter print not only mocked the idea that the slaves were being brutalized and oppressed but also presented a picture of social harmony in the West Indies in which whites admired and enjoyed the music and dancing of the slaves.

The two ideas appeared together again in Lady Nugent's journal (1801–5), after she returned from her husband's tour of duty in Jamaica: "and never was there a happier set of people than they appear to be. All day they have been singing odd songs, only interrupted by peals of laughter; and indeed I must say, they have reason to be content, for they have many comforts and enjoyments. I only wish the poor Irish were half as well off" (Wright 2002, 53). Nugent's contrast was with the Irish because the English had long seen them as poor relations.

These linked ideas were taken up again by British caricaturists as the emancipation debate heated up. A print that mocked the idea of West Indian slaves being brutalized was Robert Seymour's *Slavery/Freedom* (that is, the English poor/slaves in the West Indies) in *McLean's Monthly Sheet of Caricatures*, number 32, which came out in 1830, presenting the slaves (a merry, well-fed baby in the foreground and slaves dancing in the background) in a direct pictorial contrast with the suffering English poor. Two similar caricatures were McLean's 1833 *The Happy Free Labourers of England. The Wretched Slaves in the West Indies* and Cruikshank's 1833 *Negro Slavery. English Liberty.* The last of these was supported by eyewitness testimony from Frederic Bayley, who had spent four years in the West Indies and who, on his return to England, had aided in the creation of the image of the happy slave. Bayley (1830, 439) said:

> [The slaves] are perpetually assembling in little parties, whenever they can find time and opportunity; and none who have witnessed the joyousness of these parties can deny the happiness of the slaves. . . . The happiness appears the more complete because it is partaken by all. Old men of sixty scruple not to foot it in the merry round, with some dozen or two of their grandchildren; and if their step be not as light, and their action as lively as some of the young ones in the happy group, it is only the effect of time, for the eagerness with which they all flock to their little fêtes, and the glad smile of pleasure and good-nature that sits on every countenance while they continue, sufficiently proves them to be enjoyed.

Then, the following passage from the same Bayley was used by Robert Cruikshank (1833, 22) to support his pictorial representation titled *Negro Slavery. English Liberty*, showing that the West Indian slave was happier and better off than the English worker:

> They seize every opportunity of enjoying themselves, and the fête which is given to the master is generally likewise a source of amusement to the slave.
> "A ball is given, and while the merry guests are dancing with their fair partners in the drawing-room, and enjoying themselves within, a joyous assemblage of our darkest brethren are "tripping on their light fantastic toes," which are, indeed, fantastic to a miracle, in the great hall without, . . . with a grace, gaiety, and *goût*, equal to that displayed by their masters and mistresses.

While all of this pictorial propaganda had developed as an integral part of the need to counter the abolitionists, a more hostile and reactionary tone developed when emancipation was becoming a reality and the factor of reparation surfaced. Ironically, this reactionary hostility was responsible for the consolidation of the image of the happy slave. Emancipation of the slaves was one thing (moral), but reparation of the owners for their loss was another (money). The idea that the British public/taxpayers (presented as John Bull) had to foot the bill for do-good abolitionists and had to compensate slave owners did not go down well at all. Bear in mind that up until then the slaves themselves or some

From Africa to the Caribbean   143

Figure 7. *New West India Dance*, by J. Doyle. H.B. Sketches no. 269, 1833. Courtesy of the New York Public Library.

interested person had to buy their freedom, and this was comparatively rare. The political satirists in England made sure that the English public realized that they now had to pay for the slaves' freedom. To do this, they seized upon the image of singing, dancing and carousing slaves in the West Indies to poison the minds of the public against emancipation as costing them dearly, contributing to regression and squandering their money on the undeserving.

The pictorial caricatures presented the slaves not only as happier than workers in England but also as persons who had no knowledge of or interest in emancipation and whose only dimension was singing, dancing and carousing. A caricature titled *New West India Dance*, done by the political cartoonist, John Doyle, in 1832 (H.B. no. 269), purported to support the English public and to ridicule the slaves and all those supporting them. *New West India Dance* (that is, the freed slaves dancing) featured a scenario in which Mr Stanley (the colonial secretary, noted for his oratory in Parliament) is playing music for the slaves on a bagpipe; Mr Buxton (a prominent abolitionist) is the person who arranged for the dance to take place; and Mr Althorp (Britain's finance minister) is trying to make the English public, represented as John Bull, pay the piper for the dance (Lord Althorp: "As you called for the dance, Sir, I hope you wont have any objection to pay the piper.") However, John Bull indignantly responds

144 A RESPONSE TO ENSLAVEMENT

Figure 8. *Slave Emancipation; or John Bull Gulled out of Twenty Millions.* C.J. Grant (creator), G. Drake (publisher), c.1833–35. Courtesy of the John Carter Brown Library (Luna 11-128).

that it is Mr. Buxton who should pay the piper for the dance (John Bull: "Eh! O . . . . Yes. . . . All to oblige the big Gentleman [Mr. Buxton] in the broad rimmed hat. . . . Go to him").

Another caricature of the same type appeared the following year, titled *Slave Emancipation; or John Bull Gulled out of Twenty Millions*. What is immediately striking in this one is that the slaves and the figure representing the slave owners are presented as extremely fat and their words show them to be callous. John Bull, on the other hand, is presented as thin and the dupe of politicians and the court, who are picking £20,000,000 from his pocket to compensate the slave owners, in spite of his protests.

A sequence of illustrations by Robert Cruikshank with the same intent appeared in 1833. Cruikshank actually presented two sets of illustrations – one giving typical slave scenes and the other, *Negro Emancipation*, which gives different views of the slaves on receiving the news of their emancipation. One of the slave scenes is entitled *The Ball* and in it one of the characters says: "Keep up the ball till morning. John Bull pays the piper", which, quite obviously, perpetuates the sentiment in *New West India Dance* and *John Bull Gulled out of Twenty*

Millions. Almost identical to the latter is the *Negro Emancipation* illustration called *The Jollification*, which has the slaves saying, among other things: "John Bull be one great fool, he gib all hims money away. . . . Now we all dance and sing All Barbados bell dey ring." In the bottom right corner of the illustration is a full sack on which is written: "£20,000000 for black carrion."

In addition to publishing these images of the British public being fleeced to pay slave owners for the loss of their happy slaves, the satirists further complemented their argument with doom and gloom images (*An Emancipated Negro* and *Free Labour. The Sunny Side of the Wall*) showing the dire effects of emancipation on the slaves. They foresaw that the freed slaves after emancipation would not work, did not know how to look after themselves and, because they were ignorant, would starve to death. All these images dealing with the perceived realities of slavery, emancipation and reparation were circulated widely in popular publications and served to reinforce the image of the happy slave, which many preferred to accept as true.

However, in spite of widespread, simplistic images of West Indian slaves as "plump, active and merry figures", there were more perceptive comments made from before Brunias's paintings indicating that whites not only in the Caribbean but also in Europe had a more in-depth understanding of the slaves' behaviour. This was clearly expressed by Prévost d'Exiles (1746, 15:430): "One can also notice that, among these people, singing can be an ambiguous sign – one of gaiety or one of sadness. They sing when they are afflicted, to soften their grief; they sing when they are joyful to express their contentment; but since they have joyful tunes and lugubrious ones, you need long experience to know the difference."

The image of the happy slave came to supersede all other images because abolitionist arguments against the slave trade and then slavery made whites in the Caribbean out to be horrible. They responded angrily, claiming that abolitionists were either naive or liars. Then, in the 1830s, the created spectre of reparation produced visions of a financial burden on the British public that created resentment. The public in turn found it more satisfying to believe that the West Indian slaves were the undeserving, happy people that they were portrayed to be.

Yet the overriding economic, social and cultural argument constructed by anti-abolitionists asserted that slaves in the West Indies were workers who were better fed and clothed than their peers in Africa; in better conditions than comparable workers in Britain; more civilized than when they were in Africa; and more polished (beautiful) physically now and their children would be even more so. Anti-abolitionists were convinced that all of these benefits were evident in the fact that the slaves were always smiling, singing and dancing. For them, there was no question that profits from an economic enterprise were exclusively for those who provided the capital and took the risk. It is the puppeteer who benefits economically from the show, not the puppet.

6. Playing in Life and Death

> I perceived ... that it was on Account of the Death of an Infant one of the Negroes then had in a Coffin, carrying it to Fonte Belle for its Funeral, attended by a Number of others, rejoycing over the Dead with Tokens of exceeding great Joy. The Mother of the Child was there also. ... They jump'd, skip'd, danc'd, and sung as they went, seeming almost to be frantick with Joy.
> —Poole 1753, 295

IN THE NORMAL COURSE OF A YEAR THERE were isolated events in the slaves' lives which characteristically involved festivity. Tobin (1785, 66) noted, for example, that "the day of covering a new house is an established time of rejoicing", whereas nearly fifty years later Carmichael (1833, 1:131) related the building of a house and the celebration of its completion more directly to marriage. Such construction and festivity took place within the confines of the plantation and had to have the master's permission. It seems reasonable to assume that such milestones had always been marked in West African traditions, but that in the Caribbean slave situation it was necessary for the master to contribute materially in order to gain and retain the slaves' confidence and to make them willing to reciprocate. This symbiotic relationship between master and slave was critical in maintaining the power balance of the colonial social structure and in promoting its "sanctity".

There were other odd occasions involving the master or other whites, like birthdays and visits (*Short Journey* 1790, 88; Lewis [1834] 1969, 73–74), on which the slaves were said to celebrate with dancing. One that seems peculiar was that it was "a custom in Barbadoes, when the estate owes nothing, to whitewash the sugar mills by way of proclaiming the situation of the owner; this is followed by the mirth and festivity of the slaves" (*Authentic History* 1810, 46). Other European or "mother country" events, such as coronations and visits of royalty to the colonies, also had celebrations which filtered down to the slave population. Obviously, the slaves welcomed any opportunity to have fun, if only to get some respite from their daily routine. Of course, days of festivity also meant that they might get food and drink other than the normal fare. The encouragement of festivity as the best way to carry out patriarchal duty consolidated the masters' hold over the slaves and was infinitely more powerful than the use of the whip.

The full picture of the slaves' enjoyment of free time on weekends across the English islands was more than ordinary, if the work called *Authentic History of the English West Indies* (1810, 75–76) is to be believed: "Every saturday evening, the slaves . . . close the week with a dance – besides which, they have a grand ball, once a quarter." These words were actually copied from Stedman's account of Suriname in the third quarter of the eighteenth century. As to the "grand ball", Stedman ([1794] 1806, 2:2909) himself went on to mention that it was an event "to which the neighbouring slaves are invited; the master often contributing to their happiness by his presence, or at least by sending them a present of a few jugs of new rum". Whether or not Stedman's comments were applicable to all the English colonies, and whether or not the grand ball was a feature of all the colonies, the masters' material support of any entertainment helped and encouraged the slaves to enjoy themselves.

In the cases of slave paramours, material support was almost a moral responsibility. One can sense this in the following 1751 journal entry by Thomas Thistlewood (Hall 1999, 18), a white penkeeper in Jamaica: "At night gave Marina some sugar, 4 bottles of rum, some beef and pepper-pot, with 18 pints of corn made into fungi, to treat the Negroes, and especially her shipmates withal at her housewarming. They was very merry all night." The housewarming party was one that Thistlewood provided for after he set up a house for his slave woman.

The slaves also had "grandy balls", which contrasted with the dances encouraged by whites and materially supported by them because they were money-making ventures. Beckford (1790) was one of the first to mention them in Jamaica. Later, De La Beche (1825) and Carmichael (1833), the latter in reference to St Vincent and Trinidad, gave information about the format of the invitation and Wentworth (1834) gave details of the procedures and preparations for such dances when he visited Antigua. Social hierarchy among the slaves, which was related to occupational status on the plantation, was reflected not only in the quality of the venue for such "balls" but also in who could attend as well as the choice of food offered (see Moreton 1790, 156; De la Beche 1825, 40). The desire to establish superiority was powerful in the rigidly hierarchical plantation structure where social distinctions within race were as tenaciously held on to as distinctions across races.

Tensions which existed in the distinction between slave and freed person led to the latter not wanting to associate with the former. Moreau de Saint-Méry (1796, 39) observed that "there are balls where freed women dance only with white men, and they do not want to be asked by men of the same colour as them". He also observed that where they were rejected by the whites, freed women danced among themselves: "In certain colonies, freed negro females dance only among themselves, because the others do not admit them into their entertainment activities" (38).

After emancipation, social distinction in dances came to be associated with the venue. Breen (1844, 196n) noted that there was a difference between a "ball" (indoors) and a "bamboula" (outdoors). While Breen claimed that the difference between the two was a function of the weather and that there was a preference for the outdoor activity, Day indicated that the indoor activity was "*à la mode*" (1852, 1:46) and the outdoor one was the "real thing" (1:52). No doubt there was truth in Day's distinction, but at the same time there was a longing on his part to witness something "African", to satisfy a desire for exoticism, typical for many visitors.

Social distinction between African slaves and creole slaves was noted from early. This distinction, which was characterized generally by several writers in terms of distrust, hatred and acrimony between the two groups, in the case of dancing and singing specifically was presented as competitiveness, in the words of Monk Lewis ([1834] 1969, 344): "In the negro festivals . . . the Africans and Creoles dispute it with the greatest pertinacity."

Among the slaves themselves, there was a constant desire on the part of some to appear socially superior by following the example of their masters, for whom a successful ball was testimony of social worth. Paying dances allowed for a critical change from outdoor (public) to indoor (private) entertainment. Thus, they had a strong element of exclusiveness that fitted perfectly into the hierarchical social system which inspired social climbing and rejection of Africanness, even within the slave stratum of society. By having successful paying dances, therefore, some slaves were able to increase their self-worth and psychological well-being.

Hard Work and Merriment Together at Crop-Time

The period of the most intense activity on the plantation was crop-time, for it was during this period that a number of activities went on at the same time – cutting, transporting and grinding of the canes; boiling the juice and putting the syrup in casks to cure; taking the sugar to the port for shipment; and in some cases, distilling inferior syrup to produce rum. It was during crop-time that the slaves were under the greatest physical stress, but several writers, principally as part of anti-abolitionist rhetoric, remarked that it was during this period that slaves were happiest at work. For them, therefore, it was easy to formulate a simplistic argument that as the volume of the work increased, entertainment increased, and then to conclude that the harvesting of the sugar crop increased the slaves' happiness.

Williams (1826, 6) in Jamaica commented favourably on the atmosphere of the mill-yard ("the mill-yard was all bustle and merriment, songs and laughter") and so did Bridgens (1837) in Trinidad shortly after emancipation ("the vicinity of a mill in crop time, is generally a very gay scene"). Carmichael (1833, 1:103), in response to the charges that the slaves were overworked and brutalized during the crop season, argued strongly that "the negroes enjoy crop time, and look forward to it with pleasure: much merriment then goes on amongst them". She repeated her view several times over her two-volume work, as in the following: "It is the season of mirth and jollity; they look forward to crop-time, (the West India harvest), and speak of its getting nearer and nearer with joy, not with dread" (2:261).

Carmichael (2:29) then essentially went on to expand her point by depicting the boiling-house in the plantation complex as the entertainment centre for the slaves during crop-time: "The boiling-house is a scene of great merriment. . . . When the people are dismissed from the field or elsewhere, in the evening, the boiling-house is soon full enough: there you see negroes of all ages, drinking hot and cold liquor, singing songs, telling the jokes of the day, and sitting down enjoying themselves." Carmichael's comments on the centrality of the boiling-house in the recreation of the slaves during crop-time applied to both St Vincent and Trinidad. There is no indication in her remarks, however, that both males and females frequented the boiling-house and it may very well be that it was a meeting place for males, seeing that it was almost exclusively men who worked in the boiling-house. Another writer to comment on the happy atmosphere in the boiling-house was Bayley (1830, 86), speaking of Barbados in 1826. He claimed that the Colville estate, about which he made his remarks, "may be taken as a model of the other properties in Barbados".

That the mill-yard and boiling-house witnessed a great deal of singing during crop-time is not borne out in pictorial illustrations by William Clark and Richard Bridgens. Interestingly, the notes of the British Library curator say (regarding Bridgens's *Interior of a Boiling House*): "The boiling house was a dangerous place to work because of the intense temperatures and the hot liquids." However, even if there was chatter and singing in the boiling house, anti-abolitionist writers' conviction that it meant happiness no doubt encouraged them to mention it repeatedly. The reality was that as the stress of the work increased, entertainment increased proportionately either because of some slaves' normal inclination to sing at work or in order to salve the additional stress created.

The idea of increased merriment during crop-time must be counterbalanced by mortality statistics, which, using the classic case of St Domingue, showed that as the amount of sugar produced increased, the number of slaves dying also increased. The repeated comment that the peak period of sugar production led to an increase in merriment blithely ignores the cumulative effect on the slaves' health and well-being and naively assesses the increase only on its face value.

The Feast of Tabernacles, the Yam Custom and Crop-Over

An occasion which was fairly widely celebrated across the plantations in the English colonies was the end of the cane harvest and sugar production. It came to be known as "crop-over". One can well imagine the significance of this for the masters, whose economic futures depended on the success of their sugar production and who would have wanted to celebrate a good harvest. The slaves were not necessarily celebrating anything; they were benefiting from the "patriarchal duty" of their masters who, presumably, thought that they should give the workers a day of fun for a job (well) done.

Tobin (1785, 63), in his response to what he regarded as Ramsay's misleading information about free days for the slaves, said that in many estates in St Kitts there was "a kind of harvest-home holiday, at the finishing of the crop" and that it was accepted as one of the slaves' free days by right. Tobin's words indicate that celebration of crop-over was not universal in St Kitts and one would have to assume that it was at the discretion of the master.

The same idea of entitlement to the day is given for Jamaica by Stewart (1808, 262), who said: "This [Christmas] and harvest-home may be considered as their two annual festivals." With reference to Jamaica also, Barclay's (1826, 110) words not only indicate that it was universal but also by that time it had acquired a local name and thus, presumably, was being conceived of as a local event: "The day on which the last of the canes are cut down upon a sugar plantation, flags are displayed in the field, and all is merriment. A quart of sugar and a quart of rum are allowed to each negro on the occasion, to hold what is called CROP-OVER, or harvest-home." Barclay's words also suggest that it was a slaves' celebration. According to Stewart (1808, 263), "There is not so great a latitude for indulgence at harvest-home as at Christmas, as here the negroes are allowed only one day."

While Barclay related the start of crop-over to the end of the cutting of the canes, Marly related it to the end of the boiling of the sugar, but in both cases there was an immediate, joyful celebration, for the former in the fields and for the latter around the boiling house. Bayley said that crop-over was the slaves' "grand day of jubilee". Presumably he thought of it as a workers' day, akin to modern Labour Day, since he saw it as the end of and release from back-breaking work harvesting the sugar cane. However, judging from the remarks of the previous writers mentioned (Williams 1826; Carmichael 1833; 1:22; Bridgens 1837), who saw crop-time as the merriest time of the year for the slaves, there could have been no great joy for them in seeing it come to an end. So, in the minds of these writers, crop-over celebrations would have been similar to carnival in that both were short periods of festivity before fasting or hard times. For the slaves, however, the end of harvesting did not mean that they would be out of work, and seeing that work during the rest of the year was not as strenuous as harvesting (even with its little perks), the slaves were glad to see it come to an end.

Though celebration of a successful harvest is not restricted to any culture, in the case of the West Indian colonies it seems logical to treat it as a cultural transfer from Europe, since neither the indigenous people nor the enslaved Africans had any large scale crops to reap and celebrate. In Britain, harvest-home has always been church oriented and its nature can be gleaned from the following, taken from the *Suffolk and Essex Free Press* (19 September 1867): "this Feast of Tabernacles was celebrated with greater mirth than all the rest. It would seem that the festival partook of a patriarchal character 'Thou shalt rejoice, thou, and thy Son, and thy Daughter, and thy manservant, and thy maidservant'" (www.foxearth.org.uk). The "patriarchal character" which required the master to "make a feast for his servants" is the same that was in evidence in the Caribbean.

Crop-over celebration in Jamaica was also characterized by Saturnalian mixing and equality, as Barclay (1826, 10) says in the following: "Here all authority and all distinction of colour ceases; black and white, overseer and book-keeper, mingle together in the dance." Both Barclay and Marly described the way in which whites conducted crop-over celebrations in the West Indies, but Marly (1828, 46–48) was much more detailed in his account. Seeing that the English colonists in the West Indies were not known to be overly charitable, religious or accommodating, inversion in harvest-home or crop-over in the West Indies exemplifies maintenance of European traditions in the colonies. The kind of mixing, which was given as central to the Jewish feast of tabernacles of biblical times and also later as characteristic of Christianity (in British harvest-home festivities), would therefore seem to be a European tradition transferred to the Caribbean.

However, Edward Bowdich's (1819, 275) description and illustration of the "Yam Custom" of the Ashanti of the Gold Coast to mark the yam harvest reveals a critical similarity, for he specifically says: "The Yam Custom is like the Saturnalia . . . the grossest liberty prevails, and each sex abandons itself to its passions." Although the Ashanti Yam Custom, as illustrated by Bowdich, was a much bigger and grander outdoor activity than anything described in the Caribbean and was dominated by a king, it certainly could have been an influence on crop-over celebrations in the Caribbean, especially since many Africans were transported from that region to the Caribbean. In the final analysis, the existence of mixing and inversion in so many traditions (Roman, Jewish, British/European and West African) suggests a deep-seated human reaction at the time of harvest more so than a distinct continuity from ancestral traditions.

As to the geographical spread of crop-over across the islands and the nature of the event, some information on this comes from Bayley (1830, 436–37), who compared Barclay's Jamaican version with practice in other islands in the eastern Caribbean: "This statement of Mr. Barclay's is natural, interesting, and true; and though I believe it is more particularly relative to Jamaica, it will also apply to nearly all the other islands, differing only on one or two points of inconsiderable consequence." The evening activity in the specific islands Bayley referred to was outdoor and certainly did not have the kind of formality and sophistication to match even that described by Barclay. The difference

154 A RESPONSE TO ENSLAVEMENT

Figure 9. First day of Yam Custom. T.E. Bowdich, *Mission from Cape Coat Castle to Ashantee* (London: John Murray, 1819), between pages 274 and 275. Digitized by archive.org.

between indoors and outdoors as well as the difference in instruments, the drum especially, meant that the activity described by Bayley was essentially more of a slave activity.

Carmichael's description of the activity in St Vincent, around the same time as Bayley, specifies both outdoor and indoor features (1833, 1:175–6, 2:262, 1:293). The fiddler was the central figure in the procession and celebration and there was no sense of any equality between white and black and not much sense of wholesomeness as an event other than for the slaves to impress their masters and to receive a subvention.

As to the nature of the celebration, there is no specific feature or set of features that could be said to have identified crop-over. It is only in Carmichael's account that there is a suggestion of a special kind of dressing up. Yet it is ironic that whereas one female house servant went to great lengths and expense to humanize and dignify herself by having "her own Christian name and her master's surname marked in large letters in front of her dress", Carmichael (1833, 1:293) regarded what she did as ludicrous. Carmichael was more impressed by the "mule boys" and the fiddler dressed up with ribbons. Clearly for the slave, the public display of name must have had a double significance – a display of self as a normal human being and a sense of belonging to a plantation community.

A description of crop-over later in the century by Greville Chester (1869, 81–82) gave more festive features to the event, as if it had become a little more elaborate in Barbados:

> A kind of harvest-home generally takes place at the end of the crop-gathering upon each estate. A cart laden with last canes is drawn by mules decorated with ribbons, and attended by a crowd of labourers; the principal women being attired in white muslin. The mill and other estate buildings are gay with coloured kerchiefs which do duty as flags. Some ancient negro is put forward to make a speech to the planter, which he often does with considerable humour and address. Then the planter replies, and a glass of "falernum" . . . is handed round to each. Then dancing begins, and is carried on to a late hour to the sound of fiddles and tambourines. Sometimes the proceedings are varied by the introduction of a "trash man," a figure, i.e. stuffed with cane trash and tied upon the back of a mule, which, being finally let loose, gallops about with his incongruous burden, to the great delight of the spectators.

Several of these features have British parallels – see Strutt ([1801] 1903, 288). No doubt the unbroken connection between England and Barbados accounted for the transmission of such English features to Barbados and the maintenance of the event there.

Crop-over was an agrarian celebration in the Jewish and Christian traditions with a patriarchal element which slave masters helped to perpetuate. The slaves took to it not only because some had ancestral memory of such a celebration, but also because it had features of inversion which allowed them a sense of dignity. In northern North America, where slavery was not practised, celebration of harvests, which was initially called "harvest-home" as in Britain, is seen as one of the origins of modern Thanksgiving. However, crop-over in the Caribbean differed from Thanksgiving in North America because of its strong patriarchal element.

Celebrating Milestones in the Cycle of Life

The system of slavery had a decided effect on which milestones in life were celebrated and which were not. Whereas for some countries in Africa, the historical literature featured ceremonies associated with circumcision and with the change from puberty to adulthood, there is no clear evidence of a continuation of these rituals among the slaves in the West Indies. The enslavement process together with the family fracturing experience militated against the preservation of these rites of passage.

Marriage, too, was negatively affected by the institution of slavery. There is very little that is said generally about wedding activities, in spite of the fact that Labat (1742, 3:494) gave a contrary impression: "The most important celebration among them is that of marriage. Although the master contributes a lot, it is never enough. All the negroes on the plantation and all those who are invited bring something for the celebration as well as a gift for the newlyweds." In 1750 the Reverend Griffith Hughes in Barbados also listed marriages as one the activities that the slaves were "tenaciously addicted to" celebrating in their traditional way. The reality was that within slavery, where men were generally without economic means, marriage was an impractical and precarious undertaking.

As to the birth of children, there is no extensive evidence showing the attitudes and behaviour of slave mothers and fathers and there is very little recorded observation in the historical accounts of celebration of births. There are claims that slave mothers deliberately killed their newborns in order to spare them the experience of slavery, but this could not have been widespread. On the other hand, an early comment by Du Tertre creates a positive picture about the slaves' attitude to births. Du Tertre (1667, 528) observed that among the slaves there was major celebration at births, but he, being a missionary priest, related the slaves' practice in the early colonies to "baptisms", as if they were already Christians: "Their great rejoicings are at the baptism of their children, because for that they invite all the Negroes from their country as well as all those in their huts, and they would sell everything that they have rather than not have alcohol to solemnize their birth." During this early period of the French and English colonies in the small islands, the slaves were predominantly African and their tendency to celebrate according to ethnicity was more natural than any Christian element which Du Tertre was assuming to be present.

At the end of the seventeenth century, Labat (1742, 3:493) put the emphasis more definitely on tradition among the slaves when he spoke of them celebrating the name days, presumably, of their relatives and friends: "The majority of the Negroes, even though they are poorly accommodated, do not fail to have a small celebration for their parents and their friends on their name day: children feel constrained to do this after their father's death." Celebration of traditions in different ethnic groups is noted some decades later (1750) in Jamaica by Thistlewood, who mentions "Negro Diversions – odd Music, Motions, &c. The Negroes of each Nation by themselves" (Hall 1999, 12). Yet it is difficult to see, in that early situation of slavery, who would have been responsible for the celebration of a birth to a female slave and how the birth was seen to fit into any notion of family. Du Tertre actually said little about what such celebrations involved except to slip in the denigrating comment that alcohol was absolutely necessary.

One can interpret Bridgens's illustration *Negro Dance* as one in which a mother proudly holds up and displays her child at the door of her house, while outside joyful dancing and music take place. The child is clearly not newborn, so one would have to assume that the celebration relates to some later stage in the child's life. Inexplicably, however, neither the title of the illustration nor the comments on it mention anything about celebration of birth or "baptism", but focus exclusively on the dancing. Bridgens's illustration depicts a scene in Trinidad about one hundred and fifty years after the kind of 'rejoicing' that Du Tertre referred to in the early small island colonies. There are apparent similarities between the two. Nevertheless, the amount of conjecture required to interpret these two observations accurately leaves the matter of birth celebration among the slaves virtually in the dark.

Funerals or How the Slaves Celebrated the Release from Life

Death was a frequent and ever-present reality for the slaves: the general mortality rate was high and that for infants and children even higher. As a result of this reality, comments on funerals were common. In comparison with births, for instance, an abundance of information is given, even though most of it admits to an ignorance of the slaves' beliefs. Dancing and singing took place in a variety of contexts, but the one that was most astounding initially for European writers was funerals. For them, the slaves' behaviour at funerals was inconsistent with their own grieving response to death. As a result, the attitude of whites to funeral "festivity", which strongly reflected the traditional culture of the slaves, was to see it as backwardness. Yet the inversion it presented reinforced the conviction that blacks and whites were different beings.

In his account of early colonial Barbados, Ligon ([1657] 1970, 51) did not give the impression that slave burials were anything but simple, mournful events: "When any of them dye, they dig a grave, and at evening they bury him, clapping and wringing their hands, and making a doleful sound with their voices." This was a time when the slaves could hardly communicate with each other and had not yet formed themselves into a coherent society, so it seems logical that there was no more memorable kind of expressiveness said to be characteristic of burials then. In fact, there seemed to be little else but the burial itself. In time, however, as slave society developed, funerals became more elaborate. One of the factors that determined the character of funerals in the Caribbean was the time they took place – seeing that among slaves preservation of dead bodies was not feasible, the burial of the body had to be done soon after death, often late the same evening after work. The darkness of night added what some Europeans regarded as a surreal element to slave funerals.

A hundred years after Ligon's comment, Hughes (1750, 15n19) provided more details about funeral practices in Barbados: "Most young People sing and dance, and make a loud Noise with rattles, as they attend the Corpse to its Interrment: Some Days after, especially on their Feasts, they strew at Night some of the dressed Victuals upon the Graves of their deceased Persons, Relations, or Friends." By the end of the eighteenth century, slave funerals had become more elaborate, with wakes, punctuated processions, designated mourners, food offerings and exhortations and queries directed to the dead, most of which were accompanied by singing and dancing. The rites attached to funerals were the only ones that the slaves were allowed control over, at least for a time, during the period of slavery. It is not surprising, then, that Barclay (1826, 134) remarked that the night funeral was a "truly pernicious custom, which their native superstition regarded as a solemn rite on no account to be dispensed with". At the same time, the expressions and actions of the slaves after the death up to the time of burial caused several eighteenth-century writers to describe slave funerals as merry and festive occasions.

The descriptions had much in common with those of funerals in parts of West Africa, as, for example, the *wha'* or cry described by Matthews ([1788] 1966, 100–101) in his account of Sierra Leone: "The death of a child, friend, or relation, adds no less to the enjoyment of this pastime, by performing the wha', or cry: but, from the manner in which it is performed, a stranger to their ceremonies would rather term it a rejoicing." The word "rejoicing", which Matthews used to describe the Sierra Leone funeral, was also used to describe funerals in the West Indies.

Robert Poole, in the middle of the eighteenth century, described what he saw of two funerals in Barbados, one being that of a child in town. In both cases, Poole mentioned what happened around the grave:

> During my being at this Gentleman's came by a Negro Burial, attended by a great Number of that Complexion, making a very odd Noise and Rattling: Some beating of Sticks one against the other; others making a Gingling, like the ratling of Flints or small Stones together in a Bag, skiping and singing as they went: Which, I am informed, is the common Funeral Pomp used by these poor Slaves; who, when they come to the Grave, are said to dance round it, and then cover up the Corps. (1753, 238)

> Being come to the place, the Coffin was measured, and the Length of the Grave dug accordingly . . . during which there was continual Dancing and Singing among the Negroes, whose Number at the Grave considerably increased, many running to them from other parts, and join'd in their Mirth. (295–96)

John Singleton (1767, 114–18), a few years later, made a slave funeral in Barbados one of the outstanding events in his narrative in verse, describing it in detail and putting the slaves in a positive light. Singleton's elevation of the slaves was done by favourably comparing them with supposedly more civilized and learned Europeans ("the boasted reason of the polish'd world").

A key factor in West Indian funerals was the belief in the return to the homeland (West Africa) after death. In his narrative verse, Singleton (1767, 114) states it poetically in the words "the freed soul, Soon as it leaves its mortal coil behind, Transported to some distant world, is wrapt In bliss eternal." Death, therefore, was seen as a time for rejoicing. In the case of the funeral of a child, which Poole describes, there were varying beliefs among West Africans, but again the "death" of innocence (that is, infants especially) followed by its return to the spirit world was celebrated by several ethnic groups. In the West Indies where the infant mortality rate was high, funeral rites and practices for children thus inspired contradictory emotions.

Edward Long (1774, 2:420–21), in his comments on funerals in Jamaica, seemed to have been aware of the beliefs of the slaves, but he also saw the celebration as having a more profound function:

> Their funerals are the very reverse of our English ceremony.... Every funeral is a kind of festival; at which the greater part of the company assume an air of joy and unconcern; and together with their singing, dancing, and musical instruments, conspire to drown all sense of affliction in the minds of the real mourners. The burthen of this merry dirge is filled with encomiums on the deceased, with hopes and wishes for his happiness in his new state.

"Rejoicing" was therefore not just a continuity from African culture but a response provoked by the constant presence of death. However, in contrast to Long and others, Bryan Edwards (1793–94, 2:85–86) expressly contradicted the notion of the slaves treating funerals as a time of rejoicing, a claim which he regarded as "the dream of poetry; the sympathetic effusion of a fanciful or too credulous an imagination". He went on to say: "We may conclude, therefore, that their funeral songs and ceremonies are commonly nothing more than the dissonance of savage barbarity and riot; as remote from the fond superstition to which they are ascribed, as from the sober dictates of a rational sorrow." Edwards's rejection of the common interpretation was clearly based on his own conviction that the slaves were superstitious savages, incapable of rising to high levels of thought and behaviour.

Despite Edwards's rejection of the belief in return to the homeland, the claim, with the attendant notion of rejoicing, was still being made about fifty years later by Phillippo (1843, 246–47), for whom the slaves were "regarding death as a welcome relief from the calamities of life, and a passport to the never-to-be-forgotten scenes of their nativity". It is true that Phillippo was a religious person and might have been more inclined towards such an interpretation, in contrast to Edwards, who was more secular. Phillippo, however, had twenty years' experience to back up his statement and was probably basing his conclusion on the words and attitudes of the slaves during the final part of the event.

Barclay, whose observations and comments relate to the first three decades of the nineteenth century, described the first two stages of the night funeral of slaves in Jamaica and gives an overall impression of the effect of the music, singing and dancing. He first mentions what could be considered a bongo wake: "The whole night, or the greater part of it, was spent in drumming on the gumbay, singing, dancing, and drinking." This was followed by the punctuated procession through the plantation village which was also dominated by music (1826, 135). The overall "impression of horror", created in no small measure by the music, singing and dancing, if it is purged of all of its negativity, shows what a gripping experience the funeral, as described by Barclay (134–36), was. The idea of rejoicing at the passage of a fellow slave has therefore to be understood as a deep and heartfelt experience, not as a frivolous one, as the idea of jumping and singing, without a context, tends to create. As is clear from Barclay's experience, the continuous beating of the drum in itself had a powerful effect, one which disturbed Europeans intensely.

Edwards (1793–94, 2:85) noted the special homage, in their dancing, paid to "respected" and "venerable" persons when they died: "At other times, more especially at the burial of such among them as were respected in life, or venerable through age, they exhibit a sort of Pyrrhic or warlike dance." It is difficult to know, however, whether Edwards's observation was an example of a European projecting a Greek concept ("Pyrrhic dance") onto the culture of the slaves or whether, as he said, the kind of dancing at the funerals of important people was qualitatively and not just quantitatively different.

When considered as a continuity from West Africa, it will be seen that while in parts of West Africa the ceremony could have gone on continuously for forty-eight hours or more with the burial finally taking place in daylight hours, in the context of the plantation where daylight hours belonged to the master, the only time that the slaves had to bury their dead was when they came home from work late in the evening, if the person died during the week. The surreal dimension that the night added to slave funerals was therefore more Caribbean than African.

Barclay (1826, 162–63) noted, however, that legislation in Jamaica in 1816 made the night funeral illegal and changed the character of slave funerals, as a result of which, according to him, "the funerals of slaves in Jamaica for years past have in no respect differed from those of white people". Barclay was responding to "negative" claims about the slaves in Jamaica and wanted to show his readers how, in relation to funerals, Christianity had displaced "African superstition". Whether his last comment above was entirely true or not, it is clear from his remarks that the traditional slave funeral was strikingly different from that of the whites in the colonies and this difference was substantially due to the performances of the slaves. Phillippo (1843, 244), in an illustration, tried to give some idea of these performances, but what he succeeded most in doing was, like Barclay, to show, especially through his caption "Heathen practices at funerals", his disapproval of slave burials.

Besides the funeral as a whole and the burial specifically, Long (1774, 2:421–22) commented on a post-burial ceremony for a married woman which also involved singing and dancing. Although post-burial ceremonies came to be well known in the post-emancipation period, the remarks by Long about a married woman are practically unique for the slave period. What is significant here is that the rejoicing is said to have its final stage a month after the burial. In a context where friendship among slaves was to a great extent circumscribed by the plantation, and bearing in mind the high mortality rate, rituals of death must have been continuous and ever-present within and across neighbouring plantations. It must have been a particularly stalwart people for one to be able to say, "every funeral is a kind of festival" (2:420). On the other hand, it could have meant that they saw no real value in life and rather than the rites of life – births, attainment of adulthood, marriage – they chose to celebrate the rites of death, the ones that were most certain and real for them.

The slaves' attitude to death caused more than one European writer to philosophize about the whole matter of death itself and none more than William Beckford. First of all, he noted the importance of burials to the slaves:

> Their principal festivals are at their burials, upon which occasions they call forth all their magnificence, and display all their taste; and the expence with which the funerals of the better sort of negroes upon a plantation are attended, very often exceed the bounds of credibility; and of this position many instances might be given. Their bodies lie in state; an assemblage of slaves from the neighbourhood appears: the body is ornamented with linen and other apparel, which has been previously purchased, as is often the custom, for this solemn occasion; and all the trinkets of the defunct are exposed in the coffin, and buried in the grave with the remains. The bier is lined with cambric and with lace; and when closed, it is covered with a quantity of expensive cloth, upon which are sometimes deposited wines and other liquors for the recreation of the guests, while a hog, poultry, and other viands, are offered up as an expiatory sacrifice. (1790 2:388–89)

Then, Beckford ends with reflective comments about the difference between "negroes" and Europeans: "Happy, and in some instances enviable, is this state of insensibility! . . . As an evil, few negroes consider death in this light [regretful about death and content with life]. I never knew one who did, or who either dreaded it by anticipation, or who was apprehensive when it was hovering near" (2:390).

Beckford never seemed to consider this "festival" of death and "this [happy] state of insensibility" (that is, absence of regret or sorrow) as psychologically abnormal and to have been accentuated by relentless harshness; in fact, he seemed to regard this festivity/happiness as a characteristic feature of Africans. So, whites not only were in large measure responsible for the frequency of funerals and thus for the frequency of the festivals of singing and dancing among the slaves but also for the misleading image of happiness that they created.

"Plays", the Dance of Death, Communing with the Dead, Myal

The inescapability and finality of death have provoked varied responses in human beings from time immemorial because of the felt need to explain life and death and to link the two. Activities surrounding death and burial therefore have many features in common across all human cultures and it is basically the case that while life is associated with "reality", death is associated with "play" (that is, imagination and pretence). The association of death with play is recorded as a prominent feature in slave culture in the Caribbean.

In describing slave activities in the English islands, writers frequently used the word "play", though from the beginning it was not exclusive in its meaning. For instance, Sloane (1707, lvi), at the end of the seventeenth century in Jamaica, said that the slaves "have several Ceremonies, as Dancing, Playing, & . . .", but there is no way of knowing exactly what specific activities constituted "playing". Reverend Hughes (1750, 15) also juxtaposed the words "dance" and "play" in the same way that Sloane had done some fifty years before him: "The Negroes in general are very tenaciously addicted to their Rites, Ceremonies, and Superstitions of their own Countries, particularly in their Plays, Dances, Music, Marriages, and Burials."

By and by, it was the activities surrounding slave funerals that were specifically identified as "plays" by some writers. A significant factor in the emergence of this use of "play" is that English writers did not record any preceding or competing term from any African language spoken by the slaves as an equivalent. Neither was there any straightforward equivalent word to "play" used by French or Spanish writers, even though there were comparable activities in those colonies. The absence of a predecessor of "play" in the English, French and Spanish colonies suggests that there was no single, pre-existing African cultural activity among the slaves which gave rise to "play". There were various African ethnic groups specified or actually involved in some of the plays identified – for example, Coromantin, Ibo, Loango and Congo. These groups were at different geographical points along the West African coast and it is unlikely that they all had a specific common event.

In the Spanish colonies, or Santo Domingo specifically, the word *banco* is used for dances at wakes. Alvarez Nazario ([1961] 1974, 287) mentions it and Tejeda (2002, 45) cites it from the *Codigo Negro* (Malagón Barceló [1784], 164). The form *banco* seems to have been a formal/written Europeanization of the word *bongo*. This latter form survived in another formerly Spanish colony, Trinidad, until the twentieth century. Gayadeen (1983, 24–25, 32–33) reproduces interpretations by Alfredo Codallo of the "bongo wake".

The earliest documented statement recording "play" as a word the slaves used to refer to graveside activities appeared in a letter written to the bishop of London in 1729 by Arthur Holt (1946, 453–54), an Anglican clergyman in Barbados:

> It is a thing wished by all good Christians, that sufficient care was taken to restrain the Negroes of this island, and especially those on the Society's plantations, from what they call their plays (frequently performed on the Lords Days) in which their various instruments of horrid music, howling, and dancing about the graves of the dead, they offer victuals and strong liquor to the souls of the deceased to keep them (as they pretend) from appearing to hurt them, in which sacrifices to the enemies of souls, the Oby Negroes, or conjurors are the leaders.

Although this use of the word "play" did not become dominant in Barbados subsequently, the element of play still remained strong there, as is evident in Pinckard's (1806, 1:271) description of a funeral at the end of the century: "It seemed a period of mirth and joy. . . . the followers jumped and sported, as they passed along, and talked and laughed, with each other, in high festivity. The procession was closed by five robust negro fishermen, who followed behind playing antic gambols, and dancing all the way to the grave."

The idea that play with music and dance was a part of death was also evident

Figure 10. The English dance of death. Frontispiece in *The English Dance of Death from the Designs of Thomas Rowlandson, with Metrical Illustrations. By the author of "Doctor Syntax"*, vol. 1. (London: R. Ackerman, 1815). Digitized by archive.org.

in European cultures in the *danse macabre*, sometimes called "the dance of death". The Catholic Encyclopedia says: "The 'Dance of Death' was originally a species of spectacular play . . . traced back to the middle of the fourteenth century" (Herbermann 1907, 1620). One of the many illustrated versions of the dance of death appears on the title page of the book *The English Dance of Death* ([Combe] 1815), which shows it to be a popular topic. In other words, the dramatization of a dead person being taken away to the grave accompanied by music and dancing was equally significant in both African and European popular culture.

The practice of giving food and drink to and communing with the dead is also recognized as a feature of many cultures, including pagan Europe from which it survived into Christianity (All Souls' Day/Halloween). It is also a feature of indigenous America which survived in Latin America as the Day of the Dead. What needs to be determined is the ways in which, in the Caribbean, practices among Europeans, indigenous people and enslaved Africans overlapped or influenced each other.

The part that attracted the most attention during slave funerals was the burial, especially the singing and the offerings and exhortations to the dead person. Reverend William Smith (1745, 231), talking about Nevis, remarked that when the body was committed to the ground, those standing at the graveside would ask questions of the dead while they sang: "They sing too at burials, but get drunk, and have no sign of devotion,' calling out to the dead person, and asking him, Why he died, when he wanted nothing the world could afford, to support nature?" Atwood (1791, 261–63), in Dominica, noted a greater variety of responses from those around the grave – offerings, questions, requests, libations, goodbyes, blessings, singing and dancing.

The questions and comments directed at the dead by those around the grave, in Atwood's account, bear a striking similarity to those mentioned by Sieur de la Borde (1674, 37), speaking about the Caribs more than a century earlier. Such similarities seem to support a conclusion that there was transfer between the indigenous inhabitants and the slaves, especially in the island of Dominica, where both groups were present over a long period of time.

Asking the dead questions aloud has an element of acting in it that conjures up the idea of a "play", but the combination of "offerings, questions, requests, libations, goodbyes, blessings, singing and dancing" (identified by Atwood) certainly would have constituted a full-scale performance. In addition, the role reversals in which the dead (on the way to be buried) are said to be speaking through the living (see Oldendorp 1987, 264); Stewart 1808, 251–52) leave no doubt about the amount of imagination and ingenuity in slave activities surrounding death and burial. It was not just the living talking to the dead, but the dead being able to respond to the living. What is important to bear in mind here is that communing with the dead was an integral part of the slaves' traditional belief system in which the living honoured the dead and ancestors affected the lives of the living. For the slaves, it was no less meaningful than Christians making requests to Jesus and Mary.

Despite the fact that European religions retained pagan features of death and burial, European writers, in their ignorance, reacted to the slaves' practices as if they were from a different, backward world. This was even more so when these practices were considered harmful and hostile. For instance, Stedman's ([1794] 1806, 2:272) description of the "winty-play" among Suriname Maroons made it seem innocuous enough, but the potential for danger (to white society) becomes clearer in a later view of *winti* coming out of the experiences of Morton Kahn, who visited maroon communities in Suriname in the 1920s. He defined *winti* as "a ghost that can come into your body and make you do things you otherwise would not do" (1931, 2:139).

The winty-play among the Suriname Maroons had elements of spirit possession and immunity to death comparable to the myal dance among Jamaicans. Thistlewood mentioned the myal dance in a journal entry for March 1769: "the Myal dance had been held twice in Phibbah's Coobah's house, at Paradise Estate, as also Egypt Dago, and Job, who are both Myal-men attend these dancings" (Hall 1999, 217). Long (1774, 2:416–17) disparagingly linked it to obeah and, for him, it was "Coromantins" who were associated with myalism (2:473). He who observed that "their dances [are] entirely martial" and went on: "Their dances serve to keep alive that military spirit, for which they are so distinguished; and the figure consists in throwing themselves into all the positions and attitudes, customary to them in the heat of an engagement" (2:474).

Without using the word "myal", James Ramsay (1788, 72) mentioned the matter of its influence as one of the objections to the abolition of the slave trade that had been raised: "Many slaves die in consequence of their following the superstitious rites of the Obiah or John Crow men." Ramsay's response to this objection was to deny that "Obiah" dances had any widespread effect on the mortality rate of the general body of slaves in Jamaica: "This superstition is confined to a few, and may be easily suppressed. Perhaps among 2000 or 3000 slaves, one may be heard of who has injured his health, by strolling six or eight miles in the night time to attend one of their dances" (73). Even though Ramsay tried to downplay its influence on the physical health and mortality of the slaves, this really did not speak to the influence it had on their minds.

In spite of the fact that it was reported on by Europeans, the myal dance was mostly clandestine and it was probably because of this that it survived in slave society in Jamaica for a long time. About fifty years after Long, Lewis ([1834] 1969, 354–55) again described the dance and its context:

> The Obeah ceremonies always commence with what is called, by the negroes, "the Myal dance." . . . He [the chief Obeah-man] sprinkles various powders over the devoted victim, blows upon him, and dances round him, obliges him to drink a liquor prepared for the occasion, and finally the sorcerer and his assistants seize him and whirl him rapidly round and round till the man loses his senses, and falls on the ground to all appearance and the belief of the spectators a perfect corpse. The chief Myal-man then utters loud shrieks, rushes out of the house with wild and frantic gestures and conceals himself in some neighbouring wood. At the end of two or three hours he returns with a large bundle of herbs, from some of

which he squeezes the juice into the mouth of the dead person; with others he anoints his eyes and stains the tips of his fingers, accompanying the ceremony with a great variety of grotesque actions, and chanting all the while something between a song and a howl, while the assistants hand in hand dance slowly round them in a circle, stamping the ground loudly with their feet to keep time with his chant. A considerable time elapses before the desired effect is produced, but at length the corpse gradually recovers animation, rises from the ground perfectly recovered, and the Myal dance concludes.

While the vast majority of contexts, including funerals, related plays to festivity, the myal dance was different and it was exactly the perceived hostile element of it that Reverend Holt had foremost in mind when he used the word "play" in 1729. For Holt (1946, 454), mourners at the graveside were really offering "sacrifices" to protect themselves from the dead and this he extended to them using charms and poisons against the living, under the influence and control of "Oby Negroes". From its earliest use as a "slave" word, "play" featured ritual practice, not amusement or comedy, and it was a word used by European writers to belittle the practice and practitioners as childlike, unsophisticated and superstitious.

THE RISE AND DOMINANCE OF "PLAY", ESPECIALLY IN JAMAICA

In 1737, a slave master in Antigua regarded a slave coronation as "an Innocent Play of Courts Country" (cited in Gaspar 1985, 249). For him, *play* meant a dramatic performance similar to those in European "mock king" traditions (for example, Lord of Misrule, Feast of Fools). Other whites, however, believed that the coronation was the serious choosing of a leader to take over through rebellion. The fact that there was division of opinion then and in other cases about the true intention of the slaves means that distinguishing play from reality required more than ordinary knowledge. A corollary of this is that the variant terms writers used to describe the slaves' activities definitely revealed the limits of their knowledge.

One of the earliest terms used by an English writer (around 1650) to refer to the activities of the slaves during their free time was "sports": "I have observed that after their day labour is ended, they will not goe to their Sports, which usually they have every night, till they have in their Cottages mumbled over some prayers" (Hutson 2001, 65). This comment, made about the early slaves in Barbados, portrayed nightly communal, cultural activity as an integral part of the slaves' day. In the writer's contrast of "labour, prayers" and "sports", apparently the last word was intended to cover several kinds of recreational activities which took place in the open air in various places.

Sloane (1707, lvi), writing about Jamaica at the end of the seventeenth century, said that the slaves "have several Ceremonies". "Ceremony", which did not then have the air of solemnity it has today, was still being used in the same way more than a hundred years after Sloane: "A new ceremony was to be exhibited" (Williams 1826, 25). Sloane's use of the word, within fifty years of English colonization of Jamaica, suggests that there was already some sense of community evident in various slave events. Yet the variation in word choice ("sports", "ceremonies") by two writers in the seventeenth century, one in Barbados (see Hutson 2001) and the other in Jamaica (Sloane), attested to the absence of any generally accepted characterization of the slaves' activities, either as a whole or individually.

Writers came to favour the word "play" over "sports", especially in Jamaica, but in St Kitts it was the latter word that survived to modern times as a label for Christmas activities in which tumbling, leaping and several features of mumming featured. Note, however, that Marly (1828, 289), in early nineteenth-century Jamaica, also used the word "sports" in reference to Christmas festivities when he said: "numbers of the field negroes from the country flocked into the town to enjoy the festivities of the season, and feast their eyes with the sports exhibiting". On the other hand, in reference to Christmas activities in Trinidad, Carmichael (1833, 2:291) used the word *"play"* in an ambiguous way embracing both "playing a musical instrument" and "wassailing": "a party of negroes from Paradise, the adjoining estate, came to wish us a good Christmas.... They said they wished to come and play good Christmas to the 'young misses'.... We told them to come back and see us on New Year's day ... They went away very good humouredly, and returned ... and pleased and entertained us with their songs and merriment." The notion of "playing good Christmas to" social superiors (or people thought to have money) went beyond words (that is, simply "wishing" them a good Christmas): it meant providing them with entertainment.

A British usage of the word "play" that is relevant here is given by Strutt ([1801] 1903, 191), who observed that in the Middle Ages "the knights and the ladies are often represented dancing together, which in the MS. poem of Launfal, in the Cotton Collection, is called playing". This fifteenth-century meaning (that is, men dancing with women) that was preserved regionally in Britain no doubt found its way into the colonies. The fact that historically couples dancing together was often condemned by moral and religious people as lascivious means that it was thought to be a prelude or excitement to sex. "Play" in this sense therefore had the implication that a certain kind of dancing was overtly sexual; it also had the meaning of "playfulness", seeing that many dances were intended to entertain and amuse; and, additionally, it had the idea of pretence.

In at least one eighteenth-century piece of writing in the West Indies, not referring to slaves, the fifteenth-century meaning of "play" is preserved. The following verses taken from the *Barbados Gazette* (20 November 1731) demonstrate this:

> Nor can the Ladies pass their Hours away
> At lov'd *Quadrille*, or any other Play,
> Without their fav'rite Tam to grace the Day.
> (Caribbeana 1741, 4)

Since "Quadrille" was seen by the poet, commenting on white activities in Barbados, as a cooperative dance, it could be that "play" was used at the time for any kind of defined group dance.

The subtitle of Richardson Wright's *Revels in Jamaica 1682–1838* is *Plays and Players of a Century, Tumblers and Conjurors, Musical Refugees and Solitary Stuntmen, Dinners, Balls and Cockfights, Darky Mummers and other Memories of High Times and Merry Hearts*. Wright's topics fit easily into Strutt's headings and suggest that many of the pastimes in British towns and cities were spread to English slave colonies by white indentured servants in the second half of the seventeenth century. In any case, English writers formulated recreational/ cultural activities among the slaves according to a broad English vision which either contrasted work with play or contrasted reality with acting. Essentially, for them, the energy and the dynamism of the slaves exemplified play and justified their use of the word to label almost all of their activities. In several cases, the usage that became part of the vernacular in the West Indies actually preserved British dialectal usage, which in some cases had become obsolete and unfamiliar to some writers, who naturally regarded such usage as slave distortions or peculiarities.

The most outstanding example of usage that became obsolete in England but was maintained in the West Indies was the word "play" used to refer to activities surrounding death. In his *Dictionary of Archaic and Provincial Words*, James Halliwell (1852, 2:630) gives one of the meanings of "play" as "a country wake" and he identifies it as Somerset dialectal usage. When Rev. Holt in Barbados in 1729 referred to "what they call their plays", it suggests that the Somerset dialectal source of the usage was no longer apparent in Barbados. Attributing the source to the slaves was consistent with his view of the slaves. However, perusal of the various historical meanings of the English word "play" in the *Oxford English Dictionary* will show that none of the usages in the West Indies was a slave concoction: they all came from English dialectal sources.

If it is with Barbados that the term "play" is first identified (Holt 1729), it is with Jamaica that it is most associated in the slave period. In Jamaica, the word "play" as a label for specific cultural/recreational activities among the slaves must have become familiar by the middle of the eighteenth century, because late eighteenth- and early nineteenth-century writers, by claiming that it was the slaves' word, were indirectly implying that that meaning was no longer normal or current in general English usage. Additionally, it could have been that these writers believed that "play" perfectly represented the slaves' own view of their own activities.

Thomas Thistlewood, through his diary entries in the middle of the eighteenth century, can be best used to date the use of the word "play" in Jamaica. In his early days there, in 1751, he attended a housewarming, but he did not call it a play and he called what the slaves did "tricks" (Hall 1999, 18). Five years later he was consistently using the word "play" in his diary to refer to such events among the slaves. He identified the following activities as plays:

1. an event following the death of the infant son of a house slave: "Saturday, 24th July 1756: Nancy's play tonight. Sunday, 25th July 1756: Nancy's play ended, much music & dancing day, &c." (72)
2. an event after the death of an adult slave: "[1766] Hear that there is an information against Mr Samuel Say of Cabaritta Estate for permitting a Negro play (for Vine's mother who is lately dead) last Sunday Afternoon." (133)
3. the "christening" of a house: "Sunday, 24th September 1769: Last night Quamina at Egypt christening his house, a play, supper, &c. . . . The play continues today, a pay dinner, &c." (219)
4. an event at the burial of an adult slave: "[1771] Lincoln was at a play, at the burial of a Negro at the Retrieve all Sunday night." (182)

5. a post-burial event of appeasement: "[1771] . . . to Throw Water (as they called it) for her boy Johnie who died some months ago. . . . Many Negroes there from all over the country." (185–86)

Although there is a preponderance of post-death events referred to as plays, the term was not restricted to such events, because plays were quite frequent. In spite of the high mortality rate among slaves, it is unlikely that the nightly plays mentioned by Thistlewood (304) could have been all post-death events. Moreover, not all post-death events were identified as plays by Thistlewood, for whether in contrast or as an alternative, Thistlewood used the term "a singing" to refer to what seemed to have been events similar to what he otherwise called plays (145). Since singing presumably was the primary activity at these latter events, it would seem as if the term "play" was more normally used when dancing was more prominent. It is possible also that as Thistlewood grew older (that is, by 1785), the term "play" had come to be more generally used.

Not much information on the emergence of the word "play" is to be gained from Edward Long, who lived in Jamaica around the same time (1757–1769) as Thistlewood. Long used "games" and "plays" as alternatives, as seen in the following:

> They were formerly allowed to assemble with drums and musical instruments; to dance, drink, and be merry. . . . But when these games were afterwards converted into plots. (1774, 2:443)

> A particular attention should also be had to their *plays*, for these have always been their rendezvous for hatching plots, more especially whenever on such occasions any unusual resort is observed of their countrymen from other plantations. (2:475)

This variable use suggests that in the third quarter of the eighteenth century the term was not yet fixed.

When Marsden (1788) and Beckford (1790) mentioned the term "play", their focus was on the work/play contrast and the great physical energy involved in the activity:

> Every Saturday night many divert themselves with dancing and singing; which they stile plays; and, notwithstanding their week's labour, continue this violent exercise all night. (Marsden 1788, 33)

> And what is more extraordinary, several of them will go ten or twelve miles to what is called a play, will sit up and drink all night, and yet return in time to the plantation for their work the ensuing morning: . . . (Beckford 1790, 1:392)

It seemed striking to them both that play consumed just as much or more energy than work. What is important for dating the word, however, is that Beckford left Jamaica in 1777, which implies that the word was in common use by that time.

Moreton (1790, 155) did not give any gloss for the word, either because he assumed it would be immediately understood by English speakers or because the slave usage was well known. Interestingly enough, Moreton made a comparison between the "plays" of the slaves and the "patrons" of the Irish, noting how tiring they were. While the hard work of plays was the major focus in the citations by Marsden, Beckford and Moreton, the author of *A Short Journey in the West Indies* (1790, 88–89) was attracted by the acting and the dramatic nature of the event: "A woman is singled out by a beau-man, who exhibit all their powers of grace and activity – sometimes there are two men dance with one woman; they follow, fan her with their handkerchiefs, court her and leave her alternately, and make you understand, as perfectly as any ballet-dancer in Europe what they mean." The same is true, in the context of Suriname, when Stedman used the words "acts", "pantomime" and "actors" in his comments about slave dances, thereby substantiating the notion of "plays" in the modern English sense. Stedman went on to make light of claims of lack of propriety by situating these performances within a context of acceptability in creole society (Price and Price 1992, 159). There is little doubt that the descriptions and positive attitude of Stedman as well as the author of *A Short Journey in the West Indies* helped to solidify the concept of a slave play in the minds of European writers. Yet even if the word "play" had become the norm by the late eighteenth century, variation in preference was still evident through to the end of the century.

In the first part of the nineteenth century, the word "play" continued to be popular in Jamaica and to be associated with wakes. Michael Scott, who lived in Jamaica from 1806 to 1822, used the word as a synonym for "wake" in his fictional narrative *Tom Cringle's Log*. In describing the progress of a "negro funeral" through the streets of Kingston and the intention of the mourners to get the maximum out of it, as was the custom, by stopping as often as possible to get donations ostensibly to placate the corpse, Scott glossed "play" as "wake" in the following: "'Oh, Massa — , dollar for drink; something to hold play,' negro wake, 'in Spring-path,' the negro burying-ground" (1862, 128). In another reference he says: "The following night there was to be a grand play or wake in the negro houses" (1862, 141).

In contrast, at the same time, Stewart (1823, 272) unrestrictedly equated the word with "dance": "Plays, or dances, very frequently take place on Saturday nights." For Stewart, an outstanding feature of the creole social scene was conviviality and, for him, play was typical of occasions when people on "neighbouring plantations assemble together to enjoy themselves".

No one seemed fonder of the word "play" than Monk Lewis, and for him it seemed to mean no more than "fun". He repeated the term "play-day" several times with the following explanation the first time it occurred: "Saturday's holiday (or *play-day*, in the negro dialect)" ([1834] 1969, 89), not knowing that "play-day" was English dialectal usage. To demonstrate his benevolence towards his slaves he said he created three additional play-days in the year: "the royal play-day"; "massa's play-day"; "the piccaninny-mothers' play-day". On all these play-days there was singing and dancing and general merriment. Lewis did not use play (as a noun) to identify a specific event among the slaves or a special kind of dance. When Lewis did speak of "a play" among the slaves (56), he was talking about a dramatic presentation – that is, the most common meaning of the term.

A reasonable conclusion about the development of the word "play" is that because of the frequency and distinctiveness of the spectacle of slave burials, it was linked in the early period specifically to funerals, thus maintaining some English (Somerset) dialectal meaning. However, by the beginning of the nineteenth century, in Jamaica at least, the word "play" was most commonly being used to refer to the kind of dancing performance which was done outdoors within a ring of spectators in which the dancers acted out features of relationships between a man and a woman. Stewart (1808, 261) explained plays as follows: "The negroes have few amusements, nor have they much time to devote to amusement. Plays, as they call them, is their principal and favourite one. This is an assemblage of both sexes, who form a ring round a male and female dancer, who perform to the music of their drums, and the songs of the other females of the party." The formation and activity were sentimentally captivating for participants, including onlookers.

The defining features of plays were that they were outdoors and powerful in energy and sound. The factor of being outdoors was a direct result of the physical situation of the slaves, who had little access to large indoor spaces. The energy and sound levels were a direct psychological reaction to enslavement: people needed an outlet for their emotions and a way to enjoy their own wholesomeness. As a result of both factors, plays were substantially determined and shaped by factors in the Caribbean. It is also the case that the term "play" came to be reserved for the slaves since, in addition to the need to keep the races separate in word and deed, the slaves liked performing competitively in couples, while "ball" was used for those higher in society who, more often than not, danced in lines and groups indoors in a more "sophisticated" fashion.

The Salience of "Play" as a Descriptive and Cultural Concept

In the first two hundred years of the English colonies, writers used several terms to label cultural activities among the slaves:

Sports: Hutson 2001; *Marly* 1828
Ceremonies: Sloane 1707
Playing: Sloane 1707
Play: Holt 1729; Hughes 1750; Thistlewood 1750–86 (Hall 1999); Long 1774; Marsden 1788; Stedman 1794; Beckford 1790; Moreton 1790; Stewart 1808; Lewis [1834] 1969; Day 1852
Games: Long 1774
Festival: Beckford 1790; *Negro's Friend* 1830; Bayley 1830
Private theatricals: Resident 1828
Merry meetings: Renny 1807
Negro diversions: *Marly* 1828; Breen 1844
Slave gala: *Marly* 1828
Assembly: Wentworth 1834

It is clear from the list that, in spite of the diversity of terms, "play" was used more and longer than any of the others. Also, of all the alternatives, it was the only word whose "slave" meaning, in the context of the English colonies, had come to be as common as the regular English meaning.

Although in the middle of the seventeenth century slaves from Barbados were taken to colonize Suriname and although a significant percentage of English words form a part of the vocabularies of the major creole languages of Suriname, especially Sranan, it would be difficult to argue that there is an ethnic link between slave practices in Barbados and the scene on a Suriname plantation that Dirk Valkenburg painted in 1706–8, which Richard Price (1983, 109) refers to as "slave 'play' on the Dombi plantation". Valkenburg did not use the word "play" in the title of his painting, so Reverend Holt's 1729 use of the word in Barbados remains the first known reference to the slaves' activities as plays. Price and Price use the word "playing" as the title of chapter 7 in their 1999 book *Maroon Arts: Cultural Vitality in the African Diaspora*, but they do not do so based on bibliographical evidence. *Stedman's Surinam*, which they edited in 1992, has the term "winty-play", but Stedman's book was written at the end of the eighteenth century. Price and Price (1999, 237) identify *pêè* and *pee* as language variants in Suriname today, but these would have come from the English word "play" and there is no evidence to show that the word had any special cultural significance for the slaves at that time.

Valkenburg's painting itself does not show slaves actually playing/dancing. In fact, Lauren Freese's annotation to Rebecca Parker Brienen's article on the painting says: "Brienen argues that Slave Dance can be interpreted as a still-life painting for a wealthy slave owner and collector" (https://wiki.uiowa.edu/display/1604724/Brienen). Thus, Brienen's interpretation ("a still-life painting") quite clearly challenges Price's interpretation of the painting as a dance or play.

Price and Price (1999) use "playing/plays" with a broad, inclusive reference, in the same way that *areíto* was used as the name of a range of activities among the indigenous inhabitants of the bigger Caribbean islands. This usage is different from that of Szwed and Abrahams (1976). In this latter, written at a time when the authors still felt a need to counteract anthropologists who were negative about the contribution of Africans to American culture, they present Afro-American play in a diametric contrast with Euro-American play, using an opposition between work and play as well as between "private" and "public" behaviour. Szwed and Abrahams argue that play "is an important element of public performance of Black communities" and that "in the Afro-American order of behaviors, 'play' is . . . distinguished from "respectable" behaviour" (227). This kind of sharp contrastive argument is difficult to sustain precisely because, as they admit, "the term *play* is used by Afro-Americans with many of the same meanings as other speakers of English" (224).

Thanks, in part, to the work of Szwed and Abrahams as well as Price and Price, the term "play" has come to be a well-known feature in African American anthropology, just as *areíto* was for the indigenous people in the bigger Caribbean islands. Overall, one can argue either that these terms, through their generality, underscore the importance of play in the indigenous and African American communities, or that they are preferred terms of outsiders which created a broad, cultural concept that did not exist for the people themselves.

When all of the alternative terms used by writers on the Caribbean and all the contexts are taken together, they point to an ability to cope with and enjoy life in a situation of extreme dominance. If play had an essential, common factor in the Caribbean, it was that the activities involved imagination as well as an element of what Drewal (1992, 19–20) explained as "improvisation". The element of improvisation fitted perfectly into a Caribbean situation where everything was changing and varying for the slaves, not least of all because of their high mortality rate. They had to sustain themselves spiritually by imagining a better world and they made their world better by suppressing the harshness of life, using whatever they had inside of them, whatever material was their own, whatever they got from others, whatever the environment afforded and within the limits they could not overcome.

Impromptu, interactive, outdoor activities involving singing, music and dancing constituted play for the slaves. It was collective and individualistic at the same time: it did not strictly divide the community into participants and players (that is, all were players), it did not separate music from dancing by favouring one over the other and it allowed for turn-taking without forcing everyone to be in the spotlight. It repeatedly allowed one and all for no matter how temporary a time to cocoon themselves in fun or the imaginary in order to replenish themselves. It allowed them to create, experiment and adapt to each other.

7. Dancing in the Street
Parties, Parades, Sets and Masquerades

> Carnival, the festival of paganism, is celebrated only among enslaved people; it would be worthy of a free nation to abolish it, and there is no better occasion to do so than the dawn of liberty.
> —Marat 1789, 8

IN CARIBBEAN PLANTATION SOCIETY, PRESCRIBED FREE DAYS for the slaves were determined by the Christian calendar. Several writers identified these days – Tobin in St Kitts (1785, 63), Atwood in Dominica (1791, 260), Stewart in Jamaica (1808, 262), Carmichael in St Vincent (1833, 2:285), Bayley in Grenada (1830, 439), Lewis in Jamaica ([1834] 1969, 51) – but they seldom gave the same information. It was the major Christian feast days with their varying significance that provided a framework within which unbridled as well as organized entertainment took place. It was these major feast days that provided the impetus for the transfer of features of European festivities into Caribbean slave life. It was these feast days the slaves took advantage of to fashion festivities which drew on their varied experiences over the course of each year.

Generally, the slaves made use of the free days to do what they wanted and it did not take long for them to believe that these days were theirs by right. Admittedly, there really was no concerted move to curtail these acquired "rights" because in effect it was the masters who were trying to preserve the sanctity (or licence) of the "holy days" for themselves, even though they believed that the slaves were desecrating them and even though they were aware that the slaves at times planned insurrections on or for these days. The varying statements made by English writers about the ways in which the slaves regarded the free days leave no doubt that, for the slaves, the Christmas holidays were days of temporary freedom and the enjoyment of it and had little to do with celebrating the birth of Christ. Moreover, the various ways the slaves enjoyed themselves (rest, intoxication, dissipation, insurrection) suggest no common tradition. In fact, the "unrestrained" behaviour of the slaves can be said to have been partly caused by the slave masters because they were driven by the spirit of Christmas to be generous or merely to provide for the slaves, and the slaves were reacting to their "plenty" at that time of the year.

In contrast to "dissipation", "riots", "disorder", "revelry" and other unstructured ways in which most of the slaves were said to spend their holidays at Christmas, there was a more constructive activity among them, featuring parties, which captured the attention of the community at large. The word "parties" (similar to carnival bands today) was repeatedly used to refer to Christmas and end-of-year gatherings in Jamaica, so much so that in that context it seemed to have a specialized meaning. Though there is a semantic and some phonological similarity between "party" in this sense and Spanish *comparsa*, it would be difficult to argue that "party" was linked to the Spanish history of Jamaica.

The first mention of "parties" was by Beckford (1790, 389) in Jamaica in the last quarter of the eighteenth century. Beckford made it seem as if "the negroes upon neighbouring estates" saw each other as rivals, as if slaves had developed a competitive loyalty to their own estate. In his preceding comments, he also highlighted the practice of dressing up at different social levels as well as a spirit of competition. Though Beckford highlighted dressing up and competitiveness, he did not provide any other information about the kinds of slaves (for example, house slaves or field slaves) who made up the parties other than that they were girls from "neighbouring estates". Based on Beckford's description, "negro parties" at end-of-year festivities in Jamaica started out as rival groups of girls with each group in its own dress/costume and colour. This had to be before 1777, the year Beckford is said to have left Jamaica to return to England.

In 1808, John Stewart, who had already spent twenty-one years in Jamaica, like Beckford, portrayed the creole social scene in Jamaica as one of conviviality and one in which whites on neighbouring plantations regularly got together to enjoy themselves. As a result, Stewart used the word "party" frequently, with a variety of meanings. Therefore, when he identified two "parties" by colour in the end-of-year slave celebrations, he was using the same word for whites and slaves: he gave no sense that among the slaves parties had originated differently or that there was any permanent affiliation to one party or another.

The features of a "negro party", according to Stewart, were that the participants were all female and urban. They were decked out ("in all the pride of gaudy splendour" [1808, 263]); there was an emphasis on symmetry ("they paraded through the streets, two and two, in the most exact order, uniform in their dress, and nearly of the same stature and age" [264]); each party had a queen who was even more elaborately dressed; and each party was accompanied by a music band. Stewart showed no knowledge of any similarity between such parties in Jamaica and other islands or countries, far or near. For him, a "negro" party on New Year's Day was a local dress parade and competition among "negro girls of the towns" (263), who also sang to the strains of music provided by a band. The elements mentioned by Stewart that had not been by Beckford in 1790 were the "queen" of the party and the musical band that accompanied the party.

Subsequently, there were variations in the description of the queen. For Barclay (1826, 11), the queen was "a matron . . . who possesses some degree of authority". For Williams (1826, 62), the queens were "the prettiest and best shaped girls they can find, who are obliged to personate the royal characters". Earlier, in 1801, Nugent mentioned that groups had "a sort of leader or superior at their head" (Wright 2002, 48), even though she did not identify the person as a "queen" or even as a female.

Stewart made it seem as if the parties were under the control of the slaves' mistresses or at least actively supported by them. Marly (1828, 290), on the contrary, said that the slaves among themselves had chosen their "dignitaries" for the occasion: "Black Massa Snowball had received the suffrages of his fellow slaves in the town, and had been elected king; and Miss Strutt's black Luna was chosen queen."

Monk Lewis's description of a party in 1816 could be interpreted as a more elaborate version of Stewart's. The party now included both a king and a queen with a hierarchical retinue in attendance ([1834] 1969, 53). His interpretation of "parties" was essentially that they were originally urban, a claim that conflicts with Beckford's earlier description of them as estate-based. Lewis also seemed to be implying that the division into parties or factions reflected local preferences for one British ethnicity or another, that is, the English or the Scottish. Both Beckford and Lewis seemed to believe that parties were white groupings that spread to the slaves.

Lewis's description of the parade of parties which he happened to encounter on his arrival in Jamaica on New Year's Day in 1816 showed it to be striking. There is no doubt that he believed that this colonial town parade was a competitive celebration or "acting out" of the military successes of the mother country.

Judging from his words, the slaves were expressing their solidarity with the colonial master, with the division into parties or factions being determined by the sympathies of those in control. One gets the impression from Lewis that the parties were substantially the same from one occasion to another. However, there is not much evidence to show that Lewis moved far beyond his initial impressions in his interpretation of parties or that his comments on the origin and make-up of parties were more than speculation.

Barclay's (1826, 10) view of parties was different from Lewis's – he saw them as originally groups of uncivilized plantation Africans, but this was primarily because he intended to show that the slaves had moved away from their "bad" African ways. Two other later writers repeated the claim of African origin, but neither one is reliable. Scott (1862, 241), in describing end-of-year festivities, spoke of "the yelling of the different African tribes" as one component of the "Negro Carnival", but the problem with Scott is that it is difficult to differentiate between fictional narrative and authenticity in his work. Phillippo's (1843, 242) account is not trustworthy, seeing that he consistently copied what others before him said. Overall, in spite of the various assertions, there is not enough corroborating evidence to conclude that "parties" originated from different West African ethnic groups.

Marly, in 1828, used the term "procession" rather than "party" and, clearly, the size of what he described extended beyond the idea of a single cohesive group. He described the procession as having a "king, and queen, and court", preceded by "a very tolerable band of sable musicians" (289) and followed by "all the town negroes who could procure suitable dresses for the occasion" (290). In contrast to the early descriptions which specified only females as participants, Marly said that the "procession consisted of at least one hundred of both sexes" (289). Marly did not interpret the group he described as either European or African in origin, but saw it more as a spontaneous expression of the slaves' desires. He conceived of it as a preference on their part for "a kingly state of society". Marly, unlike Beckford and Stewart, did not describe any select set of females in the procession, but he did say that the participants generally "were skipping and dancing along, in place of walking" (293) and kept singing their favourite song. When the sun was beginning to set, they went to a house and there danced the night away. In reality, this ending of the parade was not significantly different from Williams's version (1826, 63).

Based on these descriptions of end-of-year parties in Jamaica from Beckford (1790) to Marly (1828) (which could actually have been a fifty-year span), it appears as if there was change and expansion in their size and participants. Moreover, writers were describing different places in Jamaica. Even so, it is noticeable that groups of girls dressed alike, which was central to the earliest descriptions, were absent from Marly's. Apparently, then, over time no single feature remained as a defining feature of parties.

In comparison with the eighteenth-century evidence from Jamaica, the earliest mention of street parties in Trinidad comes from a letter writer to the *Port of Spain Gazette* of 2 March 1838, who complained about "the ferocious fight between the 'Damas' and 'Wartloos'" during carnival. Day (1852, 1:314) also mentions parties as a part of the 1847 carnival in Trinidad: "Parties of negro ladies danced through the streets, each *clique* distinguished by boddices of the same colour." Here again, just as in the early descriptions in Jamaica, one of the features highlighted was female groups, each dressed in a different colour.

It should be mentioned, however, that while there were no contemporary descriptions of slave parades in Trinidad until after emancipation, the idea of "bands" before then comes indirectly from the official report of what was treated as an intended slave revolt at Christmas (1805). *Extracts from the Minutes of His Majesty's Council* (in Trinidad), dated 20 December 1805, identified the instigators of the revolt as the leaders of "regiments", which had formerly been called "convoys, which more properly may be called Societies, for the purposes of dancing and innocent amusement" (*Barbados Mercury and Bridgetown Gazette*, 1 February 1806). However, there is no indication that these regiments/convoys/societies had street parades as an integral part of their activities.

There are three facts that are significantly different about the evidence from Trinidad: first, it relates parties to carnival, not Christmas. Second, it situates the activity in the post-emancipation period, which can be interpreted to mean that during the slavery period, carnival was not a slave festival. Third, the emphasis was on masking (see Day 1852, 1:314). No such emphasis on masking is given for Jamaica. While these differences may point to different traditions, the reference in both cases to "Waterloo" is significant counter-evidence. Assuming that the "Wartloos" in Trinidad were the same as the "Blue girls of Waterloo" in Jamaica, such a similarity across the islands could hardly have been mere coincidence and especially since there were also "Wadeloes" *in* St Lucia. So, to understand the source of and *raison d'être* for parties, one has to adopt a less immediate and localized approach.

"Negro Parties" and the Ancient Greek Adonia Festival

One historical writer who, in a sense, signalled such an approach was Cynric Williams in Jamaica. He essentially associated what he called "a contest kept up by two parties of the women" on New Year's Day with a story from ancient Greek mythology: "I very much suspect this is a remnant of the Adonia mentioned by Plutarch" (1826, 62). This reference to Plutarch parallels the less explicit but similar kind of comment about the celebrations of the two rival "societies" in St Lucia made by Breen, who spoke of "primeval diversions" (1844, 198). Williams's association of the contest with the ancient Adonia festival removes it from the immediate, localized and mundane and puts it in a classical tradition.

One version of the myth behind the ancient Greek Adonia festival is that Adonis was loved by both Aphrodite and Persephone and it was decided to award him to each of the two for a different part of the year. Persephone was associated with below ground, winter and the seed whereas Aphrodite was associated with above ground, spring and the shoot or plant. The change from Persephone to Aphrodite, which accounted for the change from winter to spring, was marked by the Adonia festival (see Smith 1870, 22).

Such pagan festivals arising out of seasonal and agrarian changes (for example, winter to spring) became indistinct from religious conceptualizations of death and resurrection and were preserved in religious festivities all across Europe. Spring festivals, associated with the month of May and May Day specifically, blossomed, combining agrarian and religious elements in various ways. Spring/May queens and kings are a part of European cultural history that have come right down to modern times. However, one major difference between the contest in Jamaica with its two "parties of women" and the Adonia festival was that the date of the slaves' parties (January) and that of spring festivals (May) did not coincide.

The seasonal and life-cycle change in the Adonia myth is agrarian within the context of a temperate climate, but it is possible that the slaves could have reinterpreted or subconsciously perceived their own change of state at Christmas, even if it was temporary, as a different but more important face of their reality. In other words, the slaves' festivities could have been more than visceral enjoyment, for it is reasonable to think that the slaves reflected on what was being done to them and on what they were doing. One may ask the questions: Did the couple days of freedom loom large enough for them to make them think of them as their season of spring or renewal? Did they have ancestral memories which informed such festivals? If the answer to either question is yes, then the festivities marked a critical though temporary change of state for them and there could therefore be justification for the comparison with the Adonia festival, despite the fact that Williams was primarily highlighting the centrality of women in both.

Marly (1828, 288) indirectly gives some substance to the Adonia interpretation by presenting the slaves' experience within the framework of a seasonal contrast:

> Christmas... had come round, and in the morning of that eventful day, Singleton Hall presented a scene of gaiety, noisy hilarity, and confusion... This is indeed to them a period of exceeding joy. On that day, the following one, and the first of the new year, the bonds of slavery are loosened, and to them they are truly holidays, of freedom, happiness, and merriment. Attired in their best and gayest apparel, they seemed all life and glee, joyous gladness sparkled in their dark coloured eyes, and smiled on their black and glossy countenances, for at length the happy period had arrived, and they were on the eve of enjoying the pleasures and merriment which they had long anticipated.

Marly's emphasis on the slaves' conceptualization of the unfolding of the season moves it beyond the physical to the cerebral, especially when he concludes, "they returned to their work, many of them apparently well pleased, after having satiated themselves with such a round of enjoyment, more pleasing always in the anticipation than in reality" (296). Stewart's (1808, 262) emphasis also, though physical, essentially compares the effect of the Christmas season on the slaves to plants springing back: "pleasure animates them, and seems to throw a veil of oblivion over their cares and their condition; in short, they seem as a people recreated and renewed". The change (to spring) was no longer agrarian: it was now human. The joyful experience of inversion had brought about spiritual renewal.

As to Williams's Adonia interpretation, no support would be forthcoming from Roger Abrahams (1970a, 241), who unequivocally rejects "the explanation of these dramas as vestiges of some archetypal 'life-cycle play'". Even though Abrahams was speaking of mummers' plays and such like, his idea is that the "archetypal" kind of interpretation places what the folk do "into the sophisticated and abstract frame of reference of philosophical religion" (242).

It was Fernando Ortiz ([1951] 1981, 438), among others, who put forward a life-cycle and "archetypal" view of the origin of these festivals, saying: "Many of those primitive masquerade dances are ... originally agrarian fertility rites and resurrection rites." He also tied them to modern carnivals in Europe. Ortiz's explanation brought together both ritualistic/life-cycle notions and notions of ethnicity in performance.

Abrahams's interpretation must be considered restricted in vision when certain cultural practices are observed to have continuity and to be widespread in the Caribbean extending beyond the British colonies. While Abrahams prefers to concentrate on what participants believe themselves to be doing in a more immediate (non-reflective) sense, to reject the original or early notions behind a cultural practice that continued for centuries in varying locations is to shortchange the intellect and the traditions of the people involved. Abrahams would find it difficult to sustain an argument which deliberately dismisses interrelationships between role inversions in the Roman Saturnalia, in the English and other European versions of "the Lord of Misrule", in English masquerades and in the slaves' behaviour at Christmas.

"Negro Parties" as Possible Forms of Activism

One may ask whether, at the beginning of the nineteenth century when notions of emancipation and freedom were already in the air, parties and dressing up did not have an element of anticipation of the future. In this scenario, the participants in the two parties mentioned by Williams would have been trying to outdo each other socially to show that they were ready to take their place in the new and glorious future, well groomed by their superiors.

Another possibility is that these practices were fostered by more immediate social and political factors. Aimes (1905, 16) speaks of these "by-gone practices, which began about the middle of the eighteenth century and ceased about the middle of the nineteenth". Most of the references support this period and tend to confirm Aimes's interpretation, even though in Brazil these practices extended beyond these times in both directions and in St Lucia "societies" (= parties) persisted and actually gained strength after emancipation.

The Industrial Revolution, the American War of Independence, the French Revolution and the Haitian Revolution, covering the period 1760 to 1804, all involved deep social changes and, in one way or another, raised issues of legal status (that is, slavery) and social justice. Later in the nineteenth century, the significance of May Day changed to be related more to labour union activism and celebrations. It is the words of the French Revolution – *liberté, égalité, fraternité* ("liberty, equality, brotherhood") – that are best remembered as a beacon in the earlier period. The fight for freedom and betterment meant being politically active, a fact that became crystal clear in Saint Domingue. In the less explosive situation that obtained in Jamaica, slave parties could have been an ambivalent form of activism.

After the plantation system had become entrenched in Jamaica and enjoyed an economic and social high-point in the latter half of the eighteenth century, it is conceivable that slaves had acquired a feeling of pride in their own estate or among themselves on the plantation and tried to demonstrate it whenever the occasion arose. Alternatively, in keeping with the belief that the slaves used the Christmas holidays as a mask for rebellious activities, division into parties might not have been totally innocent and featured women because they were less likely to provoke white hostility. Or, female house slaves had become socially and politically conscious enough and savvy enough to promote their own interests in parties within the limits of white tolerance in what appeared to be white traditions.

In Trinidad in December 1805, activities in the slave regiments were certainly treated as seditious, resulting in the ringleaders being hanged and beheaded. Fraser's (1891, 1:267–72) historical interpretation of what happened accepted the general view that slaves used the holidays to plan and execute rebellions. The backdrop for the "intended slave revolt" was Christmas festivities and, whether the intentions of the slaves were innocent or not, they had what they themselves called "regiments", which Fraser referred to as "associations", "Bands" and a "Secret Society". The official version of the intended insurrection stated that "the intention of the insurrection was only known to their Chiefs, they having constantly refused admittance to women and inferior officers to their secret meetings, observing that the business which, on such occasions, occupied their deliberations, was not a matter for women or boys" (*Barbados Mercury and Bridgetown Gazette*, 1 February 1806).

The extensive presence of slave regiments in Trinidad in 1805 seems unusual when compared with other West Indian colonies, but it can be accounted for as a factor of the migration of French Roman Catholics into Trinidad and the dramatically changing economic structure of the island. As happens with migration generally, ethnic groups coming into a new situation tend to stick to their own for mutual comfort. In the case of late eighteenth-century Trinidad, this was certainly encouraged by the increasing diversity of the population. In addition, since dressing up and display were a part of the French world, including the Roman Catholic Church, it is not surprising that the "French" slaves opted to form themselves into dramatically visible groups reflecting community, plantation or Caribbean place of origin.

However, when "regiment" replaced "convoy", it clearly indicated a shift in self-perception on the part of the slaves – the convoy had now become the regiment on parade – and the disquiet this created is reflected in the official report on the intended insurrection: "The recent assumption of the name of Regiments, instead of Convoys, together with the administration of oaths for, as it was termed, of the Communion, when the crucifix, holy water, and holy bread were used, imposing obedience to their kings, and attachment to their regiments, were certainly ceremonies perfectly unnecessary for promoting the original intention of the Convoys" (*Barbados Mercury and Bridgetown Gazette*, 1 February 1806). Yet in another case some twenty years later, which Daniel Crowley (1958, 550) reports on, the official verdict on regiments was the opposite of that in 1805. It is no wonder that some historians now think that the verdict in 1805 was a case where the administration reacted with inordinate fear in the wake of the very recent events in Haiti.

In Scott's fictional work *Tom Cringle's Log*, there is another explanation of parties, one that is related to developments in the United States and Europe in the latter half of the nineteenth century. Scott identified the different parties with various crafts and trades – butchers, gardeners, workhouse people/guards. Guilds and societies are seen historically as the constituent groups of carnival in Switzerland and Germany. They also have some historical relevance to carnival groups in New Orleans and Brazil, but the groups identified by Scott were not all viable groups coming out of plantations or even among urban slaves in the Caribbean. However, constructing parties in terms of crafts and trades could have been substantially imaginative or imitative rather than being a direct reflection of reality. Even so, they would still have some vague affinity to the parades and rallies that became a feature of organized labour (made up of craftsman unions) in the United States from the mid-nineteenth century onward.

Slaves Parading as Kings and Queens: A Puzzling Phenomenon

What emerged in the second and third decades of the nineteenth century in Jamaica as what Marly called the "slave gala" or "Negro diversions" at Christmas and New Year's Day were, without doubt, "classic" examples of a kind of display that was recorded for several slave societies across the Americas. What has come to be called a "royal court" was a parade assembled in a hierarchical way with a king and queen, lesser nobles and their subjects, and a retinue. Remarkably, in this first "classic" period of festivity in Jamaica, the competition was seen to be as much between the owners of the slaves, in a vicarious way, as between the slaves themselves. Indeed, Marly, while on the one hand stressing that in the procession the slaves were performing for their own ("the negroes were only proceeding for their honorary sable dignities" [1828, 290]), on the other hand he pointed out that "this is a species of competition which yearly occurs among the native born ladies of the Island" (292).

In Day's (1852, 1:315) description of carnival in Trinidad in 1847, the "royal court" was still being identified as a feature. Day, just as Marly and Lewis had done in Jamaica, automatically assumed that the royal court was an imitation of the king and queen of England and as such essentially colonial in inspiration. The same kind of explanation is given by Abrahams (1970a, 253). However, the occurrence of similar parades among slaves and descendants of slaves elsewhere in the Americas indicates that its manifestation in Jamaica requires a more comprehensive explanation.

As a reflection of a form of societal organization, the hierarchical nature of the royal court was typical of European societies. Consequently, European maps of conquest also set out Africa in kingdoms, even though the concept of "king" in both cases was not necessarily equivalent. However, it is in relation to the Congo that African kings are most familiar in the written record and this is as a result of the association of the "Kingdom of Kongo" with the Catholic Church and the Portuguese, who established links there from the end of the fifteenth century.

Monarchy on parade was probably memorable for slaves from Benin at least, judging by the prominence given to it in Dapper's seventeenth-century account, first appearing in 1668. Dapper obviously considered the parade significant enough not only to give a written description of it but also to have it illustrated pictorially (see figure 11). His description has several points in common with

Figure 11. The City Benin (King of Benin parade). Olfert Dapper, *Umbstandliche und eigentliche Beschreibung von Africa* [. . .] (Amsterdam: Jacob von Meurs, 1670).

an earlier one by Marees ([1602] 1987, 228–229), also describing the King of Benin, in which the idea of display is very prominent. A later reference to the King of Benin's annual appearance in public is given by Bosman (1705, 465–66), but the description is somewhat different and it was on the occasion of an unexplained "Coral-Feast". An important fact supporting a link between this Benin parade and royal court parades in the New World is that Benin is located centrally along the Guinea Coast, where many of the slaves came from. In addition, certain features of the parade stand out – the king covered in royal ornaments, the dressed-up people around him, musical bands and (in Dapper's account) the retinue of infantry and cavalry. These all have parallels in the Caribbean.

Ortiz ([1951] 1981, 439), in the context of Cuba and Roman Catholic Three Kings' Day (*Día de Reyes*) celebrations, puts the slaves squarely in the middle pursuing their own African traditions. In Ortiz's interpretation two traditions, one European and the other African, converged. Evidence supporting the convergence of the slaves' celebration and Three Kings' Day comes from an observation made by Pelleprat in 1655, which is the earliest evidence on the matter in the Caribbean islands (probably in St Kitts, the island where the French started their colonization of the islands) and anywhere else in the Americas. It was an interchange between one slave speaking on behalf of a group of about forty to fifty and one of Pelleprat's fellow priests in which the priest wanted to know why the slaves were not drinking the alcohol given to them: "The Negro rejoined: 'We are also fasting today because tomorrow is [Three] Kings' Day and the black King is our patron'" (1655, 64). In this case, abstinence on the eve of the celebration of the black king on Three Kings' Day links the slaves' activities not only to the Christian calendar but to Christianity itself and specifically to the figure, Balthazar, the one of the Wise Men who was portrayed as a black person. Pelleprat's point really was that those slaves who were Christian were devout and fasted on the eve of their major occasion, but he gave no further information on the slaves or what they actually did on the following day.

There is no question that there were overlapping features in the European and African traditions. In celebrations of Epiphany/Three Kings' Day in Europe, there is clear evidence of the practice of electing a "mock" king and a royal court to rule for a day or a short period. This practice is said to have come out of the pagan festivities of the ancient Romans and Greeks. Also with reference to African traditions, Friedemann (1996, 146) cites a work on Cuba in support of a point about performances specifically by Congos in the New World as kings and queens: "J.M. Sáenz' (1961) article on the origin of masquerades (*comparsas*) in Cuba and the relationship with *cabildos* of *horros negroes* in Havana, in 1528, in which 'the negroes (male and female) of this village call themselves kings and queens and have festivities and other get-togethers and banquets which become licentious', is early evidence of support for the hierarchy of Congo kings in its American manifestation of masquerade, theatre and festival."

In Brazil, especially in the northeast, Congos are also identified with the royal court in explanations of the composition of carnival groups among slaves and Marina de Mello e Souza (2002) dedicates a whole book to the study of the history of the festival of the coronation of Congo Kings (*Historia da festa de coroação de Rei Congo*) in Brazil generally. As in the case of the royal court in Cuban and Colombian festivals, those in the Brazilian festivals have a long documented history going back to the seventeenth century.

In what was probably the earliest description of one of these festivals in Brazil, in 1688, Urbain Souchu de Rennefort (1688, 207–9) wrote the following:

> The Blacks, who are imported from Angola ... work all the time ... Their harsh captivity however does not prevent them from enjoying themselves sometimes. On Sunday, 10th September, 1666, they had their festival in Pernambuco. After

about four hundred men and a hundred women among them went to mass, they elected a king and queen and marched through the streets singing, dancing and reciting poetry which they had composed; they were preceded by oboes, trumpets and tambourines. They were dressed in the clothes of their masters and mistresses, with gold chains and gold and pearl earrings. Some of them wore masks. The parade cost them a hundred ecus. For the whole of this week, the king and his officers did nothing but parade solemnly with their sword and dagger at their side.

It is clear here that although Christianity provided the framework for the royal court parade, it was a celebration among the slaves themselves with no suggestion of any outside intervention from their masters or priests. This was a festival of remarkable durability, for in 1835, nearly a century and a half later, Rugendas (1827) produced what has become one of the most familiar pictorial illustrations of the Fiesta of Our Lady of the Rosary, featuring a black king and queen on parade with musicians and a crowd of followers (see figure 12).

Explanations of the Brazil festivals also tended to link the 'royal court' to the Portuguese, either the Portuguese rulers in Brazil or Portuguese society

Figure 12. Fiesta of Our Lady of the Rosary. J.M. Rugendas, *Voyage pittoresque dans le Brésil* (Paris: Engelmann, 1827).

in Portugal (for example, Crowley 1984, 16–17). This explanation is not only narrow but it also minimizes the role of the slaves. In other cases, it is the slave owners who, in accordance with the "divide and rule" policy, were supposed to have devised the practice for their own security. The fact is, however, that these explanations are not supported by what Urbain Souchu de Rennefort said.

The widespread occurrence of the royal court does not necessarily marginalize the significance of localized features. In Urbain Souchu de Rennefort's account, one feature that is different is the date of the beginning of the festival (Sunday, 10 September). Even though it is unlikely that the slaves had control over their own affairs to the extent that they could set the date for their celebration, it is clear that the celebration was not Christian. It is true that Roman Catholic traditions had come to assert some influence on the people of the Congo/Angola region from the end of the fifteenth century and it is true that Angola/Congo slaves were dominant in Pernambuco. However, there is no major Christian calendar date in September. Therefore, the fact that the date of the Pernambuco celebration was different lends support to the idea that the royal court parade was African inspired.

In spite of this evidence, a question that arises is whether the royal court parade came directly from Africa or came by way of Portugal and Spain, which had African slaves in numbers. Leonardo Dantas Silva (2001, 30), a commentator on the festival as it is today in Brazil, seems to be suggesting a route to Brazil through Portugal when he says: "The *maracatu*, in the form that it is known today, has its origins in the institution of Negro Kings, already mentioned in France and Spain in the 16th century." Saunders (1982, 106), in his analysis of the social history of black slaves and freedmen in Portugal during the years 1441 to 1555, writes that in 1563, "the corregedor of Colares – about 25 km northwest of Lisbon – broke up a *festa dos negros* where the blacks had elected a king and hanged a scarecrow from a gibbet". He also said: "The custom of having a ceremonial king or queen persisted in the Portuguese black community until the late nineteenth century" (118).

Instead of positing this indirect route through Europe for the royal court, it could have been simply one of the traditions Congo slaves took with them wherever they went. Additionally, Congo slaves would have fit into Christian celebrations wherever they went because they were already familiar with Christianity as there were substantial "Portuguese" settlements along the Congo littoral. A look at the periods when Congo slaves were imported into specific colonies in significant numbers can thus be used to show a correlation with the appearance of the royal court. In the case of Jamaica, the correlation seems clear. Figures of slave importations given by Handler and Lange (1978, 24) show that from the middle of the eighteenth century there was a dramatic increase in slaves from the Bight of Biafra and, more importantly, from 1781 to 1810 a considerable increase in slaves from the Central Africa and Angola region. This demographic evidence strongly supports a view that the royal court was specifically a Congo feature and that it was introduced directly into Jamaica between the middle and the last quarter of the eighteenth century.

The case of St Lucia is more problematic in that "societies" with an elaborate royal court were described there in the post-emancipation period (Breen 1844, 189). As was the case in the various islands and mainland colonies where many explanations were localized, Breen seemed to have been unaware of the royal court described by Marly in Jamaica less than twenty years earlier or any of its antecedents. He located the emergence of the Rose and Marguerite societies in the French colonies (that is, those that were or had been French). Such ignorance on the part of whites suggests, first, that there was an automatic association in their minds between a dressed up king/queen and Europe and, second, that knowledge of the royal court did not spread among the various European colonizers in the New World.

There is little actual historical documentation to show that the royal court existed in St Lucia at the time that comparable displays were described in Jamaica in the second half of the eighteenth century, but it is likely that it came into being in St Lucia in the same way or through the same forces that it did in Jamaica. There is a reference given by Crowley (1958, 551) which would support this view: "The first known mention of them [societies] occurs in a letter written by Mme. Jeanne Le Vexier, dated 15 September 1769, which Simmons reports as describing a La Rose fête held that year in Soufriere, St Lucia." However, there seems to be no other independent verification of the existence of this letter or its contents.

Some evidence of the same type is reported by Peytraud (1897) in reference to nearby Martinique a few years earlier. Peytraud got his information from a letter by the governor of Martinique, who felt disgusted, probably out of insecurity, about the activities of the slaves. Peytraud introduced his information as follows: "A letter by De Bompard, governor of Martinique, dated 20th July 1753, furnished the curious details on this subject. Having gone to St Pierre to see a parade of negroes on the occasion of Corpus Christi, found that it was most indecent" (182). As in other colonial situations, the slaves' parade was seen by the writer as a version of a European (here French) custom and having its source in the agency of local priests, but what is significant again in this French colonial situation is the date and occasion – the royal court celebration of the slaves was taking place, not at Epiphany, but on the occasion of Corpus Christi. In other words, the slaves had their celebration when the Christian calendar and the authorities allowed them to. This in itself lends support to the argument that it was the slaves' own celebration.

The royal court parade was incontestably a practice among diasporic Africans in circumstances of servitude, in Europe, Brazil, North America and the Caribbean. However it originated, the evidence shows that Africans and their descendants had a lasting attraction to it. This suggests that instead of it simply being the conscious perpetuation of a cultural tradition, it might have been basically, on the part of Africans and their descendants, a consistent psychological response to a social situation – the desire to be the social opposite to what they actually were or the need to display themselves as the converse of what they were forced to be. In Brazil, the Congo element and therefore the notion of "Africa" remained strong because of the size and pervasiveness of this African group in northeastern Brazil especially. On the other hand, in Jamaica, Trinidad, St Lucia and other Caribbean islands, where creolization was relatively more evident and where the separateness of each island tended to mask generalizations, the Africanness of the royal court parade was more difficult to perceive immediately.

From the point of view of some Europeans and whites in colonial societies, the royal court parade was a boost to their ego. In Marly's (1828, 290) estimation, it was the slaves' way of "acting" or "playing" European. Another reason for the contemporary (nineteenth-century) popularity of the royal court parade in Jamaica is that it fitted perfectly into the colonial scene with its flamboyant display of power and social hierarchy and also, paradoxically, into the continuous acculturation of the slaves, since it was interpreted as a desire on their part to reach the heights of Europeanness and to move away from Africanness.

Yet while there was this kind of favourable response to black/slave coronations and royal parades, the practice was probably never above suspicion for all whites, especially before the eighteenth century. It certainly resulted in accusations about the motives of those who participated, and led to charges, trials and executions. In the seventeenth and early eighteenth centuries, when whites were more suspicious of the intentions and motives of "Cormantee" slaves especially, intended or actual coronations were interpreted as signs of insurrection. In the 1675 slave conspiracy in Barbados, the "grand design was to choose a king, one Coffee an ancient Gold-Coast Negro, who should have been crowned . . . in a chair of state exquisitely wrought and carved after their mode" (*Great Newes* 1676, 9). In what was treated as a slave conspiracy in Antigua in 1736, a slave was "Crown'd King of the Coromantees in the presence of nearly two thousand slaves and Several White persons were Spectators of it" (cited in Gaspar 1985, 249). It is through the trial of the conspirators in the latter case that some whites became aware that coronations and ceremonial displays and dances were a part of Akan (Coromantee) culture.

The celebration of monarchy in slave galas is contradictory and paradoxical. Monarchy, in the prevailing socialist and egalitarian spirit of the day, was being called into question in Europe. It was violently removed in France, though it remained in Britain. The celebration of it by the slaves in the British colonies, financed by slave mistresses, may be interpreted as an attempt to retain and glorify the status quo. Yet slave inversions at Christmas (dressing up, parading and socializing with the masters) were in keeping with the French republican ideals of fraternity and equality, and this was in Jamaica, which was near to and influenced by revolutionary Haiti, as well as in the other French island colonies. When viewed as a continuity from Africa, the royal court parade is also ironic in that it was the very African kings who had sold their people to the Europeans and into slavery. Yet as Souza ([2001] 2006, 329) says, the royal court parade could have been a "symbol of a mythical and homogenized Africa" which the slaves constructed as a part of a common identity in a hostile environment. Thus, the slaves would have suppressed reality (that is, betrayal) in favour of a comforting fiction.

In summarizing, one has to ask the following questions: Why would imitation of a royal court parading in pomp and ceremony appeal to slaves across the Americas and why would the notion of being a King or Queen be so fascinating and abiding? In addition, if one ethnic group (Akan) or another (Congo) was the initial source of transmission of the royal court, why did its preferences become popular and dominant? The answers to these questions could not be external to the psyche of the slaves and their descendants or absent from their experience in the Americas.

Tobin, in eighteenth century St Kitts, believed that slaves in the West Indies wore clothes simply for display. He argued that their fondness for dress in the West Indies is "founded in vanity alone" and when they have an opportunity for showing it, "their passion is more for ornamental than useful covering" (1785,

62). In spite of Tobin's derisive attitude, the view of clothes as decorative more so than functional highlights an artistic view of dress that has been consistently attributed historically to the descendants of Africans in the Americas.

In the French colonial slave system, dress was not dismissed as insignificant or an unimportant element caused by vanity. Peytraud (1897, 183) reports that "an ordinance of the administration of Martinique, dated 30 May, 1776, determined that 'slaves of both sexes who took part in the parade had to wear ordinary clothes in accordance with their status'". This was the same kind of ordinance that was implemented later in Saint Domingue against the *gens de couleur*, in relation to their normal everyday wear, and helped to precipitate the revolution. Thus, "sartorial elegance" on the part of slaves and the lower classes was in most circumstances a challenge to the racial and social hierarchy: it was irksome as well as provocative. The very reaction of the slaves and the coloured to attempts to suppress expression through dress underscored its value to them.

Just before emancipation, Rolph (1836, 32) made what he considered to be a fundamental statement about slaves in Barbados: "They display a great fondness for dress, and come to the dance with a profusion of ornaments and trinkets, which you might look for in vain amongst labourers of any other countries." For him, this was a defining characteristic of the "negro character".

Resident (1828, 81), in his account of Christmas festivities in Dominica, perceptively expressed the humanizing and equalizing element of dress for the slave: "for blackey, in his way, wishes to be the very *pink of fashion*, and *to be looked at*, as well as his master or mistress". This importance of dress and the tendency to be showy and flamboyant in dress, which has been a prominent cultural feature among African descendants in the Americas, would explain the sartorial display element of the royal court parade.

"Sets" of Young Women on Show: A Display of Women's Rites

The term "set" emerged in Jamaica around 1825, overlapping with or as an alternative to "party". In its use, the word was similar linguistically to "play" in that it was an English word used to describe a colonial cultural feature and as such it brought along with it associations which were not necessarily central to its use in Jamaica and it did not highlight some that were. Writers (De La Beche 1825, 41; Barclay 1826, 11) claimed that "set" was the word used by the slaves.

Groups of girls on parade were first mentioned in 1790 by Beckford, who left Jamaica in 1777. This means that when "set" emerged as a label in the 1820s, the reality to which it referred could already have been in existence for about fifty years in one form or another. When De La Beche in 1825 and Barclay in 1826 used the term "set" or "sett", it was as if it were a fixed and accepted term, but it was not mentioned by Stewart (in 1808) or by Lewis (in reference to 1816) or by Williams (in reference to 1823). Instead, just as Beckford had done in 1790, Stewart used the word "parties" to refer to the groups of girls; Lewis also did the same and so did Williams.

From 1825 onward, both words seem to have been widely known in Jamaica even if they were not clearly separated. Waddell (1863, 17–18), referring to the 1830s, used the two words as alternatives – "two parties or 'sets' of girls". In Scott's *Tom Cringle's Log* (1862), "set" was described as if it were a component of a party. Notwithstanding the differences in definition, there was a certain consistency in the description of sets: the most consistently stated features were that a set was made up exclusively of young females and that they dressed alike. Consequently, the combination "set girl" was an equally common term.

In its most general sense in the English language, the word "set" refers to a group made up of constituents/members having one or more features in common. In contrast, in one of its specialized meanings in English, "set" refers to a dancing formation, usually involving dancers facing each other or in a square performing rehearsed movements or patterns. The usage of writers in Jamaica in the 1820s and 1830s appeared to span both the general and the specialized meanings. In reconstructing the evolution of sets, however, it is important to note that the late eighteenth-century and the early nineteenth-century Jamaican references did not associate sets with dancing – neither Beckford nor Stewart said that the girls danced. In fact, Stewart (1808, 264) said that they were selected because of their beauty and their ability to sing. Indeed, singing continued to be identified as a major feature of the set girls in the 1820s by Scott (1862, 241), who spoke of "the more mellow singing of the Set Girls".

Since neither Beckford nor Stewart used the word "set", it seems reasonable to conclude, then, that the designation "set" and the identification of the young ladies as "dancing-girls" were a simultaneous 1820s development. The most plausible way of accounting for the emergence of the word to describe the girls in Jamaica is to see it as coming out of the latest fashion in dancing in Britain, which had come over from France and found its way to Jamaica soon thereafter.

A fact that no doubt led to confusion of terms in English was that in French, the segments of the dance were called *parties de quadrille*. The French word *partie*, since it coincided in pronunciation with the English word "party", must have had some effect on the meaning of the term "party" in Jamaica, which had received a number of French-speaking refugees from Haiti. At the same time, *parties de quadrille* had been translated in English in England as "sets of quadrille" and this was the English term that was transferred to the colonies. Note, also, that French dance terms were used commonly in English. In Jamaica, therefore, the two words, "parties" and "sets", came to overlap in reference and use.

No doubt the general excitement that attended these fashionable dances in Britain, which had been brought over from the continent and in a short time found their way to the colonies, led to the application of the term "set" to the party girls in Jamaica. The party girls in Jamaica were said to parade in twos (Stewart 1808, 263; Lewis [1834] 1969, 52), which was consistent with the dance formations at the time which had two lines of dancers interacting with each other. In other words, the Lancers Quadrille, which was a specifically English and very popular variant of the quadrille in the English colonies, in one of its segments had the dancers in two columns marching like soldiers. This must have been a critical element in the development of the set girls in Jamaica. One would have to assume that, even if the party girls originally sang to the accompanying music, as a result of the influence of the Lancers Quadrille they marched/danced and in time the dancing came to supersede the singing.

Yet one may ask: "What was the model or reason for girls going on a singing/dancing parade?" There are several reasons that can be adduced, but there is no one that is overpowering. A possible model for an all-female singing group could have come out of wassailing in Britain. Stewart's choice of words ("young negresses were selected" [1808, 264]) suggests that what developed in Jamaica was a perpetuation of a tradition there, but with the twist that the only available or appropriate source for a group of young ladies to perform the ritual was among the slaves.

There is another European model deriving from the church and educational system that could have had some bearing on the evolution of all-female groups on parade. Scott (1862, 245) provided a direct comparison between the set girls and school when he said that the set on parade was "like a charity school of a Sunday, led by a rum-looking old beadle". By 1825, there were thirty-four charity schools established by British institutions throughout the West Indies and these preserved the ethos of their counterparts in Britain in that they were single-sex and, in the case of the girls, concentrated on propriety and training to be good wives. The parade, therefore, could be considered a show of achievement or a passing-out parade or a display for selection. The fact that the young ladies all carried umbrellas or parasols gives some weight to this interpretation, because the use of parasols outdoors, like the use of fans indoors, was a decidedly important factor of propriety. However, any educational model involving slaves would have become significant in the 1820s at the earliest and thus would have been an influence on and not an initial source for parties of girls in Jamaica.

Neither wassailing girls nor charity school girls on parade give a true sense of parties of girls as described by Stewart (1808, 263–65) because the prime feature in his description is "sartorial elegance". The most likely source for this was African, for several writers remarked on West African women's love of display. Indeed, it is with a Fante nubility ritual, as described by Captain John Adams (1823, 39) in the late eighteenth century, that the Jamaican parade can be best compared. It is either that the "sartorial" element of this nubility ritual was transferred to the set girls' parade or that the set girls' parade actually started out as a nubility ritual and gradually coalesced with end-of-year festivities.

The love of display among female slaves was not necessarily a borrowed or acquired feature but neither was it necessarily an element in a sex or marriage ritual. Marees ([1602] 1987, 172) conveys the idea that Fante women were fond of dancing and that they danced in groups by themselves. He went on to say that they "do not like to be watched by strangers, because they are afraid of being laughed at". Their display would therefore have to be looked at as part of their own aesthetic indulgence. With reference to the theme of symmetry, one should note that they were "keeping time with the music and one another's steps, each doing the same as the other". The uniformity in gender, dress and movement can therefore be seen as complementary features which were retained in the set girls' parade.

In contrast to the women described by Marees, there were other women who were used to entertain men as a part of social activities and especially during slaving activities. Such women were mentioned by Phillips (1732, 201) as a part of slaving activities in the Gold Coast area. Even more significant as a possible model for set girls are those mentioned in Captain John Adams's account of Benin. In this case Adams (1823, 114–15) identifies "itinerant dancing women" as a regular feature of social activities. There is no doubt that the need to entertain European men not only in the slaving ports and during the middle passage but also in plantation society in the Caribbean helped to promote the image of the woman on display.

One outdoor British festival performance which could have had some influence on the set girls' parade, as an indicator of access to whites and adoption of European culture, was morris dancing, which was typically a part of May Day celebrations. It had many variants in Britain and the manifestations of it within any one West Indian colony and across colonies would have been according to the knowledge and customs of those British people from whom the slaves acquired it. (Bear in mind that there is no actual mention of morris dancing done by whites in the colonies in any of the English accounts of the West Indies.) In many respects, morris dancing could be said to have been the obvious source for set girls. It was a festive street dance; it was a show dance or spectacle; it involved participants dressed alike; it had sets; and it was, in most cases, single-sex. The contradiction in the comparison of morris dancing with the set girls' parade is that morris dancing is widely identified almost exclusively as a dance done by men, even if sometimes they dressed as women. Moreover, in his description of a "negro party", Scott mentions "morrice dancers" (1862, 244) as separate from set girls.

Sets, therefore, can be said to have fused a number of features from a wide pool, some deriving from African and others from European traditions. What could have started in disparate ways in the 1760s as ethnic festivities among African slaves were clearly paralleled later among creole slaves of different social levels and colours on plantations and in towns across Jamaica. The most significant factor of change in the nineteenth-century, pre-emancipation period was the substantial backing provided by the white establishment for the displays. The intensity with which the plantation establishment embraced these displays must have had an element of trying to show the world and to convince themselves that their society was flourishing and healthy, especially in the face of what was seen by them as disastrous events in Saint Domingue. The image that did this best was the one they had always believed in – the various slaves dancing and singing – and in addition, now, they were well-dressed and European-like.

How the Male "Masquerader" Evolved from Grotesque to Fine

The contrast between good and bad is played out in festival celebrations in various cultures. In Europe, the contrast has a religious basis with several different manifestations, a familiar one being that between "angel" and "devil". In this contrast, "angel" is associated with female and "devil" with male. In the colonial Caribbean, the celebrations of the rites of birth, adulthood, marriage and death, which were curtailed for the slaves, were supplanted in the Christmas period by the "rights" to celebrate equality, fraternity and *joie de vivre*. In these celebrations, the set girls (female) were one side of a contrast between beautiful and ugly, with the John Connu (male) being the other.

The contrast to expensive "sartorial elegance" is valueless rags and hodgepodge, and this is precisely the picture of the earliest costumed figure that appears in the historical account. Sloane (1707, xlviii), referring to the end of the seventeenth century, described the slaves as wearing "odd things" tied to them as they danced to create a certain kind of appearance: "They have likewise in their dances rattles ty'd to their legs and wrists, and in their hands, with which they make a noise . . . They very often tie cows tails to their rumps, and add such other odd things to their bodies in several places, as gives them a very extraordinary appearance." The "very extraordinary appearance" in Sloane's description closely resembles the Cuban *kokorioko* described by Fernando Ortiz ([1951] 1981, 480):

> The kokorioko was truly a grotesque mask with formless garb; sometimes with old clothes turned inside out and generally with rags, bush, fibre of palm or "guano" and numerous ends of cloth or coloured ribbons; and sometimes hanging from the waist strings of garlic which bring to mind the skirts of fibre and grass so typical of certain African religious dances. The mask has a headpiece made of bag and cardboard, with a horrid animal face or just a frightening one, made sometimes with horse jawbones which open and shut, rattling like the jaws of a monster. . . . The kokoriokos wear rattles or cowbells around their waists and ankles which make a strange noise with every step they take.

This *kokorioko* character formed part of the Three Kings' Day parade in Havana up until 1880.

Though Sloane did not relate the wearing of these appendages to any specific occasion or festival, it is unlikely that they were just a part of weekend dancing.

In addition, although Sloane did not differentiate between males and females, subsequent descriptions suggest that these were male costumes. Therefore, one can set up, even without a direct contrast in context, an antithesis between "comely" set girls and a "grotesque" male character.

Historically, the next depiction of the "grotesque" male character is by Long in 1774. This is a much fuller but more intriguing depiction which presents the male figure with a retinue of older women as part of Christmas celebrations, although no name (like "set" or "party") is assigned to this assemblage, as if it were not a unit or cohesive:

> In the towns, during Christmas holidays, they have several tall robust fellows dressed up in grotesque habits, and a pair of ox-horns on their head, sprouting from the top of a horrid sort of vizor, or mask, which about the mouth is rendered very terrific with large boar-tusks. The masquerader, carrying a wooden sword in his hand, is followed with a numerous croud of drunken women, who refresh him frequently with a sup of aniseed-water, whilst he dances at every door, bellowing out *John Connú!* with great vehemence. (1774, 2:424–25)

The contrast is clear not only in the main figures but also in the retinue of "drunken women" here, as opposed to pretty, young girls in the sets. Long located these male African masqueraders in the towns, but no specific event is identified by name. Long does not specifically say whether they were plantation slaves who had journeyed to town or simply urban slaves.

Long's suggestion that the masqueraders were "probably an honourable memorial of John Conny" (2:424) implies that the Axim area in the Guinea Coast was their source, since that is where John Conny was from. However, in the general Congo area (from the Benin River to Cape Lopez), from which the majority of slaves came to Jamaica in the second half of the eighteenth century, similar masks are described. In other words, similarities across a wide area of West Africa suggest that the masquerader Long described was much more than a performer for a specific historical character and could well have come from the Cameroons or Congo area rather than the Gold Coast. Long (2:425) went on to say that "in 1769, several new masks appeared; the Ebos, the Papaws, &c. having their respective Connús, male and female, who were dressed in a very laughable style". The expansion can be said to corroborate the idea that such masks were common across West Africa, but the change from such descriptive adjectives as "grotesque", "horrid" and "terrific" to "laughable" indicates a difference in the appearance of these new masks.

In the general Congo area, masks were associated with circumcision rituals, boys' initiations and investiture of chiefs, among many other ceremonies and agricultural events. They are sometimes treated at the supernatural level as representations of ancestral spirits or at a simpler level as masks to frighten children. Patterson ([1967] 1973, 242–43) claims that the John Connu parade was a continuity of a traditional harvest celebration, the West African yam festival. The problem with this claim is that slaves had no compelling reason to celebrate their masters' harvest (yam, sugar or any other). It is only if they were actually celebrating the harvest on their own small plots that such a claim could have weight, or, if they were seizing every opportunity for celebration, as at the end of the sugar cane crop. Moreover, Patterson's claim would make the John Connu parade a plantation celebration rather than the urban one that Long presented it as.

Another different explanation for the John Connu parade arises out of Spanish colonial history. Long's (1774, 2:424–25) description of the Jamaican "masquerader . . . followed with a numerous croud of drunken women, who refresh him frequently" bears some resemblance to the *vejigante* followed by *locas* ("mad women") in the Loíza festival in Puerto Rico. This suggests that this parade, just like the royal court, was dispersed across different colonies. Alternatively, the resemblance may have resulted from the fact that Jamaica was directly linked culturally to Puerto Rico through its Spanish and Catholic past. However, while the group of performers in Puerto Rico includes a *caballero* (representing the Spanish), the *vejigante* (representing the Devil and the Moors), the *locas* and the *viejos* (old people), in Long's description for Jamaica it is only the equivalents of the *vejigante* and the *locas* respectively that are mentioned.

Another significant difference in Long's masquerader is that he brandishes a wooden sword. This was a part of the "terrifying" aspect of the character and contrasts with the *vejigante*, who tends to be a clown-like figure, although his devil mask may be scary to children. In spite of the differences, when the similarities between Long's John Connu band in Jamaica and Puerto Rico's *vejigante* with *locas* are taken together with Sloane's character and Cuba's *kokorioko*, the Spanish colonial source becomes a reasonable possibility.

Adding weight to the interpretation of the John Connu figure as a variant of the *vejigante* (Devil/Moor) is a view that Moorish (Islamic) influence could have come into the slave trade and into Jamaica from what is now northern Nigeria. If what Long interpreted to be John Connu could possibly have been *jinn Kano* "Kano devil", that is, a devil figure from Kano, in northern Nigeria, where Islam is the dominant religion, then it would not be necessary to route the figure through Spanish heritage. The word *jinn* (devil) is Arabic and the devil figure has a long history in Arabic literature. For example, in the 1390 work *Kitab al-Bulhan* there are a number of devil figures represented with horns which bear a resemblance to the John Connu and *kokorioko* figures.

It is possible also that the bull mask or horned masquerader came into Jamaica, in the early years of English rule, through the Leeward Islands where the bull has remained up to today a prominent feature of masquerade, in St Kitts and Antigua especially. In this scenario, one can argue that the cow-horn mask came from the more western areas of West Africa where cattle raising was normal and where the cow-horn mask was characteristically used. Here, as elsewhere, these masks were used in initiation ceremonies for boys or adolescents passing into manhood. The earliest West African example of this kind of mask is given by François Froger in a 1698 pictorial representation titled *Habillement des Circoncis* ("what the circumcised wore").

An anonymous Irish account of Christmas festivities in Kingston about ten years after Long's gave a different picture of "barbarous" costumes, one that featured urban tradesmen – tailors, fishermen, coopers, butchers and boatmen – with women by themselves providing rhythmic accompaniment:

> You cannot conceive any place more merry than the town of Kingston; at Christmas, the Negroes celebrate a kind of Saturnalia, and run about the streets in odd dresses, made up of taylor's shreds and patches; the fishermen have a fellow dressed up with nets and fish; the coopers roll an empty sugar hogshead through the streets, and at the doors of their owners customers, beat on it, in a kind of barbarous measure with their adzes, and other tools; the butchers dress up two or three fellows in cows hides, and by cracking their whips in a strange sort of concert, keep time to their singing and dancing; the wharf Negroes dance about, carrying chains, which they clank, "in transport and rude harmony. (Anon. Irish 1776, 61)

This version of the festivities in town is more comprehensive, probably more evolved and clearly shaped by the occupational structure of urban slavery. In other words, it is more creole or Caribbean than Long's, which features a single group described as African. The fact that tradesmen were higher-level slaves suggests that there was clear social distinction in the festivities in town, or that there was European influence in the featuring of trades, or that the absence from town of entities like gangs and plantations meant that the organization of the festivities had to be intrinsically different. It is obvious that the writer's reference to "Saturnalia" here had to do with slaves having fun and not with inversion (that is, sartorial elegance).

Fifty years after Long's description, the John Connu parade was augmented by Phillippo (1843, 242–43), who unabashedly used Long's text, just making some additions to it. The fulsome repetition of Long's words casts doubt on Phillippo's veracity as well as on the accuracy of same picture for 1829, some seventy years after it was first given. It is Phillippo's additions that are of greater interest, as they indicate that by that time the character had come to be called John Connu, that there was an accompanying musical band and that children were a part of the retinue.

By the second decade of the nineteenth century, the John Connu mask not only had become a headdress mask (that is, worn on top of the head) but also had changed to suit the name it had acquired in Jamaica. Monk Lewis's ([1834] 1969, 51) description of it in 1816 in Black River was as follows: "The John-Canoe is a Merry-Andrew dressed in a striped doublet, and bearing upon his head a kind of pasteboard house-boat." In other words, some time before 1820, "Connu" was being interpreted to be "canoe", a kind of houseboat. In 1823, Williams (1826, 25) confirmed this definition: "a man dressed up in a mask with a grey beard and long flowing hair, who carried the model of a house on his head. The house is called the Jonkanoo." Yet he still went on to refer to the person wearing the headdress as the Jonkanoo. Williams also cited an interpretation of it as "the sacred boat/dove" and the person wearing it as Noah (26). So, the character was now Noah, being portrayed "with a grey beard and long flowing hair", with an ark on his head. As to Marly (1828, 293) a couple years later, he spelled the name as "Canoe" and assumed that it meant a canoe: "John very prudently carried a small imitation of a canoe into which he and his wife ... danced without intermission." Waddell (1863, 17), in his account, which described activities on the north coast of Jamaica in 1829, spoke of young men parading the estates and "carrying a fanciful and gaily-painted structure, called a 'Johnny Canoe'".

Judging from Lewis, Williams, Marly and Waddell in different parts of Jamaica, by 1830 "John Canoe" was quite different from "John Connu" that Long had described: it was no longer the ugly half of an aesthetic antithesis. Yet while the appearance of the mask changed, a fundamental feature of the character remained – the display of dancing. Williams (1826, 25) stated plainly that "the bearer of it [the Jonkanoo] is generally chosen for his superior activity in dancing". To this Marly (1828, 293) added singing: "and all the while singing, or, in more correct language, roaring an unintelligible jargon, in true stentorian voices". In effect, the Jonkanoo had become musically much closer to the set girls. In Marly's description, the hideous mask (of Long) had disappeared and the characters seemed to see themselves more as comic actors (293–94). By now, in the years just before emancipation, the antithetical figure dressed in rags and wearing a horrible mask had been transformed in appearance to become more like a character in a play.

It is with Belisario (1837) that the visual representation of John Connu is associated in the years immediately after emancipation. By this time there was further change and diversification in John Connu and religious significance was no longer given to the costume. In addition to the houseboat John Connu, there was what Belisario called the "Actor-Boy". The actor, as a character in Christmas and other festivals, was not restricted to Jamaica; there were also actors in St Kitts. The putting on of warrior scenes from English literature, which the Actor-Boys in Jamaica did, was also characteristic of the Leeward Islands, Grenada, Carriacou and Trinidad. These warrior scenes are always explained as extensions of British mumming tradition, but in Jamaica, the character called Actor-Boy emerged out of or was closely related to the John Connu. This suggests some degree of amalgamation of the two traditions.

De La Beche (1825, 42) was one of the first to identify the character that later came to be called the Actor-Boy in his depiction of "a couple personages fantastically dressed to represent kings or warriors; one of them wore a mask on his face, and part of the representation has evidently some reference to the play of Richard the Third". In his presentation of these "personages", De La Beche mentions both "our Mummers and African amusements" like "Joncanoe" without any separation of the two. In Barclay's (1826, 13) account, the connection with John Connu is directly stated: "The Joncanoe-men, disrobed of part of their paraphernalia, were the two heroes, and fought not for a kingdom but a queen, whom the victor carried off in triumph." In Belisario's (1837, n.p.) comments on the Actor-Boy character, he identified it as a "class of John-Canoe". It seems somewhat ironic, nevertheless, that the two versions of the Actor-Boy he painted looked more like Aztec or other Amerindian "chiefs" than either African or European kings or warriors and the remarkable fact is that he said not a word about them and what they represented. He did explain, however, that by 1836 when he drew the costumes the Actor-Boys who were still in existence in Jamaica had "to content themselves annually with the public exhibition of their finery, and the performance of certain unmeaning pantomimic actions" (n.p.).

A simple comparison of Long's 1774 masquerader and either the House John Connu or the Actor-Boy shows the complete transformation of the costume and the role of the player. It was essentially a removal of all visible African features from the character.

Extending British Popular Culture in the Caribbean

In the historical literature, several writers compared slave performances to British mumming (for example, Stewart 1808, 252; De La Beche 1825, 41–42; Scott 1862, 244; Bayley 1830, 480). Yet no writer mentioned outdoor folk performances involving mumming being done by whites in the West Indies and there is no evidence that May Day, with which these performances are usually associated, was a celebrated event in the slave plantation colonies. One is therefore left to wonder how and when the transfer of these May Day features took place.

It is the absence of documented white lower-class models in the Caribbean that caused Abrahams (1967, 461–62) to guess about the process of transfer of "European peasant traditions". Elsewhere, Abrahams (1970b, 172) surmises why some features were acquired and not others: "But these would not have become established were there not elements in the situation of Negroes on Nevis which made the British entertainments intelligible and appropriate." Here Abrahams's explanation is limited to "the Negroes on Nevis", but the same would have applied to continuities not only in other Caribbean islands but also in North America.

Another way to account for British mumming traditions among Caribbean slaves is to posit direct transmission through British colonists of the ruling class. While describing the carnival of the ruling class in Grenada, Bayley (1830, 480) made reference to "a masked group of negro boys and girls, who danced for a while, after the fashion of the chimney sweeps on the first of May". Since the mumming traditions in Britain already included "blacks" as participants, what developed in the West Indies may have been an extension of this. In other words, (British-born) slave masters and mistresses, in endeavouring to continue ancestral traditions, could have chosen suitable slaves, put them in costumes and instructed them about their roles.

It is more difficult to account for the "literary" element of mumming. Since schooling for slaves was sporadic or non-existent and few of them could read or had access to books to read on their own, knowledge of select English literary pieces (recited in mummers' plays) would have had to come through specific and deliberate acts of coaching.

Dramatic performances were a part, even if sporadic, of white Caribbean society and farce was the most popular genre. Slaves witnessed them, participated and, according to observers, enjoyed them. It is quite likely that they reproduced their own versions of plays or parts of them for their own amusement, just as they did with foreign songs, and this must have flourished when they received pleasing reactions from whites. Also, dramatic presentations could have come out of religious drama used in informal religious education. Rote learning was a normal technique in religious education and on some slave plantations where priests and missionaries were allowed to operate, slaves were able to memorize a number of psalms and hymns and other religious material. Learning selections from Christmas and Easter plays would have been a logical extension of religious education, intended to bring the Gospel to life.

Barclay (1826, 13) boldly declared that he did not know how the slaves in their Christmas performances were able to perform scenes from Shakespeare. Bearing in mind that at that point Barclay had been in Jamaica for twenty-one years, this ignorance was astonishing. It suggests that the slaves' knowledge had been acquired in some mysterious or clandestine manner. Yet the method of transfer could not have been as mysterious as Barclay made it out to be. In the case of the people in Black River in Jamaica whom Monk Lewis spoke of, circumstantial evidence suggests that it was the power behind the "Blue Girls", Miss Edwards, who was responsible for the slaves' performances. Therefore, it must have been a case of Miss Edwards's slaves attending the plays and then rehearsing the scenes for the occasion, which would mean that they were coached by Miss Edwards herself or by someone who knew or had the text and could perform it.

Some similar process must have taken place in the case of the scenes from *Richard III*, which both De La Beche (1825, 42) and Barclay (1826, 12–13) recorded as having been performed by slaves in other parts of Jamaica around the same period, one done at Easter and the other at Christmas. The popularity of this entertainment in the rural areas means that it was not secretive and had to have the backing and input of plantation whites.

About twelve years after De La Beche and Barclay wrote, Belisario, without expressly saying so, sought to clear up a number of points which these two writers did not seem to understand. Presumably in response to Barclay's declaration of ignorance of the way in which slaves came to be acting scenes from Shakespeare, Belisario (1837, n.p.) said: "a negro who could *read*, and instruct them in committing their parts to memory, was pressed into service for the purpose ... for the four or five weeks so occupied, previous to the Christmas Holidays, at which period, the effect of his labours was manifested to a wondering and admiring audience". He also identified where the selections were taken from: "'Richard the Third' was a favorite Tragedy with them; but *selections* only were made from it ... Pizarro was also one of their Stock pieces; but whatever might have been the performance, a Combat and Death invariably ensued" (1837, n.p.).

Belisario's idea that it was the slaves' shortcomings that led to illogicalities in their presentations only reveals his ignorance, for he seemed to be unaware that the preferred scenes (that is, combat, death, resuscitation) were a part of the mumming tradition and that the slaves' performances were similar to those in Britain. Belisario was not a cursory observer; he was careful and knowledgeable, as illustrated in his depiction of typical elements in the mumming tradition (for example, milkmaids, chimney sweepers, Jack-in-the-green) in Jamaica. It is the very "accuracy" of the mumming in the Jamaican performances that makes Belisario's interpretation mystifying. It is even more so when it is noted that the morris tradition and combat, death, resuscitation performances were also popular in St Kitts and other islands.

As to the slaves' acting in the plays, however it was intended, whites regarded it as hilarious and laughable, according to Bayley (1830, 481–82). The slaves themselves no doubt wanted their performances to be liked, probably to produce mirth, but for them they were not frivolous: they were a means of increasing their valuation in the eyes of whites in the real, everyday world.

SLAVES DRESSED UP AND PARADING LIKE SOLDIERS AND SAILORS

The most potent use of colours in the colonial plantation society was the terms used to make racial divisions, that is white, black and brown or yellow. The most dominant presence of colours, of course, was in the tropical vegetation of the Caribbean, the fauna, the seascape, the sky and the dramatic changes of light. White, however, was the dominant colour worn by slaves, especially females, when they dressed up. Dressing up in bright colours, such as red and blue, was a departure from the normal, imposed, drab colours. Dressing up in bright colours, as in parades, could have been an expression of preference in dress or an attempt to match the ambient environment, or it could have been that the bright colours were due to other topical factors.

The wearing of bright colours was most likely not a continuity from West Africa because in those societies, at that time, upper-body clothing with colours was not documented as normal and widespread for the general population, but at the same time the trade in cloth seemed to suggest that fabric was a commodity in high demand. Thomas (1997, 317) states that "the cargo carried by most slave traders, and most sought after in Africa . . . was cloth". In addition, according to Thomas, "the Africans merely treated European cloth with their own dyes to make the bright products which European traders were then able to sell in, for example, Barbados".

In the Caribbean, the slaves had no control over the cloth or colour of clothes they were given. As slaves in the West Indies, the most common material they wore was osnaburg, a coarse, inexpensive linen which came usually in brown, blue and white. It is most probable, then, that one reason for the bright colours was that whenever they made their own choice, those who could afford it opted for a contrast with the everyday colours of slavery. Marsden (1788, 39), for instance, while discussing women dressing up to attract men's attention, noted that "in common they are fond of red and blue calamanco for petticoats".

There is not much evidence that high symbolic value was attached to specific colours in West Africa at the time, but Thomas (1997, 317) says that "people in the region of Guinea preferred white cloth, those in Angola blue". In this general situation of nondescript textile colours, it is noticeable that writers consistently identified two colours (red and blue) when they mentioned set girls in Jamaica (for example, Beckford 1790, 389; Stewart 1808, 263; Williams 1826, 62). The apparently sudden salience of red and blue is therefore striking.

By and large, explanations of the two colours had to do with political divisions. One was a division among the British themselves into a contrast between the (red) English and the (blue) Scottish; one was an explanation related to Jamaica specifically, where refugees who fled the revolution in Saint Domingue (Haiti) and established themselves in Jamaica created their own blue "French" set to contrast with the red set that was already there. The other explanation was a straightforward contrast between the European political rivals in the Caribbean, the English (red) and the French (blue). The fact that the Irish wore green in their St Patrick's Day parade in Montserrat (see chapter 4) supports such political and national explanations of the colours.

Barclay did not report the colours in the same way that others did; evidently, by his time there was no straightforward contest between reds and blues. Barclay's (1826, 11–12) mention of "Yellow Girls, &c" cannot be dismissed lightly because he was a long-time resident of Jamaica. In other words, "Yellow Girls" could have been just another set in a context where red and blue had lost any earlier significance.

There is a considerable amount of evidence pointing to military uniforms as the inspiration for the two set girl colours, red and blue, from the last quarter of the eighteenth century onward. The changes in colonial masters wrought by the treaties of 1783, 1797 and 1815 were of fundamental importance to the British Crown, but for the people, especially the ruling class, in the British West Indies the military victories were about them and their importance. No doubt, they were played out in the streets of Jamaica in the costumes, with rivals represented as blues and reds.

The military figures of the last quarter of the eighteenth century and the first quarter of the nineteenth were prominent in the minds of the general public as they tried to come to terms with political and social changes. When Rodney scored a great victory over the French in 1782, he had a statue erected in Jamaica and was celebrated as a great saviour. At the Battle of Trafalgar in 1805, Nelson was fatally wounded but emerged as the hero and had a statue erected in Barbados. In 1815, Britain and its allies under Wellington defeated Napoleon at Waterloo. Wellington was celebrated in song in the end-of-year festivities in Jamaica (Lewis [1834] 1969, 79–80), and groups in Jamaica, St Lucia and Trinidad were identified as "girls of Waterloo", "Wadeloes" and "Wartloos" respectively.

By the beginning of the nineteenth century, Britain's foe, France, and its former colony, Saint Domingue, had been transformed by revolutions, as a result of which many refugees entered Jamaica from the French world. So in Jamaica in the 1830s, according to Belisario (1838, n.p.), there were three sets of French Set Girls (whose colour was blue), named Royalists, Mabiales and Americans respectively. The Royalists were "Creoles of St Domingo", the Mabiales were "Africans from Congo" and the Americans were "a portion of both". Clearly, the *sets* chose names reflecting the political climate of the day and consistent with their ethnicity and self-image. Although they were all slaves of French proprietors who had fled revolutionary Haiti, their self-images were different from each other. The mulatto house slaves (the Royalists) saw themselves as sympathizers with the monarchy or the *ancien régime*, the Americans seemed to represent independent New World people, and the Mabiales seemed to put themselves in the position of the new rulers of Haiti.

In contrast to this explanation of reds and blues which revolves around the endless battles between the British and the French, Lewis ([1834] 1969, 53), in a localized explanation, related it to high society rivalry of the past between an English admiral (red) and a Scottish one (blue) who superseded him, vying to see who could set "forth their processions with the greatest taste and magnificence when both of them gave balls at Kingston to the 'Brown Girls'". Without conceding any importance to Lewis's high-society explanation, it is possible that social friction between the English and the Scottish over a long period of time could have manifested itself when plantations owners especially wanted to highlight their ethnicity through their slaves.

It was not only between the Scottish and the English that there was friction that had to do with colours but also between "liberated" Africans and slaves. Liberated Africans were "commonly black Africans, who have been taken in slave ships, and either kept in the service of the Government, or bound out as apprentices for the term of seven years, to be declared free at the expiration of that period" (Bayley 1833, 455–46). The liberated African felt himself to be superior to the plantation slave, according to Joseph ([1838] 1970, 263), he "looked . . . contemptuously on the planter's slave". The same view of the African soldier as superior to other blacks seemed to persist even after emancipation, for in the middle of the century Day (1852, 1:284) expressed this view clearly: "the black troops (being native Africans) have no sympathies in common with the colonial negroes. They are, on the contrary, extremely proud of wearing a red coat, and of being 'Queen Victoria's soldiers'." The African soldier on parade in a red coat during the period of slavery must have been an enviable sight for the creole slave, and it could have been this provocative picture of the African soldier in a red coat that inspired colour rivalry in the slave parades.

What was significant about set girls in Jamaica is that (1) the girls were dressed alike, (2) they all wore the same colours, (3) they were accompanied by a band, (4) they were preceded by flags and (5) they paraded in a kind of regimental formation. It is the combination of features that made them stand out and gave them a military aspect. Several writers stressed "marching" or "parading" in formation – Stewart (1808, 264), Lewis ([1834] 1969, 51–52), De La Beche (1825, 41), Williams (1826, 25) and Marly (1828, 293). In the same way that the military is noted for uniforms, so too were sets noted for uniformity in dress. Not only is the idea of uniformity repeatedly mentioned but it is also repeatedly explained. Almost all descriptions of set girls identified dress as their unifying factor. Stewart (1808, 264) referred to the girls as being "uniform in dress"; Barclay (1826, 11) said, "they dress exactly in uniform"; and Scott (1862, 245) spoke of them as "always preserving the uniformity of dress".

Williams (1826, 22) gave some idea of the slaves' view of dressing up and military uniforms: "They were all dressed in their best; some of the men in long-tailed coats, and one of the gombayers in old regimentals." Carmichael (1833, 1:157) noted some slaves' attraction to regimental uniforms: "such people often sell the estate's clothing, and purchase a red coat from the garrison, after it has become too shabby for the soldier". Scott (1862, 241), in his description of the John Canoe, said: "His coat was an old blue artillery-uniform one, with a small bell hung to the extreme points of the swallow-tailed skirts, and three tarnished epaulets, one on each shoulder." Belisario (1837, n.p.), in his description of the House John-Canoe, underlines the priority given to the military features of the costume: "His regimental coat and sash, are invariably retained, whatever changes may take place in the other parts of his costume." Clearly, then, the various military uniforms and their colours became a part of the sartorial imagination of the slaves and provided a template for costumes worn in street processions.

International, national (British) and local (West Indian) military factors all contributed to the emergence of reds and blues, but the most prominent contributory factor was the division in the military establishment itself – the contrast between the regiments and the navy. This is where the distinction between red and blue had always been most visible to the slaves – the soldiers in the regiments wore red and the sailors in the navy wore blue. Although, for military people, there was a distinction in terminology between army and navy positions, in the slave parades there was a mixture of terminology. Explicit instructions about formation for the set girls' parade are given by Belisario (1837, n.p.), followed by his comments on the "jumble" of terminology:

ORDER OF PROCESSION OF THE SET-GIRLS

Four Grand Masters, to protect the Set.

Adjutant bearing Flag.   Hand-drum. Singer. Tambourine. Violin. Queen. Triangle. Maam. Hand-drum. **Adjutant bearing Flag.**

Commodore.

Set-Girls in equal numbers.   Set-Girls in equal numbers.

Jack-in-the-Green.

In reference to the various titles (Grand-master, Adjutant, Commodore), Belisario commented that "no satisfactory reason has ever been assigned, for the jumble of naval, military, and other distinctions, bestowed on these Commanders". No doubt, the slaves, like most lay-persons, were attracted by the colour, appearance and suitability of a uniform as well as the sound of a title, and may have been unaware of or not interested in distinctions between army and navy titles.

Trinidad "regiments", though there is no description of them parading publicly, had some similarities of nomenclature with the set girls in Jamaica. The official report on them said: "It is also to be observed that they had adopted different degrees of rank, such as *Generals en Chef, Generals en Seconde, Ambassadors, Colonels, Aid-de-Camps, Majors, Prime Ministers, Treasurers, Grand Judges, Secretaries, Alguazils*, &c." (*Barbados Mercury and Bridgetown Gazette*, 1 February 1806). It is true, however, that these titles were both governmental and military. A comment by James (1963, 93–94) on happenings during the Haitian Revolution sheds some light on this predilection: "Like their more educated white masters, the slaves hastened to deck themselves with all the trappings and titles of the military profession. The officers called themselves generals, colonels, marshals, commanders." There was clearly a strong appeal in the image of military power and its trappings.

The colours (red and blue) worn by the girls in the sets had little to do with the African heritage of the slaves. They were symbolic of rivalry, between England and France, between the English and the Scottish and between the regiments and the navy. At the time when Lewis was describing the parade in Jamaica (1816) the military battles between the English and French had just reached their culmination. In the years following, nationalistic sentiment must have declined, even though military presence did not. So, the colours red and blue presumably no longer had their former significance for the "slave gala". In St Lucia, social and political changes had their consequences and Breen's (1844, 189) comments about "societies" indicated a move away from military and political preoccupations. Nevertheless, Belisario's description of the "order of procession of the set-girls" in 1837 in Jamaica still made it seem very military. This attraction to the trappings of the military as well as its pomp, ceremony and parades was typical of the colonies. One of the most durable examples of this kind of quasi-military, folk "institutions" is the Landship in Barbados, which has survived up to today. In the final analysis, however, it is reasonable to conclude that, for the slaves, even if they had been sucked into colonial military pageantry and its colours and thus the appearance of power and honour, their colourful performance (in red and blue) moved them away from the drab dress of slavery and made them more festive, self-confident and cohesive.

Slave Parades: Country versus Town

"Country", when it is opposed to "town", is usually associated with conservatism and backwardness. In the sugar plantation Caribbean, which had elements of feudal organization, the plantation was the heart of the economy because it was there the sugar was made that was transported to the town for shipment overseas. The cultural features that transferred from Africa and Europe to the sugar colonies in the Caribbean were remoulded there by a situation in which there was a dependency relationship between country (plantation) and town, which itself was being affected by international developments.

In Europe, through the Industrial Revolution, the town and movement to the town increasingly began to dominate society. What was happening in the colonies was therefore consistent with this. Growth through education and literacy, on the one hand, and, on the other, the build-up of military forces and the display of military might in either the consolidation of empire or the pursuit of political independence in the Americas began to convert towns into what Marly (1828, 289) called "the polar stars of attraction". Soldiers on routine assignments or executing military parades in towns, slaves parading the streets of towns at Christmas, slaves journeying to market in towns, all contributed to the image of the colonial town. Market day in the Caribbean during slavery can be described as an occasion on which slaves journeyed from their various estates and came together in a town area ostensibly to trade. It was an event which, over time, developed into a major social gathering during which displays of all types became the norm and gave the town colour and vivacity. The image of the colony in the early nineteenth century could not be presented as one of with the plantation as the absolute centre. The slaves were coming to town.

Somewhat in contrast to the country-to-town movement, which glamorized the town, was the maroon party or rural feast in which whites, usually from an urban area, went on an excursion to spend a pleasurable time in the countryside. The country, usually associated with the ravages of sugar production, thus became pastoral and bucolic in the minds of urban people. The slaves themselves had their own version of this. End-of-year slave celebrations involved a journey and gathering, but they were different from market day for the plantation slaves in that they were events during which singing and dancing took place along the journey as well as at the gathering at the end. In descriptions of these end-of-year festivities, most writers focused on the journey or procession rather than the gathering at the end: it was as if for some later writers it was principally a parade during which parties would make one or more stops to interact with bystanders or specific people. However, Beckford's (1790, 390–91) early description in Jamaica presented it as people going to a feast and from the point of view of someone living on a plantation.

Brunias's painting titled *A Negro Festival drawn from nature in the island of St Vincent*, which was reproduced in Bryan Edwards's account of the West Indies, intended to capture this kind of image described by Beckford. This gathering closely resembled the maroon parties of whites described by Singleton in Barbados and Lanaghan in Antigua. If the literary prominence given by Singleton truly reflects the actual prominence it had in colonial society, then it is reasonable to suppose that the slaves, having experienced it repeatedly as slaves, would have reproduced some features of it in their own end-of-year festivities.

Bear in mind, however, that images of "picturesque and pleasing groups" (Beckford 1790, 391) of slaves have always been subject to the charge of being propaganda, consistent with the general intention of the local colonial establishment to "rectify" the picture of "cruel oppression" (Barclay 1826, 13) that was being used to fuel the move towards emancipation. This charge was not just constantly topical but very much in the mind of Barclay (1826, 13–14) when he made the following challenge: "the description I have given of a *sett*, may appear a picture altogether imaginary: but let such persons ask any one, who has been upon a Jamaica plantation at Christmas time, if the description is not correct".

The divide in West Indian colonial societies between town and country, between males and females, between blacks and browns and between creoles and Africans virtually guaranteed that there would be diversity in manifestations of slave excursions. Of course, writers reported on these events according to where they were at the time and what they happened to see, which added to the diversity. For instance, while Beckford (1788) only mentioned parties on the estates, Long (1774) around the same time spoke only of male masqueraders in the towns. In contrast, Waddell (1863, 17–18), more than fifty years later, made it seem as if male masked players belonged to the estates while groups of young women competed against each other in the towns.

Barclay (1826, 11–12) was one of the few writers who did not make the celebrations on the estates seem inferior and, in fact, his description was virtually the only one in which there was an amalgamation of the various components on the estate:

> The young girls . . . always have with them in their excursions, a fiddle, drum, and tambourine, frequently boys playing fifes, a distinguishing flag which is waved on a pole, and generally some fantastical figure, or toy, such as a castle or tower, surrounded with mirrors. . . . they have always one or two Joncanoe-men, smart youths, fantastically dressed, and masked so as not to be known. Thus equipped, and generally accompanied by some friends, they proceed to the neighbouring plantation villages, and always visit the master's or manager's house, into which they enter without ceremony, and where they are joined by the white people in a dance. . . . A party of forty or fifty young girls thus attired, with their hair braided over their brows, beads round their necks, and gold ear-rings, present a very interesting and amusing sight, as they approach a house dancing, with their music playing, and Joncanoe-men capering and playing tricks. . . . the whole sett joins in the chorus as they mingle in the dance, waving their handkerchiefs over their heads. All is life and joy, and certainly it is one of the most pleasing sights that can be imagined.

In this wholesome description by Barclay, one gets the impression that the parade was under the control of the slaves themselves as they proceeded among their own in the plantation villages. This "country" celebration was one by and for the slaves. Within urban areas, the structure of the event, as described by Williams (1826, 62–63), was basically the same as elsewhere – a procession followed by a gathering, not under a tree or in the woods but at an appropriate house.

It was perhaps inevitable that celebrations in the town would come to overshadow those in the country. In the early nineteenth century, Stewart (1808, 263–65) contrasted towns and estates, according superiority to the former: "On new year's day it was customary for the negro girls of the towns (who conceive themselves far superior to those on the estates, in point of *taste, manners, and fashion*) to exhibit themselves in all pride of gaudy splendour." Twenty years later, Marly (1828, 289) asserted that "the towns are the polar stars of attraction to the vicinities around them" and he contrasted this with "the monotonous routine of a country life". Belisario (1837) also showed the typical direction and time lapse in the spread of influence when he said that costumes used in town one year were disposed of in the country to be used there the following year.

The country/town contrast, the male/female contrast and the old-fashioned/modern contrast were all symptomatic of the distinction between African identity and creole identity as well as lower and higher status among the slaves. Parties reflected social level. Most of the indicators in the descriptions point to this and, more so than most, the support accorded the set girls by "browns" and "whites" and the absence of such support for the John Connu. The value system embedded in the white-to-black colour scale, and, within that, the creole-to-African scale, is implicit in the following description by Stewart (1808, 263–65): "The most comely young negroes were selected, and such as had a fine and tutored voice . . . they generally sung together different songs which they had learned for the occasion, or those which they had caught up from the whites, in a style far superior to the negresses on the plantations. Their appearance, in short, was splendid, elegant, and tasteful, such as would surprise and delight a stranger." Williams's (1826, 62–63) comment on the selection process also corroborates this value system.

The criteria used in making selections and choices among the slaves were consonant with white colonial values and the majority of slaves gradually embraced them. The result was that this acculturation process caused the slaves' own traditional activities to decline, as is evident in the following observation by De La Beche (1825, 42): "The various African amusements, in which the negroes formerly took so much delight, are not now kept up with spirit, and Joncanoe himself is getting out of fashion." Speaking about the slaves as people, Marly (1828, 290) was even more explicit about the perception of change:

> The appearance of a number of blacks, of both sexes, thus habited, shewed better than would be generally conceived. The glossy deep black, when one is a little accustomed to it, looks well – the features and forms of numbers of the females were more European than African, and among the males, numerous figures were to be observed, that, for manly strength and proportions, might be placed in comparison with the great portion of white people.

Such praise for being more white no doubt began to resound in the ears of some slaves who consequently redoubled their efforts to effect the cultural "amelioration" process.

The fundamental element of the colonial (hierarchical) power structure that came to characterize slave parades was separation according to racial features and economic status. In reference to groups, Beckford (1790, 391–92) specifically remarked: "though a general resemblance of colour and features may be thought at a little distance to prevail, – yet the most common observer will, upon a near inspection, perceive a very striking discrimination of both". This element is also highlighted in Scott's (1862, 245) version of sets: "There were brown sets, and black sets, and sets of all the intermediate gradations of colour. ... But the colours were never blended in the same set; no blackie ever interloped with the browns, nor did the browns in any case mix with the sables, always keeping in mind, black *woman* – brown *lady*." Belisario (1837, n.p.) presented the separation in a slightly different way in speaking about those who came from Haiti: "They formed themselves into three Bands or Sets at Christmas. ... The former was composed wholly of Creoles of St Domingo, who considered themselves on that account of the highest grade – the 2d, of Africans from Congo, and the latter of a portion of both."

Since appropriate behaviour was an index of social status, sets differed in what they did or did not do during the procession. Belisario (1837, n.p.) points out that "there is another Set, denominated 'House-Keepers', who never dance in their progress through the streets". This was because, according to observers of taste and decorum, it was "derogatory to dance elsewhere than in dwelling-houses, or within walled premises". Of course, "house-keepers" were those brown females who managed the affairs in the house and were close to the master.

As the towns expanded as "artistic" centres of attraction, the streets became the domain of the lower classes. Whites had their carnival indoors; the slaves and former slaves had theirs in the open air, in the streets of towns and where they could be generally seen. Those who had them indoors intended to be sophisticated and exclusive and to be like the whites in the society.

"The Carnival Is Dead! Long Live the Carnival!"

In 1837, Isaac Belisario spoke of "the by-gone days of merriment in Jamaica, when the streets were thronged ... and the scene might not inaptly have been styled a *Tropical Carnival*" (n.p.). Although it seems odd to identify Jamaica as the location of the first carnival of the people in the Caribbean, the fact is that this is exactly where it was. In contrast to other islands where (pre-Lenten) carnival changed from an upper-class affair to a people's event and prospered, in Jamaica, Christmas and end-of-year festivities started with the slaves and became more grand and urbanized up until after emancipation before they declined.

Belisario (1837, n.p.) attributed the decline of carnival in Jamaica to what he called "the powerful influence of the *March of Intellect*". He went on to say: "Some few tribes of Africans, may still be found enjoying their song and dance to the *Gumbay*, after the manner of their native country, but such instances are rare". Belisario's association of the "Tropical Carnival" with African customs was typical for his day, and his claim that it had virtually disappeared was also a typical response to the criticism by abolitionists that nothing had been done for the improvement of Africans and their descendants. The decline of the Tropical Carnival for him therefore meant that the descendants of Africans had become intellectually brighter and socially more sophisticated.

Claims of decline as a result of "progress" and missionary work have to be taken cautiously because end-of-year festivities among the slaves were never universal and regular. Some evidence of this comes from Stewart (1808, 264–65), who already in his time, was talking about decline: "This spirit of emulation, in these parties, for finery and shew, is, however, less prevalent now than it used to be. For some years back, no exhibitions have taken place." Overall, festivities had an up-and-down existence.

As with any kind of show, a critical factor in staging the Tropical Carnival from year to year was economic. As several writers observed (Lewis [1834] 1969, 56–57; De La Beche 1825, 41; Williams 1826, 26; Marly 1828, 294), collecting money was the main objective of some participants and it was done in haphazard ways. Most likely, the amounts collected varied considerably from one performer to another according to their acts. In general, the money that performers received could hardly have lasted from one year to the next and it was probably not intended to. It is not surprising, then, that in cases where the slaves had to provide their own outfits, it led to pilferage and robbery (Stewart 1808, 265). To control such practices, slave owners did sometimes provide funds.

More substantial financial support for the slaves came as a result of vanity and competitiveness among the ruling class. One consequence of white men keeping slave women is that they had to provide for them to the extent, in some cases, that they were treated as special: "These beau-girls . . . are the mistresses of the overseers and other white men, who think they cannot be too lavish in adorning their persons" (*Short Journey* 1790, 89). In the triangular relationship that ensued, the women used some of the money they were given to provide for their own men: "the beau-men are the favourites of the beau-girls, who secretly furnish them at the expence of their keepers" (90).

Even in cases where no sexual relationships were involved, owners still wanted their slaves to look better than those on other plantations, as Stewart (1808, 264–65) observed: "These girls were wont to be decked out with much taste, sometimes at the expence of their white or brown mistresses, who took a pride in shewing them off to the greatest advantage." De La Beche (1825, 42) gave a good indication of the actual cost of some of the components of outfits (and note that he was speaking of girls on the estates): "Their dresses on these occasions are very often very expensive, hats cost a doubloon (sixteen dollars) and blue or white kid shoes at fifteen shillings per pair are by no means uncommon; those that wish to be particularly smart carry parasols."

Lewis ([1834] 1969, 53) identified what seemed to be a further expansion of financial support beyond the direct provision for the outfits of the slaves: "This year, several gentlemen in the neighbourhood of Black River had subscribed very largely towards the expenses of the show." Around the end of the first quarter of the century, Marly (1828, 295) seemed to confirm this kind of support: "It is almost unnecessary to say, that the expenses of these amusements are contributed by the opulent among the white and brown population – the negroes contributing very little among themselves." Thus, the shows and the queen contests specifically came to be fostered and financed by whites (and probably some coloureds), who used the slaves as surrogates in their in-group rivalries. It is the shift in focus from the doings of the field slaves on the estates to those of the domestic slaves and town slaves that promoted the financial role of the establishment in the sustenance of the galas.

Conspicuous wealth was an important measure of standing among creoles in colonial Caribbean society, so much so that it bred vicious competitiveness. Lewis gave an amusing account of the competition in 1816 (between Miss Edwards of the blue party and her opponent of the red party) in which he referred to "the scornful animosity and spirit of depreciation" (Lewis [1834] 1969, 53) that Miss Edwards expressed towards the rival and the reverse. Marly (1828, 292–93) did the same later, identifying the nature of the competition between three combatants: "and as each of these three ladies had expected to have their favourite slave better and more richly dressed than the others, Miss Strutt formed a subject of envy to those who proved unsuccessful". It is not surprising, then, that after emancipation, when there were no longer any captive surrogates and whites had to find other ways to compete with each other, the gala declined.

In the towns, therefore, where the slaves increasingly became surrogates and pawns with little or no control over what were called "slave galas", players were performers providing entertainment for whites. Events involving inversion and dressing up gave them a feeling of what it would be like to be white. Female slaves were dressed up like dolls in a white competition and had to wait for words of praise and handouts in appreciation of their efforts. Female slaves became mock soldiers dressed in red and blue because they had become transfixed by uniforms. John Connu was converted into a European illusion. On the eve of emancipation in Jamaica, therefore, "upper-class" slaves were fiercely ready to move into the positions of their masters and mistresses.

In St Lucia, where participation in the two rival societies increased across the population after emancipation, there was also a rise in the incidence of open friction and exploitation. It was almost inevitable that the level of rivalry between the two societies would have been sharpened by what Breen (1844, 200) called "the intrigues of interested partisans". The instance which Breen gives is particularly interesting because of the element of race and the echoes of slavery that it involved:

> Thus in 1840, an attempt was made by an unscrupulous planter to set one society in opposition to the other. . . . The object was to allure the labourers to his estates and get them to work on his own terms: for this purpose he took one of the societies under his special protection; had himself elected their king; purchased superb dresses for the queens; and got up splendid fêtes for their entertainment.

Breen's reaction of mild outrage suggests that even before emancipation the societies were not estate-based but were like fraternities related to the Roman Catholic Church.

In spite of this incident and its disastrous consequences, in St Lucia the societies consolidated themselves as independent entities, where, according to Breen, among other things "the women, whose attendance is much more regular than that of the men, assemble in the evening to rehearse some favourite 'belair' for their next dance, or to receive a *lecture* from the king" (193). The societies' involvement with the Roman Catholic Church (in which they had patron saints) as well as with the Catholic tradition of carnival (in that both had costumes and parades), neither of which parties in Jamaica had, meant that they had a measure of institutional stability.

In Trinidad, where regiments had neither church support nor white support, they had little chance of survival after emancipation as the kinds of ethnic institutions identified in 1805 (Martinique, Guadeloupe, Danish), especially when the attractiveness of differences in origin receded. However, the Carenage area, which was specifically identified as the source of the 1805 plot, continued to be vibrantly associated with African traditions and also with the conversion of carnival into a popular festival.

The expression "The king is dead! Long live the king!" highlights the idea of immediate and automatic institutional succession, but the antithesis in it embodies the same contrast that is in the Adonia myth – the cyclical manifestations of Nature. Frazer (1925, 307) portrays carnival similarly in popular European culture: "Sometimes at these Shrovetide or Lenten ceremonies the resurrection of the pretended dead person is enacted." In the case of the Tropical Carnival in Jamaica, however, cyclical resurrection was not everlasting. Popular street performance blossomed in the revolutionary era and had its first classic manifestation in Jamaica, but its decline there was due to the very revolutionary changes that promoted it.

The book *Goya: The Last Carnival* (Stoichita and Coderch 1999) has a chapter titled "The Carnival Is Dead, Long Live the Carnival". The back cover blurb for the book says: "the authors show how obsessions with the notions of 'revolution' and 'Carnival', both inversions of the established order, characterized Spanish culture at the end of the eighteenth century". If the Tropical Carnival in Jamaica is taken as representing the same revolutionary spirit, it is logical that the post-emancipation years saw its decline. However, if the carnival died in Jamaica, it burst forth in Trinidad with renewed vigour as a post-emancipation people's festival. Its resurrection as a pre-Lenten festival in Trinidad (which was Spanish until 1797) revealed its immediate *raison d'être* as being more directly associated with the Roman Catholic Church, but its dynamic root (play) was still there – its shoot was undergoing a metamorphosis, which paradoxically was to become institutionalized.

But what of Jean-Paul Marat's (1789, 8) argument: "Carnival, the festival of paganism, is celebrated only among enslaved people; it would be worthy of a free nation to abolish it, and there is no better occasion to do so than the dawn of liberty"? Though Marat was speaking of post-revolution France as a "free nation", his view was essentially the same as that of Belisario and Barclay in Jamaica, who saw the slaves' festivities as African backwardness which should not have been carried forward into the post-emancipation period. It may be that this view does not take into account Alphonse Karr's "the more things change, the more they stay the same" or that the word "revolution" (< revolve) started with the meaning "going right around and coming back to the same place", which makes disturbing the status quo perpetually necessary.

8. "Dancing with Soul in It"

> The lady keeps her face towards him, and puts on a modest demure look, which she counterfeits with great difficulty. In her paces she exhibits a wonderful address, particularly in the motion of her hips, and steady position of the upper part of her person: the right execution of this wriggle, keeping exact time with the music, is esteemed among them a particular excellence.
>
> —Long 1774, 2:424

AS WITH OTHER FEATURES OF CULTURE, MOST European descriptions of dances in the early colonial period were generalizations from limited observation and subsequent repetitions of these generalizations. However, there were some that were detailed. Observations focused on dance formations, for example, whether males and females danced together, whether they touched, whether they formed a circle or were in a line. Writers also spoke of the energy of the dances, the positioning and movement of parts of the body, and general reactions created by the dancing. There were also observations about the intent of the dancers, elements of competitiveness where they existed, the skill of the dancers and impressions of their mental state.

The enslaved African enjoying a weekend feeling of freedom was not in any sense constrained by formalism. Especially in the early colonies, there were mostly ad hoc situations of entertainment with a fair measure of ethnic diversity. Dances would have been modified according to how strikingly beautiful or novel a movement was seen to be or felt. No doubt, there were differences between contexts, as between funerals and completion of a house. Naturally, some slaves would have remembered the details of formations and movements from their own ethnic traditions, but even in these cases their own individuality and creativity would have modified them. One has to speak of dancing rather than dances; one has to start by identifying features that were repeatedly mentioned and others that were noted, without trying to reconstruct prototype dances. Set combinations of features could not have been characteristic of a (Caribbean) situation without a history of itself and generally characterized by variety. One can at best only piece together dances according to the details or features of them that writers gave.

In commenting on slaves dancing in Barbados between 1647 and 1650, Ligon neither described their movements as parts of or as whole dances nor did he refer to any dance by name. Unremarkable performance within a small space outdoors, with movement of the head and hands and occasional jumping into the air with rhythmic precision, was the summary picture in Ligon's description ([1657] 1970, 50); it was as if it were a long, continuous and non-provocative experience.

Stamina was being given as one of the notable features of the slaves' dancing, for, overall, Ligon's representation indicates a preference, on their part, for a moderately energetic but long-lasting activity. Since the slaves divided themselves into males and females, it suggests that, in the societies they came from, dancing differed according to gender, status and roles and also, in the case of females, according to notions of modesty and physical capability. Even so, the description given probably applied to both genders except for the "leaping bolt upright" (Ligon [1657] 1970, 50), which may have been restricted to the men.

There is no way of knowing whether the level of energy and long duration of the dancing were a carry-over from Africa or represented a conditioned response to the experience of slavery. In any case, it was neither the energy nor the duration that bothered European observers but the sexuality of it. Ligon, being aware that Europeans were more concerned about the sanctity associated with Sundays, was intent on showing that the slaves were not acting in a heathenish manner. It is therefore difficult to tell the extent to which he moderated his description.

What Richard Blome (1672, 86) wrote fifteen years later was merely a paraphrasing and repetition of Ligon's words – Blome used the phrase "antick actions" to try to sum up Ligon's words "rather what they aim at, then what they do" ([1657] 1970, 50). Blome's phrase suggests not only excessive, demonstrative behaviour but also movements intended to convey a message. Unfortunately, there is no further evidence to make it clear whether the emphasis was on flourish or mimicry. At the end of the century the idea that the slaves' dancing required great body strength was what Hans Sloane (1707, xlviii) highlighted when he said: "Their dances consist in great activity and strength of body, and keeping time, if it can be." In fact, the last phrase seems to suggest that though rhythm or timing was a prerequisite, it was subordinate to body movement.

French reactions to the slaves' way of dancing were more in line with Sloane's, judging by the following comment by Du Tertre (1667, 527): "They assume such unnatural postures and dance with such violent contortions of the body that I am often astonished how they can move after finishing this painful exercise. However, on leaving there, they are so fresh and appear so little tired that you would not think on seeing them that they had been dancing." Here again, what seemed strange to this French writer was the amount of independent and vigorous movement of individual parts of the body and that the dancers did not seem to tire in spite of the considerable energy they expended. In all these descriptions there is no assertion or even suggestion that the dance movements expressed joy or happiness – they were presented as expressions of physical ability. Yet the illustration of the batuca by Dessalines d'Orbigny (1836),[1] although it refers to Brazil almost two hundred years after Ligon's description of the slave dance in Barbados, allows for a point of

Figure 13. The batuca of Sao Paulo. Alcide Dessalines d'Orbigny, *Voyage pittoresque dans les deux Ameriques* [. . .] (Paris: L. Tenré, 1836). Digitized by archive.org.

---

1. This is a variant of an illustration by Johann Baptist von Spix appearing five years earlier.

comparison (see figure 13). It is the prominence of the hands with "antics" in the batuca that seems comparable, even if the other features are later than Ligon's description. Since upraised hands are associated with "jumping for joy", it is possible that the early dancing that Ligon described was an expression of joy rather than being mostly ritual.

In these English and French descriptions, the difference between the European conception of dancing and what the Africans did was presented as basically a difference between foot movement or space covered (European) and upper-body movement and stamina (African). Blome, for instance, repeated the word "antique" that Ogilby had used the previous year to describe the dancing of the indigenous people. Where Blome used the word "antick", Du Tertre used the French equivalent, *postures*, with the added comment that the dance seemed tiring, which is exactly what Du Tertre said about the dancing of the indigenous people. As elsewhere, this word choice could have been a case of lumping together all "others" and describing them in the same way.

Projecting the African Record on to Caribbean Dancing

The most prominent claim made about the slaves' dancing was continuity of heritage, because virtually everything the slaves did was assumed or said to be African. In Du Tertre's (1667, 526–28) account it is even more precise – there is a sense of a carry-over from West Africa of the practices of individual ethnic groups: "Hardly a festival or a Sunday passes without several Negroes from the same tribe or from neighboring ones assembling to entertain themselves, and on these occasions they dance the dances of their tribe. . . . Their greatest festivities are at the baptisms of their children, for on those occasions they invite all the Negroes from their tribe as well as those from their estate."

Labat (1724, 2:53) at the very end of the century also highlighted different ethnic groups: "Congo negroes have a dance that is the exact opposite of that [of the Aradas]. . . . Mine negroes dance around in a circle but looking outwards. Cape Verde and Gambia negroes have their own specific dances." The problem with these claims of ethnic continuity is that while it is quite normal for people in a foreign land to seek their own, it is unlikely that such a desire was realized in many islands since the Africans periodically available for purchase were not numerous enough or homogeneous enough to allow for preservation of ethnic groups. Note, for example, that in the tiny island of Carriacou there is a well-known and researched tradition of "nation" dancing in which at least nine different West African ethnic groups are identified and intertwined.

Validity of claims of West African continuities in dance in the Caribbean can be assessed by comparing statements made about Caribbean slaves with those made about West Africans through the seventeenth century by Marees ([1602] 1987, 171–72), Jobson (1623, 107), Villault (1670, 208–9), Phillips (1732, 223) and Barbot (Hair, Jones and Law 1992, 2:564–65). The overall evidence shows that over the period 1602 to 1732 there is filling out of the African scenario with details, a filling out that was as much the result of consulting previous sources as it was a matter of independent eyewitness observation. No concerted effort was made to differentiate ethnicities.

The following is a list of the significant features of West African dancing that these accounts provide:

- active use of hands/snapping fingers/clapping hands to keep time
- stamping the feet on the ground
- jumping up in the air
- bending over at the waist
- approaching one another and withdrawing
- bringing stomachs close together and sometimes knocking bellies together
- uttering words or talking to each other/singing or reciting verses
- dancing as if possessed (through words and speed of movement)
- gender differentiation to form lines or couples
- (women) playing games
- (men) dancing with swords/cutlasses

Close textual comparison shows that European writers used features from this body of information on Africans in Africa to describe slaves dancing in the Caribbean, for features given above appear in various combinations in descriptions of Caribbean dancing throughout the slavery period. In other words, some European writers were not really giving eyewitness accounts of Caribbean dancing, but just repeating a vision of African dancing formulated in earlier or contemporary accounts. In addition, European accounts of the Caribbean maintained details of descriptions according to their own respective traditions. For instance, French accounts over time repeated names of dances and these names did not occur in English accounts.

Labat's Notorious but Influential *Calenda*

The first detailed description of a slave dance in the Caribbean appeared in the account of the French priest Jean-Baptiste Labat, who also later published work on Africans in Africa. Labat's description was first published in 1722, but referred to his experiences twenty-five years previously in Martinique. Labat (1724, 2:52) commented on dances of various African groups, but the dance he highlighted was from among the Aradas, or that is what he said: "The one that pleases them the most and is the most common is the calenda; it comes from the Guinea coast and, from all appearances, from the kingdom of Arda."

Even though Labat repeatedly said that the dance was the most popular among all the Africans, his association of it with the Aradas was not totally unrelated to the fact that he claimed to know more about them than any other group. He said (2:46) that in 1698 he learned the language of the Ardra slaves so that he could find out more about them. Labat's description of the dance may have contained features he actually observed, but there is little doubt that he was influenced by previous and contemporary accounts, especially French ones (for example, Villault, Barbot), for several features identified by these writers are in his description:

> The dancers are in two lines, one facing the other, the men on one side and the women on the other. . . . As to the dancers, they hold their arms almost like people who dance and play castanets. They jump, spin around, go forward two or three feet from each other, then withdraw until the sound of the drum tells them to touch each other by bumping their thighs against each other, that is the men's against the women's. On seeing them do this, I thought it was their bellies they were bumping, but it was only their thighs. They withdraw immediately pirouetting, to begin again the same movement with totally lascivious gestures, as often as the drum gives the signal, which it did several times one after the other. Occasionally, they would hook their arms and do two or three circles always bumping their thighs and bending over. (2:52)

The notable features of Labat's calenda, which were also in those of the earlier French writers, Villault and Barbot, were: the men and women in two lines respectively facing each other; the approach of the dancers with arms half raised, the bumping and the withdrawal; the pirouetting and other movements; and repetitions of the procedure.

There are two significant features which Labat gives that are not directly identified in the seventeenth-century African descriptions. The first is that the spectators formed a circle around the performers. In fact, in his account Marees ([1602] 1987, 172) reported that the African women "do not like to be watched by strangers". Jobson (1623) mentioned spectators, but did not give the impression that they encircled the dancers. The circle around the dancers is not mentioned until later, by Atkins ([1735] 1972, 53), referring to Sierra Leone in 1721. It is mentioned later still by Matthews ([1788] 1966, 101) and again in reference to an area in Sierra Leone. Since the historical record before Labat did not provide him with the idea that the formation in which the spectators enclosed the performers in a circle was typical in the slaving areas of West Africa, it lends some credibility to Labat's description as that of an eyewitness in Martinique.

The second significant feature of Labat's calenda not directly mentioned in previous French descriptions of West Africans dancing is that they sometimes hooked arms and danced in circles. Barbot, however, compares the Africans' dancing with the *filoux* (who in this case would be the gypsies) and one of the best-known gypsy dances is the flamenco, which involves a high outward-pointing elbow posture and movement in a circle. It is possible that Labat also became aware of this feature from Barbot's description.

The calenda, as described by Labat, involved physical prowess and display, but it was seen mostly to exude a strong sexual element. Other African dances presumably lacked the energy and sex appeal of the calenda. It was this element, a focal one in European perceptions of the dance, that dominated their comments, in spite of the fact that in most of the descriptions of West African dances mentioned previously, there was no overt or repeated reference to a strong sexual element. Presumably the touching and bumping of thighs and the hooking of arms and dancing in a circle had become more prominent in Caribbean slave society in which women, because of their relative shortage, had come to be identified even more in terms of their sexual function. It may also be that the black male figure interacting directly with a woman in an outdoor space constituted an unacceptable image for white society in the Caribbean (in a way that it could not have done in West Africa) and for that reason provoked a hostile reaction. Ironically, the name *calenda* became notorious far beyond Martinique principally because of Labat's detailed documentation of it as African lewdness.

Forging the Name of a Dance

In spite of his professed expertise in the language of the slaves and in spite of his use of African sources, there is enough evidence to show that *calenda* is a word that Labat projected onto the Caribbean from Romance sources. Such "creativity" was not foreign to Labat, who, in his reconstruction of Des Marchais's 1725–27 voyage to West Africa, liberally used material from earlier explorers to fill out his account.

As to the probable sources of *calenda*, first, Bishop Asterius of Amasea on 1 January 400 preached a sermon against the evils and immorality of the Festival of the Calends: it is likely that Labat knew of this. Second, there was a well-known twelfth-century French troubadour, Raimbaut de Vaqueiras, who composed a song called *kalenda maya*, which became famous at the time. Third, an even more common and everyday use of the word was in the Roman concept *kalends* that occurred in dates of documents and travelogues written in Latin, which was the contemporary language of scholars. *Kalends* was the word the Romans used not only for the first day of the month but to locate other days preceding. It is not just coincidental that the name that Labat gave to the dance is similar to *kalends*, bearing in mind that, as the *Catholic Encyclopedia* points out, the Feast of Fools (which is related to the Feast of the Calends) took place on or about 1 January (Thurston 1909), and bearing in mind also that in his first mention of the word Labat links it to celebrations at Christmas, or, in other words, the kalends of January.

Fourth, there was another source that must have influenced Labat – the etymologies of Isidore of Seville. In Isidore's discussion of the etymology of musical terms (*Etymologiarum sive originum*, c.630, book 3, xxi), the Latin verb *caleo, calere* ("to burn, to be full of ardour") is identified as the source of *calendo*, a textual variant. (The form *calendo* is one inflexion of the verb *calere* which has *calenda* as another inflexion.) It could hardly be that a form of this common and regular Latin word, which was used by Isidore of Seville in his influential treatise on music, bore no relation to an 'African' dance described by Labat as "lascivious" (= hot).

Fifth, research sources do not really provide a word similar to *calenda* with an appropriate meaning in the languages of Dahomey, an absence which in itself raises the matter of the geographical source Labat gives for the calenda. He claimed that the dance came from the Kingdom of Arda, which was in Dahomey (modern-day Benin). Labat's location of the origin in Dahomey was substantially based on the fact that that is where, he said, a great number of the slaves on his plantation came from. However, in contrast to Labat, other writers link the calenda to the Congo and it is hardly surprising that Labat's word (*calenda*) was not truly corroborated as the name of an observed dance and that other names came to be used instead.

One writer who blindly helped to perpetuate what Labat said was Antoine Pernety, another French priest, whose observation was made about sixty-five years after Labat's in the context of Montevideo. Describing an incident which he witnessed while walking around, he said: "one of the mulattos, who looked like a hispanicised Indian, took the negro woman by the hand and the two of them began to dance for a full quarter hour the dance called *calenda*" (1769, 1:299). Then, in order to substantiate the indecency of the dance, Pernety proceeded to reproduce (without actually mentioning Labat by name) Labat's full description of the calenda that he had read. The fact of the matter, however, is that Pernety was labelling the dance which he saw merely by reputation: there was no other evidence given to confirm that what he saw was what Labat had described for Martinique.

This did not prevent André-Pierre Ledru (1810, 2:75), another Frenchman writing some forty years later, from consolidating this notion of the calenda being danced in Montevideo, by paraphrasing what Pernety said and representing it as a direct citation from Pernety: "There is however a very lively and lascivious dance which is danced sometimes in Montevideo; it is called 'calenda', and the negroes as well as the mulattos, whose temperament is hot, love it to death." Thus the notion of the calenda in Argentina became a reality.

French corroboration of Labat's calenda continued in 1783 when François Dumoulin, who spent some time in Grenada in 1773, produced a painting with slaves dancing, which he titled *Calinda: Danse des Nègres en Amérique* (see figure 14). As in Pernety's description, Dumoulin's painting featured a man and a woman dancing, much like in the paintings of the Italian, Agostino Brunias, who was in the islands at the very same time. Unlike Brunias, however, Dumoulin in his title identified the slaves' dance by name and as common across the Americas.

It was from Moreau de Saint-Méry, a French creole born in Martinique, that doubt about Labat's calenda first emerged. Moreau de Saint-Méry gave a detailed description of dances in Saint Domingue in a 1796 article called *Danse* and it had to be that Moreau de Saint-Méry did not completely believe what Labat had said which caused him to give his own etymology for the word

Figure 14. *Calinda: Danse des Nègres en Amérique*, by François Dumoulin, 1783

calenda. In spite of the fact that he said that "the *calenda* belongs to Africa", he still went on, in a footnote, to give the name itself a Celtic derivation. Even though this etymology had little to sustain it, it clearly indicates that Moreau de Saint-Méry did not think that *calenda* was an African word.

Beside the etymology, there was some ambiguity or overlap in the way that Moreau de Saint-Méry used the term *kalenda*. In *Danse*, it is as if Moreau de Saint-Méry divided Labat's calenda into two different dances – the kalenda and the chica. In his later book on Saint Domingue, Moreau de Saint-Méry (1797, 1:45) said: "Another negro dance in Saint Domingue, which is also of African origin, is the *chica* which is simply called *calenda* in the Windward Islands, *congo* in Cayenne, *fandango* in Spain." Here he said that the dance was called *calenda* in the Windward Islands but in the earlier work he said that it was called *chica* in the Windward Islands. Moreau de Saint-Méry makes much of the chica, and, without referring to Labat by name, he repeats (in *Danse*) what Labat said about the dance being borrowed by the Spanish throughout the Americas, even mentioning the nuns dancing it at Christmas behind their grills.

Some modern commentators, probably not paying attention to the deceptiveness of dance names, have tended to read more into the differences between the slaves' dances than the earlier writers did. Carlos Esteban Deive (1977,

35–36), for example, has classified the calenda and chica as fertility dances with detailed significance: "the calenda ... originally was a dance of a sacred nature, an expression of a universal life force, a fertility rite in which each position, each step and gesture had a symbolic and well defined meaning. ... What is evident in it [the chica] is the 'fertility dance' nature of it, in which the dancers simulate the sex act by means of pelvic thrusts."

Rosemain (1986, 19–20), for her part, has argued that the kind of confusion and ambiguity found in explanations of calenda and chica stem from early historians' ignorance of the religion of the slaves and their different fertility dances. Contrary to what Rosemain assumes, there could not have been a clean and direct transfer of distinctive African dances to the Caribbean: slaving and slavery did not allow for it. The fact is that *calenda* was mostly a concoction by Labat – the name was not African or original, the source he gives is questionable and the movements of the dance were taken from previous sources.[2] Above all, European familiarity with the word and its lascivious connotations helped to popularize and reify the idea of African lewdness in dance.

Continuities and Adaptations in Dance

As time passed after the early English and French descriptions, changes in the ways of dancing began to be reported. Oldmixon (1708, 2:123) said, for example: "In Mr. Ligon's time, the Men danc'd by themselves, and the Women by themselves, but 'tis not so in ours." Here there is a simple assumption that all the slaves' dances had been seen and reported and that they all had had the same formation. It was not even the case that Oldmixon had been to Barbados and had witnessed the dancing himself. His comment was probably based on what Sloane (1707, lvi) had said shortly before, referring back to his stint in Jamaica during the last decade of the seventeenth century: "'Tis true they have several Ceremonies, as Dances, Playing, &. but these for the most part are ... mixt with a great deal of bawdry and Lewdness."

Now, the slaves' dancing was being deemed immoral and lewd, partly due

---

2. This position is supported by an observation made by Maureen Warner-Lewis (2003, 237–38): "Clearly, the term *kalinda*, just like *bambula*, served as generic labels for activities that spanned a wide spectrum of kinetic performance, dance in one context, and sport in another, or even referred to several types of vocal display."

to the fact that it took place on Sunday. Sloane's attitude and conclusion at the end of the century therefore directly contrasted with Ligon's in the middle of the century, but what actual changes in the slaves' dancing had taken place is not evident. Nevertheless, the sight of male and female slaves doing their dance moves in public, in urban areas especially, must have been upsetting to those who were concerned about propriety and public order.

Movement towards European practices was inevitable. Because of the domestic roles they had to perform and because they had to service white social events, slaves became familiar with white dances and in many cases learned to master them. As a result, African dancing lost its distinctive features as the slaves adapted to European modes of dancing. A factor that certainly would have brought about change was one that Du Tertre (1667, 527) noted: "while the men and women dance and jump with all their might, the little children make up another dance to the side, and one can get pleasure seeing them imitate the postures of their fathers and mothers, and mimic their actions". This suggests that children born in the Caribbean were creating their own dances while imitating the movements of their African parents. The consequences of this creolization over two or three generations would have been quite apparent, in spite of the constant introduction of new Africans into the situation.

According to Labat (1724, 2:52), the slave masters, for reasons of modesty, wanted to ban the calenda, or probably it was Labat masking his own thoughts about what he should do in the case of the slaves at the monastery at Fonds Saint Jacques. In order to move the slaves away from the "lewd" calenda dance, slave owners, according to Labat (2:53), went as far as to encourage the slaves to learn French dances "such as the minuet, the courant, the *passe-pied* and others, as well as reels and round dances, so that they can dance several at the same time, and jump as much as they want". It is hardly likely that the mass of slaves would have abruptly changed to dances in which they could not express themselves, in spite of Labat's condescending notion that the substitute European dances allowed them to jump as much as they wanted to.

According to Labat (1724, 2:52), prohibition was extremely difficult also because the calenda had become an integral part not only of the adults' life but also that of their children from early on. It is significant that what Labat said about children imitating their parents was exactly the same as what Du Tertre had said a few decades earlier. This was an informal and no doubt what was regarded as "natural" transfer from one generation to the next; it contrasted with the idea of a school for dancing, which was mentioned in relation to

Africans in Africa and whites in the Caribbean. It demonstrated the early exposure of children in slave society to adult life and their early socialization into courtship, sexual practices and display of prowess.

In the English islands, even if differences between contexts were becoming clearer, descriptions of dancing in the eighteenth century continued with the same emphases made by earlier English writers generally. Poole (1753, 295), referring to Barbados, became more dramatic: "Such gestures, such Distortion of Limbs, such different Positions of Body were shewn, that they seemed as tho' they were acted by a Spirit of Frenzy; a Madness that stung them into strong convulsive Motions, rather than the natural Act of the Will. But tho' there was so much Agitation of Body shewn, which they call Dancing, yet they scarcely moved out of their Place." Here, the "Spirit of Frenzy" was being associated with a funeral and was induced, in Poole's interpretation, by the belief in migration of the soul back to the homeland. European fascination with "agitation of the body" and dancers remaining in the same spot continued through until the end of the eighteenth century.

In his description of funeral dances for important persons among the slaves which he described and labelled as "Pyrrhic" or "warlike", Edwards (1793–94, 2:85) also used the word "agitated": "they exhibit a sort of Pyrrhic or warlike dance, in which their bodies are strongly agitated by running, leaping, and jumping, with many violent and frantic gestures and contortions". These words by Edwards are virtually identical to those of Hughes (1750, 16–17), about fifty years previously and referring to Barbados: "they have a sort of *Pyrrhic*, or a Martial Dance, in which their bodies are strongly agitated by skipping, leaping, and turning round". One difference is that Edwards adds the burial context which Hughes did not specify. A pyrrhic dance is also mentioned by Williams (1826, 22) three decades later and again the word "agitated" is repeated: "Others performed a sort of pyrrhic before the ebo drummer, beginning gently and gradually quickening their motions, until they seemed agitated by the furies." A problem here is that even if all these writers concurred about the concept of "agitation", there must be doubt about its validity as a defining feature if it was just a matter of repetition from previous works rather than independent reaction in different places.

Europeans were very much inclined to associate this kind of dancing, especially at funerals, with spirit possession. The notion of being "agitated by the furies" must have been disturbing to whites and so, as a result, there was a concerted effort to move the slaves away from this kind of dancing. However, while in reference to funeral dances the idea of "agitation" was repeated, for other dances it was the idea of "gestures". Not only did Poole and Edwards above use the word but also Luffman (1789, 135) in the following comparison of slave dancing in Antigua with European performances: "to this music ... I have seen a hundred or more dancing at a time, their gestures are extravagant, but no more so than the principal dancers at your Opera-House". So, from the time of Ligon (mid-seventeenth century) to the end of the eighteenth century, European writers across the islands were also noticing an element of acting in the slaves' dancing.

There was also another element that was noted. Even though, as shown, Edwards's words ("Pyrrhic or warlike dance") mimic those of Hughes in Barbados, there was another difference between the two in their views of the dance. Edwards, as in many other instances, was directly influenced by his predecessor in Jamaica, Edward Long, and it was Long who associated that specific kind of dancing not just with the supernatural but more pointedly with an ethnic group he regarded as very dangerous – the "Coromantins". It was a designation which he admitted was vague and could include various groups, but he warned that they were a grave threat to the security of whites. He said (1774, 2:474) that "their dances [are] entirely martial. . . . Their dances serve to keep alive that military spirit, for which they are so distinguished; and the figure consists in throwing themselves into all the positions and attitudes, customary to them in the heat of an engagement." For Long, then, Coromantin dancing was a matter of preparation for war.

It was a view of Coromantins taken directly from Bosman's (1705) account of Guinea and it showed that there continued to be a transfer of beliefs from Europeans writing on Africa to those writing on the West Indies. Of some significance also is the fact that characterization of dancing as practice for war goes right back at least to Plato and his identification of "gymnastic" as preparation for soldiers. It is also the case that the indigenous people of the islands were seen as using dance to whip themselves up into a frenzy so that they could go off into battle to avenge their fallen peers. The connection between dancing and fighting therefore needed no bolstering in Long's eyes.

Yet it seemed as if, from the point of view of the slaves themselves, a man dancing with a woman, performing different but complementary roles, emerged as the most popular kind of dancing. This was what struck Leslie (1740, 310) most in Jamaica when he said: "Sunday Afternoon the Generality of them dance or wrestle, Men and Women promiscuously together." The notion of promiscuity is one that Sloane had presented earlier and it was one that was featured by Labat, but it basically arose out of the sight of a man dancing with a woman. The same view is presented by Marsden (1788, 34) in Jamaica a few decades later: "two of them generally dance together". It was also noted by Stedman ([1794] 1806, 2:299) in Suriname: "The negroes dance always in couples, the men figuring and footing, while the women turn round like a top, their petticoats expanding like an umbrella; and this they call waey-cotto" and, as was the case with most of what Stedman said, it was repeated almost word for word in the work *Authentic History of the English West Indies* (1810, 74) for Jamaica. Though the last citation was not a direct observation of Jamaica as it purported to be, dancing in couples is confirmed for Jamaica by Stewart (1808, 261): "When two dancers have fatigued themselves pretty well, a second couple enter the ring, and thus the amusement continues." This development was Caribbean, for there is no mention of such dancing in the African accounts.

Another significant feature which emerged in an activity which had an audience and a spirit of display was competitiveness. Moreton (1790, 157) made the following observation: "It is very amazing to think with what agility they twist and move their joints:– I sometimes imagined they were on springs or hinges, from the hips downward; whoever is most active and expert at wriggling, is reputed the best dancer." The dancers, spurred on by the crowd encircling them, tried to outdo each other and to win the cheers of their peers. It is in this way that the individual's skill could triumph over social and racial impediments.

The movement of certain parts of the body according to the rhythm of the music, the closeness of the dancers and their suggestive gestures, the active participation of the crowd all together heightened the sexuality of slave dancing. At the base of it was the music, which European writers continued to call "African" music. Consequently, the notion of lasciviousness, which Labat's description of the calenda had already broadcast far and wide, came to be the hallmark of slave dancing through to the late eighteenth century. Young (1801, 276), while visiting one of his estates in St Vincent, directly associated lasciviousness with "African" music even in a dance which seemed to have been done by females alone: "This moment a new party of musicians are arrived with an African *Balafo*. . . . They played two or three African tunes; and about a dozen girls, hearing the sound, came from the huts to the great court, and began a curious and most lascivious dance, with much grace as well as action; of the last plenty in truth."

Around the same time in Jamaica, Edwards (1793–94, 2:85) escalated this perception of lasciviousness when he said: "but most part of their songs at these places are fraught with obscene ribaldry, and accompanied with dances in the highest degree licentious and wanton". What Edwards found it difficult to go beyond was what Pinckard (1806, 1:265–6) later described as "the twistings and turnings of the body – they writhe and turn the body upon its own axis".

Some writers managed to move beyond being sanctimonious to being appreciative of the slaves' ability to entertain (Marsden 1788, 33–34). Moreton, while repeating how entertaining the dancing was, shifted the main focus in the dance to the female, where earlier it had been on both sexes or on the vigorous movements of the male. The seductive movements which others assumed to be directed at the dancing partner, Moreton (1790, 157–58) suggested that they were directed at specific spectators. Moreton's picture was consistent with his view of creole females generally, whose behaviour he associated with the root of degeneracy in the slave colonies.

Also in reference to the slaves' acting as a feature of their dancing, Long (1774, 2:424) had earlier observed a suggestive contrast between the serious appearance and the real intent of the female: "The lady keeps her face towards him, and puts on a modest demure look, which she counterfeits with great difficulty." This contrast between the facial appearance and presumed real intent of the dancers is also an idea which is later repeated by Pinckard (1806, 1:266):

> Their approaches, with the figure of the dance, and the attitudes and inflexions in which they are made, are highly indecent: but of this they seem to be wholly unconscious, for the gravity – I might say the solemnity of countenance, under which all this passes, is peculiarly striking, indeed almost ridiculous. Not a smile – not a significant glance, nor an immodest look escapes from either sex: but they meet, in very indecent attitudes, under the most settled, and unmeaning gravity of countenance.

Pinckard's major point, expressed as "gravity of countenance" masking "indecent attitudes", repeats Long's "modest demure look, which she counterfeits with great difficulty". This feature of the dance involved play-acting or playing a part. There is no question that as the dances changed to focus on the interchanges between a man and a woman dancing, the "antick motions" of the mid-seventeenth century became more intelligible to European and other onlookers and in essence constituted unscripted ballet.

Throughout the eighteenth century, features of the dance Labat called the calenda appeared in French and other accounts describing dancing in various places on both sides of the Atlantic, but in no account does any writer duplicate fully what Labat said. The name that several later writers used for the kind of dance Labat named *calenda* was *chica* or the Spanish version *sicá*. The earliest mention of this name seems to have been not until about a hundred years after Labat, by Ledru, who, on a trip in 1797 to collect information, visited several places, one of which was Puerto Rico. In describing the celebration of the birth of a first born near Loisa, Ledru (1810, 2:75) said: "The mixture of Whites, Mulattos and free Blacks formed quite a pleasant group . . . they executed in turn Negro and Creole dances to the sounds of the guitar and the drum popularly called *bamboula*." The accompanying footnote elaborated: "The *chicca* and the *calenda*, voluptuous dances, a little lascivious."

As to the authenticity of what Ledru said, there is no evidence to suggest that Ledru's knowledge of Puerto Rico was more than that of a visitor, but it seems unlikely that the celebration which he described was fictitious, even though the names *calenda* and *bamboula* could have been reproduced from earlier works. Ledru gave the impression that *chicca* was African and *calenda* was Creole, but from that point on *chica* superseded *calenda* as the popular name for the "lascivious" kind of dance described, especially in the Spanish Caribbean. Though the names *calenda* and *baboula*, which first appeared in Labat's 1722 account, became popular as names for various dances in the colonies which had major French influence, in the English colonies with little or no French influence these names were seldom used by English writers. In fact, no Caribbean dance names were recorded in the eighteenth century in the English colonies.

In the course of the eighteenth century, even though no writer was comprehensive, the historical record shows that different kinds of dances had developed. The feature outline that follows gives an idea of the variety of formations and motions that slave dancing was exhibiting:

Motions of the Body

Face	normal
	blank
	pretending
Head	steady
	bobbing
	from side to side

Hands/arms	up or down
	waving
	elbows out
Shoulders	forward
	upright
	backward
Torso/pelvis	straight
	bumping
	thrusting
	writhe/wriggle
Feet/legs	(variable speed)
	leaping
	pirouetting
	skipping/stepping
	circling

Formations

Performance within a ring/circle

Individuals	in sync
	flexible
Men vs. women	separate
	facing
Couple	in sync
	taking turns

Dancing was serving various purposes. For instance, as a result of the high mortality rate among slaves, dancing as a part of funerals became distinctive and more observable. The movements of this kind of dancing were linked to the supernatural and attracted such descriptive words as "frenzy", "fury" and "convulsion" from whites who witnessed it. Another kind of dancing, which incorporated some of the movements of funeral dancing, was what Long regarded as martial dancing. Even if the hostile intent specified by Long was questionable, there is no doubt that there was a kind of gymnastic dancing, not associated with funerals, that required a high level of (leg) dexterity, physical coordination and energy. The other major kind of dancing that was evident was the interactive dancing of a man and a woman. This kind of dancing involved several elements, for example, sexual overtones, competitiveness, acting and aesthetic display. This variety in dancing signalled the expanding role that it was playing in slave life.

The Joan-Johnny and the Bamboula

The first mention of the name of a dance within the period of slavery that did not come out of Labat's description of the calenda or was not identified with a specific ethnic group was by Captain J.E. Alexander (1833), in the context of Barbados in 1831. The name "Joan-Johnny" recorded by Alexander was uncontentious as a dance name in that it had no deceitful history, but the fact that the name was so English raises questions about its source or it signals the extent to which Barbados was culturally anglicized. As with the words "dance" and *calenda*, Joan-Johnny had a double meaning – it was used to refer to an event as well as to a specific manner of dancing.

There is some question as to whether the name (Joan-Johnny) Alexander recorded was exact since some writers after him called it "Joe and Johnny". However, references in the 1830s support Alexander's version of the name. Rolph gives the name as "Joan and John" and his reference is to the year 1833. The journal of J.B. Colthurst (1835–38), a special magistrate who worked for some time in Barbados after emancipation, referring to the year 1836, said: "The Sabbath day is now respected; no Sunday markets, no Joans and Johnnies on that day" (Marshall 1977, 65). So, the name was not fixed; it varied slightly from one citation to another.

If Alexander's version of the name was the original one, it points to a dance done by a man and a woman in a kind of courtship display. The name seemed to have originated in Barbados and taken later to Demerara (Lloyd 1839, 56–57). It could have developed in the prime English colonial setting of Barbados as a nationalistic alternative to dance names used in the French and other colonies. Seeing that the name is particularly English in all of its variants, it is reasonable to conclude either that the event/dance was an imitation of an English event/dance or, more likely, that the name was modelled on English dance names and was not one coined by the slaves. Lloyd labelled it "the African dance, called 'Joe and Johnny'" (56) – but for him "African" probably just meant "former slave".

As an event, it was variable. Rolph (1836, 21) mentioned a planter in Barbados inviting him in 1833 to "a festival amongst his negroes, called Joan and John. It was on the birthday of his daughter." Having witnessed the "Joan and John",

Rolph concluded, "Indeed it was altogether a very gratifying spectacle." It was clearly not an in-group or restricted affair and Rolph's description of it made it appear respectable and pleasant with the only possible objection to it being that it took place on a Sunday. The urban variety appeared to be somewhat different and, especially after emancipation, became the social opposite of a "grand(y) ball" in more ways than one: it was outdoors, it was a pay-to-participate event, it was competitive, it attracted a crowd of onlookers and it provided a great deal of entertainment for all present. It seemed to have some exotic appeal for the otherwise cynical English author Charles Day (1852, 1:47), who, in the 1840s, said: "Hearing that a 'Joe and Johnny' was to be held at a place called Cullumore Rock, a short distance from Bridgetown, I resolved to attend it", and also: "I went on New Year's Day, in the evening, to another "Joe and Johnny" (1:52).

The dance was identified by name from the 1830s to the 1850s. In the demographic situation in Barbados, where by this time there were few Africans, it had to be a creole dance. In addition, in most references to it, the dance was located not on the plantation but in more urban settings. The lifespan and relative longevity of the dance, starting before emancipation and ending after, meant that it was not fundamentally affected by the political and economic changes that occurred. The fact that it was mostly an urban event was probably crucial in this connection. There seemed to have been some importance also in the fact that it was a paying affair and an artistically competitive one.

Features of the Joan-Johnny that writers highlighted occur in dances associated with Africa, Europe and other parts of the Caribbean. Alexander (1833, 1:158) gave what he probably considered the basic features of the dance: "a couple would twist their bodies, thump the ground with their heels, and circle round one another". The man and woman danced as a couple, but each one displayed individual skills either in turn or simultaneously. There is no mention of the man holding the woman or guiding her by the use of the hands. Stamping the ground (with the heels) and circling around the partner were features of the fandango (one of the oldest Spanish dances) and the flamenco (an old gypsy dance). Twisting their bodies had long been noted as a preferred feature of slave dancing in the Caribbean. Circling round one another seemed to be a new feature and could have been critical in the identification of the dance as Joan-Johnny.

A look at descriptions by Long (1774, 2:424), Pinckard (1806, 1:265–6), Alexander (1833, 1:158), Lloyd (1839, 56–57) and Day (1852, 1:47–49, 52–53) gives a picture of both continuity and change in this dance for couples, which came to be called Joan-Johnny in Barbados in the early 1830s. By the 1840s, the dance had become more European, as is attested by the dance terms which Day used to describe it and the fact that it was being done by mulattos. Moreover, when Day (1852, 1:49) observes that the dancers "went through all the steps as accurately as do 'my lord and my lady' on May Day", it suggests that this was really a European dance, despite the fact that Day himself said that it was "a real negro dance". It seemed to be only the "wriggle" that maintained it as "negro". Yet Day (1:50) remarked that a visiting mulatto "'ladeé' from Trinidad" had a "slightly disdainful expression, as if she scorned the vulgar 'Joe and Johnny set out'". Another contradiction was that, although Day identified the "Tum-tum" as the principal instrument in the Joe and Johnny, Alexander, ten years earlier, had identified the fiddle, the banjar and the calabash.

As a result of his fascination with the Joe and Johnny, Day gave a fair idea of the venue and atmosphere of the event on two different occasions in urban Barbados in the 1840s:

> A "Joe and Johnny", being a real negro dance is always held in the open air. The "Tum-tum" was an old familiar sound, and guided by its spirit-stirring thump, I found a numerous assemblage of ladies of colour, forming a ring in the unenclosed "back-yard" of a negro hut. (1852, 1:46–47)

> When I arrived, the rays of a sickly moon were gleaming on the broad-leaved plantain which waved over the heads of the dancers; some were of the πολλοί – no fine madams – no jewellery – no Eau de Cologne – but negro girls, few of whom boasted shoes or stockings – most of them their everyday rags, and everyday smell. This was the "real thing". How the band did work! – how they stamped, and wagged their heads in all the extasies of intense excitement, feeling to the full as much delight as the dancers. (1:52)

Day's comment – "This was dancing with soul in it" – was one of the earliest characterizations of the music and dance of the descendants of Africans in the Americas as having "soul".

There are critical features which distinguish the Joan-Johnny of the 1830s and thereafter from Labat's calenda of the 1690s. The latter was a group dance in a line formation; the former was a dance for couples. Though there was advancing and retreating in both dances, there was no bumping in the Joan-Johnny as there was in the calenda. The leaping and pirouetting, which were features of the calenda, were not typical of the Joan-Johnny. It was the bumping that made the calenda "lascivious" in the eyes of Europeans, whereas it was the wriggle that did it for the Joan-Johnny. However, it was the man and woman circling around one another which seemed to be the key feature in the identification of the dance as Joan-Johnny.

The name Joan-Johnny (and its variants) seemed to have been restricted to Barbados and Demerara. In St Vincent, the equivalent may have been what Day recorded as "da caffee treat"/"the coffee treat". The forms "caffee" or "coffee" are variants of the more general "Cuffy" (sometimes written as "Kofi"), a name, often of disparagement, given to Africans in the New World, even though originally it was simply a West African male name given according to one's day of birth. The idea of "treat" comes out of the situation of slavery and refers to the "subvention" that slave masters gave to slaves to allow them to hold dances. Unlike Joan-Johnny in Barbados, the way of referring to the event and way of dancing in St Vincent was initially by way of a descriptive circumlocution.

Day (1852, 2:120–21) distinguished between a "fancy ball" and a "coffee treat" and also went on to record local beliefs about which dances were "decent" and which were "vulgar":

> On inquiring the kind of dances, I was answered "quadrilles," but, as the black lady continued, "only *decent* dances were permitted, not dem wulgar, like de caffee treat." The coffee treat is equivalent to an English hop, where drinking and fighting are the accompaniments. The banjo, or tum-tum, supplants the more refined fiddle and triangle and dancers pay ten dogs, or sixpence, each time they dance. The coffee treat takes place in each locality about once a-week; the fancy-ball about once a fortnight.

Day does not give any details of the movements and formation of the "caffee treat", but his social description of it as well as the very designation of it as "wulgar" and obviously popular suggests that it was the Vincentian equivalent of the Joan-Johnny.

In Jamaica, there seemed to be no named equivalent of the Joan-Johnny, but Williams (1826, 22) uses the international term "bolero" to refer to a "sort of love-dance". Presented in the way that it is, the Jamaican "version" carried no immediately obvious social stigma and in fact the term "bolero" makes it seem sophisticated. In the decade before that, there was even more favourable treatment of slave dances by Lewis ([1834] 1969, 79–80), who made them seem like a form of ballet. What Lewis described, involving, as he says, three people in some cases, differed from a courtship dance between couples, like the Joan-

Johnny, and seemed more like a dramatic scene acted out through dance. For these writers to have commented so favourably on slave dances meant that there must have been at least a fair degree of competence in the performances of the dancers. Yet one has to bear in mind that some writers were more interested in defending slavery and therefore in making the slaves seem as accomplished as possible, thereby suggesting a state of contentment among them.

The Bamboula

In the French colonies and those with significant French influence, the bamboula was the parallel of the Joan-Johnny. The bamboula had eclipsed the dance that Labat called calenda, but the name *calenda* had survived and was being used to refer to other performances. As with Joan-Johnny, the term *bamboula* referred to both an event and a way of dancing. As was the case with Labat's name *calenda*, *bamboula* had also varied in meaning.[3] Originally, Labat (1724, 2:52) identified *baboula* as the smaller drum used by the drummers in the calenda, but subsequently the form *bamboula* was used, to refer to a dance. The mid-eighteenth-century song from Haiti "Lisette quitté la plaine" relates the protagonist's loss of happiness to Lisette's absence ("Since I lost Lisette, I don't care about the calinda . . . I don't beat the bamboula" (Moreau de Saint-Méry [1797] 1958, 81). Presumably, at the time the "calinda" was the happiest dance and bamboula still referred to the instrument (drum). The connection between drum and dance is evident in Puerto Rico where the name *bomba* came to be used for both. In the Danish islands of St Thomas and St Croix the word *bamboula* was used for the dance.

Max-Radiguet gave a dramatic description of a bamboula he saw in Martinique on New Year's Day, 1838 (Max-Radiguet 1842, 4:335–36). This dance was quite different from the one Labat had described more than a hundred and forty years earlier and it was also different in several respects from the contemporary Joan-Johnny in Barbados and Demerara. It was a dance between a man and a woman, but the bumping of bellies/thighs, which was the most significant feature in Labat's description of the calenda, was not a feature of this bamboula. In fact, as was the case in the Joan-Johnny, there was no touching (except when

---

3. Weeks (1914, 291) identifies *bambula* as a Congo verb, but the meaning ("to deflect, to transfer in a mysterious way") and the context he gives seem to have nothing to do with the Caribbean word.

the woman wipes perspiration from the brow of the male dancer) as the two circled around each other and perform their courtship routines.

According to Max-Radiguet, the male dancer was the dominant figure in the bamboula and he seemed to be more of a performer/entertainer than the male dancer in the Joan-Johnny. The characterization of the performance of the dancer as "gymnastic" (doing cartwheels and walking on the hands) took it far beyond what was said of the Joan-Johnny, but, quite remarkably, these gymnastic elements were very similar to what constituted dancing in Britain in earlier centuries, according to Strutt ([1801] 1903) and the word "gymnastic" also recalls Plato's characterization of dance. In the Joan-Johnny the faces of the male and female were said to be very serious; in the bamboula the male dancer feigned fear and joy and other emotions, presumably according to the reactions of the female. The characterization of the bamboula as "frenetic" establishes a parallel with the concept of St Vitus dance, which Day used to describe the Joan-Johnny.

Belisario's *French Set-Girls* probably gives a good idea of the bamboula dance (the position of the elbows, knees and feet) seeing that this band was meant to represent slaves who came over from Saint Domingue after the Revolution. Overall, the bamboula in the French-influenced islands was more flamboyant than the Barbadian Joan-Johnny as a dance and as an event, but not very different, judging from Long's (1774, 2:424) description, from a comparable dance in mid-eighteenth-century Jamaica – "the man, all action, fire, and gesture". Partly responsible for the flamboyance of the event in the French-influenced islands and Jamaica was the stronger presence of Africans there: in the case of Barbados, the importation of Africans had started to decline towards the end of the eighteenth century and in the case of Martinique, slavery lasted longer.

The influence of the physical context within which the bamboula was done was also much more powerful. At night, it was dramatic, as Max-Radiguet (1842, 4:336) explained: "That noisy scene at that hour of the night . . . that hellish music; that frenetic and lascivious dance; those characters in strangely variegated costumes made more phenomenal by the flickering red light of the torches from which the wind dislodged sparks and smoke, [all this] gave me, more than any description, an idea of what it was like on those dreadful nights of the Sabbath presided over by Satan on the magical mountain of the Hartz!"

Breen (1844, 196–97) recorded a similar reaction created by the physical context of the bamboula in St Lucia: "A circle is formed in the centre of some square or grass-plot. . . . and as the groups of dancers advance in all directions,

Figure 15. *Negro Figuranti.* R. Bridgens, *West India Scenery* (1836). Courtesy of the New York Public Library.

the darkness of the night disappears before the blaze of a thousand flambeaux. ... To a superficial observer these exhibitions present somewhat of a profane and even heathenish appearance." Remarkably, Breen was so impressed by the totality of the dance that he felt compelled to defend it in the face of a "Christian moralist", but this in itself tells what an overpowering effect it must have had and how exotic or "heathenish" it must have looked to a visitor. Breen himself might have underestimated the connections that this kind of performance might have had with supernatural practices in the French-influenced islands. So, if the dance between the man and the woman was central in the Joan-Johnny, thereby putting them into focus with the rest being subsidiary, in the case of the bamboula, the entire event was more memorable because of the dramatic and flamboyant setting and other-worldly atmosphere.

The work which gives the best idea of the moves and the postures of the dancers in the bamboula is Bridgens (1837) (see figure 15). It provides pictorial illustrations in the context of Trinidad, which, with its dominant French influence at the time, had a bamboula like Martinique and St Lucia. Plate 22 in Bridgens 1837 is titled *Negro Figuranti*, a title that immediately establishes a comparison with Italian and, more generally, European dance movements and postures. It was a comparison that had been already favourably made about fifty years before by Luffman (1789, 135) in Antigua. More importantly, however, observations made by previous writers were now further clarified by Bridgens's (1837, n.p.) illustrations and explanations:

> It will appear to the most cursory observer, that all their movements in dancing are marked by great activity. . . . The bending of the body forwards, shewn in two female figures, which is accompanied by an indescribable wriggling motion from side to side, is worthy of notice. . . . The putting one leg over the shoulder, and dancing on the other, will be recognised as a common trick with clowns and mountebanks at our fairs.

Bridgens's illustrations of gymnastic positions graphically depicted what other writers described.

There is, as elsewhere, the element of literate influence in descriptions of the bamboula. It is verifiable not only in the repetition of basic features but also in the repetition of minor gestures. One such gesture is mentioned by Stedman ([1794] 1806, 2:299) at the end of the eighteenth century: "the girls encourage the performance, and wipe the sweat from the brows and sides of the unwearied musicians". Some years later it is repeated by Cynric Williams (1826, 22), speaking of Jamaica: "the gentleman occasionally wiped the perspiration off the shining faces of their black beauties, who, in turn, performed the same service to the minstrel". There is also a French version of it given by Max-Radiguet (1842, 4:335–36): "then, at a convenient moment, the black Veronique wipes the perspiration which is running down the face of her partner". The gesture helped to paint a picture of caring characters, but it is also a reminder of the presence of previous literature in contemporary accounts.

It seems almost incredible that people who were constantly being brutalized and traumatized could execute dance movements and routines with such panache and fire as to attract the attention of writers and artists for over three succeeding centuries (mid-seventeenth to mid-nineteenth century). There was no equivalent depiction of dancing in West Africa, even though the basic features of Caribbean dance were associated with West Africa.

The following summary of features with illustrations gives some idea of the various movements and expressions that constituted slave dancing in the

Caribbean. Unfortunately, there was little or no recognition on the part of writers of the degree of adaptation that had taken place, that is, the extent to which creole slaves had developed the dancing of their parents and grandparents principally in response to slavery. The irony was that the dancing of creole slaves continued to be referred to as "African". However, we can now compare the features in the table that follows with those given earlier as African features to see the adaptations made in early Caribbean dance.

List of Features	The Features Described
a. Remaining in the same place	"yet they scarcely moved out of their Place" (Poole 1753, 295)
	"and sometimes do not move six inches from the same place" (Marsden 1788, 34)
	"I must not omit to remark that the feet did not take the most active part in the dance" (Day 1852, 1:48)
b. Jumping in the air/ leaping/ pirouetting	"one of the activest amongst them will leap bolt upright" (Ligon 1657, 50) "While the men and women dance and jump with all their might" (Du Tertre 1667, 527)
	"They jump and pirouette" (Labat 1724, 2:52)
	"They withdraw at once, pirouetting" (Labat 1724, 2:52)
	"they exhibit a sort of Pyrrhic or warlike dance, in which their bodies are strongly agitated by running, leaping, and jumping" (Edwards 1793, 2:85)
c. Advance and retreat	"they come within two or three feet of each other and withdraw in rhythm" (Labat 1724, 2:52) "slowly advancing towards each other, or retreating to the outer parts of the ring" (Pinckard 1806, 1:266)
	"slowly advancing towards each other, or retreating to the outer part of the circumference" (Phillippo – cf. Pinckard)

Table continues

List of Features	The Features Described
c. Advance and retreat (*cont'd*)	"The first movement was an en avant by both, the feet close together toeing and heeling it very gently, the retirez the same" (Day 1852, 1:47)
	"the en avant deux, the retirez" (Day 1852, 1:52–53)
d. Stamping	"The dance consists of stamping of the feet" (Pinckard 1806, 1:265–66)
	"Occasionally they change the figure by stamping upon the feet" (Pinckard 1806, 1:266–67)
	"a couple would . . . thump the ground with their heels" (Alexander 1833, 1:158)
	"the dance consisted of stamping the feet" (Phillippo – cf. Pinckard)
	"how they stamped" (Day 1852, 1:52)
e. Head erect	"The head is held erect, or, occasionally, inclined a little forward" (Pinckard 1806, 1:266)
	"the head of each dancer was erect, or occasionally inclined forward" (Phillippo – cf. Pinckard)
f. Knocking their bellies/thighs	"knocking their thighs against each other, that is, the men against the women" (Labat 1724, 2:52)
g. Moving without lifting the feet from the ground	"the whole person is moved without lifting the feet from the ground" (Pinckard 1806, 1:266)
	"the whole person was moved without raising the feet from the ground" (Phillippo – cf. Pinckard)
	"then the feet were straddled in a somewhat indecorous manner for ladies, moving along and round à la fandango,

Table continues

List of Features	The Features Described
g. Moving without lifting the feet from the ground (*cont'd*)	with a motion similar to that exceedingly droll one used by tragic actors in a booth, 'bent on deeds of blood', who sidle up to their victims by an alternate action of the heels and ball of the foot, without lifting their pedal extremities off the ground" (Day 1852, 1:47–48)
h. Writhe/wriggle	"there was so much Agitation of Body shewn" (Poole 1753, 295)
	"she exhibits a wonderful address, particularly in the motion of her hips, and steady position of the upper part of her person: the right execution of this wriggle, keeping exact time with the music, is esteemed among them a particular excellence" (Long 1774, 2:424)
	"and shake their hips" (Marsden 1788, 33)
	"It is very amazing to think with what agility they twist and move their joints:– I sometimes imagined they were on springs or hinges, from the hips downward; whoever is most active and expert at wriggling, is reputed the best dancer" (Moreton 1793, 157)
	"they writhe and turn the body upon its own axis" (Pinckard 1806, 1:266)
	"the twistings and turnings of the body seeming to constitute the supreme excellence of the dance" (Pinckard 1806, 1:267)
	"a couple would twist their bodies" (Alexander 1833, 1:158)
	"various contortions of the body" (Phillippo – cf. Pinckard)
	"they writhed and turned the body upon its axis" (Phillippo – cf. Pinckard)

Table continues

List of Features	The Features Described
h. Writhe/wriggle (*cont'd*)	"an indescribable wriggling motion from side to side" (Bridgens 1837) "That wriggle transcends description: none but itself could be its parallel" (Day 1852, 1:48)
i. Circling around each other	"a couple would . . . and circle round one another" (Alexander 1833, 1:158) "and then 'slueing round' each other" (Day 1852, 1:48) "They circle, violently, together" (Pinckard 1806, 1:267)
j. Appear serious/solemn cast of countenance/gravity of countenance	"The lady keeps her face towards him, and puts on a modest demure look, which she counterfeits with great difficulty" (Long 1774, 2:424) "for the gravity – I might say the solemnity of countenance, under which all this passes, is peculiarly striking" (Pinckard 1806, 1:266) "an indispensable requisite which also seemed to be a solemn cast of countenance" (Day 1852, 1:48)
k. Elbows fixed/elbows pointing outwards	"they hold their arms almost like those who dance and play castanets" (Labat 1724, 2:52) "the hands nearly meet before – the elbows are fixed, pointing from the sides" (Pinckard 1806, 1:266) "the hands nearly united in front; the elbows fixed, pointing from the sides" (Phillippo – cf. Pinckard) "arms a-kimbo, the palms of the hand turned outward" (Day 1852, 1:49)

Table continues

List of Features	The Features Described
1. Holding the frock and waving it up and down	"holding up their frocks à la minuet de la cour, with their heads looking down at their feet" (Day 1852, 1:48) "the arms (holding the frock) wagging up and down, much as we see done in the negro dances on stage" (Day 1852, 1:53)

The list in table 1 gives features of various dances, but in most of them it was the engaging encounter between man and woman inside a ring of "spectators" that defined slave dancing, especially the movement that writers referred to as "writhing" or "wriggling". The execution of intentions and attitudes through body movements was a reaction to enslavement: dance had become a crucial medium through which the male slave could rise to any height, and the female was reacting to the man that she really understood and could match her. While some white observers saw ribaldry and lasciviousness, the participants saw impressive, desirable physiques in motion, at play and on display. Rather than being tired at the end of their activity, the participants would have all had a cathartic experience which lessened their stress and revitalized them, making them better able to face another day and week. For those other slaves who were influenced by churches and who poured out their soul in religion, the experience was similar.

Carlo Blasis's Negative Branding of African Dances

One of the most prominent literary exponents of dance in the early nineteenth century was Carlo Blasis and his text *The Code of Terpsichore*, first published in 1828, was the handbook of dance for generations of students. In this book he spoke of the negative influence of African dances on European dances, stating in almost every case that African dances lacked propriety. Some of the significant statements he made were the following:

> The art of dancing in Spain became a degradation and a vice ... This corruption in style and taste among the Spaniards, must be chiefly attributed to the *Chica*, a dance of a very immoral nature, which the Moors had brought with them from

Africa. The native of the Peninsula, under the influence of the climate where he is born, and with the natural heat and vivacity of his constitution, eagerly received the *Chica*, which soon became one of his chief delights. To this dance I therefore ascribe the indelicacy, and sometimes even the lasciviousness so common in Spanish dancing. The *Chica* afterwards changed its name to that of *Fandango*. (1831, 16)

The Fandango, we thus perceive, again changed its name, but suffered little variation in its character. It was introduced into Italy but performed with more restraint. Almost every Spanish dance, such as the *Bolero*, the *Cachucha*, the *Seguidillas*, of Moorish origin, are imitations of the African *Fandango* or *Chica*. They are therefore all marked with that voluptuousness, I might even say obscenity, which characterised their model. (17)

The *Chica* was brought to us from Africa, where every tribe dances it, particularly the Congos. The Negroes carried it with them to the Antilles, where it soon became naturalized....

The woman holds one end of a handkerchief, or the two sides of her apron, and the chief art on her part consists in agitating the lower part of loins, whilst the rest of the body remains almost motionless. A dancer now approaches her with a rapid bound, flies to her, retires, darts forward a-fresh, and appears to conjure her to yield to the emotions which she seems so forcibly to feel.

When the Chica is danced in its most expressive character, there is in the gestures and movements of the two dancers a certain appearance more easily understood than described. The scene offers to the eye, all that is lascivious, all that is voluptuous. It is a kind of contest, wherein every trick of love, and every means of its triumph, are set in action. Fear, hope, disdain, tenderness, caprice, pleasure, refusals, flight, delirium, despair, all is there expressed, and the inhabitants of Paphos, would have honoured the inventor of it as a divinity....

The Chica is now banished from the balls of the white women of South America, being far too offensive to decency; and is only sometimes performed in a few circles, where the small number of spectators encourage the dancer. (28)

A number of Blasis's points require careful scrutiny. First of all, it is clear that Blasis used Labat as his initial fount of information, for he repeats (that is, translated almost verbatim) some of his details, among which the one which betrays his plagiarism most is: "The nuns during the night of Christmas eve showed themselves to the public through the gratings of their convents" (28). His most significant change is not only that he used *chica* rather than *calenda* as the name of the dance but also that he makes no mention of the word *calenda*. Indeed, in all his other comments, he treats *chica* as the original name of the dance, thereby discounting Labat's name, *calenda*. It is probably this more than anything else, considering the influence of Blasis, that led to the rise in the name *chica* and the decline of *calenda* as the name of the dance. Another difference in Blasis's explanation of the chica, which, in contrast to Labat's restricted vision, really showed a typical kind of European shallowness, was the statement that the dance came from Africa "where every tribe dances it". However, it is his following remark ("particularly the Congos") that was influential in subsequent written accounts and shifted the dance from being Dahomean to Congo.

The fundamental flaw in Blasis's presentation is that although he copied Labat's remarks about the Spanish together with some other details, the dance he described differed significantly from Labat's and actually resembled the kind of dance for couples, like the Joan-Johnny and the bamboula, which writers in the Caribbean were describing at the beginning of the nineteenth century.

Another major point, one which transcends Blasis, is that there was a long history among European writers of damning the Spanish and Portuguese by stating that they were "tainted" with African blood and that because they were closer to the tropics than other Europeans they were like other tropical people, controlled more by physical, beast-like tendencies than intellectual ones. Blasis, an Italian, was clearly a writer in this tradition.

One therefore has to be careful with Blasis's facile claim that the chica became the fandango and the fandango became the bolero – in short, that Spanish dances were basically African dances. One also has to be careful with his acceptance of Labat's claim about the pervasiveness of the chica throughout South America. One also has to avoid the knee-jerk reaction to such claims, typical of Spanish writers, that nothing in Spain or the Spanish colonies had anything to do with Africa. It is probable that the noted similarities in dancing between Africans and their descendants and Europeans can be explained as both continuities and universals.

The Encounter between "African" and "European" Dancing

The value system that became established in Caribbean societies meant that European dances were considered more sophisticated than all others. In addition, the desire to be fashionable meant that the colonies were always seeking to adopt the latest crazes from Europe. By the end of the eighteenth century, reports indicated that the enslaved Africans and their descendants had already incorporated European dances into their "repertoire". The fact that in 1791 Young makes no negative comment about the competence of slaves on his estates in St Vincent dancing European dances indicates that these dances had already become normal for them (Edwards 1801, 3:273). This is even more evident when he himself danced with slaves in Antigua: "I danced a country dance with old Hannah, and a minuet with long Nanny" (3:283)

Moreau de Saint-Méry (1789, 186) pointed out how important it was for manumitted slaves especially to be European in their dances: "They follow whites in their choice of dance and this is so for all of them." It may be that this social drive was more intense in the French islands than in the English ones. Generally, however, it was of course part of the acculturation process. Soon, the European type dances were being referred to by freed blacks and slaves as more "refined" and "decent" than the traditional African dances.

The desire not only to be refined but also fashionable was quite evident from the end of the eighteenth century onward, according to observations made by several writers: "at the time to which these remarks chiefly apply, reels were the favourites; to these, have succeeded the country-dance, and even the quadrille", said Resident (1828, 37), referring to Dominica in 1796; "the festival concluded with a grander ball than usual, as I sent for music from Savanna la Mar to play country dances to them", said Lewis ([1834] 1969, 240), referring to his slaves in rural Jamaica in 1816/1817; "they dance Scotch reels, and some of the better sort (who have been house servants) country dances" (Barclay 1826, 10), the reference to "the better sort" further highlighting the relationship between fashion and class; and "I recollect obtaining the following information from B. as to one of those dances. 'How many had you at the dance?' 'More than two hundred.' 'What did they dance?' 'Quadrilles and waltzes.' 'Did you not dance the English country dance?' 'No, they no fashion now-a-day'" (Carmichael 1833, 1:292). These reported responses from a slave about which European dances were fashionable at the time among the slaves underlines the extent to which European dances had become part of the repertoire of slaves in St Vincent.

For a long time, from the late eighteenth century through the mid-nineteenth century, "African" and "European" dances coexisted in slave entertainment, even though some dance features were not restricted to any one culture. Many slaves were proficient in both "African" and "European" dances. Carmichael (1833, 1:319), for instance, mentions an African slave with varied competence: "he was uncommonly handsome, and reckoned a first-rate dancer, both of creole and African dances: it was indeed surprising to witness the grace, gravity, and majesty of his demeanour". However, De la Beche (1825, 41) observed that preferences were shown for African or European dances according to age: "those of the old school preferring the goombay and African dances, and those of the new, fiddles, reels, &c.". The generational changes were of course a reflection of changing social preferences and the acculturation process.

Derision is an element which always arises in behaviour contrasting social classes and it was no different in the dynamic encounter between the dancing of the slaves and that of the slave owners. The contradiction, however, is that all classes seemed to be laughing at each other. Normally, it is the lower-class person who is identified as gauche and becomes the butt of the ridicule. On the other hand, several writers portrayed the slaves as mocking whites for their elaborate way of dressing and their peculiar way of dancing. Yet it is contradictory that the slaves would on the one hand be trying to appear sophisticated and at the same time be mocking what was considered sophistication. It could have been symptomatic of a tragic and ironic psychological malaise. The fact that in the early years it was done for the amusement of whites makes it seem even more poignant.

In the following description of Christmas celebrations in Jamaica by Marsden (1788, 33) during the last quarter of the eighteenth century it is difficult to tell who has the last laugh: "The prime negroes and mulattoes pay a visit to the white people during the festivity . . . They dance minuets with the mulattoe and other brown women, imitating the motion and steps of the English, but with a degree of affectation that renders the whole truly laughable and ridiculous." The feature – "a degree of affectation" – is little different from "a modest demure look, which she counterfeits with great difficulty" (Long 1774, 2:424), "unmeaning gravity of countenance" (Pinckard 1806, 1:266), which continued to be identified as a feature of the most popular slave dances. Indeed, then, this simulated serious demeanour or play-acting was a part of the slave tradition; it was more than the comic relief Marsden thought it to be. It reinforces the notion of "play" rather than simply "dance" as the primary focus.

When balls took place, many slaves were outside the ballroom looking in and then imitating what they saw. An idea of this is adapted from Bayley (1830, 428–29) by Robert Cruikshank (1833, 22), in which there is no ridicule of the dancers, but apparent admiration for their skill and knowledge. It should be borne in mind, however, that Cruikshank was a satirist and one of the ideas that he was depicting was that the slaves in the West Indies were happy and better off than poor people in Britain. His intention was to demonstrate that the slaves were no different from their masters. Even in spite of the exaggeration, apparently by the 1830s the slaves were executing the latest European dances (the Lancers) through observation of them. So, the slaves knew how to dance the latest European dances, but it was because they were not formally taught these European set dances that their acquisition of these dances automatically attracted attention.

Instead of the slaves always being outside and dancing the European dances in their own way, Marly (1828, 47–48) gives what were apparently typical scenes at a crop-over dance where slaves danced inside the hall, with black women partnering white men or with the slaves dancing with each other when the white men withdrew to have supper. It is white men, not the "negro girls" or "their own black countrymen", who are portrayed as gauche in dancing. The slaves were equally at home inside, dancing "reels or country dances".

The transition from dancing outdoors to dancing indoors was the fundamental indicator of the changing values of the slaves. It is ironic that it was not a new or urban event that was symbolic of the critical stage in the process of change, but one related to the lifeblood of these societies – sugar. The crop-over event was a plantation event, which meant that the acculturation process by now had virtually affected all the slaves in the society, as though it had to be completed before the emancipation of the slaves so that no other options would be available to them when presumably they could follow their own preferences. It is interesting to note that the bamboula, which seemed to be the quintessential outdoor event before emancipation, also came indoors after, as illustrated in Larsen (1928, 261) in the Virgin Islands in the 1860s.

Making the Body Talk in the Context of Slavery

Slave dancing in the West Indies developed as an interactive, outdoor spectacle with dancers surrounded by a crowd forming a ring. It was like a small version of matadors fighting bulls in a ring in Spain or gladiators fighting lions in the Colosseum in Rome and it basically performed the same function of central, popular entertainment. However, unlike those bigger, more structured activities, it was an open space event that allowed for changes in participants, involvement of children on the periphery and, overall, greater individual

Figure 16. *Contests and Plays of the Negroes*, by François Dumoulin, 1788.

freedom. It was an inclusive, 'peaceful' event. Interestingly enough, the name *kalenda*, which Labat had identified as the name of the first popular slave dance in Martinique, was also used as the name for a kind of African performance/dancing that featured (mock) fighting between men with swords or cutlasses, which developed in the Caribbean into stickfighting. As depicted by both Dumoulin (see figure 16) and Brunias, it seemed more like a contest of artistry and skill, almost in the form of a dance, rather than a contest of violence. It did, however, involve an element of physical injury because it was intense. It was definitely a variant of the ringed performance.

The ringed performance was different from the round dance (dancers forming a circle). In contrast to Moreau de Saint-Méry, who saw the circle dance as primitive, Gikandi (2011) commented positively on it, but his argument is diminished by his misinterpretation of the source he cites. Gikandi (2011, 265) writes: "Reporting on the West Indies, the French priest Jean Pierre Labat did not find the Calenda, a Congolese dance, entertaining, but he did notice both the organization of the dancers in a circle and the intimacy it engendered: 'The dancers, men and women, form a circle, and without moving about do nothing else but to raise their feet in the air.'" Contrary to what Gikandi writes, Labat's (1724, 2:53) argument was that the Congo dance (which he did not name) paled in comparison with the universally loved calenda (an Arada dance) – "Congo negroes have a dance that is the exact opposite of that [of the Aradas]." Moreover, the calenda which Labat described was neither a circle dance nor a ringed dance – the dancers were in two lines. There was no circle dance described for Africans in the Caribbean.

The ringed performance involved either individuals or couples – the former gymnastic in appearance and the latter more elegant and stylistic. These variants have survived, not necessarily distinct from each other, especially in the bèlè in several French-influenced Caribbean islands, where individuals, taking turns, perform before a crowd to show their own special dance moves and postures in a competitive manner.

Dancing in which a man and a woman respond to each other's moves is in structure the same as call-and-response in singing, but the difference in this kind of dancing is that there is a strong element of exhibitionism and a desire to match or outdo the other – it is thus both complementary and competitive. It can be said that part of what is read into the female dancer's performance is an indication of sexual readiness and competence and, as to the male dancer, an indication of his sexual prowess. Some of the indigenous dances involving males and females were said to imitate birds, but no details are given. In the case of the slaves, the performance of the male dancer in this dance has an element resembling the pre-mating ritual of a peacock or that of some doves. It is quite likely that, probably like the indigenous dance, the slave dance drew some inspiration from the behaviour of birds. Bear in mind, however, that this kind of dance was not exclusive to West Indian slaves and the worldwide popularity of the fandango, for example, indicates that mating ritual dances have universal or fundamental roots.

What the mating ritual dance shows is that dance is used to effect non-verbal communication. What it also shows is that the beauty of the dance is thought to affect the partner – whether the partner is supposed to be dazzled into submission by the beauty of the dancing body or the visual pleasure is meant to make the partner more receptive is debatable. In the context of slavery in the West Indies, where there was a high degree of language diversity and difficulty in verbal communication, the communication achieved by beauty in dance was extremely advantageous in overcoming verbal limitations: it compensated for the linguistic skills needed in courtship. Ironically, it also led to the stereotyping of the male slave body during the period of slavery and afterwards as one with unusual sexual power.

Over time, female slaves especially were able to display their attributes through dancing when they took part in indoor social events put on by whites. Close-quarter, approved contact with whites publicly conceded that slaves were human beings with social skills. Some slaves would certainly have been elated by this recognition of their humanity and would have valued dancing as the medium through which they achieved it, even if exclusive, indoor events afforded them less freedom in their dancing.

Slavery took away from the slaves the use of the intellect to govern themselves, to judge and arbitrate their own matters, to feed themselves and to formally educate themselves. Furthermore, they no longer had the hierarchical age and ancestral structure with its acquired wisdom to manage their supernatural beliefs. In these ways they were dehumanized. However, one area of activity which allowed them some latitude to express their humanity was entertainment and, ironically, they not only entertained themselves but they also had to entertain their masters. It is in dancing that their aesthetic sensibility became most apparent and dominant. In spite of the fact that whites regarded dancing as physical rather than intellectual activity, the slaves themselves drew an inner strength from it and relied on this to defend their humanity.

9. Singing to Survive and Jive

PAUL LAURENCE DUNBAR, AN AMERICAN AND SON OF SLAVES, has a poem "Sympathy" (1913, 102) which asserts: "I know why the caged bird sings!" Dunbar gives the reason as:

> It is not a carol of joy or glee,
> But a prayer that he sends from his heart's deep core,
> But a plea, that upward to Heaven he flings

Maya Angelou has a similar poem, "Caged Bird" influenced by Dunbar's poem, which proclaims:

> But a caged bird stands on the grave of dreams
> His shadow shouts on a nightmare scream
> His wings are clipped and his feet are tied
> So he opens his throat to sing.

In other words, for Maya Angelou, singing is a response to loss of freedom.

The Jamaican duo the Blues Busters used Psalm 55:6 ("Oh, that I had the wings of a dove! I would fly away and be at rest") as one line in their 1965 song "Wings of a Dove". They finished the verse by adding: "Since I have no wings, I have to sing, sing, sing, sing, sing." The idea here is that singing is an escape from the trials of life and that it is a facility of humans; but birds have the better, enviable option – they can just fly away.

Without using any bird image, R.C. Dallas (1823, 145) boldly stated: "the fact is that the negroes are a singing race". For him, then, they were always singing, which, taken literally, would mean they were like songbirds, innately programmed to sing. On the other hand, Edward Long (1774, 2:410) reported that the "Creole Blacks" contemptuously called the Africans among them "Guiney birds". Now, guinea birds are not known for singing sweetly; they are more like noisy watch dogs and one may be tempted to infer from this that singing sweetly did not apply to Africans, only their descendants, and furthermore that happiness through singing was a feature of the descendants only.

This metaphorical use of birds adds an imaginative element to the discussion of singing in the context of slavery, but it also shows contradictions of symbolic representation. Basically, it is necessary not only to consider whether singing was magnified as an emotional outlet, whether it was joyful or sorrowful, but also to explore the difference between the reaction of captured and enslaved Africans and that of persons born into slavery.

In the historical literature, the factor that brought the slaves' singing and music to the attention of Europeans was that it was inescapable in the plantation setting. Several writers described their music and singing as loud. The sound of their voices was said by Moreton (1790, 156) to be "so loud, that of a calm night they may be heard at about two miles distance". What contributed to the loudness was the interaction between the participants, which probably made it sound tumultuous to Europeans. The musical instruments, the hand clapping, the dancing, the exchange of dancers and the singing made for an affair that resounded.

However, this vibrancy and loudness was not immediately apparent from the beginning, according to some seventeenth-century accounts. For example, Labat (1742, 4:467), in describing a dance, referred to the dancers as "mumbling some story which one of the company relates, to which the dancers reply with a refrain, while the spectators clap their hands". Apparently, in the seventeenth century, individual ethnic groups were not substantial enough to create loudness and vibrancy.

The interactive way of singing came to be the factor that was the most often noted down, presumably because it was most striking to Europeans. The call-and-response format was a feature of various situations – work songs, recreational singing and funeral singing. Labat (2:463) identified it at the end of the seventeenth century as an integral part of the calenda dance: "The most accomplished sings a song . . . the refrain of which . . . is sung by all the spectators." The same kind of comment was made in *Short Journey* (1790, 90–91) as well as by Monk Lewis ([1834] 1969, 80). These descriptions, covering more than a century, presented a kind of interaction in song which Europeans found powerful for the most part and uncomfortable.

Added to the pervasiveness, interactivity and loudness of the singing, what must have been intriguing was that the language of the slaves was different and in large measure not intelligible to whites. In summary, then, according to the historical literature, slave singing was a major feature of colonial life which increased in impact, especially when experienced as part of a viewed event, as slave activities became more established and as the percentage of creole slaves increased.

LABELLING ALL THE SLAVES' SINGING AS AFRICAN

It would seem reasonable to assume that whatever songs captured Africans sang on board ship and when they reached port were African. However, this may not be completely true, for it is more than coincidental that the soldier James Aytoun (1984, 21) referred to the slaves' arrival song in Dominica in the late 1780s as a "yo yo" and Sir William Young (1801, 268) in St Vincent thought the slaves arriving in St Vincent in the early 1790s were singing "yah yah". Young said that he thought the word meant "friends" and Maureen Warner-Lewis (2003, 311–12) gives "yaya" as a term of address in Trinidad Koongo which she glosses as "friend" and identifies as a respectful title for an honoured person in Koongo. It is highly unlikely that slaves arriving in different ports from different African sources at different times would automatically choose to sing the same (type of) song.

In this case, it is not a matter of one writer copying the other, because not only were Young and Aytoun far apart socially but also their recollections came to light at different times and in different ways. It does not seem far-fetched, therefore, to suggest that some simple song of arrival had become customary among ships' captains and that arriving slaves were instructed to sing it. Indeed, the strict regimentation of the slaves on arrival points to a strong input from ships' captains rather than a spontaneous outburst of song from the slaves. In short, right from their arrival the slaves were being seasoned into their new environment and being led to believe that singing was advantageous in this new situation.

At the beginning of the eighteenth century, transcriptions of pieces identified as slave songs in Jamaica were published for the first time in a book in a formal manner, with music score and words. Only a few of the transcriptions which appeared after that during the period of slavery were the result of the kind of zeal that Hans Sloane (1707, 1) exhibited when he said: "Upon one of their festivals when a great many of the Negro musicians were gathered together, I desired Mr. Baptiste, the best musician there to take the words they sung and set them to musick." There were actually three tunes ("Angola", "Papa" and "Koromanti") appearing in Sloane's work, although the second one is extremely brief. From the titles given to each piece and from the words in the score of the first and the last, Sloane obviously meant that each piece was from a specific ethnic group among the African-born slaves in Jamaica. Sloane must have had some specific way of identifying the ethnicities given (he did say that the "Papas ... have ... scarifications" [1707, liv]), but the sketchy way in which the words are inserted on the score especially in the third piece is not reassuring of a high level of linguistic competence on his part.

If the festival that Sloane recorded took place in 1688, that was only thirty-three years after Jamaica became an English colony, which means that the majority of slaves at the time had African languages as their first language. However, during that period a significant number of colonists and their slaves came to Jamaica from the smaller English islands, which also means that some acculturation had already affected most slaves. So, beside the fact that whatever words the slaves were singing were being mediated through a transcriber who presumably did not fully understand their languages, it is possible also that the Africans involved could already have been separated for some years from the languages and contexts of the songs they were singing.

In one of the many general statements about "the Negros" preceding the presentation of the music scores, Sloane (1707, xlviii) said, "their songs are all bawdy, and leading that way", but the full meaning of the words of the transcribed songs is not clear. Nevertheless, Lalla and D'Costa (1990, 128), with the help of a native speaker of relevant West African languages, suggest that the third song ("Koromanti") is a "children's play song", though it is difficult to see how and why in the context specified by Sloane the musicians would be playing a children's play song.

Bryan Edwards (1793–94, 2:85), in another sweeping statement like Sloane but a few decades later, adds a further dimension without bringing any clarification: "Their tunes in general are characteristic of their national manners; those of the Eboes being soft and languishing; of the Koromantyns heroic and martial." So, from these different sources, songs of at least one ethnic group (Koromantyn) could have been children's play songs, bawdy songs and heroic and martial songs. It is not only that these comments do not bring clarity but also that even if one could unequivocally characterize these songs or any one or two songs recorded in the literature, one would not know how representative they were of slaves' songs generally.

By specifying ethnicities in their comments, Sloane and Edwards created a notion of precision, in contrast to the vague notion of "African", as in the following citation from Pinckard (1806, 1:272), speaking of a slave funeral in Barbados: "During this process an old negro woman chanted an African air, and the multitude joined her in the chorus." Barclay (1826, 136n) provided a music score for an "African" song, but neither he nor Pinckard proffered words for what they heard – probably the words did not sound like English to them.

It is interesting to contrast Pinckard's notion of "African" songs with Barclay's. For Pinckard the song that he heard was "loud and lively", whereas "wild and melancholy" was "African" for Barclay, in keeping with the vision of "savages interring their dead at the midnight hour". Pinckard also noted that everybody joined in the singing, which suggests that they knew the words and that the songs were familiar, which could have been typical for funerals. A notable factor in this case is that the people involved were not plantation slaves. Yet in this comparison of Pinckard and Barclay, it could have been the difference between "urban" Barbados and plantation Jamaica that accounted for some of the variety in "African" funeral songs at the end of the eighteenth century.

When Long first mentioned John Connu in 1774, he identified and associated the masquerader with a famous person from Axim on the Guinea Coast. Long himself did not record any songs sung in the parade, but Phillippo (1843, 242), more than fifty years later, repeated much of what Long said, applying it to early nineteenth-century Jamaica. He introduced what he regarded as festivities similar to "the wild festivals of Africa", saying: "On such occasions each of the African tribes upon the different estates formed itself into a distinct party." However, these were actually Barclay's (1826, 10) words which he copied. Phillippo (1843, 242) then proceeded to reproduce Barclay's (1826, 12) music score for one of the songs sung by the set girls as if it applied to the songs sung by the John Connu players. Clearly, then, what Phillippo reproduced as possibly an "African" tune was really creole, because the criteria used to select those specific singers would not have allowed for African slaves.

Handler and Frisbie (1972, 16) reproduces the score and words of what is referred to as "An African Song or Chant. – taken down in Notes by G.S. [Granville Sharp] from the information of Dr. Wm. Dickson", who was in Barbados during the years 1772 to 1785. The major contradiction with this "African Song or Chant" is that the words are not African – they are creolized English. In a case like this, the most "African" could mean is that musically it sounded African.

Another instance of an "African" song is referred to by "A Scotchman" in a letter to the editor of the *Port of Spain Gazette* of 2 March 1838. In this letter, the "Scotchman" complained about the desecration of the Sabbath, mentioning "the African custom of carrying a stuffed figure of a woman on a pole, which was followed by hundreds of Negroes yelling out a savage Guinea song". The ironic fact about this is that the "custom of carrying a stuffed figure of a woman on a pole" may well have been a cultural practice brought from Europe, but the "Scotchman", in typical fashion, assuming "barbaric" things to be African, identified it as African. Frazer (1925, ch. 28, sec. 2) gives several examples of stuffed figures on poles in Europe as part of the cultural practice of "Burying the Carnival". Since the "Scotchman" went on to say that "nine-tenths of these people were creoles", it is quite likely that there was little that was "African" in what he described, except the tune or beat of the song.

A description of interest, though it does not mention the word "African", is Max-Radiguet's (1842, 4:335–36), in his description of a bamboula. It is his way of describing the sung parts in the bamboula that closely resembles typical remarks by Europeans about Africans: "he sings some weird words at the top of his voice"; "the old black furies . . . burst out in shouts of strange joy, sang with fury . . . they kept on yelling"; "men, women and children . . . yelled strange things, . . . they all shouted and yelled together". Max-Radiguet could have meant that the performers had become possessed and were producing abnormal sounds, but there is the more evident suggestion of "African savages" speaking (unintelligible) languages in the heat of passion.

There is still another dimension to the continued labelling of songs as African and it has to do with the perceptions of the slaves themselves. It seems reasonable to assume that in the early colonial years especially, when the majority of slaves were African-born and were bonded together in a foreign situation, they themselves regarded their singing as African. Following Parncutt and Dorfer (2011, 404), one could argue that the music generally would have sustained them psychologically in exile and created feelings of solidarity. Yet as the vilification of "African" intensified over the years, some creole slaves, who, according to the social hierarchy, were culturally superior to African slaves and who believed that they were showing superiority in their singing, would have been distressed when their singing was dubbed African.

The continual designation of songs as "African" covers up the transition among the slaves from many different African languages and song types to creole ones. Examples from the historical record reveal that the notion of an African song was vague and impressionistic throughout the slavery period and was not intended to capture any distinction between what was typical of enslaved Africans as opposed to creole slaves. In any case, because of the ever-present diversity in situations, people and song types, it would have taken a musically astute person to identify musical features of songs which differentiated African from creole. Many writers simply used "African" emotively as a term to brand the slaves as uncivilized or partly civilized and, from the point of view of the slaves, it constituted a belittling of linguistic and acculturative differences among them that were important to them. The continual use of "African" with reference to singing masked the transitional stage of communicative difficulty, loss of expressiveness and declining capability in African singing that would only have become less debilitating with increasing competence in the evolving creole language and creole singing.

STARTING A SINGING TRADITION: IMPROVISATION

In the early colonial context, there was no available tradition on which enslaved Africans could draw as a matter of course. The areito tradition of the indigenous inhabitants of the islands did not have any possibility of being revived among the slaves, principally as a result of the dramatic decline of the indigenous people. The griot tradition of Senegal and other traditions of ethnic groups in West Africa were rendered virtually useless as a result of ethnic fragmentation. Furthermore, the varieties of language that enslaved Africans were speaking in the early colonial situation were themselves new and developing, which meant that the words of songs were new. In addition, the contexts and situations were new, which meant that the topics had to be new. In short, writers in the eighteenth century were witnessing the start and creation of a tradition. Moreover, there was little or no scribal tradition to set down the music and words and provide a written repository from which further selection could be made. Impromptu and the perception of impromptu, therefore, were the order of the day.

In his description of the calenda dance, Labat (1742, 2:463) noted that "the most able one sings a song which he composes there and then on whatever subject is appropriate". A few decades later, Long's (1774, 2:423) general comment on the slaves' songs was that "their songs, as they call them, are generally *impromptus*, without the least particle of poetry, or poetic images, of which they seem to have no idea". Edwards's (1793–94, 2:85) comment about two decades later was a repetition and embellishment of Long's and Renny (1807, 168) repeated almost verbatim what Edwards said without addition.

Long's view that the songs were "without the least particle of poetry", if taken in a non-prejudiced sense, basically meant that the slaves' songs did not have the rhymes, beat and line length that Europeans were accustomed to. This perception could have been partly caused by the fact that the singers were at the time using a variety of language that as yet had not moved far beyond its basic communicative function or that the singers who were most noticeable were using a non-native variety of language which they had not yet mastered. Of course, Long's assertion that there was an absence of "poetic images" may also mean that whatever nuances there were in the songs were beyond his comprehension. In any case, what seemed obvious to Long in the middle of the eighteenth century was that singers were making up songs as they went along and they did not sound very poetic to him.

Towards the end of the first quarter of the nineteenth century Wentworth (1834, 1:240–41) was still highlighting creativity and even repeating the word "improvisatore" used by Edwards and copied by Renny. The persistent element of improvisation testified to a functional need for adaptation to suit varied situations and changing participants. A case identified by Wentworth was during a crossing in a boat from one island to another when singers/rowers were directing their songs and remarks to specific passengers. This need to personalize songs and make them relevant, interesting and funny therefore led to constant improvisation.

Carmichael (1833, 1:103) also commented on the impromptu nature of the slaves' songs, but she saw this not as a consequence of their circumstances, but as a factor of their mentality: "Negroes have fertile imaginations; and it is not unusual for them to compose impromptu, words to their songs, very often of the most ludicrous nature." Carmichael's vision of the black slave fit into the general picture of the simple, amusing, contented and playful being, but in itself this does not deny the probability that culturally improvisation may have been a prominent feature among West African communities. Bear in mind the following perceptive remark by Jobson (1623, 105–6) in the context of slaving on the West African coast: "singing likewise *extempore* upon any occasion is offered; wherein diverse times they will not forget in our presence to sing in the praise of us white men, for which he will expect from us some manner of gratification".

Some other comments about improvisation give an idea of both the process of composition and the social process of learning involved. Lanaghan (1844, 2:107) noted that a familiar tune could be used, one person would make up new words and the group would then repeat them, thus making a topical and fresh song. A remark by Thomas Cooper (1824, 18n) shows that subjects which, for the slaves, were topical and important could be considered by Europeans to be trivial and not substantial enough for songs: "On one occasion, I listened to a party of old women, boys and girls, singing the following in our kitchen: O massa! O massa! one Monday morning they lay me down, And gave me thirty-nine on my bare rump. O massa! O massa!" Ironically, the whole thrust of Cooper's thesis was the brutalization of the slaves by the slave masters and this very example was given to show the frequency and severity of flogging of slaves (that is, a stated maximum of thirty-nine lashes). Yet Cooper could dismiss the slaves' song as "making a song out of anything".

As to the slaves themselves, they probably saw the improvised song as a safe way of making complaints or a way of using levity to mask pain. In summary, one could argue, then, that improvisation was a popular technique for two complementary reasons – circumstances required it and singers had a cultural predilection for it.

Structural Simplicity with Rhythmic Repetition

There seemed to be no significant body of African songs that survived as a part of the daily lives of the slaves in the Caribbean, as a result of which there was the heavy dependence on improvisation. This meant that in the linguistic development of songs there was more emphasis on creativity than on ancestral continuity. Even though ancestral knowledge would have remained in their heads, singers drew on what was around them to compose their songs and, in time, this substantially affected their repertoire. Perhaps there was an unconscious recognition on the part of Thibaut de Chanvalon (1763, 67), a creole in Martinique, that the slaves were by force of circumstances at the beginning of a new tradition, for in 1751 he compared their songs to poetry from the first age of Man. Even though his comments referred to a period when these colonial slave societies had already been in existence for more than a hundred years, it was still a time when traditions were beginning to emerge. Thus,

Chanvalon's notion of slave songs was that they were basically dynamic, embryonic compositions:

> They are at one and the same time poets and musicians. The rules of their poetry are not rigorous; they are always subject to the music. They lengthen or shorten the words as is necessary to fit them into the tune for which the words must be composed....
>
> If an object or an event strikes a negro, he immediately makes it into the subject of a song. Three or four words, which are repeated by the spectators and the singer in turn, make up the complete poem; five or six beats make up the full extent of the song....
>
> What seems unique is that the same tune, though it may be just a continual repetition of the same notes, keeps them busy, keeps them working or dancing for long hours; the tune, neither for them nor even whites, does not result in the kind of boredom that such repetitions should cause. Sustained interest is no doubt due to the warmth and expression they put into their singing. (67)

The fact that Chanvalon was a creole meant he had a reasonably good understanding of slave songs, but what is also evident in one of his comments is that creole whites enjoyed them.

European writers were of the same view that the topics of slave songs were simple, but they were not necessarily as appreciative as Chanvalon. For example, Cooper's words ("Negroes will make a song out of anything") are dismissive in tone. Long (1774, 2:408–9) expressed his view with more or less the same kind of attitude: "Their ideas seem to be confined to a very few objects; namely, the common occurrences of life, food, love, and dress: these are frequent themes for their dance, conversation, and musical compositions." However, most of the songs of the world are "confined to ... food, love and dress" because these are the fundamental needs of human beings and thus the things that have the greatest potential for making them happy or sad. The striking simplicity of the slaves' songs was therefore in the basic themes, uncomplicatedness of language and their rhythmic structure.

A recorded song which exemplifies simplicity in verbal and musical composition as well as rhythmic repetition is the following:

> Guinea Corn, I long to see you
> Guinea Corn, I long to plant you
> Guinea Corn, I long to mould you
> Guinea Corn, I long to weed you

Guinea Corn, I long to hoe you
Guinea Corn, I long to top you
Guinea Corn, I long to cut you
Guinea Corn, I long to dry you
Guinea Corn, I long to beat you
Guinea Corn, I long trash you
Guinea Corn, I long to parch you
Guinea Corn, I long to grind you
Guinea Corn, I long to turn you
Guinea Corn, I long to eat you.
(*Columbian Magazine* 2 [May 1797]: 766, quoted in Brathwaite [1971] 1981, 18)

Clearly, the transcription converted the song into English, but the pattern of repetition is what is dominant, as is the amusing last line which the whole song has led up to. Songs with such a structure allowed for additional or new lines and that is one of the main features that kept them alive – their adaptability and potential.

It would be unrealistic to expect slaves, except those with an aptitude for music and singing, to produce more than simple songs in a new linguistic and social situation where there was a severe time constraint and a limitation of resources. Few, if any, would have had time to sit down, compose, practise and refine songs. Linguistic subtlety and nuances would have come gradually mostly through actual singing and playing at events. In any case, the utility value of a song such as "Guinea Corn" was much higher for the slaves than "refined" songs.

In the literature, certain slaves were identified as musicians to play at white balls, but there is no mention of recognized singers whose performance was requested or whose job it was to sing, as was the case in certain West African communities. In contrast to dancing, there is no mention in mid-eighteenth-century literature, for example, that singing was competitive or that one singer surpassed the others in any special way. It is only later, in the selection of set girls in Jamaica, that singing was identified as a criterion. Singing, therefore, for the slaves, was not a specialized or display activity and, more than any other artistic form, allowed for general participation. Yet one should note that while slave songs recognized and to some extent catered for the widespread limitations in verbal competence among the slaves, on the other hand, it was those very limitations that delayed the development of singing into a specialist and competitive activity.

Consolidation of a Singing Tradition: Singing on the Job

The image of the slave that European writers developed across the eighteenth century and into the nineteenth was one of a being who sang at work. Singing at work was characteristically portrayed as a group event, but even where a group was not identified, singing and work were seen as complementary. In 1763 Thibault de Chanvalon said: "They don't do any job which requires exercise unless they do it with rhythm, and almost always singing" (67). Twenty-five years later came Marsden's (1788, 36) significant comparison of the slaves singing at work to a swarm of bees (see chapter 4). After emancipation, Belisario (1838, n.p.) noted that "the Milkmaid of Jamaica travels along at a rapid rate, and beguiles the way with snatches of songs, in a style peculiarly her own". A few years later, Lanaghan (1844, 2:106–7) in Antigua remarked that work required an accompanying song. That the slaves sang while working was a consistent observation – it is as if one had approached a plantation during a working day, one would have heard choirs of slaves singing everywhere.

The slave spent a considerable part of the day at work, and singing certainly filled out time and space for many slaves. The work song, therefore, in the case of all workers and especially the single worker, can be said to have created a more amenable work space, as opposed to the hollowness of silence or the rough noises of the environment. Yet even though singing and work went together, the relationship between the two was such that it was not immediately clear whether singing was additional to work, a response to work or provoked by work. This question was raised early in the colonial period by Du Tertre (1667, 497): "I don't know if the songs they mutter while working come from the gaiety of their temperament, or if they sing them to soothe their tiredness." This difficulty in fathoming the reason for singing indicates, more than anything else, that the idea of universal singing by the slaves would have been at best an exaggeration and at worse a reduction of the slave to an instinctive or mechanical simpleton.

Music, in one form or another, as an accompaniment to work has never been restricted to any one set of people and it is not necessarily spontaneous. For centuries, precise rhythmic beats have been used to keep rowers in unison, and military bands, with the drum as the dominant instrument, have been used to keep soldiers going and together. Singing could have become functional and effective for the same reasons among the slaves, but this would not have been essentially different from the practice of "singing the slaves" on board ship during the middle passage (that is, an imposition intended to achieve an economic objective), and it is difficult to see why the slaves would have imposed such a regimen on themselves. For, rather than there being any claim in the historical literature that singing was imposed on the slaves by the masters, there is the repeated idea that singing was spontaneous among them. Therefore, it must be that slaves were using singing for their own benefit: in essence they were using this medium aesthetically to restore their equilibrium and enliven their working hours.

When the slaves worked in groups, the pace of the work was in harmony with the rhythm of the songs sung and when the work was done in unison, the weight and manoeuvrability of tools or implements used determined the pace of the work. There was therefore a direct relationship between work and song structure. Presumably, a double-time beat would have accommodated many of the heavy tasks requiring strength which the slaves had to do and this is probably why it became a common beat in the slaves' music. The slave in this way became acclimatized to the common rhythm of the tools, which made them less onerous.

Chanvalon (1763, 66) explained what he thought to be the centrality and basic function of the rhythm in the work song in the following way: "It is an advantage in most jobs. Singing enlivens them and the beat becomes a controlling force. It forces those who are indolent to keep up with the others." The social function and the effectiveness of rhythmical singing thus did not escape the notice of some whites, who were noting this equal and full participation in work with satisfaction. As to the slaves themselves, one can only speculate about the cumulative effect of being controlled by a beat while working and the extent to which this affected psychological well-being, especially each individual's tendency to freedom or conformity.

Singing was also an interactive experience in which status and competence determined who sang and when as well as who were the main singers and who formed the chorus. Slaves thus recognized artistic levels among themselves and, no doubt, lead singers in work songs were accorded some measure of respect. In addition, since it was normal for the slaves to target whites in the subject matter of their songs, those slaves who were better composers were likely given preference to sing. However, as a group, the slaves must have prided themselves on being able to perform their songs skilfully and artistically and thus lessen the probability of retaliation from their superiors. In short, work, art and consciousness of status were intricately intertwined. Overall, however, singing among West Indian slaves was the province or the art of the acquiescent, as a result of which observers formed the impression that the performers were all cheerful and contented.

Du Tertre (1667, 497), in the early years of the small island colonies, identified cheerfulness as the most visible feature in the slaves' demeanour when they were singing, even when they were singing about their masters' (mis)treatment of them. Seeing that Du Tertre commented on the topics of the songs rather than the music, it could be that even at this early stage the work song had its subject matter in focus and was sung in such a manner as not to be openly threatening. Since Du Tertre could specify the subject matter, apparently the songs were being sung in language that was intelligible to him, which suggests that the songs were intended to be overheard by the very persons who were the culprits. Yet Du Tertre's overall reaction was that the slaves were merely making fun of their masters. Two forces seemed to be operating. First, the slaves believed that a cheerful critic had a good chance of being heard and, second, they derived (mischievous to sadistic) pleasure and satisfaction from being able to get back at their superiors.

Long (1774, 2:423), in a comprehensive summary of the nature of slave songs, explains the interactivity and subject matter but finishes by highlighting the element of fun:

> The tunes consist of a *solo* part, which we may style the recitative, the key of which is frequently varied; and this is accompanied with a full or general chorus. . . . Instead of choosing panegyric for their subject-matter, they generally prefer one of derision, and not unfrequently at the expence of the overseer, if he happens to be near, and listening: this only serves to add a poignancy to their satire, and heightens the fun.

It is significant that Long considered the slaves to be negative (choosing derision) rather than positive (choosing panegyric) in their subject matter: it is as if they preferred making fun rather than engendering pride. It is as if all the divisive elements of slavery and their loss of status had overpowered them or wiped all ideas of positive identity from their minds.

Moreton (1790, 152), in his account of Jamaica in the last quarter of the eighteenth century, reiterated the idea of amusement in identifying what he saw as "witty" work songs, sung by females in the fields. Moreton's reaction, like that of Du Tertre and Long, was to see the songs as amusing even though they were critical of the masters. The examples strengthen the argument that the slaves focused on artistry in their singing to counterbalance any perceived negativity in the message.

Another example of a work song in which the singer is commenting on the master comes from William Dickson and is reproduced by Handler and Frisbie (1972, 16):

> Massa buy me he won't killa me Oh
> Massa buy me, he won't killa me Oh
> Massa buy me, he won't kill me Oh
> 'for he kill me, he ship me regulau

This song is cynical and witty, but there was a certain "safety" for the slave in singing work songs critical of a master, seeing that the slave could be said to be singing a song about someone else (possibly dead and gone). At the same time, the slaves among themselves could cleverly change the words of a song to make it relevant to their own situation, a fact that led writers repeatedly to point out that the songs were improvisations. In a song like the one above, in which the slave is cynical enough to argue that his master was not going to kill him because he had bought him, it is evident that slaves felt some measure of security in their economic worth. Slaves, in their singing, no doubt had to walk a thin line between amusement and provocation and it is no doubt because of this that they had to develop cleverness in language use.

Another work song, one that was quoted in more than one work and seemed to be widely sung and recognized, ostensibly showed a more reflective and philosophical slave accepting the inevitability of death. Bayley (1830, 358) cited it in the context of Grenada:

> Sangaree da kill de captain,
> Oh lor, he must die
> New rum kill de sailor,
> Oh lor, he must die
> Hard work kill de nigger
> Oh lor, he must die[1]

---

[1]. Phillippo's (1843, 189) version of the song, said to be recorded in Jamaica, has "dear" instead of "lor" and it also has a (chorus) line at the end, "La, la, La, la etc.". However, since Phillippo extensively copied remarks on dance from Pinckard's account of Barbados, there is no guarantee that what he says here about this song is genuine.

Actually, in spite of the apparently morbid predictions, this song had an element of fun in it in that, according to the slave, as opposed to the slave who would be worked to death, all the whites were going to drink themselves to death. So, in that sense, it fitted into the witty type of work song that made fun of the masters.

Even more than wit, the artistic element in work songs that is best known is the call-and-response structure. Reverend William Smith (1745, 230–31), in Nevis about the middle of the eighteenth century, gave an early explanation of this element in work songs:

> The Negroes, when at work, in howing canes, or digging round holes to plant them in, (perhaps forty persons in a row) sing very merrily, i.e. two or three men with large voices, and a sort of base tone, sing three or four short lines, and then all the rest join at once, in a sort of chorus, which I have often heard, and seemed to be, La, Alla, La, La, well enough, and indeed harmoniously turned, especially when I was a little distance from them.

Early descriptions of this kind no doubt led to and inspired the pictorial illustration appearing in the *Illustrated London News* (9 June 1849) a hundred years later, showing women with hoes all upraised in unison. The sound of forty singers interacting as a group in a cane field, complemented by the noise of the hoes striking the ground as one sound, could not have been far removed in its visual and aural effect from many a formally choreographed performance.

The chorus ("La, Alla, La, La") sounds like the one given by Sloane in his "African" songs in Jamaica, but Smith gave no information about the content of the "three or four short lines" probably because he did not understand the words. The pattern of the call-and-response described by Smith for this song, which is interactive, differs from that in the song "If me want for go in a Ebo", which is in its message outward-directed. The latter is not a conversation, for there is only one voice; there is a statement and a refrain in alternate lines which complement each other. It is true that while there may be one singer throughout, the "me" shifts from being "Ebo" to "Guinea" to "Congo" to give an idea of the different slaves, but there is no sense of a genuine call followed by a response. This shows that what may be generally and vaguely referred to as a call-and-response format can be differentiated into types, some having a discourse format and others a complementary one. In addition, the variety of the work song described by Smith was probably more characteristic of gangs, whereas predominantly witty work songs were typical of jobs with small numbers of workers.

The interactive work song was celebrated in verse by Grainger (1764, 89), who spoke of "the laughing, labouring, singing throng" and also said:

> While flame the chimneys, while the coppers foam,
> How blithe, how jocund, the plantation smiles!
> By day, by night, resounds the choral song
> Of glad barbarity;
>
> (102)

The beauty of the scene clearly affected Grainger and he therefore tried to capture in his own verses what he obviously saw as poetic – a plantation scene dominated by the slaves' call-and-response choral singing. His remark – "the plantation smiles" – may better be interpreted to refer to the plantation owner, more so than the slaves, but it is the slaves whom he and many others saw as smiling, cheerful and full of mirth as they performed their choral singing. The tone of the songs, the nature of the interchanges between the singers and their reactions would therefore have had to bring about this perception. One gets a prosaic, but no less positive, version of whites' reactions to the slaves' singing performances in the fields as well as the general atmosphere of "mirth" from Bridgens's description of a scene in Trinidad in 1837 (n.p.): "The Negroes comfort themselves in the increased labor ... by a boisterous mirth that knows no relaxation. Some gifted individual extemporizes a line or two, when he is joined by the whole gang, with a power of lungs that would cause the despair of a chorus at a minor theatre." This is a rare case where a writer was sufficiently impressed to refer to the lead singer as a "gifted individual".

Carmichael (1833, 1:103) recorded the same remarkable marriage of *mirth* and call-and-response singing in the fields during crop-time in her account of St Vincent in the 1820s. Wentworth (1834, 2:66–67) not long after also presented a crop-time picture of "poetry and music", but he also pointed out contrasts between gangs in what they were singing: "Here is a song, or rather a *chorus*, which the negroes sing on such occasions, being a fair sample of their poetry and music; kept up, perhaps, by a few of them working together, whilst the others at the same time sing some popular English tune, recently imported, something like that delectable compound of harmony and discord, a 'Dutch Medley'."

Another positive reaction to the slaves' performance while working is evident in comments made by Atwood (1791, 258), who seemed to have been impressed by the creativity and competitiveness in work songs which he heard in Dominica. In this case, women and men were working together and the call-and-response format seemed to have assumed its own form as a kind of competitive fun between the sexes.

Singing among the slaves was therefore in nature dramatic performance or "play" in which there was, among other things, an artistic relationship between song structure and the nature of the work, between the singer and the group and between the group and some intended target nearby. Even if there were complaints in some of the songs, there is enough evidence to argue that singing was typical of the acquiescent slave who tried to make the most of an inescapable situation. It is unlikely that rebellious or recalcitrant slaves would have been singing.

From the examples given, one can conclude that the slaves' interactive way of performing and their exuberant way of expressing themselves, which occasioned the simple reaction "it is pleasing to see them at work" (Atwood 1791, 258), were remarkable and demonstrated the positive power of art in combatting oppression. Paradoxically, then, the slaves' performances while working were so accomplished and successful that it was their cheerfulness that shone through and it must have given them a great measure of stoic comfort that neither their masters, overseers, drivers nor anyone else could see any trace of their pain. Indeed, some of them may have convinced themselves that they were happy.

Forging a Spiritual Space in Song

West Africans who came to the New World as slaves were confronted with a monolithic religion the likes of which few of them had ever experienced before. Most of them came to accept it for one reason or another. There is no clear record of the functions that singing played in supernatural practices across the many cultures of West Africa that the slaves came from, and so the rituals of European practice, which included addressing the deity in song and with music, could have been not just new but could have constituted an empty experience for those Africans who had not been exposed to such European religious practice in Africa. Yet though the state or established versions of Christianity constructed a hierarchical world with the slave at the bottom, some Protestant groups championed a world of penury not far removed from the reality of the slaves and the critical feature of Christianity was that it was messianic, which seemed to cater to the slaves' plight. Thus, in spite of its strangeness, the slaves took to this religious singing and its messianic message because singing was already so much a part of their work life, because the idea of returning home after death was a part of the cultural beliefs of some of them, and because the redeeming element of Christianity was appealing to them in their circumstances.

While the Methodists, Baptists and Moravians made many converts of adult slaves, the state or established church believed that the best way to control the workers in the society was to concentrate on children – to school them into obedience and the proper way they should act as slaves and workers. The Anglican Church therefore produced literature specially for the slaves, such as "Directions for catechists for instructing Indians, Negroes, &c.", "A form of divine service for the use of the Negroes", "Bishop Ken's Morning, Evening, and midnight hymns for the use of the catechists in the diocese of Barbados and the Leeward Islands".

Phillippo, in mentioning the successes of Metropolitan schools in Spanish Town, Jamaica, in the years after emancipation, cited several examination performances by the children of former slaves. Being able to recite a considerable amount of information from memory was seen as a high point in examination performance. As evidence of this, Phillippo (1843, 197) reported that "one little boy repeated two hundred and thirty-eight hymns and three chapters [of the Bible], comprising sixty-six verses, almost without mistake or hesitation. A little girl recited, with equal facility and correctness, forty-nine hymns and eight chapters of the Bible." Whether or not this phenomenal performance was true, it showed, without a doubt, the centrality of hymn singing in the variety of Christianity the slaves were inducted into.

Much earlier, the Reverend James Ramsay (1784, 162) was moved to comment on the extent to which this singing came to dominate the lives of slave converts in St Croix: "When they go to, and leave off work, they sing in concert a few hymns drawn up in the common language. Singing makes a considerable part of their common worship." Lewis ([1834] 1969, 174) made a similar kind of comment about the function of singing in the context of Jamaica: "One poor negro . . . told the overseer that he knew himself to be so great a sinner that nothing could save him from the devil's clutches, even for a few hours, except singing hymns." Granier de Cassagnac (1844, 101–2), from his observations in Antigua and some of the French islands, came to the conclusion that "provided that you give negroes music and let them sing, you will always have as many of them as you want in the churches". To substantiate his argument, he directly related the growth of the church in one island to the "negroes'" love of singing: "Two years ago the curate at St Francis in Basse Terre put an organ in his church. Since then, it is never without negroes. Mass after mass is said and they always find themselves there on condition that they are given two or three turns to sing" (102). This provision of more opportunities for singing during the church service seemed to be the first noted example of the kind of significant changes brought about by former slaves' participation in European religions in the colonies.

In addition to comments on the love of singing, there were comments on the nature and quality of the singing. Lloyd (1839, 8) remarked that in the Methodist chapel in Barbados "the singing was louder than in England, from the very powerful voices of the Negros" and also that "Negros . . . all join in, whether they know the words or not" (46–47). This reaction to the slaves' singing voices is similar to an early comment made by Ligon in the seventeenth century: "For their Singing, I cannot much commend that, having heard so good in *Europe*; but for their voices, I heard many of them very loud and sweet" ([1657] 1970, 52).

European reaction to the slaves' loud and enthusiastic singing generally tended to be extreme, positively or negatively. Granier de Cassagnac (1844, 101), by using the words "shouts" (*cris*) and "howling" (*hurlent*), not only gave a clear indication of the force with which singing was produced in Antigua but also his negative reaction to it. Day (1852, 2:111) remarked on the "piercingly shrill" voices of singers in St Vincent, whereas Lanaghan (1844, 2:107) in Antigua had a more favourable reaction: "They are also great psalm-singers, the streets often resounding with this peculiar species of harmony." There is no question that the slaves and former slaves gave full vent to their emotions in their singing and, as Lloyd said, they were not put off by not knowing the words of the songs. However, there is no indication in the comments of whites that the slaves' singing was an expression of pain and a cry for immediate, earthly relief.

After emancipation, with changes in behaviour and circumstance, came new contexts for singing which were even more European in nature. Reverend Hope Waddell (1863, 115), as an agent of the Church of Scotland Missionary Society in northwestern Jamaica, in 1836 was moved to have a "temperance soiree" for members of his flock at which "with the singing of hymns and prayer we mingled free conversation, stories, and unpremeditated addresses". According to him, the success of that "soiree" led to others. In Antigua, Lanaghan (1844, 2:171–74) reported on the development of Methodist "tea parties" or "tea meetings". Provision of social entertainment for church people was an aim of such events described by Lanaghan and Waddell, to compete with dances and balls, which were seen as immoral. Essentially, it meant that religious singing and secular singing were dividing the slaves into two different camps.

One index of development in the lives of the slaves and their descendants was the movement from outdoor to indoor life and religious singing was a part of this movement. Most European religious services took place indoors and the slaves were now for the first time transferring their singing indoors. European perception that their singing was loud was therefore not unexpected, for the slaves were accustomed to singing outdoors where more force was needed to counteract the higher level of noise. In addition, the feeling that the slaves put into their singing was directly related to the stressfulness of their lives and the appeal-to-deity which they believed their singing to be performing in this new religious context. Consequently, while the slaves and their descendants were being transformed by European religious practices, they were also transforming the same practices.

The singing of European hymns and other religious songs with set music and words added a new dimension to the slaves' singing, one that was easily received by those slaves and subsequently former slaves who saw themselves becoming more civilized and less heathen. Actually, it created or restored a "serious" dimension to the slaves' singing, one that had been virtually lost when the slaves were deprived of most of their supernatural practices by enslavement. In the kinds of secular singing the slaves were allowed to indulge in on their own, cheerfulness and fun were central; in the religious singing that Christianity brought to them, seriousness and formality were self-evident. Protestants especially tended towards asceticism and abnegation, which affected those who came under their influence. So, while the new adherents were enthusiastically singing, they were gradually being schooled away from the carefree lifestyle that was thought to be characteristic of them.

Singing the Blues Away

As a result of their experiences of being captured and enslaved, followed by the taxing middle passage and then the ravages of slavery in the Caribbean, the emotional response that one would expect to be most commonly expressed in the slaves' songs was one of melancholia, and some writers made this point. However, several other writers, especially anti-abolitionists, created the impression that the slaves were always carefree and happy, with a *carpe diem* philosophy of life. Rather than being totally contradictory or paradoxical, it may be that the slaves, through peer-group pressure, came to transition away from sadness and morbidity and even if their songs were melancholy, the singing of them brought about a change in the singer. Singing is a transforming medium, for, as Plato argues, the lullaby causes the baby to fall asleep. In like manner, one can argue that singing brought about a decrease in slave melancholia and moved slaves towards "peace and calm in the soul" (Plato 2009, book 7). One can therefore argue for a distinction between the melancholia in the songs and the effect of singing.

Most of the songs that can be identified as melancholy were direct responses to bad treatment, harsh experiences or problematic situations. Dickson (1814, 209) made the following comment about two songs sung by slaves in Barbados between 1772 and 1785: "They have a song, the burden of which is 'Plantation broke, O! poor me one Quaco O!' But it is not so affecting, at least to me, as 'Grace Jones de Regulà', one of their most beautiful ditties." No further details of these songs were given, but they were being cited in a context lamenting the plight of the slaves when their masters went broke and the deplorable conditions attending their sale to pay debts. Singing in this case was an expression of helplessness rather than of complaint.

By and large, most of the melancholy songs were sung with passive resignation rather than aggressive bitterness. Chanvalon (1763, 67), referring to slaves in some of the smaller islands in the middle of the eighteenth century, said: "Their songs are almost always in double time. . . . Those that are made for tenderness inspire rather a sort of languor and sadness; even those that are the gayest carry a certain imprint of melancholy." In his reaction to songs from about the same period in Jamaica, Long (1774, 2:423) said: "Some of them are not deficient in melody; although the tone of voice is, for the most part, rather flat and melancholy." Edwards (1793–94, 2:85) not only characterized the songs themselves but also the effect they had: "At the same time, there is observable, in most of them, a predominant melancholy, which, to a man of feeling, is sometimes very affecting." A few years later, the same comment was elaborated on by Renny (1807, 168). In Chanvalon's comment there is a contrast between "tender" and "gay" songs, while Renny highlights the individual slave singing. The argument here is that in spite of their melancholy tone, these songs brought about peace through reflection rather than caused incitement to action.

Consequently, the following song given by Moreton, which is angry and aggressive, seems suspect. Moreton (1790, 152–53) claimed that he was "struck with deep melancholy" on hearing a slave sing a song like the following:

> Tink dere is a God in a top,
> No use me ill, Obisha!
> Me no horse, me no mare, me no mule;
> No use me ill, Obisha.

Moreton's intention in his book was to create sympathy for the slaves and to show up their masters for their brutality and so the given song is deliberately cited with that intention. It does not seem that in reality a slave could have sung such a song openly without being deemed insubordinate and without being brutally punished. If the song was sung in the safety of the slave's dwelling, then it would have been particularly pathetic. If the song just added weight to the emancipation side of the debate, then it may have achieved Moreton's purpose, but that does not corroborate its status as a genuine slave song.

Not unexpectedly, Samuel Mathews, a creole from St Kitts who supported the status quo, did not identify any of the songs he presented as melancholy. In fact, he introduced the following song as one "in great vogue amongst the Negroes" in St Kitts, as if it was happy and amusing:

> Shatterday nite aucung lau town,
> Chan fine my deery honey,
> Run round de lebin street,
> Chan fine &c.
> Look behind de guaba bush,
> Chan fine &c
> Vosh me pot, au vosh um clean,
> Chan fine &c,
> Au put in paze, au put in poke,
> Chan fine &c.
> Au bine me pot, au bine um sweet,
> Chan fine &c.
> Au sweep me ouse, au sweep um clean,
> Chan fine &c,
> Au clean me knife, au clean um shine,
> Chan fine &c.
> Au mek me bed, au mek um soff,

Chan fine &c,
Au mek um up, au shek um up,
Chan fine &c.
(1793, 138)

This song, a classic case of the absent man-of-the-house on Saturday night, seems to have had a long and popular life because it was reproduced by Mathews in 1822 with some modifications in the spelling of the words. It was later copied in its 1822 form by Wentworth (1834, 2:67), whose comment on it underscored the fact that it was the chorus that was dominant. What is suspicious about Wentworth's version, however, is that, except for the addition of a music score, there is nothing to indicate change over the years. In spite of the fact that Wentworth claimed that it was a work song "kept up, perhaps, by a few of them working together" (2:66), it seems to be the straightforward copying of a previous document rather than a transcription of a song actually heard.

Monk Lewis, almost a champion of the "happy slave" image, recorded songs that were examples of "singing the blues", although he never said so. The following, involving a form of control by obeah, is explained as "The song of a wife, whose husband had been Obeahed by another woman, in consequence of his rejecting her advances": "'Me take my cutacoo, (i.e. a basket made of matting,) and follow him to Lucea, and all for love of my bonny man – O – My bonny man come home, come home! Doctor no do you good. When neger fall into neger hands, buckra doctor no do him good more. Come home, my gold ring, come home!'" ([1834] 1969, 253). This is truly a melancholy love song that reveals a strong belief in the supernatural. Unlike in the previous song, in which the protagonist "chan fine my deery honey", this is a case where she knew where her "bonny man" was, but she could do little to make him come home in the face of the powerful obeah that was "tying" him.

Another song recorded by Lewis (254) reveals a different feature of the slaves' belief systems and practices – the belief in trial by ordeal. The words of the song are implicitly a declaration of innocence from an accused person: "If da me eat Mammy Luna's pease – O, / Drowny me water, drowny, drowny!" (If it is I who ate Mammy Luna's peas, / May the water drown me.) This protestation proved to be a case of false bravado because the person was swept away by the rising water, which meant that the song had a strong element of pathos. More importantly, the song was an integral and typical part of a "nancy" story and as such exemplified singing as a narrative device within storytelling which could be exploited at will by the storyteller.

Another song recorded by Lewis (292) seems to be little more than a plaintive cry:

> Ho-day, poor me, O!
> Poor me, Sarah Winyan, O!
> They call me neger, neger!
> They call me Sarah Winyan, O!

There is no clear reason given for the self-pity in the song; one has to assume that the status ("Negro") and the name (Sarah Williams) are particularly traumatic for some reason. In comparison, another song which is explicitly more tragic but which Lewis (322) introduces as "a popular song" is one in the form of a discourse involving the slave master and the victim/slave:

> Take him to the Gulley! Take him to the Gulley!
> But bringee back the frock and board." –
> "Oh! Massa, massa! Me no deadee yet!" –
> "Take him to the Gulley! Take him to the Gulley!"
> "Carry him along!"

In a dramatic, interactive structure, this song illustrates the ability to make fun of the most tragic circumstances, not just mistaken death but the fact that "the frock and board" were more valuable to the master than the dying slave. Such an appearance of levity virtually removes any element of self-pity on the part of the slave and becomes almost like an amusing play mocking the master.

The topics of the songs given were not as frivolous as whites claimed, but it was the treatment of the topics, especially serious ones, that made them seem so. The slaves endeavoured to minimize sadness instead of wallowing in it, to make fun of suffering, to convey in their reactions that it was frivolous, and to obtain some feeling of triumph over it. This they did through tone, interactivity and, judging by reports, genuineness and directness in expression. So, "singing the blues" became the most popular genre because it allowed the slaves to do their best singing, to rise above their situation and be appreciated for it.

Satirizing the Master[2] and Poking Fun at Others

In the middle of the seventeenth century Du Tertre (1667, 497) made the following observation about the slaves: "As they are great satirists, they point out the smallest flaws of our Frenchmen and they cannot see them do anything reprehensible unless they take it among themselves and make it the subject of their amusement and entertainment." Labat (1742, 4:480–81) also made a similar claim about the slaves in the French islands, referring to the year 1698. At the end of the eighteenth century, in his comments on the black slave in Saint Domingue, Moreau de Saint-Méry ([1797] 1958, 1:61–2) repeats the word *railleur* ("satirist") used by his French predecessors. Edward Long (1774, 2:423), speaking of Jamaica in the middle of the eighteenth century, highlighted derision. Bryan Edwards (1794, 2:85) said that there was among the slaves "a talent for ridicule and derision, which is exercised not only against each other, but also, not infrequently, at the expence of their owner or employer". A few years later, Robert Renny (1807, 169) repeated Edwards's words. No doubt in their social intercourse the slaves had a particular liking for biting, satirical remarks, but the expression of them in song must have been exceptional in its execution and impressive, as evidence of a keen intellect, for it to be so carefully noted down by various writers.

This penchant for ridicule fitted in with the literary behaviour of the local whites, which in turn was consistent with the spirit of sharply worded criticism typical in Europe in the eighteenth century. While satirical features among the black section of the population were part of their traditional culture, they may have survived other non-satirical features not only because they found some form of encouragement in the general critical atmosphere of the time but also because they were explicitly and implicitly encouraged by the social situation.

From early, writers noted that the slaves chose singing as one way of commenting on their situation and also as a way of informing the master and others of the iniquities of it. For instance, Du Tertre (1667, 497) referred to "a song in which they repeat all the good or bad that their masters or overseers do them". Since European writers continued to make this kind of comment, it means that what the slaves were doing was overheard by masters and overseers and was intelligible to them. There are no reports of hostile reaction on the part of masters, which suggests that reality proved it to be a safe method of criticism or

---

2. Piersen (1976) refers to this as "puttin' down Ole Massa".

assessment of masters. There is no good way of determining its effectiveness. Even so, Resident (1828, 234–35), in Dominica, noted that slaves were cautious when singing songs about whites and in some cases had to be requested to do so, which they did reluctantly. The implication here is that whites enjoyed hearing such songs about themselves and their peers, but this also meant that the slaves' comments had to stick within the bounds of amusement.

In his comment on the slaves' use of derision in the plantation setting, Long (1774, 2:423) identifies "mill-feeders" specifically: "In the crop season, the mill-feeders entertain themselves very often with these *jeux d'esprit* in the night-time; and this merriment helps to keep them awake." Here the practice is seen as partly functional and as if inspired by the job itself. This contrasts with the more general situation where the slaves were reacting to abuse or what they considered to be punishment, as in the following case in Barbuda noted by Day (1852, 2:296–97) in the 1840s: "The negro population of Barbuda does not differ essentially from negroes elsewhere. They are very civil but steal wherever they can, and, when detected, make satirical songs on the manager for stopping their pay. . . . a song is immediately made on the poor manager: 'He 'top me pay for *one* head of *carn*,' making him out to be a very hard taskmaster." Both of these cases refer to the work situation, where there was usually more direct confrontation with the authority they were attacking.

Satire, however, was also a part of their plays, as is pointed out by Edwards (1793–94, 2:85): "At their merry meetings, and midnight festivals, they are not without ballads of another kind, adapted to such occasions; and here they give full scope to a talent for ridicule and derision." Renny (1807, 169), a few years later, repeated the same words, adding at the end: "they amuse themselves, . . . at the expense of the awkward *new-come* Negro". Another instance of a satirical song directed at peers is given by Lloyd (1839, 56–57): "Each one recites what he likes; perhaps ridicules the 'true Barbadian', who assumes considerable consequence, from its being the oldest British Colony." The location here was Georgetown, British Guiana, to which many Barbadian former slaves had begun to migrate after emancipation. Here, the "true Barbadian" native of "the oldest British Colony" had become the butt of jokes in what was a case of displaced animosity towards the British master.

One of the best known and simplest of the satirical slave songs can also be classified as principally urban and involving visitors. It ridicules the European who lands in the New World for the first time and does not survive very long. The song was recorded by Renny (1807, 241) as follows:

> New-come buckra
> He get sick,
> He tak fever,
> He be die;
> He be die.
> New come, &c.

Imagine being a European who has just arrived in Port Royal in Jamaica about 1800 and you are confronted by women near your ship singing this song. The background situation was that many Europeans arriving in the New World were struck down by yellow fever and soon died, after suffering horribly. On the other hand, Africans and their descendants in the New World seemed not to be severely affected by the disease. Was this song meant to be just poking fun at new arrivals or was it a cruel threat? It should be noted, incidentally, that the same subject was presented in a narrative comic caricature titled *Johnny New-Come in the Island of Jamaica* done by "JF" and published in 1800 by William Holland. This suggests that the song was not seen as any more cruel than the caricature and both were probably just treated as acceptable fun.

An urban satirical song aimed at an innkeeper was recorded by Colonel Thomas St Clair in Barbados. St Clair (1834, 373) introduced and explained the song this way:

> I put up at an inn kept by Nancy Clark, a black woman of considerable celebrity, on whom the Negroes of this island made the following song:
>
>> If you go to Nancy Clark,
>> She will take you in the dark;
>> When she get you in the dark
>> She will give you aquafortis.
>
>> If you go to Susy Austin,
>> She will take you in the parlour;
>> When she take you in the parlour,
>> She will give you wine and water.

These verses, on my landing, were howled out by every Negro in the place, and on inquiry, I found them to have originated in the conduct of Nancy Clark towards a young girl of colour; she having, in a fit of jealousy, taken an opportunity of throwing in her face some aquafortis to destroy her beauty, which she succeeded in doing most completely. Susy Austin, another woman of colour, kept the other inn, and perhaps, might have bribed the poet for the second stanza.

The writer must have gotten the impression from the local situation that a singer could be paid to advertise products and services. It shows the commercial power that songs could have in the urban setting where business competition must have been keen especially for the patronage of visiting military people.

In 1993 Boehm listed "criticism and ridicule" as one of four mechanisms that societies across the world have used to bring about egalitarian behaviour in cases of extreme dominance. In the case of the slaves in the Caribbean it was a mechanism that they used generally in their songs. It was even used very strategically by white caricaturists who portrayed the slaves as ridiculing "John Bull" around the time of emancipation and specifically in relation to reparation. No doubt, slave satire would have had a powerful effect in intra-slave matters, but how effective it was generally in moderating the behaviour of whites is not clear. Phillippo (1843, 200–201) suggests that it was when he gives the following case of a drunken planter:

> Hearing on a certain occasion the sound of considerable merriment in the direction of his negro settlement, curiosity induced him secretly to ascertain the cause, when he beheld a negro personifying his own gestures and habits when in a state of intoxication, amidst the convulsive laughter of the multitudes of men, women, and children gathered around him. The whole scene had such an effect upon him that he never again indulged in similar excesses.

One can argue that if the British caricaturists "imitated" the slaves in this way, then it must have been effective, but there is no clear evidence that it was effective politically, that is, in bringing about a change in the treatment or status of slaves.

Singing about Liberation

There are few songs of liberation associated with slave rebellions in the Caribbean, but this is not strange since recording and preservation of such songs would have been alien to the sentiments of colonial administrations as well as to European interests. In any case, while the historical record highlighted drums and other musical instruments as media connected to rebellion, it did not characterize songs as important in slave uprisings or singing as a mask for revolutionary activity.

One exception to this was in 1805 when the Trinidad administration condemned four slaves to be hanged for inciting insurrection and gave the following as supporting evidence:

> Such circumstances, combined with the barbarous expressions lately publicly sung by the huckster negro women and other slaves . . . – *"Pain c'est viande Beque, Vin c'est sang Beque; nous va mange Pain Beque, nous va boir Sang Beque*, et les autres compagne repondirent avec le refrain *St Domingue."* puts it beyond a doubt that (the insurrection once broken out) measures had not been neglected to prepare the minds of the slaves in general for such an event. (*Barbados Mercury and Bridgetown Gazette*, 1 February 1806)

This was a unique claim by the administration that the slave population was being prepared for a revolution by a song being publicly sung. The highlighted words in the citation (*"Pain . . . Beque"*) derive from the Roman Catholic Eucharist and are in the language (French Creole) that the slaves in Trinidad would have learned and therefore show the influence of the church on the slaves. One would have to assume that it was the refrain (*"St Domingue"*) and a clear element of mockery in the way that the words were being "publicly sung" for the lieutenant governor and his council to come to the conclusion that the slaves were being prepared for rebellion. If indeed this interpretation was correct, it shows an admirable level of courage on the part of the singers.

Another song of rebellion was identified by Monk Lewis ([1834] 1969, 228) as "Song of the King of the Eboes". Lewis, who was speaking of events before his visit to Jamaica in 1816, introduced the song by saying "a copy of the following song was found upon the King":

> Oh me good friend, Mr. Wilberforce, make we free!
> God Almighty thank ye! God Almighty thank ye!
> God Almighty, make we free!
> Buckra in this country no make we free:
> What Negro for to do? What Negro for to do?
> Take force by force! Take force by force!
> *Chorus*
> To be sure! to be sure! to be sure!

This refusal to continue being a slave and to seize freedom was in effect a declaration of rebellion through song. It was indeed treated by the authorities in Jamaica as evidence of intent to rebel and the participants were dealt with accordingly. This song, for whites, would have been comparable the Daaga "war song" recorded by Joseph ([1838] 1970, 264) in Trinidad some years later. The liberation sentiments in it must have raised visions of nearby Haiti. However, apart from these examples there are no other songs that can be called songs of rebellion, not even what Carmichael (1833, 2:301–2) referred to as "an insurrectionary song" in the 1820s in Trinidad, which simply relates to a plot to steal money.

There are other songs that can be obliquely associated with liberation. For example, Cynric Williams (1826, 299) provided a cynical, anti-abolitionist song said to have been sung by a slave. The slave was one of a group of washerwomen in Turtle Crawl in northeastern Jamaica who said that the song was composed by a freed slave who had spent six to seven years in England training to be a missionary. The song, which features a female slave/white man/male slave triangle, contains a mischievous element that is doubly ironic. The double irony is that the church is seen to have worked against the interests of the slaves in its functions as a status quo institution and at a personal level it corrupted the people, especially women, with "roguish" preachers. The main force of the song, however, is that it equates Wilberforce ("Massa W-f-e") with this "roguish" behaviour and, as such, is a backhanded attack on him and the abolitionists. It may really then be classed as anti-abolitionist propaganda rather than a genuine slave song opposing Wilberforce and liberation.

Renny (1807, 24) introduced what could have been an "egalitarian" song in the following way:

> The following was, in the year 1799, frequently sung in the streets of Kingston:
> One, two, tree
> All de same;
> Black, white, brown,
> All de same:
> All de same.
> One, two, &c.

In Jamaica, so near to revolutionary Haiti, for slaves to be making such a statement about colour had to be provocative. Yet nothing is said about the reaction of whites to this song and there is no indication of its context or the circumstances of its origin. More than thirty years later, Phillippo (1843, 190) repeated what Renny said without adding anything particularly informative about the significance of the song.

Expansion of the Repertoire: Europeanization in Slave Songs

Although throughout the slave period, evidence of whites singing is sparse, it is clear that the slaves not only were liberally exposed to English, Scottish and Irish songs but also that they reproduced them in one way or another for various reasons. It was not just house slaves who were involved, because Wentworth (1834, 2:66–67) mentions slaves in the fields singing "some popular English tune, recently imported". It was especially at festivals or major celebrations that slaves produced versions of British songs which came to be noticed by European writers. Several of these occurred in the literature around the time of emancipation, not necessarily because they were more popular then but because writers wanted to include "eyewitness" material to make their work appear more genuine and to make themselves seem more knowledgeable, especially when they were promoting one side or the other in the abolition debate.

Overhearing, probably the most common method by which slaves expanded their musical repertoire, is explained by Carmichael (1833, 2:152): "Very often, when I had finished their lessons for the evening, I sat down to play on the piano-forte. On such occasions they remained about the house, listening to the music. . . . They soon had a large addition of tunes added to their stock of negro airs; and I have heard sundry airs from Hadyn and Mozart, chanted by the boys when cleaning their knives, with astonishing accuracy." This method of expansion was typical of an acculturation process in which the piano-forte and sheet music would have created a strong attraction as elements of sophistication. Yet the fact that the slaves retained "their stock of negro airs" indicates that expansion of their musical repertoire was an index of their open-mindedness rather than a desire to become European.

During the festival that Monk Lewis witnessed on New Year's Day, 1816, he saw slave "actors" doing an English play and "set girls" singing songs about the Duke of Wellington and the Battle of Waterloo. He also mentioned the singing at the end of the performance when the girls came around to collect money and especially the lead singer, whose "first song was the old Scotch air of 'Logie of Buchan', of which the girl sang one single stanza forty times over" ([1834] 1969, 57). What was significant about a slave girl singing "O Logie o' Buchan" (composed before 1756) was that it would have taken some familiarity with the Scottish dialect to reproduce it. For a slave girl to be able to sing a verse of this song meant that there was more than a passing Scottish influence on the slaves from among whites who were interacting with them and teaching them or providing models of the words of songs.

About a decade later, Marly (1828, 293) also mentioned the singing of British songs by slaves during the end-of-year "negro festival". It seems as if different "parties" had a preference for specific songs and sang them repeatedly during the procession. The song of one party caught his attention and he introduced it in the following way: "The greatest number of them were skipping and dancing along, in place of walking, and kept singing . . . lines of the Woodpecker, in chorus, which, from its universal use, seemed to be their favourite." This ballad ("The Woodpecker"), originally composed by Thomas Moore (1861), was made into a song which seemed to have become very popular. As is the case with set pieces learned by heart, there is the clear suggestion, in the writer's transcription, that some of the original words and meaning of the song had eluded the grasp of the slaves. Nevertheless, what must have been appealing to them in their rural setting were the words "If there's peace to be found in the world / A heart that is humble might hope for it here." There is no sense here of rebellion, but peaceful acceptance of a humble life.

Another festival song from Jamaica, given by Belisario (1837, n.p.), contains some liberation sentiment, but Belisario disregarded this and dismissed the song as unintelligible:

> There is a Regiment of the 64th, we expect from home,
> From London to Scotland away they must go,
> There was one among them, that I really love well,
> With his bonny Scotch plaid, and his bayonet so shining,
> Now pray my noble King, if you really love me well,
> Disband us from slavery, and set us at large."
> Chorus. – La la la, la la la.

Belisario's scathing remarks on the song were: "The incongruities to be found almost in every line, never strike these folks, on the contrary, they are perfectly satisfied with this style of arranging their ideas, without for a moment stopping to consider, if it be prose, or poetry. – Here we have a love-sick *fair-one*, absolutely enamoured of a soldier she has *never seen*, and in conclusion, presuming the King is in love with her." Belisario's problem was that he was distracted by the form and structure of the song and paid little attention to and had little sympathy for the slave's words at the end, which had a clear message – "Disband us from slavery and set us at large."

Versions of celebratory war songs also appeared as "negro festival" songs in Jamaica. The originals were clearly inspired by the British military victories over its main colonial rival, France, especially the Battle of Waterloo in 1815 and the deeds of the Duke of Wellington. Lewis ([1834] 1969, 57–58) gives an introduction and explanation to examples of this kind of song which were topical and apparently popular:

> The second [song] was in praise of the Hero of heroes; so I gave the songstress a dollar to teach it to me, and drink the Duke's health. It was not easy to make out what she said, but as well as I could understand them, the words ran as follows:
>
> "Come, rise up, our gentry,
> And hear about Waterloo;
> Ladies, take your spy-glass,
> And attend to what we do;
> For one and one makes two,
> But one alone must be.
> Then singee, singee Waterloo,
> None so brave as he!"

Most likely the slaves were attempting to produce a dramatic version of military songs they heard to suit the festival, but the poetic structure of these British songs and the ethnic features present did not always allow for easy conversion and intelligibility. Nevertheless, for them, the element of drama and perhaps parody were more important than accurate mimicry.

In contrast to this dramatic adaptation, Bayley (1830, 437–38) gave a blatant anti-abolitionist parody of a popular English song ("I'd be a butterfly, born in a bower...") saying that it was popular among slaves in Grenada. The parodied version fits squarely into the material produced or sanctioned by anti-abolitionists, which immediately makes it difficult to tell whether it was really sung by Grenadian slaves, and especially since the parody does not engage with the line in the original, which says: "I'd never sigh to see slaves at my feet." Perhaps Bayley thought that the slaves were so happy that sighing for them was illogical. More than likely, what Bayley gave as the slaves' version of the song was his own anti-abolitionist doctoring of it.

In addition to expanding their repertoire, the singing of British songs with many of the words and most of the verse structure intact reflected the degree of acculturation that the slaves had undergone by the time of emancipation. More than one writer, with a sense of approval, observed that the slaves had lost much of their Africanness in their cultural performances, which essentially meant that they had become more creole. The most critical factor in the acculturation process was that the slaves had fewer and fewer models of Africanness to emulate and correspondingly more and more European ones. In effect, their singing was being changed and, even if they maintained for some time a range of cultural influences in their singing, overall it was moving towards European norms.

Singing of foreign songs became an integral part of formal education for the children of former slaves after emancipation. The following information about singing and foreign songs taught in Mico schools in St Vincent is given by Charles Day (1852, 2:274):

> Singing seems to be the grand feature, and I hear the children singing in chorus half the day. Pious ejaculations are accompanied by the drollest tunes. As a specimen, I may mention one of the St Vincent melodies:
> "Holy Bible, book divine, tural-ural,
> Precious, precious, thou art mine, tural-ural, tural-ural."
> The tune was "Bonnie laddie, sodger laddie.
> "A boat, a boat unto the ferry," is another infantile chorus, whilst the children promenade round the school-room.
> When the children were dismissed, the seminary was attended by adult teachers from seven p.m. until nine o'clock, and then I had the benefit of the full choir.
> "Here's a health to all good lasses," was a favourite glee. Coloured ladies as teachers joined the class, and gave the "Canadian Boat Song."

The image of the slave as a being who liked to sing and dance was therefore integrated into the school system with a heavy concentration on singing, which involved learning both conceptual and language elements as well as accepting the philosophy of life inherent in the songs.

The Significance of "Slave" Songs in the Mouths of Whites

J.B. Moreton's book *Manners and Customs in the West India Islands*, which first appeared in 1790, was more disturbing to the ruling class of whites in the West Indies than any other previous work. In it there were a number of songs, most of which negatively portrayed the sexual behaviour of women in Jamaica. It was the ridiculing of creole women of all colours that most likely helped to provoke the ire of creoles against Moreton, who cited the songs in most cases to illustrate social behaviour and attitudes. What he succeeded in doing by the use of his illustrative material was to give what seemed like an in-depth and accurate picture of creole ways. Even though Moreton, in his introductory statement to some of the shorter songs, gave the impression that he was merely transcribing what he had heard, overall, the format (metre and rhyme scheme) and the length of the pieces suggest that they were Moreton's own creations.

Moreton's transcription of the "negro dialect" was typical for the time – an anglicized version which partly was intended to reflect the speech of the slaves and partly to make the language intelligible to English readers. There is no question that Moreton had learned a lot about Jamaican speech and customs, but his claim to be presenting actual songs from Jamaica is suspect. While the songs could have been accurate in subject matter, they were not a good reflection, in their form and structure, of the songs sung by slaves at the time. In fact, it is not unreasonable to see some of them as a sophisticated form of doggerel that Moreton and others would have thought to be a good image of slaves.

Samuel Mathews's 1793 book and the "slave" compositions in it were a direct response to Moreton, whom Mathews (1793, 134) branded as "the lying hero" and regarded as "an ignorant, disappointed adventurer". Mathews made the following preliminary statement about Moreton: "Apropos, the Lying Hero then gives you what he calls a negro song; if the reader understands any thing of their lingo, he will find there appears nothing of the negro language in this song. This is as much like a negro song as I am like a poor man." Mathews then went on to record his own songs, saying: "to convince you, my worthy fellow, attend to the two songs which I wrote in the year 1786, and had the honour of singing both, for His Royal Highness Prince William Henry, the last day of Feb. 1787". He then proceeded to give two songs ("Buddy Quow" and "Kibenna"), both of which featured a slave cuckolded by his white master or overseer.

This was not the first time that the first of these two songs had appeared in print. The *Barbados Gazette*, 11 and 15 August 1787, printed the song, which was titled "Buddy Quo" and except for a few variations in spelling was the same as the one in Mathews's book. In the *Barbados Gazette*, the "Buddy Quou" song is not explicitly credited to Samuel Mathews. However, there is circumstantial evidence to support Mathews's claim to the authorship of the song and the context for it. The *Antigua Chronicle* of 8 December 1786 carried news of

Prince William Henry's visit to the Caribbean islands. The prince was captain of HMS *Pegasus*. He visited St Vincent on 18 November 1786; Barbados on 27–29 November 1786; Dominica on 1 December 1786. He was to go on to Antigua and other islands after that. This gives credibility to Mathews's claim that he sang the songs for the prince at the end of February. It is probably Mathews's presence in Barbados that led to the publication of "Buddy Quou" in the *Barbados Gazette* in August 1787, before it appeared in his own book in 1793.

The question whether a white Kittitian could compose and sing genuine slave songs is an interesting one. Clearly, as a white person he did not have the same experience in St Kitts as a slave, but if, as he claimed, he had a long and close association with slaves even as a singer, to what extent would his songs have differed from theirs? What is revealing, however, is that when "Buddy Quou" was first reproduced in the *Barbados Gazette*, it was said to be "sung to the tune *What cheer Old Messmate Jack*", which was a British sailor's song. Not only was the tune therefore not modelled on the slaves' songs but also the form and tone of the song bore some similarity to the song ("The sailors' dialogue") which provided the tune. The second verse of "the sailors' dialogue" between two sailors, Tom and Jack, goes as follows: "What cheer, old messmate Tom? You look as if you'd cry now; / But I have news from home will make you jump mast high now, Messmate Tom" (Firth 1908, 227), which is virtually the same in structure, rhyme scheme and tone as Mathews's "Vos motter Buddy Quow? Aw bree Obeshay bong you, / You tan no sauby how daw bocra mon go wrong you, buddy Quow."

It would seem, therefore, that Mathews's claim to be singing genuine slave songs really meant that the language of the songs was the dialect that the slaves spoke, for, according to his very words, "negro language" determined "negro song".

It is possible nevertheless that in addition to the "negro language" Mathews may also have been able to capture some of the style of the slaves in his live performance since he claimed that the slaves did not realize he was a white man when he sang for them. It could also mean, since Mathews was so convinced that he sang like the slaves, that the singing of the slaves was already significantly creolized, that is, affected by British songs by the end of the eighteenth century. An additional factor is that "Buddy Quou" uses derision as a weapon: it has two voices, without being a dialogue – that of the "victim" as well as a person, in the first and third stanzas, who is goading the "victim". This use of derision seems to have entrenched itself in the behaviour of the slaves from early in the West Indies. It is a factor which also adds some substance to Mathews's claim to genuineness.

Unlike Mathews's first song/story which follows the format of an English tune, the second one is not dominated by a regular rhyme scheme or lines with a symmetrical beat. In fact, the lines as transcribed by Mathews give no idea of the rhythm or the tune. This is a case of telling a story and a joke with musical accompaniment where the "singer" clearly had to perform the piece, taking the audience through all the trials of the protagonist and giving the punch line at the very end. Perhaps it was this second song that was closer to typical slave songs. Charles Day (1852, 2:121) reproduced an adapted version of the song and introduced it in the following way: "As we have heard something lately of negro melodies, I subjoin a genuine St Kitts negro song, by Sam Matthews." While it is possible that the song was popular in the 1840s, more than fifty years after it first appeared, it is more likely that Day had come across it in the printed literature and reproduced it to bolster the authenticity of his account, which in itself undeservedly promoted the song as a "genuine negro song".

Mathews, in his own mind and probably that of most other whites who heard him, composed slave songs and, more significantly, performed slave songs for a white audience in an important formal context. One of the ways in which this can be interpreted in historical perspective is that it was a transitional stage of "negro" music, with songs and other artistic creations being performed first by white entertainers before the very creators were accepted on white stages to perform them. In this sense, Mathews was a precursor of Al Jolson. In all such songs involving white performers, the intent that is almost exclusively dominant is to create a feeling of happiness, even converting suffering into comedy and jokes.

"The Bonja Song" (cited in chapter 3) presents problems similar to Moreton's compositions. The most striking feature is that it is very regular in its metre and rhyme scheme, which suggests a white rather than a slave source. The British Library catalogue says the following about the song: "A favorite Negro air for the piano-forte, etc [Words by C.F.D.] London: Broderip and Wilkinson. [WM 1802]." Dallas (1823, 145) himself said: "The melody of this song, which was published some years ago, by Broderip and Wilkinson, is, with very little variation such as was caught by ear from some of the negroes. The writer of the words took down the notes, and added the harmony." So, it seems as if the element of the composition that came from the slaves was the music. The words reflect a familiar contrast between whites and blacks that was put forward by whites. In this case, the focus of the song is equally on the "unhappy" white man as it is on the "happy" slave. It fits into that European tradition of using the "uncivilized" to show up the shortcomings of the "civilized".

Like "The Bonja Song", the Jamaican song "Quaco Sam" (in its reconstructed form in Lalla [1981]) is difficult to accept as a slave composition because of the regularity of its rhythm and rhyme scheme. The probable date of composition of this song is given as between the years 1814 and 1823 (Lalla and D'Costa 1990, 143), but if it was composed then, the structure of it must have been different because there are no extant slave songs from the eighteenth and nineteenth centuries that are so uniform. Indeed, Long's comment that slave songs were "without the least particle of poetry" (1774, 2:423) and Chanvalon's that "the rules of their poetry are not rigorous" (1763, 66), both essentially meant that they differed in form from English verse. Even though slaves were undergoing constant English influence, it seems unlikely that they would have changed so completely. The song was clearly modified over time and acquired several versions. It is interesting to note that Walter Jekyll's (1907) version of the song is even more anglicized and relates only to the chorus of the Lalla versions (1981, 1990). No doubt, the popularity of the song among all Jamaicans and others led to its constant re-creation.

Another very symmetrical piece of seven stanzas, said to be composed by "the people of colour in Jamaica" in 1806, was published in 1830 in a book written by Captain Hugh Crow, who is the subject of the song. Crow (1830, 124) introduced the song in the following way: "This was an original song, of which the following is a copy, verbatim, and which is submitted to the reader as a specimen of the literary abilities and good humour of the blacks." Here again, this composition is suspect. First, it is too uniform in its structure, and, second, circumstantial evidence suggests that Crow wrote the poem about himself intending to create the impression that he was a benevolent slaver whom the people he dealt with remembered fondly.

Another set of songs presented in the "negro dialect" occurs in Scott's narrative work, but the writer in this case did not explicitly claim to be recording verbatim. These Scott songs have familiar topics set in a simple verse structure and rhyme scheme. It is as if this combination had become the accepted literary version of slave songs. Judging by some of Moreton's compositions, Mathews's "Buddy Quow", the "Quaco Sam" song, the Hugh Crow song and Scott's songs, it is obvious that there was a belief, probably widespread, that the simple ditty with rhymes could be used to represent slave songs. There was a naive appeal in the use of a simple and innocent person, going about happily from day to day, as a mouthpiece for making social and political comments, because such a person would have been seen as without malice and as merely a messenger. The rise of this kind of "slave" song was contemporaneous with the rise of newspaper dialect all across the Caribbean as a form of social commentary. It signalled the early assertion of certain ethnic features of "national" identity, features that were rising up from the bottom of the society.

Bees, Caged Songbirds and Eagles

Western European countries that colonized the Americas promoted songs of war and military achievement as an important part of their national heritage; in the Caribbean songs of enjoyment and happiness have become a well-known part of the general image of the people. The difference between the former and the latter may be seen as a distinction between captors and captives and may be symbolized as a difference between eagles and songbirds. The singing that is most important to the former is enshrined in the opening words of Virgil's classical text, the *Aeneid*: *"Arma virumque cano"* (I sing of arms and the man). Because most of the slave rebellions in the Caribbean colonies, with the notable exception of Haiti, were abortive, there is no tradition of singing war songs (that is, calls to war) and virtually none of celebration or victory. The warlike songs the slaves came to know were Christian, as in the Psalms, and even though the "battle hymn" "Onward, Christian soldiers, marching as to war" was composed in 1864, it gives some idea not just of the mentality of Christianity as a religion of colonization and empire but also the kind of warrior song that the slaves were exposed to.

Whites were divided in their reactions to the slaves' singing. Grainger (1766, 102) spoke of "the choral song of glad barbarity"; Renny (1807, 168) spoke of "the dismal melody produced by the Negro"; Lanaghan (1844, 2:107) spoke of "this peculiar species of harmony". Indeed, no matter how the slaves' singing was characterized, it was never regarded generally as hostile, threatening or warlike. When Dallas (1823, 145) characterized "negroes" as "a singing race", he was implicitly comparing them with other races, even though his conclusion was based on his experience in Jamaica and not on any universal observation. While his claim was exaggerated and dramatic, it pointed to a kind of singing that was wholesome.

No human groups are singers by nature and the slaves' natural physical environment did not make them singers. Dallas's conclusion combined three realities: whites were unaccustomed to the volume and variety of sounds (including singing) they heard in the Caribbean, the historical record exaggerated singing among the slaves and the psychological privation the slaves underwent promoted an accentuated and compensatory role for singing.

There were three features of the slaves' singing that were outstanding – its salience, its artistic and linguistic structure, and its general appeal. In the early years of the nineteenth century and before, the British public was fascinated by oral performance, especially public oratory. In the West Indian colonies, it was also oral performance that was dominant, not by the sophisticated in the society, but by those at the bottom, who, ironically, were constantly challenged by a polyglot situation in which communication was severely limited for many. For them, singing had to become multidimensional in order to effect maximum communication. Thus, singing involved interactivity (in which there was a balance between the individual and the group), inclusivity (through which the spectator was treated as a participant); intensity (which created a sense of energy and genuineness) and verbal cleverness (which involved simplicity and indirection). The fact that whites among themselves were doing "negro" dances to "negro" tunes shows the extent to which the art of the slaves had become an integral and popular part of white entertainment, no matter what attitude they had to it. Samuel Mathews singing "sex" songs for Prince William Henry (later King William IV) was more intriguing than it first appears, for not long after Mathews performed for the prince, the prince was boldly featured in a 1788 British etching titled *Wouski* (see figure 17). It is described as follows: "Prince William Henry seated in a hammock tenderly embraces a pretty African or mulatto girl; they gaze into each other's eyes." Clearly, Mathews was aware of the prince's amorous exploits in the Caribbean and that his songs would appeal to him.

The etching *Wouski* highlighted the theme of the white man and the amorous black woman that is not only in Mathews's song but came right down to two historically significant calypsos of the twentieth century: Lord Invader's "Rum and Coca Cola" and the Mighty Sparrow's "Jean and Dinah" both feature white American military men being happily embraced by local women. Note that the non-white female character "Wowski", who originally appeared in Colman's *Inkle and Yarico* in 1787, ending up marrying white Trudge to the strains of the now familiar song "Come let us dance and sing / While all Barbadoes

304   A RESPONSE TO ENSLAVEMENT

Figure 17. *Wouski*, by James Gillray, 1788.

bells shall ring". This English image of the black woman and the white man became so attractive that an 1827 publication of Colman's libretto featured a single (frontispiece) pictorial illustration – Trudge and Wowski dancing to that song (see figure 18). Ironically, the same (white man/black woman) image was in the years preceding caricatured just as strongly, as in the *Johnny New-Come* (1808) comic strip and "Tit bits in the West Indies" (1798).

What is intriguing about Mathews himself is that he was a contemporary of Alexander Hamilton in St Kitts, Nevis and St Croix, though there is no evidence that the two knew each other or that they had much more in common than writing. The fact is, however, that Hamilton, a Nevisian who became a founding father of the United States, is the inspiration for the Broadway musical *Hamilton*, which captures the revolutionary spirit of the period as well as budding US nationalism in play (acting to hip-hop music with roots in Jamaica). In other words, Mathews, a white Kittitian who entertained the future King William IV with "negro" songs, resurfaces in the spirit of his countryman more than two hundred years later. Ironically, Hamilton, whose life did not really exhibit any significant level of play, died from a gunshot wound sustained in a duel, an event typically associated with the defence of honour.

Figure 18. *Trudge and Wowski*, by Robert Cruikshank/G. Bonner, 1827. Page 1 of George Coleman, *Inkle and Yarico: An Opera in Three Acts, in Cumberland's British Theatre with Remarks, Biographical and Critical: Printed from the acting copies, as performed at the Theatres Royal, London*, compiled by John Cumberland, vol. 16 (London: John Cumberland, 1827).

Individual writers tended to make general statements characterizing the slave songs in one specific way, but the various generalizations collected together show that there were several types of songs, with the majority being melancholy, satirical and amusing. The recorded songs were all social as opposed to being purely lyrical or philosophical, with the most common preoccupations stemming from man-woman relationships and master/overseer-slave relationships. Whether or not it was simply because whites were the ones from whose work the evidence is taken, there is no record of songs of vengeance or songs of nostalgia in remembrance of Africa or a homeland or songs of achievement. A telling observation made by Chanvalon (1763, 67) in reference to the slaves' songs is that "none inspire pride". This is the other side of Long's observation that they preferred derision to panegyric, for even when their songs contained praise, it was just amusing flattery to get some benefit.

Interestingly enough, there are varying views among philosophers about laughter and derision. In his discussion of Quintilian's statements on laughter and contempt, Quentin Skinner (2002, 142) says: "When we laugh, we are usually glorying or triumphing over others as a result of having come to see that by comparison with ourselves, they are suffering from some contemptible weakness or inferiority. As Quintilian summarizes, 'the most ambitious way of glorying is to speak derisively'." Hobbes's interpretation of laughter and derision is different, for as Skinner says: "Hobbes is clear, then, that laughter is fundamentally a strategy for coping with feelings of inadequacy" (163). Skinner goes on: "[Hobbes] declares that laughter 'is vaine-glory' and that 'much laughter at the defects of others, is a signe of Pusillanimity'" (164). So, where some may see derisive slave songs as stemming from feelings of superiority, others may see resort to laughter at the expense of others as a sign of weak, cowardly minds.

Loudness, pervasiveness and interactivity certainly made the slaves' singing stand out, but the attractive edge that some slave songs had was that they featured sex and race. The adage that "sex sells" was as true then as it is now, and sex between black and white was even more compelling. White men's penchant for slave women was repeatedly mentioned in the historical literature. It was deplored by some writers, while others, like Isaac Teale, were not to be denied and believed that there was "No difference, no – none at night" between black and white ("The Sable Venus: An Ode", in Edwards 1793–94).

Slavery deprived Africans and their descendants of a great measure of intellectual stimulation. First, by bringing people into a polyglot situation in which they could not converse normally, it promoted a sense of linguistic incompetence, intellectual inferiority and effectively reduced intellectual stimulation. Second, slaves were not generally allowed to make basic decisions about getting their own food, shelter and clothing. They were not allowed to make their own decisions about work. Even though in the normal run of things, these everyday preoccupations are seen as chores, they are the very chores that take up a great percentage of the normal, free person's mental activity and lead, as with all intellectual exercise, to the sharpening of the intellect. Slaves were also barred from interacting directly and consistently as peers intellectually with other ethnic groups in the society. As a result, slaves were left with a great deal of intellectual emptiness and boredom. Singing, for them, was a natural artistic medium through which they openly compensated for deprivation and established solidarity.

Because of their strong attraction to Christianity, the image that might have been most applicable to the descendants of slaves in the Caribbean was that of the eagle, if one were to use Isaiah 40:31 as the critical criterion: "But they that wait upon the LORD shall renew their strength; they shall mount up with wings as eagles; they shall run, and not be weary; and they shall walk, and not faint." However, there is no such image of the slaves or their descendants in the historical literature. Images that have been applied to the slaves are of the bee and the songbird – the one to them at work and the other to them both at work and at play – were both positive images from nature, but they refer to creatures that are much smaller and less powerful and deadly than the eagle. In fact, one can set up a contrast between the powerful (eagle) and the meek and mild (bee and songbird) to show that the philosophy of life that applies to the one does not apply to the other, as was the case with the master (honour) and the slave (happiness).

10. Various Faces of Virtue and Honour

> But the real miracle was that these young men [that went by names like Desperadoes, Invaders and such, who had no school to go to, no job to go to] pointed the way forward, which is that they laid down their guns and knives of steel and did combat with each other on drums of steel through music.
> —Minshall 2014

THE PICTORIAL CARICATURE OF THE "NEGRO" GRINNING, dancing and singing is indelibly etched in the historical record. It is as if this was the essential "negro", even more so than the disfigured "negro" maimed, brutalized and vilified by Europeans and others in the process of enslavement. It is as if neither slavery nor deprivation could contain this bubbly character whose *gaieté de coeur* had to burst forth. It was a kind of postcard image and portrayal that were significantly different from those of all other ethnic groups. Even the British medallion that was struck on the occasion of the abolition of slavery in 1834 presented the former slaves as a dancing people (see figure 19).

Misrepresentation of the slaves was typical in both the negative and positive views of them because, in most cases, both were inseparable from political postures. It is true that many of the cultural practices that the Africans and their descendants acquired had to have emerged in conditions of positive communication and cooperation. It is true also that acculturation could not have come about unless there was a high degree of acquiescence on their part and a generally positive outlook on life among them. Yet there is a problem equating the positiveness and pragmatism of the enslaved with glowing or exaggerated abolitionist assertions about their competence or characteristics. For instance, Rolph (1836, 32), after seeing a "negro dance" in Barbados during the years 1832–33, made the following summary conclusion, which is essentially a cultural generalization involving exaggerated claims: "The extreme accuracy with which they preserve the time in the dance – their intense devotion to music

Various Faces of Virtue and Honour 309

Figure 19. Slavery abolished by Great Britain medallion, 1834. Courtesy of the New York Public Library.

– their extraordinary vehemence – the violence of their gesticulations are eminently characteristic [of negroes]."

In this cultural generalization Rolph identified four elements of what he regarded as "the negro character", namely (1) an "extreme" sense of rhythm, (2) an "intense" devotion to music, (3) a show of strong emotion and (4) highly demonstrative behaviour. The first two relate to music and dancing while the last two are given as more general characteristics. All four are European visitor reactions to "negro" behaviour, the kinds of reactions which through repetition, writing and pictures helped to generate the postcard image of the happy dancing "negro", which is still fashionable today. The similarities between Cruikshank's image (figure 20) and the tourism image "Jamaica. No problem" (figure 21) are striking.

Writers in the earlier centuries of colonization (for example, Las Casas, Labat) spoke of distortion in the historical record for personal and political gain, but deliberate distortion in pictorial representations in the late eighteenth and nineteenth centuries became the norm in Britain as a result of the popularity of satire and caricature in the media. A picture was therefore not worth a thousand words: pictorial representation was even more distorted than verbal. The ignorance and fanciful imagination which devalued early illustrations of New World "realities" gave way in favour of blatant political intent. Thus, images of well-being and happiness as well as the opposite were inaccurate because they were essentially propaganda.

Since work was the central activity of slaves, abolitionists concentrated on the brutality that it occasioned. Take, for example, the use of chaining to punish and control. Note that it has come to be associated with singing in unison, but there is no evidence of this aspect of it in the image *Slaves Chained Together and Driven to Work on the Roads*, which was produced by an anti-slavery organization in Birmingham and was based on the words of the anti-slavery writer Richard Bickell (1825, 14–15), who observed: "Sometimes for greater safety, and an increase of punishment, they . . . are worked in pairs, chained together by the

Figure 20. *Negro Slavery*, by Robert Cruikshank. Left side of *Negro Slavery: English Liberty*, in *The Condition of the West India Slave Contrasted with That of the Infant Slave in Our English Factories. With Fifteen Illustrations from the Graver of Robert Cruikshank* (London: W. Kidd, 1835).

Figure 21. No problem, Jamaica.

neck; in this manner they go out to work on the roads, or in the streets, with a workhouse driver after them, who lashes them pretty sharply to urge them on."

However, though Cynric Williams (1826, 263) corroborates the use of chain gangs in Jamaica, he minimizes the effect of the chaining and asserts that the ones he saw were in good spirits: "I passed a gang of negroes mending the roads in chains, two and two, linked together, some by the necks, others by the legs. The chains were light, but still chains, although the weight did not affect the spirits of the wearers."

Anti-abolitionist caricaturists were more extreme than Williams – they avoided the image of work and punishment and created a picture of slavery with festivity as the central activity and concern. The addition of reparation added a further dimension of hostility to their portrayal of the slaves, as is clear in Cruikshank's depiction of the ball.

Then, not satisfied with the callous image of the slave they created, they resorted to scare tactics to unsettle those who would support the abolitionist cause by depicting what would happen to people who did not have enough sense to support themselves on their own, in images such as *Free Labour: The Sunny Side of the Wall* (which shows free slaves now starving to death) and *An Emancipated Negro* (which shows an emaciated figure trying to capture a bug to eat).

The happy image of Caribbean people, ironically, is restricted to the African-derived part of the population, even though the European-derived part was always in a better social and economic position to evince it. It actually started as a feature of the French imagination of their initial encounter with the natives of the smaller Caribbean islands, a vision that was deliberately opposed to that of the Spanish. It was an image that goes back to Hesiod's (1978) conception of the Golden Age of Man and one that is related to the "noble savage" concept usually associated with Jean-Jacques Rousseau (1755). The French priest Du Tertre (1667 2:357) started his account with an image of the islands as "a little paradise always verdant and washed by the most beautiful waters in the world". He then proceeded to characterize the indigenous people as morally and socially perfect: "they are as Nature produced them, that is, having a great natural simplicity and naivety: they are all equal, almost without knowledge of any kind of superiority or servitude".

In the same way that the French replaced the Spanish negative view of the smaller islands with their own "paradise" view, the anti-abolitionists later countered the "brutalized" view of the slave with their own "happy" view, and so emerged the image of the "negro" grinning, dancing and singing. Perhaps the massive and pervasive presence of slaves in plantation society made whatever the slaves did appear larger than life and, specifically from what some foreign observers preferred to see, their joy en masse was more memorable than the pain of a few. Additionally, since the slaves were socially restricted and had few avenues to express themselves culturally, music and dancing were disproportionately observable and prominent and for that reason came to be exaggerated.

However, European writers did not characterize both "others" in the New World in the same way. From the initial encounters in the Caribbean, Spanish writers produced images of the indigenous people in the smaller islands that reflected their own hostility, limited access and language limitations, all of which revealed a narrow *conquista* mentality. As to the French, in spite of Du Tertre's preliminary idyllic image, the indigenous people were described foremost as an alcohol-dominated people, as dissolute and then later as reticent. French information on the indigenous people either came from singular, special studies (for example, Breton [1665, 1666]) or referred to what could be observed from a distance at "big" or special gatherings. There were almost no regular, close-up, eyewitness statements characterizing daily routines of the indigenous people. In fact, in several of the accounts of European encounters with the indigenous people, the latter were described as appearing and disappearing unexpectedly, as if they were phantom-like and nomadic and as if they could not have had routine cultural activities or an artistic sensibility.

As to European images of their own people and descendants, you see little in the historical record that suggests that music and dance were "bursts of emotion" or reflections of *joie de vivre*, because what appears in the record shows almost no evidence of this. There is little to indicate, from an English perspective, for instance, the joy of the experience of nature revealing itself as beautiful or bountiful and the consequent admiration of it and expression of it in music and dance; and there is little to indicate the sorrow of the experience of nature revealing itself as harsh and the consequent attempt to overcome it or drown it in song. It is only occasionally that one gets a muted comment about nature, as that by Wentworth (1834, 2:66): "the mill vanes rustling in their revolution, and the confused clamour of voices in dialogue and song, present a singular contrast to that calm repose which nature seems to claim for herself in these clear and ardent climes". In short, there is no dominant image of happiness or sophisticated sensibility or cultured urbanity or honourable achievement through work.

It is in part because of the narrow interests of the colonists that life among whites in the island colonies is thought of as driven by a frontier mentality, as aesthetically impoverished, and as having little that was intellectually or culturally uplifting. It is because of the dependence on slaves that whites were seen as indolent and lacking in virtue. "Revels" is the word Wright (1937) and others applied to highlight the sole spark of colonial social life among the ruling class, and Patterson ([1967] 1973) characterized these activities negatively as being nothing but debauchery. In fact, one is left to wonder whether the image of constant carousing and debauchery among the ruling class was not partly intended to create an exotic contrast for readers in Europe or was not a repudiation of sudden and undeserved wealth and of the parvenu.

Consistent with the image of debauchery, social and political histories of the West Indies created a picture of early colonial society as adversarial and rife with hostility. This is due to the fact that such accounts were preoccupied with power relationships involving different ethnic and racial groups; social stratification; repressive, often inhumane, methods of retaining control; and other negative aspects of human behaviour. Invariably, this preoccupation with competitiveness and strife led to misrepresentation in the written record and showed the European writer to be just another soldier in the colonies, with a prejudiced vision, fighting for the mother country and creating images of the colonies that served the interests of the mother country. A perfect example of this kind of writer is Jean-Baptiste Labat, whose accounts of the early colonies dominate the historical record. He is described biographically as a priest, a writer and a soldier, the last presumably because he was actually involved in the military defence of Guadeloupe.

Jean-Paul Sartre ([1949] 1966, 42) argues not only that the writer is a soldier but that the writer fights for freedom within a context of democracy:

> One does not write for slaves. The art of prose is bound up with the only regime in which prose has meaning, democracy. When one is threatened, the other is too. And it is not enough to defend them with the pen. A day comes when the pen is forced to stop, and the writer must then take up arms. Thus, however you might have come to it, whatever opinions you might have professed, literature throws you into battle. Writing is a certain way of wanting freedom; once you have begun, you are engaged, willy-nilly.

Europeans writing about the colonies might have seen themselves as operating freely in democratic societies, but they certainly were not writing for West Indian slaves and the writing of most of them could hardly have been seen as "a certain way of wanting freedom" for slaves. For instance, Mrs Inchbald claimed that Colman's *Inkle and Yarico* was "the bright forerunner of the alleviation in the hardships of slavery" (Colman 1806, 3), but it is doubtful that is what Colman had in mind, and Richard Cumberland's play *The West Indian*, one of the most successful plays in eighteenth-century Britain, did not make an issue of slavery. Contrary to what Sartre intended, his words "One does not write for slaves" are ironic.

René Magritte's painting of a pipe with the words below it *Ceci n'est pas une pipe* (referred to in English as *The Treachery of Images/This Is Not a Pipe*) challenges the viewer to be always conscious of the difference between images and reality: it reminds the viewer that the image is not to be taken as the reality. The French have an old proverb, *"A beau mentir qui vient de loin"*, which basically means that a person coming from faraway places can get away with telling lies about those places because no one can disprove what he is saying. In effect, the proverb is warning the listener to be wary of "eyewitness" accounts.

Stolen information, falsehoods and lies serve to embellish an account and thus the standing of the storyteller, or they serve to bolster a viewpoint. In most cases, however, increase in knowledge shows up early distortions and careful research reveals features plagiarized from elsewhere. For example, one does not even have to use current scientific knowledge in order to refute colonial writers' reports of continuous dancing and playing among the slaves. The claim of continuous motion and lack of rest cannot square with the growth in the muscular physique of the slaves over the period of slavery. Furthermore, in the pictorial contrast of the poor in Britain with the slaves in the West Indies in which the slaves are presented as plump, there is a somatic non-sequitur: the slaves would have had to be physically lean at most since their work was long and hard and if they were said to be dancing non-stop for days.

Whether it is in relation to Europeans, indigenous people or Africans, misrepresentation and subsequent repetition of it are typical in the written record. However, a major redeeming factor that supports some level of reliability is that early colonial writers did not conspire together and, in many cases, they were hostile towards and envious of each other. In addition, desire for dominance caused each European nation to try to enlist the support of subordinate groups in their struggle against competing European nations. Another factor is that although all European nations operated with a sense of racial superiority when faced with indigenous groups, Africans and others, none wanted to be characterized as brutal and inhuman in their treatment of subordinate groups. Starting with Las Casas and his attacks on Spanish colonial practices and, much later, the emancipation forces in Britain and Schoelcher and others in the French world, there were contending opinions that moved the written record towards an increased level of sensitivity and reliability.

As far as lacunae in the written record are concerned, it is instructive to bear in mind what Donald Thompson (1993, 194) says: "a great deal of what we do read in accounts of Taino music and related matters in regional histories may have been spun out over the centuries from what are offered at third hand as the words of a single writer". This stretching out the little to make it big is of course not restricted to Taino music. In fact, it is a general tendency, one which attends all situations where there is a dearth of information, where there are relatively few writers providing information on a variety of places over a long period of time. When writers repeat not only the same observations but also specific words and combinations of words, it is more than likely that what they are all saying has come from one source and one context. Thus, for example, in the propagation of the cultural history of the indigenous people of the Caribbean, two priests, Father Ramón Pané (in the bigger islands) and Father Raymond Breton (in the smaller islands), came to have a disproportionate prominence.

Repetition from previous sources, especially among French writers over the years, resulted from a belief that uniform and simple images of others, especially Africans, were good enough because these people lacked intellectual breadth and depth. The case of Labat's (1722) description of the calenda dance in Martinique and Mellet's ([1824] 1913) description of the lariate dance in Chile a hundred years later is a prime example. Tauzin-Castellanos (2014, 150) comes to the following conclusion about Mellet's book: "*The Journey through South America* is both a mine of information and an unfathomable source of disinformation." Since this conclusion can be applied to several writers, it means that European writers from early preferred a simplistic, stultifying fiction about Africans, one feature of which is that they could be linked across the Americas by their dancing. It consolidated and generalized an essence for them.

The belief in African homogeneity and essence in dancing is still being proclaimed (Daniel 2011, 13–16). This argument does not show much change from a half century ago when Lisa Lekis (1960, 54), using Kaigh (1947) as her authoritative source, wrote: "The music of western civilization has developed and changed over the centuries both in form and instrumentation, but African rhythm remains much as it was when King David danced before the Sacred Arch. It has been remarked [Kaigh 1947] that the children of Africa were dancing the Charleston when Julius Caesar had hardly heard of the Gauls – and the curious thing is that today they are still dancing it."

The fact is, however, that since dance and music are conditioned by social mores and are dynamic in nature, and since the dispersal of Africans across the Americas was not uniform, differential retention/loss of Africanness and diversity in play are the norm everywhere. Dance and music in the Americas are a result of variegated social life in the Americas. Derek Walcott (2007, 3) said in his Nobel lecture: "The stripped man is driven back to that self-astonishing, elemental force, his mind. This is the basis of the Antillean experience, this shipwreck of fragments, these echoes, these shards of a huge tribal vocabulary, these partially remembered customs, and they are not decayed but strong." To assert that African rhythms were preserved unchanged for thousands of years is to treat Africans and African descendants in the Americas as mindless. To belittle the variety and richness of mixture that the slaves and their descendants created in the Americas in favour of some protypical African essence is misguided. It is the music and dance that were created in the Caribbean and the Americas more generally; it is what they used to do in slave society and how they affected people that reveal virtue and have brought honour.

Playing the Game and Making Much Out of Little

The indigenous word *guatiaos*, which was used to refer to indigenous and Spanish people who established a bond of fellowship between themselves, was known throughout the Caribbean region and survived, with some modification, for centuries. It was Peter Martyr (Anghiera 1628, 11) who first spoke of this bond of friendship and then, more explicitly Las Casas (1986, 2:37), who, in describing early Spanish encounters with the indigenous people in the first decade of the sixteenth century, said: "This exchange of names in the common language of this island is called *guatiao* . . . a bond of perpetual friendship and a league." This New World bond of fellowship came to be known even in France, for Montaigne, in his essay "Des Cannibales" (circa 1578), reinterpreted *guatiao* as the French word *moitié*, in reference to indigenous people from Brazil who were brought to France.

Successful French colonization in the New World began in the smaller Caribbean islands but soon spread to Hispaniola. Many of the migrants involved in the emergence of a French colony in Hispaniola were adventurers who came to be known as *boucaniers*. The situation of those who left St Kitts to settle in Tortuga was one that required a tri-partite division of labour and partnership for survival. Oexmelin (1686, 1:29–30) explained it thus: "the small number of adventurers was divided into three bands: one dedicated themselves to hunting and took the name of 'boucaniers'; another to running routes and they got the name 'freebooters' . . . ; and the last devoted their time to working the land and they were called 'habitants'". They all had indentured servants who served them for three years.

It is the private relationship between *boucaniers* that is significant. About it, Oexmelin (1:151) said in the middle of the seventeenth century: "they always joined together in twos and called each other 'matelot'. They pooled everything they owned." Oexmelin (1774, 1:100) said that the *habitans* had the same *matelot* relationship among themselves. This kind of partnership and interdependence was not new because the system of *matelotage* had been introduced among young, unmarried Frenchmen in St Kitts for their mutual support and was maintained among those who migrated to Tortuga. Before it was mentioned by Oexmelin, *matelot* had previously been mentioned by Du Tertre (1667, 452) and by De Rochefort (1658, 461): "This word 'matelot' is commonly used among the French colonists to mean a partner. And when two colonists have bought or cleared a plantation, you say that they have become partners."

The most significant alliance among enslaved Africans in the New World came out of their middle passage experience – those who went through it together on the same ship regarded themselves as inseparably bound. In Cuba, according to Pichardo ([1875] 1976, 140), the word *carabela* was used to mean "My countryman, who came with me from Africa". The word *carabela* in its basic meaning was one that occurred in the very early literature of discovery and declined in use thereafter – it referred to the kind of light sailing-ship used by Columbus and the early explorers. Apparently, then, the concept was incorporated into their language by the slaves in the Spanish colonies with the specific meaning of "fellow sufferer" from as early as the sixteenth century and later spread across the other European colonies in different forms (for example, French *bâtimens* and English "shipmate").[1] The significance of "shipmate" in Jamaica was explained by Bryan Edwards (1794, 2:78):

---

1. A number of variants based on the same concept are given for different Caribbean societies in Mintz and Price ([1976] 1992, 43–44).

and accordingly we find that the Negroes in general are strongly attached to their countrymen, but, above all, to such of their companions as came in the same ship with them from Africa. This is a striking circumstance: the term *shipmate* is understood among them as signifying a relationship of the most endearing nature; perhaps as recalling the time when the sufferers were cut off together from their common country and kindred, and awakening reciprocal sympathy, from the remembrance of mutual affliction.

The importance of the term "shipmate" is evident in the fact that it continued to appear in the literature past emancipation (for example, Waddell 1863, 107).

The argument here is that there is a common thread linking the *guatiao* (indigenous), *matelot* (European) and "shipmate" (African) relationships and it is that bonding as peers was seen as the best way to survive (and prosper) in a new, prospectively difficult situation of migration. The greater similarity in concept between *matelot* and "shipmate" (where both sides were new to the environment) points to the establishment of a similar community structure different from the familiar one based on the nuclear family unit, which traditionally is hierarchical (father–mother–children). In the case of the *boucaniers*, it was an alternative, peer-group society which is described without any reference to women or children, in which men formed economic marriages with other men, usually as couples. In the case of the Africans brought to the Caribbean, they were not only cut off from their ancestors but, as human machines, little attention was paid to preserving or creating any normal nuclear family relationship among them. They were therefore operating for the most part as a peer-group community with loose and unpredictable relationships between men and women and children. For them, important 'institutions' were the coffle, the shipmate experience, the plantation gang and the slave yard.

The peer-group community encouraged gregariousness through communal activities, the prime ones being playing, dancing and singing, especially in ringed performances. This contrasted with a community based on consanguinity or religion (like Jewish communities in exile). In a sense, the gregariousness of the peer-group community was consistent with the Epicurean doctrine, which said: "Of all the things which the wise man seeks to acquire to produce happiness of a complete life, by far the most important is the possession of friendship" (Cassius Amicus 2011). In other words, if friendship could produce happiness generally, it was even more important for solidarity and happiness in new societies made up of different ethnic groups.

However, there were also negative consequences of the peer-group community. Playing, music and dance produced some measure of happiness in the case of the slaves in the Caribbean, but there was no sense of lasting achievement not only because there were no material gains in these communal activities but also because competitiveness was constant and the mortality rate was high. Music and dance may have bonded the slaves in the present and to the immediate past, but not to an ancestral past and any sense of continuity and heritage peculiar to a group, because music and dance eliminated ethnic differences as they created new common identities. A ringed performance was a continuous interchange of peer performers and critics and, because in most cases there were no winners and losers, it fostered a Sisyphus-type mentality. The Tropical Carnival was also an annually repeated illusion of happiness.

The peer-group community intersected with the traditional family community and was variably influenced by it. The planters fostered the peer-group community with its playing, dancing and singing, but the churches promoted the traditional family through Christian practices, like monogamous marriage and propriety. The practices of the two types of community could not exist peacefully together resulting in destabilizing tensions and conflicting attitudes to play.

When captured Africans came into Caribbean ports and were being prepared for sale, they must have suspected that they were being forced to sing and dance to look good to prospective buyers and they must have had some psychological reaction to this dilemma. The fact that they were subjected to various other indignities to see how sound they were complicates the matter of understanding how they felt and reacted. One can use two types of draft in the United States to try to locate the dilemma of the slaves when they were put up for sale – a military draft and a sports (National Basketball Association/National Football League) draft. In the latter, the individual is desirous of being selected early, whereas in the former, many individuals (for example, during the Vietnam War) try to dodge the draft by all means possible. Yet even in the worst circumstances, human vanity or pride (Brown and Levinson [1987, 62] speak of "positive face") operates. So, the Africans may or may not have wanted to be chosen early, but at least they did not want to suffer the further indignity of being repeatedly rejected or completely disregarded. The Africans, by the time they were bought, knew that they could not escape a life of slavery, so many would have decided to accept their fate. Having reached this state of mind, they most likely decided to make the most of it, to join in the "play", to dance and sing, in order not to languish ignominiously and be faceless.

The bonding or shipmate experience which captured Africans underwent en route to the Americas was violently fractured when each slave was put up individually for sale. However, this traumatic middle passage experience made peers of all African slaves who, going forward, would have been bolstered by a sense of fortitude in survival and probably affected by some notion of being among those who were supernaturally favoured to reach the other side.

Stephen Levinson (1979) uses Wittgensen's concept of "language-games" to show how language communication works pragmatically. Levinson argues that one has to know the rules of language, just as one has to know the rules of any other game (for example, basketball) to play it successfully. It is not just a matter of knowing the meanings of words and structures but understanding what can and cannot be said within a certain context, and how what one says will be understood. In their communication with their masters in this new situation, the enslaved Africans had to learn to make those decisions in order to survive and prosper. Thus, in their singing they were not just learning/creating new structures for their music but using all the means they had at their disposal to present an intelligible image of themselves. They not only wanted to be understood by their superiors but also to be appreciated by their peers and to make a contribution to their own well-being. Composing and singing songs of derision, for example, would have had more than one objective – to overcome extreme dominance (as Boehm [1993] specifies) and to achieve honour among peers.

An old joke explaining the difference in temperament between Barbadians and Jamaicans goes back to the slave trade and the choices that buyers/masters made. It states that because the slave ships reached the island of Barbados first, the Barbadian planters were able to choose the best behaved slaves as opposed to the Jamaican planters who, by the time the slave ship reached Jamaica, which was the last stop, had nothing but the worst behaved slaves to choose from, and this explains the difference today between docile Barbadians and rebellious Jamaicans. In spite of the frivolity with which this joke has always been told, it is clear that subjective judgement played a critical role on both sides and that the attitudes of the buyers were paralleled by the emotions and attitudes of the human merchandise, and even if singing and dancing cannot be shown to have had a major role in creating a good image of self, there had to be some measure of "play" in the slaves' behaviour to achieve it. In fact, in the case of slaves who were the first to be selected, they must have experienced some degree of pride and attributed it to their physical appearance or their ability to perform well.

The argument here is that this early competitive and subjective selection process fitted integrally into the system of favouritism that dominated the relationship between the slaves and their master and mistress. Since festivity seemed to be the easiest way to demonstrate contentment, enslaved Africans realized from early that "playing the game" for the master and mistress in whatever ways they thought best and in the ways they could most impress was key to their survival and "improvement". Those whites, like Monk Lewis, who regarded the slaves as happy simpletons and who saw festivity among them as a genuine expression of contentment, accepted the slaves' play as genuine and they benefited from it. On the other hand, since from the earliest years there were those slaves who would not play the game, who caused whites to be always suspicious of their motives and to see festivity as a cloak for nefarious activities, pictorial illustrations at the time of emancipation (for example, by Doyle, Cruikshank, Grant) showed slaves in their festivity saying that "John Bull" was a fool, that they were fêting at his expense and were going to do violence to him in retaliation for all he had done to them. So, the two contending views of slave festivity made the image of contentment and the prospect of rebellion a constant reality.

For some slaves, the appearance of happiness was a mask they put on when they dealt with whites, but for the majority of slaves, who were more removed from the master in their everyday lives, the ability to enjoy themselves among themselves (which whites frequently saw or overheard) was not an illusion. It was their greatest strength and saviour. They did not emerge from slavery with the destructive bitterness which is attributed in Psalm 137 to the Jews of old as they contemplated their retaliation after deliverance out of bondage. While in one sense, the dancing and singing slave may have been a cruel caricature, in another sense, playing the game was less suicidal and more practical than other means of trying to survive an impossible condition. Ambivalent and duplicitous actions persisted after slavery as an integral part of play and the masking behaviour that became entrenched among Africans and their descendants in the Americas as a way of saving face.

In explaining the games people play in competing for honour, Huizinga (1980, 65) identifies the contest of words and says about it: "This boosting of one's own virtue as a form of contest slips over quite naturally into contumely of one's adversary, and this in turn becomes a contest in its own right. It is remarkable how large a place these bragging and scoffing matches occupy in the most diverse civilizations. Their play-character is beyond dispute." The best known example in the Americas of the "scoffing matches" that Huizinga talks about is "playing the dozens" among African Americans in the United States. Though no similar feature was recorded for the slaves in the colonial Caribbean, derision was identified as one of their most prominent features. A successful song of derision would have raised the status of the singer within the community in the same way that an extempore song praising a superior would have raised the standing of the singer in that person's eyes.

It was therefore as an everyday activity that music became pervasive among the slaves, although it is unlikely that the slaves saw themselves as a singing people. Dancing was frequent but less pervasive and it is even less likely that the slaves considered themselves to be a dancing people. Even in cases where they did walk miles to attend a dance, it was most likely to support a shipmate or countryman in a money-raising venture or a celebration of some type.

Perhaps Du Tertre (1654, 476) was unwittingly pointing to something significant about the enslaved Africans when he said: "They make every land their homeland, provided they find food and drink there." The slave owners knew that if the slaves were constantly hungry or underfed, they would have been unable to do the amount of work required. As far as they were concerned, they needed a diet that would give them a considerable amount of energy. At first, slave owners administered rum every day, but this probably did not have the desired effect. It may just have been accidental that the foods available from the land (that is, yams, sweet potatoes, cassava, coco, tania, corn, Guinea corn) were high-energy foods, and that these, together with salted fish/meat and sugar (both of which may have caused the slaves to eat and drink more), came to be the slaves' regular diet. There is reason to believe that, over time, the average height and size of the slaves increased and, more immediately, the daily hard work and high-energy food caused their strength and stamina to increase. In 1837 Bridgens (n.p.) said: "They seem to seek in muscular exertion a means of letting off a portion of the superabundant animal spirits of which they appear to keep a supply in reserve for such occasions." Disregarding Bridgens's racist mindset and substituting "energy" for "animal spirits", it seems reasonable to argue that the slaves' dancing was a way of letting off steam psychologically and physically.

For many of the slaves, dancing was not glamorous and not without a hurtful history. Perhaps for the African slave who crossed the Atlantic and had to dance in pain every day on board ship, dancing came to be associated with suffering and cruelty. Perhaps for the African slave who had to dance to display soundness after arriving in the West Indies, dancing was an embarrassment.

Perhaps for some female slaves who had to dance to please men, dancing was humiliation. However, in all these cases, the African slaves were conscious that music and dancing were being used by an "enemy" as a tool to achieve an objective. It is that the objectives or functions were negative, but music and dancing in themselves may not have been permanently and irrevocably tainted in the minds of those who were forced into doing them. It is probable that when they started to participate in community activities in the Caribbean, the scars of music and dancing lessened. Yet even after slavery, during the apprenticeship period, "dancing" did not always have positive connotations, for James Williams (1837, 9, 10) spoke of and illustrated "dancing the treadmill" as a form of severe punishment.

There is no evidence that African slaves in the West Indies perfected their dancing, songs and music in schools, in the manner of professionals. The very claim, on the part of Europeans, that the slaves had "natural" musical and dancing proficiency indicates that for the slaves, principally because of time constraints, there was no separation of practice and performance/event. For them, there was admiration of wit and humour in songs, there was admiration of flair in dancing, there was admiration of the musician's ability to transport participants beyond the mundane. On the other hand, there did not seem to be any great preference for individual music playing – music and dancing were predominantly part of group activities.

There is no question that much of what the slaves produced was ad hoc, that is, in response to their conditions and experiences. In some cases, they sang the blues and in other cases, they sang happy songs. They also used songs to show their ingenuity, wit, humour, satirical intent and also as means of protest. Furthermore, one could argue that they chose to sing rather than to talk in all these cases because singing was not only more expressive but was also safer for their own self-preservation – it had a built-in veil of duplicity.

Singing and rhythm were an integral part of work for many slaves who worked outdoors. It is also likely that the kinds of singing and drumming activities that were a part of funerals affected most people, seeing that funerals were a regular part of slave life. Presumably, songs of different types could be sung or hummed by most slaves whether they were alone or in groups.

But everyday does not necessarily mean mundane or dull, for the slaves and their descendants had a strong imaginative element in their performance culture. Gabriel García Márquez (1982) speaks of imagination and make-believe (fiction) almost as prerequisites for happiness and suggests that they were not made use of in the past because people had other more pressing needs. Now, though in the historical record of the slave period there is no detailed presentation of storytelling among the slaves as a major feature of their activities, there is good reason to assume that it was always there though initially not well developed because of language communication difficulties. The integration of song and dance into storytelling and the acting out of story characters like Anancy and Brer Rabbit was typical and continued strongly into the twentieth century. At least two of Derek Walcott's plays (*Dream on Monkey Mountain* and *Ti-Jean and His Brothers*) have links to this tradition.

The well-reported playing that was a part of Christmas celebrations and other festivals, the attraction to parading as kings and queens, and the "Saturnalian" features of inversion exhibit the slaves' powerful use of imagination, make-believe and creativity to give regular injections of enjoyment and happiness to their daily and yearly cycle of life. Even a street character such as Isaac Belisario's Lovey sang and performed his puppets as he sold his flowers, and through his imagination and creativity gave enjoyment to those he came into contact with every day. Make-believe was a simple world that slaves and their children slipped into on a regular basis because they could control what happened in it, it did not require capital or sacrifice, it was gregarious, and it was amusing and enjoyable. The gregarious or society-building element is scientifically argued by Dissanayake (2014, 54) in her artification hypothesis when she says: "Not only are brain chemicals like cortisol suppressed by participating with others in formalized and rhythmically repeated activities, oxytocin and other endorphinic substances are secreted, creating pleasurable feelings of unity with others, strengthening their commitment to each other."

Distinctiveness, Virtuosity and Independence in Art

If one were to go by the comments of those European writers who seemed more balanced in their assessments, one would have to conclude that the slaves were very sophisticated in some of their dancing. Repeatedly and over a long period of time, writers favourably compared slave performances to European performances, not just generally but by using specific European terminology to describe details of their movements. For example, Hughes (1750, 16–17) in Barbados used the term "pyrrhic" to describe a specific slave dance. Edwards (1793–94, 2:85) in Jamaica used the same term. The same "pyrrhic" is also mentioned by Williams (1826, 22) in Jamaica. Whether or not this was a case of plagiarism, the fact is that all three writers over the last seventy-five years of slavery chose to use the Greek term.

An explanation of "pyrrhic" and its significance are given by Plato (2009, book 7). The source and significance of "pyrrhic" are further explained by Gallini (1770, 25–26), who at various places in his work draws on Plato to explain classes of dance in Ancient Greece: "The . . . *pyrrhic* was danced by young men armed cap-a-pee, who executed to the sound of the flute, all the proper movements, either for attack, or for defence." And later:

> The true military dance is the pyrrhic, of which Pyrrhus passes for the inventor. There were several kinds of them, which all had the same name. According to Xenophon, where he speaks of the Thracians who danced at the entertainment of their Prince, Seuthes, armed men danced, bounding lightly to the sound of the flute; they parried with their shields strokes which they commutually aimed at each other with the greatest dexterity. (113–14)

It is quite likely that when Hughes, Edwards and Williams chose to use a Greek term to describe a slave dance, it reflected the customary tendency to use the familiar to describe the foreign. One can argue that, notwithstanding the "praise", what these descriptions with their European terminology did was to make the slaves' dancing appear European-like, as is the case with a similar dance among West Africans, which Barbot compared to the "ballet de Mars . . . performed at the Opera" (Hair, Jones and Law 1992, 2:565). However, in circumstances where the strongest European tendency was to regard the slaves and all their practices as uncivilized, using a Greek term to describe their dances reflected a highly appreciative response and the more so because the dance could have been deemed warlike and threatening.

Also commenting on slave dances, Luffman (1789, 135) in Antigua enthusiastically said: "I believe, were some of their steps and motions introduced into the public amusements at home, by French and Italian dancers, they would be well received." This kind of connection between European dance movements/ postures and those of the slaves was also made later by Bridgens (1837) in Trinidad when he used the term *Negro Figuranti* to label the different dance postures of the slaves there. Likewise, Williams (1826, 21–22) in Jamaica used the international term "bolero" to describe a slave dance. In all these cases the common notion of "uncivilized Africa" is absent: it is as if the slaves were trained international dancers.

The high opinion of performances continued even after emancipation significantly enough in the work of Charles Day, who was otherwise extremely hostile to everything West Indian. He commented that a certain "motion was similar to that exceedingly droll one used by tragic actors in a booth" (1852, 1:47–48) and that the waving of a skirt was "much as we see done in the negro dances on stage" (1:53). Though in these cases Day was describing the former slaves' execution of European dances, what was important was his comparison of it to greater or international performances.

As to songs, it is important to note that during the visit of royalty to one colony, a white man composed and was allowed to sing "negro songs" as part of the entertainment package. There is no question that this was an early indication of the "national" distinctiveness of "negro songs" and the popularity they were beginning to have in the Caribbean.

Exceptionalism has been a topic of interest over the years, but it is usually discussed in terms of individuals. What is peculiar about black exceptionalism in the Caribbean historical record, as it applies to music and dance, is that it is presented in terms of an area of expertise characteristic of a whole race. This generalization may be explained as "a characteristic of play" in the way that Huizinga (1980, 50) expresses it: "Winning means showing oneself superior in the outcome of a game. . . . In this respect he wins something more than the game as such. He has won esteem, obtained honour; and this honour and esteem at once accrue to the benefit of the group to which the victor belongs. Here we have another characteristic of play: success won readily passes from the individual to the group." Yet, contrary to what Huizinga argues, attributing honour and esteem in singing and dancing to the slaves did not "confer upon the winner a semblance of superiority in general".

What is even more important is to separate virtuosity from black exceptionalism. While it was normal for writers who were not familiar with the slaves personally to generalize about slave performances, it is obvious that virtuoso performances, then as now, can only be done by a small percentage of any population. In the case of the slaves, the public, interactive nature of performances, the turn-taking and the fact that there was no identifying of individual performers created the impression that all the slaves were exceptional, which clearly could not have been so. The other factor that bolstered this perception was the general admiration of virtuosity among the crowd that encircled the performers, which is what added to the overall pleasure derived from these competitive performances.

There were eighteenth-century individual Africans (or descendants) in the Americas who were identified as exceptional in the arts, but these were no more than test cases for the belief that blacks could excel intellectually. Francis Williams was a free black in Jamaica whose language and literary skills made him exceptional at the time. The same is also true of the African-born American Phillis Wheatley, whose poetry made her famous in England and the colonies. To what extent in the era of slavery Caribbean free blacks and slaves were aware of Williams and Wheatley is impossible to know, but on each plantation and in each colony, slaves would have known who were the outstanding dancers.

In contrast to the cases of Francis Williams and Phillis Wheatley, the competence of "negroes" in singing and dancing was seen as physical and the transition from some "negroes" to all was also based on the perceived muscular physique of "negroes" in general and their adaptability to the hot, tropical environment. Moreover, in the context of slavery in the tropics, where whites cultivated an image of physical fragility or delicacy, the slaves and their descendants believed they were physically superior and came to believe also in their superiority in dancing and their powerful voices.

The problem, however, is that writers were seeing these accomplishments as "natural", and this reaction was just a consolidation of the notion of uniform, almost impermeable African characteristics. When Dallas dubbed Africans a "singing race", he made them into "gifted" people, although not to the extent of savants. The English word "gifted" and the French word "savant" may at first appear to be positive characterizations, but "savant" especially has strong negative connotations in that people so characterized are otherwise seen as having severe mental or psychological deficiencies. Their artistic gift is seen as the result of a brain abnormality and not as the result of cognition and training. When used to refer to a race, the "exceptional" tag carries similar connotations. In the case of slaves and their descendants, the most critical factor in the emergence of "exceptionalism" is that play was the facility that was most freely available to them. The activities in play were meaningful, constantly and widely practised as a result of which expertise in them increased. They defended the slaves' virtue as human beings.

At the opposite end of the social spectrum was the immigrant planter, who was the major formative figure in the early years of West Indian colonial society. It is unlikely that in 1650 dancing and music had as yet become popular social activities in the West Indian colonies, but the early planter's love of drinking and entertaining was already pointing in that direction. There is nothing in the description of the "character" of the early planter (see Hutson 2001, 64) that suggests a leaning towards intellectual pursuits, a preoccupation with fine arts or scientific sophistication.

There were plantation owners who spent almost all of their lives in the West Indies. On the other hand, there were many plantation owners in the West Indies who sought to be, and some actually became, part of the aristocracy in Britain. So, if one were to try to assess the character of colonial society from the point of view of the preferences of plantation owners, then it would have been a continuum between the one extreme (focus on local pursuits) and the other (focus on returning "home" to Europe). However, to a much greater extent, it was the institutional framework and the nature of colonial society that determined the character, pastimes and sports of the plantocracy. Governors, administrators and military officials were responsible for most major social functions, which virtually had to be attended by the local administration and plantocracy. The same is true, if to a lesser and varied extent, of the events of the established church and the schools. It would have been difficult for creoles to promote their own kinds of entertainment as alternatives, even if they wanted to. Thus, the entertainment structures that developed were largely bureaucratic, with the participants being always a mixture of the foreign and the local, with varying tastes.

The fact that the foreign and more powerful element of colonial society was always changing or moving from one place to another meant that there was variation more so than constancy and uniformity in the social sphere. With every change of administrators and military people, with every boat bringing migrants or returning creoles came the latest styles in clothes, music and dances, which percolated through the society even to the lowest levels. Yet there was a certain measure of conservatism in rural plantation life, which replicated notions of the landed gentry in Britain. Rich planters in the Caribbean had free time and facilities to indulge themselves and strove hard to preserve their privileged way of life. Unlike their counterparts in Europe, however, they did not pursue as wide a range of activities, for literary and artistic endeavours did not take up as much of their time since colonial societies generally were not culturally sophisticated.

Strenuous outdoor activities were avoided from the beginning of colonization and this did not change significantly over the years among creole whites. Ironically, in the early years, even dancing was thought to be impractical in the hot tropics. Those fewer activities that whites pursued naturally received greater emphasis. A reasonable argument can be made therefore that in the

Caribbean whites actually preferred those indoor activities from which they could get greater and more immediate gratification (for example, drinking, womanizing, gambling and dancing). One exception to this was the rural feast, a quiet outdoor excursion with elements of exotic escape from everyday life (like sophisticated maroons) that were greatly facilitated by the climate and scenery of the islands.

Concerts and serenades were sedentary and often indoor activities but they required, for full enjoyment, a level of musical expertise that was not common in the colonies. Even if, for those who were involved, these activities gave a sense of superiority, and probably a feeling of being closer to Europe, overall they did not seem to be typical or popular like masquerades and pantomimes, which attracted wider participation and required no expertise to enjoy.

The preferred social pursuits among the planter class or "colonial gentry" retained elements of hierarchy and power, factors that were extremely important in their world. For instance, the ball was an exercise in management and organization in which protocol, deference, social recognition and etiquette were in full view for all to comment on and judge. One's standing was enhanced or diminished according to one's performance at a ball because the ball involved various aspects of display and performance on which one was judged – greeting, poise, decorum, dancing, drinking, conversation, social knowledge, "sexual" skills (coquetry) and physical beauty. Thus, social skills were more relevant and important to creole whites than intellectual skills.

Yet dancing was not a sterile, bland activity executed in the pursuit of higher goals. Creole whites developed a love of dancing and seemed to marry the European preoccupation with form and their slaves' preoccupation with verve and enthusiasm. So, while they adopted European dances from the mother country, they executed them with a kind of panache that could be said to have modified and improved them. The gratification from dancing came not from a slavish imitation but from individualistic execution which was, to some extent, fired by a competitive element. Whether or not there was actually a greater degree of enjoyment of dancing, creole whites, in their visible behaviour, certainly exhibited a greater degree of it than European whites seemed to do and they were very proud of their competence.

Of course, the way that English readers interpreted such behaviour was to believe that a people indulging in too much dancing and singing were not to be taken seriously, since they were consuming their energy in frivolous pursuits. The idea of creole whites dancing with abandon and leaving the dance hall dishevelled was therefore consistent with this belief. Creole whites were thought by Europeans generally to be idle (their work being done for them by slaves) and therefore to have ample time for balls and entertainment. The women especially, many of whom seemed to have little to do, were said to be roused from their lethargy only by dancing. The idea was that such a people would not build great civilizations, would not contribute to the development of world knowledge and would leave nothing permanent behind them. Thus, they were essentially peripheral to the world stage.

Some European writers bluntly stated that the Caribbean did not produce great writers and Wentworth specifically associated musical people with low mentality. His conviction stemmed from his belief about Africans and their descendants, a belief that music and dancing were activities typical of the happy and carefree, typical of people with no economic and political responsibilities to exercise their brains. This view of music and dancing, diametrically opposed to that expressed in Plato, was probably more English (than French or Spanish) and reflected a European view of the English as a people with a low level of desire for and competence in music and dancing.

The idea that people who loved to dance and sing were frivolous and unintelligent is also argued by claiming that they could be easily manipulated and controlled, without them even knowing it, because of their "addiction". Hannibal Price (1900) asserted that dancing was one of the keenest passions of the frivolous colonists of St Domingue and this could have been extended to colonists across the Caribbean. Lady Nugent came to believe that, for her social gatherings, she should not attempt conversation but have dancing instead and, furthermore, that dancing should be used to keep up the spirits of her guests. In other words, by generalizing Lady Nugent's policy, one could argue that it was creole whites who were manipulated to dance and party by a colonial administration which did not think them capable of much else.

In the final analysis it is the comparison of whites with the slaves that sheds light on dancing as a vehicle for group or national expression. Creole whites were not enslaved but were said to be passionate about dancing, just like the slaves. It is clear that dancing improved social relations in both groups and it is also clear that dancing was the most powerful, readily available and freest medium for doing so. It may simply be that the primordial purpose of dance as a society-strengthening medium is most evident in transitional stages of non-uniform societies. The 1775 to 1845 era of revolution, independence and emancipation had its peaks at various times across the Americas; it was the era that American space rather than Europe started to be proclaimed as "home" by white creoles. Slaves began to sense a change from bondage to freedom. It was a time when people were emboldened to express themselves in their own way and dancing and singing were centrally involved in this transition.

Acting out Primeval and Ancestral Beliefs

As far as any possible direct and immediate correlation between climate and music and dancing in the Caribbean is concerned, one can argue that if the indigenous inhabitants of the smaller islands were not a musical people and the African slaves living in the same islands were, then environment was not a powerful agent in causing the latter to be musical. One may further say that if a people living in their own habitat/environment were not musical and another people coming into it were, then the environment was not a critical deterrent. In short, the climate in the Caribbean, as an agent, was neutral. Another element of climate that did have a significant effect was the tropical night, with its orchestra of sounds and illusion of sights. These seemed to fire the imaginative element of the folk culture that emerged, heighten belief in the supernatural, and enhance the aura of dances, slave plays and performances related to funerals. More generally, however, it is not climate in itself but points in the cycle of crops possible in the climate that are related to festivities and rituals.

For the Africans who came to the West Indies, many of whom were from in and around Nigeria and Ghana, the yam festival, taking place at the beginning of August, had been (that is, in Africa) the most important feature of their yearly agricultural cycle. It involved music, dance and plays. Since little is said directly in the historical literature on the West Indies about the yam festival, it is difficult to gauge the extent to which the culture of the yam festival operated and persisted in the minds of the slaves in the Caribbean. Most of the slaves worked in the fields, but since they did not derive their food directly from the main crop they produced, since they had no vested interest in it and since their traditional cultures did not coincide with its cycle, the times of planting and harvest did not initially have any spiritual significance for them. What seems logical to assume is that festivities and features of the yam festival and other such festivals remained in the consciousness of Africans who were enslaved as adults and that some of these festivities and features were introduced into the agricultural cycle that developed in the colonial Caribbean. It is those features that had relevance to the Caribbean slave colony that would have prospered.

Europeans were, by and large, an agricultural people whose religious and non-religious beliefs and festivities were determined in large measure by their climatic cycle – spring, summer, autumn and winter – the most perceptible change in vegetation being from winter to spring. The changes in season had an effect not only on the state of mind of the people, their behaviour and dress but also on crops – absence, planting and harvest – and thus on times of celebration and festivity. When the Europeans established and consolidated their culture in the Caribbean, Africans and others were essentially being ruled by the dictates of a different climate.

Though the Europeans themselves were forced to modify their culture to make it fit the realities of a tropical climate, they did not substantially change their religious beliefs and festivities and they were not fundamentally influenced by or wholeheartedly accommodating of the tropical cultures of others in their colonies. The fixed and moveable feasts of the Christian calendar, which involved music, dance and plays as the major elements of celebration and festivity, became the established pillars for the colonies.

Plays in Europe are traced back, in part, to religious performances and activities within and outside the church. For instance, early theatre in France is linked to activities associated with church feasts, and the twelfth-century play *Le Mystère d'Adam* is usually cited as an example of the kind of Bible-related work out of which formal French theatre emerged. In addition, practices with street theatre, like the Lord of Misrule and others with a pagan history, continued to be popular though controversial as church-related festivities in France and across Europe from the Middle Ages onwards. In other words, they were an integral part of the popular culture of Roman Catholics.

In the Spanish American colonies, according to Labat (1722, 4:156–57), the African dance, the calenda, was so much to the taste of Spanish American creole Catholics that by 1698 they were dancing it in their churches and processions, and their nuns danced it on Christmas night so that people could see how joyful they were at the birth of the Saviour. Although there was no independent verification of this claim before or after Labat and although it might just have been Labat's own way of trying to denigrate Spanish creoles, as it almost shockingly displays the link between play and religion in the Roman Catholic Church in the Spanish American colonies, which, according to Labat's account, had acquired African (and thus pagan) features.

Describing traditional activities at Christmas in seventeenth-century

England, Nancy Egloff (n.d.) mentions the various pagan elements included: "At court and in towns and cities, players prepared plays and masques, or performances with dance, song, spectacle and costuming. . . . Certain activities enjoyed by folk of both high and low status included wassailing and mumming, which could be performed at various times throughout the two-week period. . . . Other activities enjoyed during Christmas revels included caroling, dancing and gaming." Most of these traditional features of play were transferred from England to its colonies in Virginia and the English Caribbean. However, the Puritans were opposed to much of the ritual, ornaments and pagan residues in the Roman Catholic Church and its festivals and decided to get them out of their worship and their life. They disapproved of Christmas celebrations, for example, regarding them as pagan, and banned them. In a simple sense, one of the intentions of the Puritans was to remove pomp, ceremony, symbolism and acting, which were integral components of Roman Catholic worship and which were not fundamentally distinct from the pretence which is theatre.

In the same vein, the Church of England and other Protestant churches reduced the amount of pomp and ritual practices associated with worship and Christian life. Changes in practice and philosophy of the Protestant churches, some being more restrictive than others, were transmitted to the colonies in North America and the Caribbean, and, in fact, it was the Puritans who founded the English colony of Massachusetts in the seventeenth century to practise their form of religion more peacefully there. In the English colonies in the Caribbean, converts from among the slaves and their descendants were gradually moved in the direction of this kind of Puritan asceticism.

It is the different practices of the Protestant churches and the Roman Catholic Church respectively that determined to a large extent the developmental route of play in the Caribbean. As adherents of the Protestant churches got religion before and after emancipation, the nature of their play changed, whereas the activities of those in the Roman Catholic Church expanded with increased participation from members of the society formerly excluded. Jamaica started with a Spanish and thus Roman Catholic history and it also had close connections with Haitian émigrés after the Haitian Revolution at the beginning of the nineteenth century. The Jamaican population as a whole was not under the dominance of the Anglican Church in the way that Barbados was. It is especially in the rural areas where the church was not as dominant and where African influence was still strong that play continued to flourish. In the islands where Roman Catholicism dominated because of the French presence historically (Trinidad, St Lucia, Dominica, Grenada), play flourished. Getting religion, in the sense of becoming Protestant, for the slaves and their descendants meant removing Africanisms and not indulging in the ceremonial rituals and pagan festivities associated with the Roman Catholic Church.

"Getting religion" also has the more general meaning of seeing the light or becoming more enlightened, and in the nineteenth century, which produced two of the world's most radical and influential thinkers, Charles Darwin and Karl Marx, being enlightened meant being more rational. From the 1820s onward, the phrases "the March of intellect" and "the March of the mind" became popular, signalling an increasing belief that progress meant embracing the power of science and technology. The nineteenth century also included the era of Victorian morality which deeply influenced Britain and its colonial possessions, especially in the areas of religion and sex.

In relation to the former, attempts were made, starting from before the Victorian era and continuing after it, to stamp out pagan practices (including those of people in the colonies) and to move towards "proper" religion (meaning Protestant ones) and then later to embracing science as a replacement for irrational (that is, religious) beliefs. The power of science appeared to be glorious and boundless and the idea of replacing human labour with machines was appealing, especially to those who wanted to get rid of "unpleasant" and demanding workers. The effect of scientific development was most dramatically realized in the Caribbean when human slave labour began to be replaced by machines with engines.

In relation to sex, dignity and restraint were the watchwords. This meant that dress and behaviour had to be "proper". In the British Caribbean colonies, it meant that African practices, festivities like carnival, dancing and all activities thought to be lascivious were discouraged. On the other hand, play flourished in those communities in the British colonies which had been, and still were, to some extent, outside direct and heavy British moral and philosophical influence and they also managed to preserve more of their non-European cultural practices under the aegis of the Roman Catholic Church.

Among the slaves, obsequies for the dead came to constitute a community event, even though slave quarters were initially inhabited by culturally varying and even disparate individuals. The events surrounding death involved supportive peer-group activities in which at first there had been no common tradition among human beings who had been brought from various ethnic backgrounds.

The ancestral practices that survived were modified by constraints of time, resources and the need to be meaningful across differences. It was a situation in which rituals couched in specific African languages could not work. It is because music, dancing and playing were flexible, expressive media that could communicate deep emotions and promote feelings of solidarity across ethnicities that they came to be dominant.

Slave "plays" also had an element of fictional creativity that is said to be universally important to human beings. One of the many claims about the European *danse macabre*, for example, is that it prepares the living for death. This in itself is just one example of a more universal claim that theatre and fictional narratives constitute practice for the challenges of life. This is strongly argued by Jonathan Gottschall (2012, 67), who says: "Fiction allows our brains to practice reacting to the kinds of challenges that are, and always were, most crucial to our success as a species." One could argue then that slave plays served to desensitize slaves or reduce the level of trauma occasioned by constant death among them to make it more manageable. Since Singleton (1767, 114) spoke of the slaves' "calm deportment" at their funerals and since Beckford (1790, 2:390) spoke of their "state of insensibility", it would seem as if the slave plays were achieving their goal.

Rites of passage mark the movement from one stage of life to another, as if the human being is on a journey and has to note and cross over a number of "water jumps". For the slaves, death was just the last in these "water jumps". In his article "Death and the Afterlife in African Culture", Kwasi Wiredu (1992, 137) explains the "crossing" that is occasioned by death as follows: "In traditional Africa boundaries are often marked by rivers. Not surprisingly, the high point of the postmortem journey is the crossing of a river. Once having crossed the river, one enters the land of the departed and joins the society of the ancestors."

Clara Ward's gospel song "How I Got Over" gives an idea of "crossing a river" and, more specifically, what funerals and crossing over mean for African Americans. The following selected lines show how the song presents the African American idea of the soul going home to a land of rest after a hard life and the powerful role of singing inherent in it:

> How I got over
> How did I make it over
> You know my soul look back and wonder

How did I make it over
Had a mighty hard time coming on over
I've been falling and rising all these years
I had to cry in the midnight hour coming on over
. . . .
I'm gonna wear a diamond garment
In that new Jerusalem
I'm gonna walk the streets of gold
It's the homeland of the soul
I'm gonna view the host in white

They've been traveling day and night
Coming up from every nation
They're on their way to the great Cognation
Coming from the north, south, east, and west
They're on their way to a land of rest
And they're gonna join the heavenly choir
You know we're gonna sing and never get tired
And then we're gonna shout all our troubles over

Two of the most dramatic and moving performances of "How I Got Over" were done by Mahalia Jackson – one at the March on Washington in 1963 and the other at Martin Luther King's funeral in 1968. The fact that the song was selected for these two momentous occasions and performed by arguably the greatest gospel singer underlines the significance of it as a testimony of the arduous achievement of American Americans as a people coming out of a history of bondage. What is important here is that singing as an experience that transcends the earthly as well as the idea of death as a crossing over to "the homeland of the soul" and a "land of rest" would have come right down from the slaves themselves. No doubt, Plato would have supported the notion that singing and dancing calm the soul as it crosses over. For the slaves, the other major crossing in their memory was from Africa to the Americas (the middle passage), which occasioned the "shipmate" relationship, and for some of them, the return journey also may have been a sustaining hope for post-life.

It was in the funeral procession and burial that elements of play were most prominent. The funeral procession with fellow slaves bearing the coffin aloft from the slave yard to the burial place was the person's final earthly journey during which the pall-bearers sought to execute the dead person's will by resolving outstanding debts. At the graveside, communing with the dead person and making requests of them is consistent with a point that Wiredu (1992, 138) makes in the section of his article titled "The This-Wordly Character of the Afterlife in African Thought": "Now, the significance of the ancestors consists simply in this, that they watch over the affairs of the living members of their families, helping deserving ones and punishing the delinquent. . . . There is, of course, a reciprocal side to this. . . . Accordingly, the living feel not only beholden to the ancestors for their help and protection, but also positively obliged to do honor to them." Thus, whereas in Western culture it is just that one must not speak ill of the dead, according to Wiredu, in African culture death brings honour to the dead. Even if it is only in death, slaves become honourable through an act of sublimation.

The committal of the body to the ground and the release of the soul constituted the final exchange or crossing over and this was celebrated accordingly: "the drums resound with a livelier beat, the song grows animated and cheerful; dancing and apparent merriment commences" (Stewart 1808, 251). A slave play for a person who died was a community send-off in which the community provided psychological support for the immediate relatives before, during and after the burial. The immediate relatives also honoured the departing dead by welcoming the community to a get-together with performances. A successful play was a memorable honour to the relatives of the dead. Above all, the ritual of crossing over was the slaves' supreme experience of spirituality.

SEARCHING FOR WHOLESOMENESS AND CREATING A SENSE OF IDENTITY

Blasis (1831, 18) presents the following argument about dancing among the Spanish: "Dancing, far from being, as among other nations, an innocent amusement is, with the Spanish an excitement to vice and immorality." He argues further that "this corruption in style and taste among the Spaniards, must be chiefly attributed to the *Chica*, a dance of a very immoral nature, which the Moors had brought with them from Africa" (16). He goes on to argue that the Spanish style of dancing influenced the Italian (19). From the very early description of the calenda dance by Labat, West Indian dancing was described as having some of the same features given by Blasis as characteristic of Spanish and Italian dancing, which, according to him, came from Africa. Ironically, except in Cavazzi 1687, no such features had been consistently highlighted historically in African dancing and it is clear that Blasis took much of what he said about the chica from West Indian descriptions like Labat's and not from African ones.

One of the powerful realities of slave and colonial society in the West Indies was sexual relations within and across the racial barriers set up. Indeed, Doris Garraway (2005, xiv) argues that "the 'libertine colony' thesis thus offers a means of understanding the centrality of desire and sexuality to notions of white Creole identity and political legitimacy in Saint-Domingue". Sexual relations across races in the New World started with the invading Spanish forces, which contained few or no women, seeing local women as fair game. There was not much difference in the gender composition of the early colonizing groups, which again meant that European men expected to satisfy their sexual needs with local women. A gradual increase in the number of European women coming to the New World did not significantly alter a practice that had established itself and neither did the shift in some colonies from a dependence on indigenous labour to African slave labour. African women were forced into the same sexual role in the slave colonies in the New World as indigenous women had been previously. Though brute force and coercion were means used to obtain women, it was the more common and socially acceptable means used that featured dancing.

Two factors are especially relevant in an assessment of dancing in the West Indian island colonies – the dance as a kind of sexual marketplace and the role and behaviour of women at dances. Accordingly, the various dances which took place in the slave colonies can be subdivided into (1) dances among whites only, (2) dances where coloured women were the focus, (3) festival dances (for example, crop over) where white men danced with black women and (4) slave dances. In (1), all non-whites were peripheral. In (2) and (3), white women were most likely excluded or simply did not take part. It is only in (4) that black men could participate freely, though in (3) they were given an occasional chance to participate. In (2), (3) and (4), and often in (1), black men were the musicians.

The hierarchical structure of slave society made the white man supreme and it was from the white man that women obtained status. Dancing in these contexts was often presented as a display of self and was often competitive. For coloured women, a ball was an occasion to acquire a white keeper. For some slave women, a dance was a way of attracting the attention of white males to get favours from them. For white women, dances were opportunities to show themselves as prospective wives, and, for those who were already wives, to consolidate their position. Yet because dancing was in part a physical activity, there was often a concessionary belief that Africans and their descendants had an advantage over Europeans in this respect, but in the minds of Europeans this superiority, being non-intellectual, did not amount to much.

One of the accepted roles of dances among whites was to facilitate the coming together of (young) women and men as couples in an organized and approved manner under the supervision of their elders. Dances also allowed for the development of liaisons between white men (masters on the plantation as well as other high-level whites) and potential mistresses. Thus, dancing became virtually compulsory for creole whites (male and female). The dance as a venue and context for such meetings was advantageous because of the constant movement of white males into and out of the colonies either as military persons or potential senior level plantation administration. Newcomers were thus given the chance to select from the local pool of females and, in reverse, local females could accept or reject from among those males on offer. The unpredictable element in all this, however, was the dancing competence of visiting whites (males), who were the most critical factor in the situation. While creole ladies had to be able to dance to display their attributes to the fullest, foreign males who were not competent in dancing could restrict themselves to talking to achieve their objective. The foreign addition to the local mix was no doubt exciting and exhilarating for females – it gave them the power of choice and maintained a competitive and provocative tension between creole and foreign males.

The features of character that emerge from this scenario of dances in the early colonial West Indies are desire for "otherness", preoccupation with display of self and competitiveness. From the early colonial period onward these were features that became entrenched in coloured females across the society. For males and females respectively, there developed a spirit of vengefulness resulting from being consistently overlooked – that is, foreign white men being preferred over local white men, coloured women being desired more than white women, white women being off-limits to non-white men. For white males, the coloured female body must have had a special appeal and the fact that there was an extreme, paranoid attempt to keep white females away from coloured males suggests that the body of the black male especially, on display and in motion, must have been thought to be magnetic and intoxicatingly erotic.

The rules of the "marketplace" were protected by stewards and dominant females in the case of white and indoor dances, but outdoor dances, as ringed performances, were self-regulated. The fact that the real marketplace after a time became a venue for dressing up and fashion underlines the fact that tasteful performance and display were not separable from marketing. The dynamic relationship between taste and the marketplace is admirably captured not only in the mulatto woman's concept of "dignity" balls but also in Brunias's representation of the mulatto woman strutting her stuff.

Plato spoke of singing and motion being used to quiet and bring peace, but writers on the early colonial Caribbean presented music and dance in many ways. One that was common and persistent was that music and dance induced frenzy and madness: this was first said about the indigenous people and then later about the slaves. In reference to the former, Picart (1735, 116) spoke of songs and dances in which people foamed at the mouth and shook like demons. In reference to the latter, European writers were so convinced of their view that they repeated it over a hundred-year period:

> they seemed as tho' they were acted by a Spirit of Frenzy; a madness that stung them into strong convulsive motions (Poole 1753, 295)

> these sage matrons dancing and whirling round in the middle of an assembly, with amazing rapidity, until they foam at the mouth, and drop down as convulsed. (Stedman [1794] 1806, 2:272)

> At 6 a party of singing men and women at our door, and all our servants, &c. dancing mad, I think. ([Nugent] Wright 2002, 50)

> gradually quickening their motions, until they seemed agitated by the furies. (Williams 1826, 22)

> a novice might conjecture that dancing had become epidemic, and that the whole black multitude . . . had become inoculated for it by a tarantula . . . (Wentworth 1834, 1:283)

> It is madness, delirium, a people possessed (Max-Radiguet 1842, 4:336)

> Day: St Vitus seemed to pervade the whole company (Day 1852, 1:53)

For these writers, therefore, and probably their readers also, the evidence was clear that beating drums and dancing were intoxicating forces that agitated the minds and bodies of the slaves.

The notion of ecstatic frenzy induced by music and dancing has been reported for cultures all over the world, but the way that it is usually reported makes it seem pagan, backward and without virtue. Ecstatic frenzy is often given as a climax in a ritual, but in the case of the slaves it is invoked to present a picture of unbridled zest, intensity and acceleration in their music and dancing. This kind of description was consistent with Blasis's (1828, 6) belief that "music and dance have a strong ascendancy over our intellectual faculties". It followed, then, that since music and dance had such power over the slaves, these activities could lead to dangerous and harmful consequences, just as was already happening among them with the myal dance. In short, European readers could easily conclude that people who had so little control over themselves really needed to be monitored carefully, for intoxication could make them docile or dangerous.

Ironically, it was in Haiti, according to Hannibal Price (1900), that a dancing policy was implemented with the objective of keeping the slaves happy and harmless. The way Price phrased this idea made it seem as though whites deliberately and consciously encouraged their slaves to dance in order to control them. While it is likely that whites thought that the happier the slaves were, the less rebellious they would be, at the same time, whites were aware that many slaves were spending their energy and free time dancing and they were concerned that this would dissipate their energies and would prevent them from doing their plantation work. It is unlikely that a plantation owner knowing the pros and cons of dancing would have encouraged his slaves to dance more.

The reality was that what would happen when slaves got together in groups was not always predictable. So, throughout the colonial period, many laws were passed banning certain musical instruments, and various types of curfews were instituted to prevent assemblies that could lead to rebellions. This was because, both among the indigenous inhabitants and among the Africans and their descendants, incitement to war or plots to rebel were associated with dances or what looked like festive occasions. On the other hand, over the years there developed among whites the belief that the slaves were happy among themselves when they were dancing and singing. In fact, it seems that, by and large and over time, the prevailing feeling among whites towards the slaves' dancing and singing was one of comfort rather than fear. Yet the idea that colonial whites consciously used the slaves' greatest passion and weakness, that is their singing and dancing, to preserve the status quo and, for themselves, social stability is not verifiable from opinions expressed in the historical record.

Another view of dance, one that is widespread across cultures, is that it is is good for body and soul. When slave boat captains resorted to "dancing the slaves" to keep their "goods" in saleable condition until they reached port, this was hardly a brainwave, even if they were partly persuaded this way because they believed that Africans liked to dance. The same can be said about the practice of making the slaves dance after they reached port, to show how sound they were. What is unusual about the use of dance in these cases is that the negative context of enforcement seems incongruous with what is normally accepted as healthy activity.

It is unlikely that the slaves themselves thought of dancing in the way Plato (2009, book 7) did when he said "the other [sort of dancing] aims at producing health, agility, and beauty in the limbs and parts of the body, giving the proper flexion and extension to each of them, a harmonious motion being diffused everywhere", because they suffered from no shortage of exercise to keep their muscles and limbs in order. Whether the slaves consciously considered that dancing was good for their souls and therefore actively sought to do it for this reason is doubtful. Indeed, whether slaves thought of music and dance in terms of some deep and lasting effect is doubtful. Their immediate intention was to enjoy themselves or at least to socialize with their peers.

In the popular inspirational song "His Eye Is on the Sparrow", the line "I sing because I am happy" succinctly captures the belief of some whites that blacks sing and dance because their natural disposition causes them to. The identical belief was expressed during the days of slavery in "The Bonja Song" (referred to in chapter 4), which has the refrain "Me happy, so me sing". The belief is also implicit in Dallas's assertion that "negroes are a singing race" and it is manifest in Du Tertre's words "they are no less joyful being enslaved than if they were perfectly free" (1667, 2:526). However, the notion of natural happiness as a characteristic of Africans and their descendants has been discredited.

Arguments for happiness being the result of some experience are more widely accepted. The use of alcohol or other mind-altering drugs, as by the indigenous people of the islands, can reasonably be interpreted as a desire on their part to reach a higher reality or to shorten the path to happiness. In this case, happiness is the result of drugs. The same is true of religion, according to Marx, who compares it to opium. The African American spiritual "There Is a Balm in Gilead" recommends salvation through Jesus Christ as a spiritual medicine that heals sinners and so makes them happy. Here again, it is the idea of happiness as result that is prominent.

Considering dancing and singing as media for a "religious" or transporting experience is one way to see them as having a therapeutic effect on a widespread and consistent basis. Frequency and duration of dances support the idea of social catharsis. However, the view expressed by Native (1783, 14) that the slaves performed better the next day than if they had rested the whole night long is without scientific support – the release of endorphins during exercise may bring about temporary highs, but there is no evidence that these highs can substitute for rest as a means of the body revitalizing itself. The idea of "frenzy", when applied to the slaves, suggests a transporting experience comparable to what one would get in certain religious contexts. It can be said that music and dance came to be a substitute for religion for many slaves or constituted the heart and soul of religion. Granier de Cassagnac's comment (1844, 101–2) that church attendance grew through organ music and singing supports this argument. Note also Phillippo's statistics (1843, 287–96) about and illustration of the phenomenal post-emancipation growth of the church.

There are many other claims made today about the curative powers of music and dance. If all the said benefits of music, especially drumming, and dance were inevitable and automatic consequences, the slaves would have been cured of and free from most physical and psychological illnesses and disorders. But even overdoses of music and dancing could not counteract the overdoses of brutality they received. The fact is that even if music and dance give the body a jumpstart, the body then has to restore itself on its own.

Yet the oft-repeated observation by eyewitnesses that the slaves looked happy counteracts any argument that they were generally depressed or showed high levels of malaise, as was said about the indigenous inhabitants, because it does not seem possible, whatever mask one wears, not to show signs or results of depression over a long period of time, and the historical record was not so skewed as to be totally unreliable. There was no reported high suicide rate among slaves in the colonies, which also suggests that, despite their enslavement, something constantly caused them not to choose this option. The observation that the slaves sang at work, while it does not prove that work/exercise had a hedonic effect on them, does not disprove it. It could be that singing accompanied by comforting thoughts in a situation of fellowship made it efficacious. From his observation of slaves singing in church, Lloyd (1839) noted that some of them sang lustily even though they did not know the words. For them, it must have been the music and singing and the spirit of communitas that were critical.

Work was bolstered by camaraderie, especially among field slaves working in gangs, which would have lessened the negativity of the situation. It seems reasonable to argue that generally, even if the daily work/exercise in itself did not have a hedonic effect, it kept the slaves sound and psychologically allowed them to dance in their free time, and this sequence, over time, produced a hedonic effect. The argument here is that the slaves' experience of music and dance, except probably in the case of funerals, was more pleasurable than numbing.

Bob Marley, in his song "Trench Town Rock", says "Hit me with music" because "One good thing about music, when it hits you feel no pain." Marley is obviously extending the metaphoric expression "Hit me" from gambling's "Hit me with another card" and drinking's "Hit me with another drink" to music. The implication is that, in contrast to gambling and drinking, music will cause you no pain and, furthermore, it will make you feel good. In the depressed urban area of Jamaica that is Trench Town, gambling and drinking would be normal, so Marley was proposing a better alternative for dealing with life in such a context. This role for music was equally applicable in the case of the slaves in the Caribbean and music is recognized as a remedy for pain that is superior to several others, If Marley's words are taken as a twentieth-century restatement of traditional medicine, then it means that this remedy is a part of the folk knowledge of the Caribbean.

Division among the slaves is usually supported by claims that two policies were repeatedly practised by those in control. First, there is the familiar divide-and-rule policy that external or controlling forces deliberately foment strife among different ethnic groups in a country to prevent them from coming together to voice concerted opposition. Second, there is the policy related specifically to the slaves in the Caribbean that they were consciously selected from among different ethnic groups in Africa to keep them from plotting rebellions. As to the first claim, it is true that the hierarchical plantation system was controlled to a great extent by the practice of idiosyncratic favouritism on the part of the masters, a practice which pitted slave against slave and led to constant conflict and disquiet among slaves. As to the second claim, diversity in ethnicity was a reality irrespective of whether it resulted from any specific policy; a consequence of it was that there was vacillation between loyalty to ethnicity and loyalty to peers on the plantation.

Added to the general elements of division in Caribbean slave society, singing and dancing became divisive in at least three ways – in relation to race, social class and religion. First, the belief that Africans and their descendants were "gifted" meant that they were naturally different human beings from whites.

Second, the hierarchical contrast that was set up between European civilization at the top and African savagery at the bottom did not constitute a continuum but two mutually exclusive cultural classes of people within the same society. Third, European churches frowned upon (certain kinds of) singing and dancing, but where the church allowed for singing as a part of worship, what was preferred (the service of song) was diametrically opposed to what was not (the African "play"). So, singing and dancing created a barrier between "saved souls" and "heathens" within the same social class.

In spite of these discordant elements associated with singing and dancing, structures and practices evolved within slave societies which facilitated cultural accommodation and social well-being. For the slaves, who generally arrived in the Caribbean as disparate individuals, dance was a critical force in social bonding, as set out for example in the theses of Sacks, Ehrenreich and Dissanayake. Sacks (2008, 269) argued that rhythm, as evidenced in the "synchronized efforts of a group of people at work, binds together the individual nervous systems of a human community" and this argument amplifies, as a subset, the thesis repeated by Ehrenreich (2007, 23) that "the evolutionary function of dance was to enable – or encourage – humans to live in larger groups".

The "shipmate" experience, "seasoning" (that is, placing new slave with old slave), the gang system, plays and parties, all, at different levels, facilitated the bonding experience. "Parties" exhibited elements of entertainment, display, gregariousness, rivalry, political organization and economic benefit, which were attestations of a constructive process that counteracted differences among the slaves themselves as well as with the rest of society. "Set girls" appear in various forms in different contexts in different islands and, no doubt, the "Landship", which has survived in Barbados, was formed on a similar basis. From their inception, set girls came together not only as a social set but also to collect money. This "friendly society" element strengthened in some islands as the colours and military aspects of their organization lessened or changed.

Some social cohesion also began to creep across the racial divisions because there was some inclusiveness and openness in dancing and at plays. In addition to the occasional Saturnalian activities that involved interracial interaction, the slaves' activities themselves were not exclusive. The 1792 satirical print *Cruelty and Oppression Abroad* shows "enslaved Africans happily watched by two white men and a white woman" (British Museum description) and Dickson (1789, 92) speaks of the slaves welcoming "a well dressed white man" to enter their dancing ring. No doubt, some slaves felt good at having their social superiors enter and participate in their world. Honourable or not, it led to better understanding on both sides and less fear.

Another constructive activity was the Tropical Carnival, which was not a religious, pre-Lenten festival in its early, popular manifestations in Jamaica. The New World experience of enslavement had to be a critical in blacks' appropriation of it. In other words, the dehumanization caused by enslavement heightened the attraction to carnival for Africans and their descendants in the Americas: the elements of choice and freedom, which are fundamental to carnival, were the antithesis of the experience of enslavement. Even if it was only for a couple of days, slaves could dress up and parade and believe themselves to be normal human beings by organizing themselves in groups, acting in concert together and competing against each other. Robert Dirks (1987, 187) argues, however, that this was really a matter of covert slave behaviour becoming overt: "Reversals, then, did not consist of negations. They were the playing out, collectively and conspicuously, of what otherwise went on covertly. The invisible scramble became the explicit contest."

Emancipation in Jamaica shifted the balance from a house slave (set girl) representation of carnival (with white input) back towards a lower-class, "grotesque" John Connu version, not determined by the plantation. The fancy Actor-Boy and set girl costumes were beyond the pockets of the former slaves, so the imagined face of reality was honourably and pleasurably achieved by masking and "dressing down".

The slaves were afforded choice within the general need for assimilation – individuals could introduce some of their own ethnic features into a whole which was not overburdened by the features of any one ethnic group. In addition, there was no dominant formality that prevented them from changing the features of their festivities from year to year. Moreover, the pre-emancipation period allowed for greater adoption/adaptation of more European pagan celebrations among the slaves. In fact, the constant presence and influence of the European as colonist or foreigner/tourist, the constant influence of the returning creole and the continual movement of people from one island to another made for a dynamic culture.

This culture, in spite of or probably because of its sharp contrasts and violence, gradually exhibited a non-sadistic and non-suicidal level of accommodation and over time, to a great extent through festivity, achieved a workable measure of racial cohesion. Rather than becoming just receptacles for brutality and depravity and being reduced to being in a state of social non-existence, slaves became more human (not just service beings and sex objects) in their masters' eyes through their singing and dancing in their straitened circumstances. So, though some masters and mistresses were severely corrupted and damaged by the institution of slavery and the feeling of power, they were not totally impervious to the image of joy in adversity.

Colonies were basically business ventures for European nations and within colonies, plantations were business ventures for individuals. The need to make money from investments therefore determined how colonies and plantations were governed. It is the owners or representatives of owners who made the decisions. There was no thought that consensus was necessary for decision making in the colonies because there were no other stakeholders than those who had land, business, or other property. The most that owners and managers would have done was to have informal consultations with whomever they chose. Yet in the Caribbean, workers devised non-threatening ways to be heard without being openly rebellious. It was a precarious situation for slaves, who were both property (that could be disposed of) and human workers (who had views and feelings). The historical record shows that one way the slaves achieved their desire to be heard was through their songs. Ridicule and satire in song exposed bad treatment and bad ways of masters to the public and whether or not it generally caused the respective persons to make modifications, it would have given them reputations that affected their standing in the community. It is in this indirect and haphazard way, working within the system, that slaves contributed to the well-being of their societies. Satirical and derisive songs have proved durable as a "safe" and virtuous way for the otherwise faceless mass to counteract extreme dominance.

Happiness and Virtue in a Situation of Extreme Dominance

One may argue that the image of the dancing and singing "negro" during the period of slavery was a baseless caricature or, in fact, an unfortunate case of obsequious acquiescence. One may argue that the postcolonial Caribbean person singing, dancing and fêting is a continuation of the dancing and singing "negro", or that it is a case of cultural liberation and the two were produced by particular circumstances that were not comparable. One may argue differently by saying that circumstances are not responsible for the love of festivity among sub-Saharan Africans and their descendants because their love of festivity is an irrepressible cultural characteristic. Some may argue that there is a little of all these arguments in Caribbean festivity from the start right up to today. Since migration and conquest are a part of the history of all human societies, the basic question is: how are a conquered or oppressed people supposed to react – to accept their lot or to violently overthrow their oppressors or to work within the situation to bring about a resolution?

In looking at the alternative arguments given above to explain festivity in a context of oppression in the Caribbean, the idea of an irrepressible cultural characteristic is problematic because culture does not operate in a vacuum. Social, political and economic circumstances for slaves in the plantation Caribbean would have had to be similar to those of West Africans living within their normal traditions for there to be a substantial overlap in culture and this was clearly not so. Consequently, those West African cultural features which were not unsuitable in the Caribbean situation had to change to fit slave plantation societies and the rest disappeared.

As to a supposed difference between the "dancing and singing negro" before emancipation and the Caribbean person of today, national political independence in the twentieth century and the economic need to be fully self-supporting as countries constitute a clear parallel with emancipation of a multitude of individuals in the nineteenth century and their need to assume full responsibility for themselves. Admittedly, the assumption of responsibility for self after emancipation operated within the same general political and economic box that obtained before emancipation, whereas with political independence the assumption of responsibility for nation forced Caribbean people across the social classes to move towards promoting those things they were familiar with, could rely on, market and manage. For local cultural development as well as to boost tourism all year round, music, dance and festivals came to be seen as having great economic and social benefits, especially for those in the lower classes of society. These artistic activities became transformational in appearance by changing the image of the islands away from being sugar (or banana) colonies tainted by slavery to tropical island nations providing recreational and entertainment services.

As to the question of obsequious acquiescence, one has to consider the way that it is raised by Patterson (1982, 78) and others in terms of slaves not preferring honour to life. Except in the case of Haiti, the majority of slaves in the islands chose acquiescence, they chose to live as slaves rather than die "honourably", they chose with "degraded minds" (Patterson's formulation) to dance and sing. Was it that whether the slaves were strong- or weak-willed when they arrived, their spirits were broken by the system of slavery in the Caribbean and they consequently became acquiescent? Was it that they were indoctrinated by religious beliefs (their own or European) to see their happiness after death and to be acquiescent during life? Or was it that the areas that they were allowed to indulge in (singing and dancing) as slaves gradually removed turmoil from their minds and made them 'acquiescent'? The psychological changes at the heart of these questions cannot be fully explained by the historical evidence available, but this book has made a case.

One fundamental fact about human beings is that self-preservation is instinctive; honour is not. Honourable suicide is more characteristic of people with a warrior mentality, such as the Japanese Kamikaze suicide bombers of the Second World War and the Muslim suicide bombers of today. Note that these are just an extreme form of a common idea of national heroism – giving up one's life for one's cause or country – that is inculcated, not innate. In other words, unless there is a perceived cause and unless it is rallied into action by leadership, people under normal circumstances will be governed by self-preservation. In the case of the colonial Caribbean, especially the smaller islands, circumstances made invocations to honourable suicide practically very difficult.

In spite of the fact that self-preservation is instinctive, the desire to live is affected by the perceived value that is placed on human life. If one sees, every day, people killed in gang violence in urban areas, in battles fighting the national enemy, in extreme religious causes, in natural disasters and epidemics, in massacres by the mentally ill and in domestic disputes, one (especially the youth) may come to the conclusion that being "involved", becoming a warrior, is what life is about and that living safely is not living at all. In fact, for many young people in today's world, honourable suicide is becoming less and less distinct from national heroism as a way to overcome a perceived dangerous dominant force or as a way to justify life.

The most influential, interwoven factors in the colonial history of Caribbean societies were the dramatic implosion of the indigenous populations; the migration from Europe to the Caribbean of people with adventurer and capitalist ideals; the severing of Africans from their heritage and the destruction of their ancestral family structure; the negative consequences of ethnic diversity and culture contact; the (attempted) imposition of a monolithic European model on the whole society and the acquiescence of enslaved Africans in a system of slavery; and the hierarchical subordination of the population. All these have their parallels in today's world. For all groups involved in Caribbean colonialism, the basic impulse was to try to rise above the conflicts and their stigma by creating salutary images of themselves and by learning to live with each other.

In contrast to Europeans who operated by themselves within their own geopolitical ignorance and were in their own comfort zone at home in Europe, creole whites saw themselves as part of a new world made up of various people and they believed that, by their own means, they had managed to construct and establish a society with themselves on top. Generally, they saw themselves as adventurous, tested by reality, creative in a context of newness and transparent in their behaviour. Whereas, for Europeans, a colonial ball was testimony of a spoiled and indolent people whose main concern was frivolity, for creole whites, a successful ball was a perfect manifestation of social and managerial prowess and racial ascendancy.

As to the Africans and their descendants, faced with a continuous, everyday process of dehumanization, they had to recover their equilibrium by humanizing themselves in accessible ways, principally through festivity. No doubt they saw these avenues of expression in festivity as equally available to all and not providing anyone (master or slave) with either privilege or restriction. For them, good performance emerged through competition that was public and beauty was determined by consensus. Of course, the ravages and inequities of enslavement (as well as the reduction of economic responsibility for self) provided slaves and their descendants with a powerful spur to prove themselves and showcase their talents.

The slaves' humanizing of themselves is different from the notion of being driven by a fanciful belief or the argument that the vision of an inverted world occurs automatically to the downtrodden or that the slaves recreated the festivities issuing from a temperate climate and an agricultural people as performances related to a future world where bounty, enjoyment and freedom reigned. The slaves' humanizing of themselves was a matter of them using every occasion to restore or maintain their version of what the classical paradigm calls "mens sana in corpore sano" – that is, a positive mind in a strong body. The fact that singing functioned as an antidote to stress and everyday toil almost paradoxically converted work into play in the view of white observers who could only see groups of happy people. The slaves sang, danced and performed with genuineness, passion and enthusiastic expression, consciously or not, to sustain themselves. This was the "zest" that Bertrand Russell saw as a prerequisite for happiness. It was pervasive, as evidenced in a typical remark such as "They do not do any work which requires some effort without doing it in rhythm and almost always singing" (Chanvalon 1763, 67).

While the institution of slavery occasioned different responses in whites and blacks, the specific colonial context as well as a generally favourable environment led to similar ones. Entertainment and a welcoming disposition seemed to be important to all groups and this could be said to be a factor of the early colonial context, introduced by the indigenous people as *guatiao* to all who came from the Old World. The reality was that for migrants (forced or free) faced with an unfamiliar environment, there was a human need for a welcoming and helping hand as well as for succour and protection. Even in the case of the indigenous people, welcoming and entertainment were a normal part of their lives when they visited others on another island.

The apparent lack of visible effort and strain on the part of the slaves while they were working, coupled with their smiling faces made Europeans think that they did everything naturally and instinctively. Because of their unbridled enthusiasm for what they had access to and inspired them, whites wanted to believe that singing and dancing were their only concerns. The desire to preserve their dignity when they felt the sting of the whip contributed to the idea that dehumanization did not bother them. The fact that they were deprived of responsibility for their own economic well-being convinced Europeans that they had a "No problem, man" mentality. In sum, then, Europeans were inclined to see nothing in the slaves' general demeanour and behaviour that caused them to think they were anything but how they were in their pastimes and entertainment, that is, "carefree", "easy-going" and happy.

The contrast between European opinions, the self-concept of creole whites, white concepts of Africans and their descendants and the reverse reveals suspicion and hostility always actively at work pushing apart the racial and ethnic groups that made up Caribbean society. This negativity needled all of them, especially those at the bottom, who, paradoxically, even came to regard themselves as superior because they would pride themselves on having their own culture and being able to outdo their social superiors at theirs, specifically dancing and singing. Over time, more positive elements of human behaviour allowed for a greater and more dynamic fusion of cultures that reflected the most malleable of various worlds, but the antagonistic spirit never waned and continued to push individuals in myriad little social events to try to outdo each other.

Overall, then, the combination of characteristic features of the various groups produced a society made up of constituent groups that continually wanted to prove themselves to others. However, it is as if the only areas in which such a society could do this and in which it was not already at a disadvantage were those (singing, dancing and playing) which, for a long time and in many parts of the world, were traditionally regarded as frivolous. It is as entertainment, tourism and the Arts have begun to grow as major areas of the global economy that many Caribbean people have been able to move towards satisfying the desire to prove themselves and to see that this is the most viable way to go forward.

Even though this study has tried to dispel the simplistic historical image of Caribbean people as a happy, singing, dancing and playful people by looking at it critically and in detail, it is still interesting to compare the simple image of Caribbean people with that of others. Strutt ([1801] 1903) argued that one sees the character of a people better when they are at play, but the general consensus may be the opposite – that is, that a people's true character shows itself when they are "at war" and that it is this kind of image that surfaces repeatedly and shapes international behaviour.

There are two common images of Jews – one stemming from Psalm 137 and the other made famous in Shakespeare's *Merchant of Venice*. Psalm 137 presents the Jews as unforgiving, and their happiness as revenge. This vengeful image of Jews has persisted up to modern times, as evidenced in the relentless Jewish pursuit and punishment of Nazi war criminals. Unger's (2014, 44) words "vindictive reassertion of one's place with regard to others" may be borrowed to sum it up. The related image, portrayed in Shakespeare's Shylock, is the Jew as mercenary, demanding his pound of flesh. These responses are seen as un-Christian, based on Paul's letter to the Romans in the Bible which says: "Vengeance is mine. I will repay, saith the Lord" (12:19).

Popular images of the French relate to food, romance and language, but images of the French as a people under pressure are quite different. A negative image of them, as a broken, nihilistic people, comes out of Vichy France (1940–44) and the works of French writers and philosophers after the Second World War. The philosophy of the absurd is exemplified in Camus's *L'Etranger* and Ionesco's theatre. From the latter the following quote is typical: "No society has been able to abolish human sadness, no political system can deliver us from the pain of living, from our fear of death" (Ionesco 1958, 14). So, the image of the French under pressure is one of sadness and life as "absurd".

The British are commonly seen as a people conditioned by their weather, which is often gloomy and rainy. The popular image of the British under pressure is one of a people with a "stiff upper lip". This image is best exemplified in the 1940 Second World War speech by British prime minister Winston Churchill (1940), when he said: "I have nothing to offer but blood, toil, tears and sweat... You ask, what is our aim?... It is victory, victory at all costs... however long and hard the road may be; for without victory, there is no survival." Abnegation and resolve are admirable qualities for a warrior, but psychological repression in the average citizen is often seen as leading to mental illness.

In each of the cases above, studies can explore these images to reveal how invalid they are, but these studies would not alter the fact that such images of peoples persist in the popular imagination and act as powerful spurs and catalysts. Yet all of these simple images are strikingly different from the one which says: "In no country in the world are there stronger or more unequivocal indications of happiness and enjoyment than in the West Indies" (Resident 1828, 234). It is a formulation that has persisted up to today. In the final analysis, one has to conclude that, in the popular imagination, it is a virtuous character that reacts positively, with some recrimination but without violence, under long and intense pressure.

The Roman poet Horace is noted for his pieces of advice about using time wisely and pleasurably, especially "Carpe diem quam minimum credula postero" ("Seize the day, trust little in the future") and "Nunc est bibendum, nunc pede libero pulsanda tellus" ("Now is for drinking, now is for beating the ground with a free foot"). On the other hand, Virgil was catering more to the warrior mentality when he started the Aeneid with "Arma virumque cano" ("I sing of arms and the man"). Empires will come and go, and there will always be happiness on one side and conflict and killing on the other because that is the way of nature. There will always be philosophies justifying the one side or the other, but, with the escalation in the will and power to destroy, there must be a more concerted and heartfelt attempt to tip the balance in favour of well-being through play.

Productive existence or development in new and difficult situations necessitates improvisation, especially when violent solutions are suicidal. Improvisation requires imagination and the will to experiment to achieve satisfaction. Play (fun + improvisation + imagination) facilitates the development of procedural knowledge that can be generalized to manage many different situations. That is a virtue of play.

References

Abbad y Lasierra, Fray Iñigo. (1788) 1966. *Historia geográfica, civil y natural de la isla de San Juan Bautista de Puerto Rico*. Rio Piedras, PR: Editorial Universitaria, University of Puerto Rico.

Abrahams, Roger D. 1967. "The Shaping of Folklore Traditions in the British West Indies". *Journal of Inter-American Studies* 9 (3): 456–80.

———. 1970a. "British West Indian Drama and the 'Life Cycle' Problem". *Folklore* 81:241–65.

———. 1970b. "Patterns of Performance in the British West Indies". In *Afro-American Anthropology: Contemporary Perspectives*, edited by Norman Whitten Jr and John Szwed, 163–79. New York: The Free Press.

An Abstract of the Evidence Delivered before a Select Committee of the House of Commons in the Years 1790, and 1791 on the Part of the Petitioners for the Abolition of the Slave-Trade. 1791. London: James Phillips.

Acosta, José de. (1590) 1894. *Historia natural y moral de las Indias*. Madrid: Ramón Anglés.

Adams, Captain John. 1823. *Remarks on the Country Extending from Cape Palmas to the River Congo*. London: G. and W.B. Whittaker.

Aimes, Hubert H.S. 1905. "African Institutions in America". *Journal of American Folklore* 18 (68): 15–32.

Alexander, Captain J.E. 1833. *Transatlantic Sketches, Comprising Visits to the Most Interesting Scenes in North and South America, and the West Indies: With Notes on Negro Slavery and Canadian Emigration*. Vol. 1. London: R. Bentley.

Alvarez Nazario, Manuel. (1961) 1974. *El elemento afronegroide en el español de Puerto Rico*. 2nd ed. San Juan de Puerto Rico: Instituto de Cultura Puertorriqueña.

Angelou, Maya. "Caged Bird". Poetry Foundation. https://www.poetryfoundation.org/poems/48989/caged-bird.

Anghiera, Pietro Martire d'. 1628. *The famous historie of the Indies: Declaring the adventures of the Spaniards, which have conquered these countries, with the varietie of relations of the religions, lawes, governments, manners, ceremonies, customes, rites, warres, and funerals of that people. Comprised into sundry Decades. Set forth first by Mr. Hackluyt, and now published by L.M. Gent*. 2nd ed. London: L.M. Gent.

———. 1989. *Décadas del Nuevo Mundo*. Santo Domingo, DR: Sociedad Dominicana de Bibliófilos.

[Anon. Irish]. 1776. *An Account of a Voyage to Jamaica, with a Description of Some of the Caribbee Islands, and Various Matters Relative to the Island of Jamaica, and Its Inhabitants, &c. &c. in a Series of Letters from a Young Gentleman (Who Lately Went to Reside There) to the Author.* Dublin: J. Sheppard and G. Nugent.

Arber, Edward. 1885. *The First Three English Books on America. [?1511]–1555 AD Being Chiefly Translations, Compilations,* &c., by Richard Eden [. . .]. Birmingham: Turnbull and Spears.

Atkins, John. (1735) 1972. *A Voyage to Guinea, Brasil, and the West-Indies; in His Majesty's Ships, the* Swallow *and* Weymouth. Northbrook, IL: Metro Books.

Atwood, Thomas. 1791. *The History of the Island of Dominica.* London: J. Johnson.

Authentic History of the English West Indies with the Manners and Customs of the Free Inhabitants including Their Civil and Criminal Laws, Establishments, &c. a Description of the Climate, Buildings, Towns, & Sea Ports; with the Treatment and Condition of the Negroes: An Account of the Lands in Cultivation and the Natural and Vegetable Productions, Exports, &c. 1810. London: Printed for the author.

Aytoun, James. 1984. *Redcoats in the Caribbean.* Lancashire, UK: Blackburn Recreation Services Department.

Bachiller y Morales, Don Antonio. 1883. *Cuba primitiva: Origen, lenguas, tradiciones e historia de los indios de las Antillas Mayores y Las Lucayas.* 2nd ed. Habana: Libreria de Miguel de Villa.

Barbot, Jean. 1752. In *A Collection of Voyages and Travels, Consisting of Authentic Writers in our own Tongue, which have not before been collected in English, or have only been abridged in other Collections* [. . .], compiled by A. Churchill. Vol. 5. London: T. Osborne.

Barclay, Alexander. 1826. *A Practical View of the Present State of Slavery in the West Indies; or, An Examination of Mr. Stephen's "Slavery of the British West India Colonies": Containing More Particularly an Account of the Actual Condition of the Negroes in Jamaica.* London: Smith, Elder.

Bayley, F.W.N. 1830. *Four Years' Residence in the West Indies during the Years 1826, 7, 8 and 9.* London: William Kidd.

———. 1833. *Four Years' Residence in the West Indies during the years 1826, 7, 8 and 9.* 3rd ed., enlarged. London: William Kidd.

Beckford, William. 1788. *Remarks upon the Situation of Negroes in Jamaica, Impartially Made from a local Experience of nearly Thirteen Years in that Island.* London: T. and J. Egerton.

———. 1790. *A Descriptive Account of the Island of Jamaica* [. . .]. 2 vols. London: T. and J. Egerton.

Belisario, I. 1837–38. *Sketches of Character, In Illustration of the Habits, Occupation, and Costume of the Negro Population in the Island of Jamaica, Drawn from Nature, and in Lithography.* Nos. 1, 2 & 3. Kingston: N.p.

Bennett, Louise. 1966. *Jamaica Labrish*. Notes and introduction by Rex Nettleford. Kingston: Sangster's Book Stores.
Benoit, P.J. 1839. *Voyage à Surinam; description des possessions néerlandaises dans la Guyane. Cent dessins pris sur nature par l'auteur, lithographiés par Madou et Lauters*. Bruxelles: Société des beaux-arts (De Wasme et Laurent).
Bickell, Richard. 1825. *The West Indies as They Are; or A Real Picture of Slavery: But More Particularly as It Exists in the Island of Jamaica*. [. . .]. London.
Bilby, Kenneth. 1985. "The Caribbean as a Musical Region". In *Caribbean Contours*, edited by S.W. Mintz and S. Price, 181–218. Baltimore: Johns Hopkins University Press.
Blasis, Carlo. 1831. *The Code of Terpsichore: The Art of Dancing, Comprising Its Theory and Practice, and a History of Its Rise and Progress, from the Earliest Times*. Translated by R. Barton. 2nd ed. London: Edward Bull.
Blome, Richard. 1672. *A Description of the Island of Jamaica; With the other Isles and Territories in America, to which the English Are Related, viz, Barbadoes, St. Christophers, Niebis, or Mevis, Antego, Barbuda, St. Vincent, Bermudes, Dominica, Carolina, Montserrat, Virginia, Anguilla, New England, New Foundland* [. . .]. London: L. Mibbourn.
Boehm, Christopher. 1993. "Egalitarian Behavior and Reverse Dominance Hierarchy". *Current Anthropology* 34 (3): 227–40.
Borde, Pierre-Gustave-Louis. (1876; part 2, 1882) 1883. *Histoire de l'île de la Trinidad sous le gouvernement espagnol*. Paris: Maisonneve et Cie.
Bosman, Willem. 1705. *A New and Accurate Description of the Coast of Guinea, Divided into Gold, the Slave, and the Ivory Coasts* [. . .]. London: James Knapton and Dan. Midwinter.
Bouton, Le P. Jacques. 1640. *Relation de l'Etablissement des Francois depuis l'an 1635. En l'isle de la Martinique, l'une des antilles de l'Amerique. Des moeurs des Sauvages, de la situation, & des autres singularitez de l'isle*. Paris: Sebastian Cramoisy.
Bowdich, T.E. 1819. *Mission from Cape Coast Castle to Ashantee*. London: John Murray.
Boyer, Paul. 1654. *Veritable relation de tovt ce qvi s'est fait et passé au voyage que Monsieur de Bretigny fit à l'Amerique Occidentale. Auec vne description des mœurs, & des prouinces de tous les sauuages de cette grande partie du Cap de Nord: vn dictionnaire de la langue, & vn aduis tres-necessaire à tous ceux qui veulent habiter ou faire habiter ce païs-là, ou qui desirent d'y establir des colonies. Le tout fait sur les lieux, par Pavl Boyer, escuyer, sieur de Petit-Puy*. Paris: P. Rocolet.
Brathwaite, Edward. (1971) 1981. *The Folk Culture of the Slaves in Jamaica*. London: New Beacon.
Breen, Henry H. 1844. *St. Lucia: Historical, Statistical and Descriptive*. London: Longman, Brown, Green and Longmans.

Brehaut, Ernest. 1912. *An Encyclopedist of the Dark Ages: Isidore of Seville*. New York: Longmans, Green.
Breton, Raymond. 1665. *Dictionaire Caraibe Francois. Meslé de quantité de Remarques historiques pour l'esclaircissement de la Langue. Composé par le R. P. Raymond Breton, Religieux de l'ordre des Freres Prescheurs, & l'un des premiers Missionaires Apostoliques en l'isle de la Gardeloupe & autres circonvoisines de l'Amerique*. Auxerre: Gilles Bouquet.
———. 1666. *Dictionaire Francois-Caraibe*. Auxerre: Gilles Bouquet.
Bridgens, R. 1837. *West India Scenery, with Illustrations of Negro Character, the Process of Making Sugar, from Sketches Taken during a Voyage to, and Residence of Seven Years in the Island of Trinidad*. London: Robert Jennings.
Brown, P., and S. Levinson. 1987. *Politeness: Some Universals in Language Usage*. Cambridge: Cambridge University Press.
Cahusac, Louis de. 1754. *La danse ancienne et moderne ou Traité historique de la danse*. Tome premier. Lahaye: Jean Neaulme.
Calderón de la Barca, Pedro. (1635) 1831. *La vida es sueño*. In *El teatro español, ó coleccion de dramas escogidos de Don Pedro Calderón de la Barca*. Vol. 2. London: J.Y.C. Adlard.
Caribbeana: Containing Letters and Dissertations, Together with Poetical Essays, on Various Subjects and Occasions; Chiefly Wrote by Several Hands in the West-Indies and Some of Them to Gentlemen Residing There. Now Collected Together in Two Volumes. (1741) 1978. London: T. Osborne et al. Reprint, Millwood, NY: Kraus Reprint.
Carmichael, Mrs. 1833. *Domestic Manners and Social Condition of the White, Coloured, and Negro Population of the West Indies*. 2 vols. London: Whittaker, Treacher.
Cassius Amicus. 2011. *The Doctrines of Epicurus – Annotated*. Cassius Amicus.
Castle, Terry. 1986. *Masquerade and Civilization: The Carnivalesque in Eighteenth-Century English Culture and Fiction*. Stanford, CA: Stanford University Press.
Cavazzi, Giovanni. 1687. *Istorica descrizione de' tre' regni Congo, Matamba, et Angola sitvati nell' Etiopia inferiore occidentale e delle missioni apostoliche esercitateui da religiosi Capuccini, accuratamente compilata dal p. Gio. Antonio Cavazzi da Montecvccolo, sacerdote capvccino, il qvale vi fv' prefetto. E nel presente stile ridotta dal p. Fortvnato Alamandini da Bologna [. . .]*. Bologna: Per Giacomo Monti.
Chanvalon, Jean-Baptiste Thibault de. 1763. *Voyage a la Martinique, Contenant Divers Observations sur la Physique, l'Histoire naturelle, l'Agriculture, les Moeurs, & les usages de cette Isle, faits en 1751 & dans les années suivantes*. Paris: J.B. Bauche.
Chapman, Matthew James. 1833. *Barbadoes, and Other Poems*. London: J. Fraser.
Chester, Greville. 1869. *Transatlantic Sketches in the West Indies, South America, Canada, and the United States*. London: Smith, Elder.
Churchill, Winston. 1940. *Hansard*. House of Commons Debate, 13 May 1940, vol. 360, cc1501–25, 2:54 pm. http://hansard.millbanksystems.com/commons/1940/may/13/his-majestys-government-1.

Clarke, Eric. 2011. "What Are the Important Questions? A Reflection". In Deliège and Davidson 2011, 17–28.

Clarke, Grant, and Roy Turk. 1924. *"I'm a Little Blackbird Looking for a Bluebird": A.H. Woods Presents Florence Mills in Dixie to Broadway*. Music by Arthur Johnston and George W. Meyer. New York: Irving Berlin, Inc.

Clarkson, T. 1839. *History of the Rise, Progress, and Accomplishment of the Abolition of the African Slave Trade by the British Parliament*. London: J. W. Parker.

Colman, George. 1806. *Inkle and Yarico; An Opera in Three Acts; As Performed at the Theatres Royal Covent Garden, and Haymarket. With Remarks by Mrs. Inchbald*. London: Longman, Hurst, Rees and Orme.

———. 1827. *Inkle and Yarico: An Opera in Three Acts*. In *Cumberland's British Theatre with Remarks, Biographical and Critical: Printed from the acting copies, as performed at the Theatres Royal, London*, compiled by John Cumberland, vol. 16. London: John Cumberland.

Colthurst, J.B. 1835–38. "Journal as a Special Magistrate in the Islands of Barbados and St. Vincent, July 1835–August 1838". Boston Public Library, MS.U.1.2.

[Combe, W.] 1815. *The English Dance of Death from the Designs of Thomas Rowlandson, with Metrical Illustrations. By the Author of "Doctor Syntax"*. vol. 1. London: R. Ackermann.

Cooper, Thomas. 1824. *Facts Illustrative of the Condition of the Negro Slaves in Jamaica: With Notes and an Appendix*. London: J. Hatchard and Son.

Coppier, Guillaume. 1645. *Histoire et voyage des Indes Occidentales, et de plusieurs autres regions maritimes & esloignées*. Lyon: Jean Huguetan.

Crow, Captain Hugh. 1830. *Memoirs of the Late Captain Hugh Crow of Liverpool*. London: Longman, Rees, Orme, Brown and Green.

Crowley, Daniel J. 1958. "La Rose and La Marguerite Societies in St Lucia". *Journal of American Folklore* 71 (282): 541–52.

———. 1984. *African Myth and Black Reality in Bahian Carnaval*. Los Angeles: Museum of Cultural History, UCLA.

Cruikshank, Robert. 1833. *Cruikshank's Comic Album*. London: W. Kidd.

———. 1835. *The Condition of the West India Slave Contrasted with That of the Infant Slave in Our English Factories. With Fifteen Illustrations from the Graver of Robert Cruikshank*. London: W. Kidd.

Dallas, R.C. 1823. *Adrastus, a Tragedy; Amabel, or The Cornish Lovers and Other Poems*. London: James Cawthorn.

Daniel, Yvonne. 2011. *Caribbean and Atlantic Diaspora Dance: Igniting Citizenship*. Urbana: University of Illinois Press.

Dapper, Olfert. 1686. *Description de l'Afrique, contenant les noms, la situation & les confins de toutes ses parties, leurs rivières, leurs villes & leurs habitations, leurs plantes & leurs animaux; les mœurs, les coûtumes, la langue, les richesses, la religion & le gouver-*

nement de ses peuples.... Amsterdam: Wolfgang, Waesbere, Boom and van Someren.

Darwin, Charles. 1871. *The Descent of Man.* Vol. 2. London: John Murray.

Day, Charles William. 1852. *Five Years' Residence in the West Indies.* 2 vols. London: Colbourn.

De La Beche, H.T. 1825. *Notes on the Present Condition of the Negroes in Jamaica.* London: T. Cadell.

De Léry, Jean. 1578. *Histoire d'un voyage fait en la terre du Bresil, Autrement dite Amerique. Le tout recueilli sur les lieux par Jean de Léry natif de la Margelle, terre de Sainct Sene au Duché de Bourgougne.* N.p.: A. Chuppin.

De Rochefort, Charles. 1658. *Histoire Naturelle & Morale des Iles Antilles de l'Amerique.* Rotterdam: Arnould Leers.

Defoe, Daniel. 1718. *The Family Instructor.* Vol. 2. London: Eman Matthews.

Deive, Carlos Esteban. 1977. "Sobre el origen del merengue". *Ahora!*, no. 716 (1 August): 30.

Deliège, Irène, and Jane W. Davidson, eds. 2011. *Music and the Mind: Essays in Honour of John Sloboda.* Oxford: Oxford University Press.

Dickson, William. 1789. *Letters on Slavery [...] To which are added, Addresses to the whites and to the Free Negroes of Barbadoes, and accounts of some Negroes eminent for their virtues and abilities.* London: J. Phillips.

———. 1814. *Mitigation of Slavery, in Two Parts. Part I: Letters and Papers of the Late Hon. Joshua Steele, Vice President of the London Society of Arts, Etc and Member of His Majesty's Council in Barbadoes. Part II: Letters to Thomas Clarkson, Esq. M.A. by William Dickson, LL.D. Formerly Secretary to His Excellency The Late Hon. Edward Hay, Governor, &c. of the Above Ancient and Important Colony.* London: Longman, Hurst, Rees, Orme, and Brown.

Dirks, Robert. 1987. *The Black Saturnalia: Conflict and Its Ritual Expression on British West Indian Slave Plantations.* Gainesville: University of Florida Press.

Dissanayake, Ellen. 1995. *Homo Aestheticus: Where Art Comes from and Why.* Seattle and London: University of Washington Press.

———.. 2014. "A Bona Fide Ethological View of Art: The Artification Hypothesis". In *Art as Behaviour: An Ethological Approach to Visual and Verbal Art, Music and Architecture,* edited by Christa Sütterlin, W. Schiefenhövel, Christian Lehmann, Johanna Forster and Gerhard Apfelauer, 43–62. Hanse Studies, vol. 10. Oldenburg: BIS-Verlag der Carl von Ossietzky Universität.

D'Orbigny, A. 1836. *Voyage pittoresque dans les deux Amériques.* Paris: L. Tenré, H. Dupuis.

[Doyle, John]. 1832–42. *A Key to the Political Sketches of H.B.* [i.e. John Doyle]. London: T. M'Lean.

Drewal, M.T. 1992. *Yoruba Ritual: Performers, Play, Agency.* Bloomington: Indiana University Press.

Du Puis, Le F. Mathias. (1652) 1972. *Relation de l'establissement d'une colonie francoise* dans la Gardeloupe isle de l'Amerique, et des moeurs des Sauvages. Reprint, Basse-Terre: Société d'Histoire de Guadeloupe.

Du Tertre, le R.P. Jean Baptiste. 1654. *Histoire generale des Isles de S. Christophe, de la Guadeloupe, de la Martinique et autres dans l'Amerique.* Paris.

———. 1667. *Histoire generale des Antilles habitées par les François.* Vol. 2, *Contenant l'histoire naturelle, enrichy de cartes & de figures.* Paris: Thomas Jolly.

Dunbar, Paul Laurence. 1913. *The Complete Poems of Paul Laurence Dunbar.* With an introduction to "Lyrics of Lowly Life" by W.D. Howells. New York: Dodd, Mead.

Edwards, Bryan. 1793–94. *The History, Civil and Commercial, of the British Colonies in the West Indies.* 2 vols. London: J. Stockdale.

———. 1801. *The History, Civil and Commercial, of the British Colonies in the West Indies.* 3 vols. 3rd ed. London: John Stockdale.

Egloff, Nancy. n.d. "Christmas in 17th-Century England and Virginia". Exploring English Customs and the Lord of Misrule". http://www.historyisfun.org/jamestown-settlement/a-colonial-christmas/christmas-traditions.

Ehrenreich, Barbara. 2007. *Dancing in the Streets: A History of Collective Joy.* New York: Metropolitan Books.

Fernández de Oviedo y Valdés, Gonzalo. (1526) 1996. *Sumario de la natural y general historia de las Indias.* Edited, introduced and annotated by J. Miranda. Biblioteca Americana. Mexico: Fondo de cultura economica.

———. 1535. *La historia general de las Indias.* Seville.

———. 1959. *Historia general y natural de las Indias.* Biblioteca de Autores Españoles. Vols. 117–21. Madrid: Ediciones Atlas.

Fink, Eugen, Ute Saine and Thomas Saine. 1968. "The Oasis of Happiness: Toward an Ontology of Play". *Yale French Studies*, no. 41: 19–30.

Firth, C.H., ed. 1908. *Naval Songs and Ballads.* Vol. 33. London: Navy Records Society.

Fraser, Lionel Mordaunt. 1891. *History of Trinidad.* Vol. 1, *(First Period) From 1781 to 1813.* Port of Spain, Trinidad: Government Printing Office.

Frazer, J.G. 1925. *The Golden Bough: A Study in Magic and Religion.* Abridged ed. New York: Macmillan.

Friedemann, Nina S. De. 1996. "El Carnaval Caribeño: Ritual contemporáneo de comunicación". *Revista mexicana del Caribe* 2:140–57.

Froger, Francois. 1698. *Relation d'un voyage fait en 1695, 1696, & 1697 aux Côtes d'Afrique, Détroit de Magellan, Brezil, Cayenne & Isles Antilles, par un Escadre des Vaisseaux du Roy, commandeé par M. DeGennes. Faite par le Sieur Froger Ingenieur volontaire sur le Faucon Anglois. Enrichie de grand'nombre de figures dessinées sur les lieux.* Paris: M. Brunet.

Froude, James A. 1888. *The English in the West Indies or, The Bow of Ulysses.* Longmans, Green.

Fyfe, Christopher, ed. 2000. *Anna Maria Falconbridge: Narrative of Two Voyages to the River Sierra Leone during the Years 1791–1792–1793, and the Journal of Isaac DuBois, with Alexander Falconbridge: An Account of the Slave Trade on the Coast of Africa.* Liverpool: Liverpool University Press.

Gallini, Giovanni-Andrea. 1770. *Critical Observations on the Art of Dancing.* London: The author.

Garraway, Doris. 2005. *The Libertine Colony: Creolization in the Early French Caribbean.* Durham: Duke University Press.

Garvey, Marcus. 1938. Speech made in Sydney, Nova Scotia. *Black Man* 3, (10): 7–11. Reprinted 1990, *The Marcus Garvey and Universal Negro Improvement Association Papers,* edited by Robert A. Hill, vol. 7. Berkeley: University of California Press.

Gaspar, D.B. 1985. *Bondmen and Rebels: A Study of Master-Slave Relations in Antigua with Implications for Colonial British America.* Baltimore: Johns Hopkins University Press

Gayadeen, Holly. 1983. *Alfredo Codallo: Artist and Folklorist.* Trinidad and Tobago: The Author.

Gikandi, Simon. 2011. *Slavery and the Culture of Taste.* Princeton: Princeton University Press.

Gill, John. 2009. *Andalucía: A Cultural History.* Oxford: Oxford University Press.

Glissant, Édouard. 1990. *Poétique de la relation.* Paris: Gallimard.

Goldenberg, David M. 2003. *The Curse of Ham: Race and Slavery in Early Judaism, Christianity, and Islam.* Princeton: Princeton University Press.

Gottschall, Jonathan. 2012. *The Storytelling Animal: How Stories Make Us Human.* Boston: Mariner Books.

Grainger, James. 1764. *The Sugar-Cane: A Poem.* London: Dodsley.

Granier de Cassagnac, Adolphe. 1842. *Voyage aux Antilles françaises.* Vol. 1. Paris: Dauvin et Fontaine Libraires.

———. 1844. *Voyage aux Antilles. Deuxieme partie. Les Antilles anglaises, danoises et espagnoles, Saint Domingue et les Etats-Unis.* Paris: Au Comptoir des Imprimeurs-Unis.

Great Newes from the Barbados, or, A True and Faithful Account of the Grand Conspiracy of the Negroes against the English and the Happy Discovery of the Same. With the number of those who were burned alive, Beheaded, and otherwise Executed for their Horrid Crimes. With a Short Description of that Plantation. 1676. London: L. Curtis.

Gumilla, Joseph. 1741. *El Orinoco ilustrado, historia natural, civil, y geographica, de este gran rio y de sus caudalosas vertientes: govierno, usos, y costumbres de los Indios sus habitadores, con nuevas y utiles noticias de animales, arboles, frutos, aceytes, resinas, yerras, y raices medicinales: y sobre todo, se hallaràn conversiones muy singulares à nuestra santa fé, y casos de mucha edificacion escrita por el P. Joseph Gumilla, de la Compañia de Jesus.* Madrid: M. Fernandez.

Hair, P.E.H., Adam Jones and Robin Law, eds. 1992. *Barbot on Guinea: The Writings*

of Jean Barbot on West Africa 1678–1712. Vols. 1 and 2. London: Hakluyt Society.
Hall, Douglas. 1999. *In Miserable Slavery: Thomas Thistlewood in Jamaica 1750–86*. Kingston: University of the West Indies Press.
Halliwell, James Orchard. 1852. *Dictionary of Archaic and Provincial Words, Obsolete Phrases, Proverbs, and Ancient Customs from the Fourteenth Century*. 2 vols. Brixton Hill: C. and J. Adlard.
Handler, Jerome S. 1991. *Supplement to "A Guide to Source Materials for the Study of Barbados History, 1627–1834"*. Providence, RI: John Carter Brown Library and Barbados Museum and Historical Society.
Handler, J., and C.J. Frisbie. 1972. "Aspects of Slave Life in Barbados: Music and Its Cultural Context". *Caribbean Studies* 11:5–46.
Handler, J., and F. Lange. 1978. *Plantation Slavery in Barbados*. Cambridge, MA: Harvard University Press.
Harris, Leonard. 1997. "Honor, Eunuchs, and the Postcolonial Subject". In *Postcolonial African Philosophy: A Critical Reader*, edited by Emmanuel Chukwudi Eze, 252–59. Cambridge, MA: Blackwell.
Hazard, Samuel. 1873. *Santo Domingo: Past and Present, with a Glance at Hayti*. New York: Harper and Brothers.
Helm, Alex. 1981. *The English Mummers' Play*. Suffolk, UK: Folklore Society.
Henríquez Ureña, Pedro. 1938. *Para la historia de los indigenismos*. Buenos Aires: Universidad de Buenos Aires.
Herbermann, George. 1907. "Dance of Death". In *The Catholic Encyclopedia*, vol. 4, 1620–22. New York: Robert Appleton. Available online through Christian Classics Ethereal Library, https://www.ccel.org/.
Hesiod. 1978. *Works and Days*. Edited with prolegomena and commentary by M.L. West. Oxford: Clarendon.
Histoire naturelle des Indes: The Drake Manuscript in the Pierpont Morgan Library. 1996. Preface by Charles E. Pierce Jr; foreword by Patrick O'Brian; introduction by Verlyn Klinkenborg; translations by Ruth S. Kraemer. New York: Norton.
Holt, Arthur. 1729. Letter to Bishop Gordon, Barbados, 7 March 1729. Lambeth Palace Library, London. Fulham Papers, vol. 15, folios 266–67.
———. 1946. "Arthur Holt, Anglican Clergyman, Reports on Barbados, 1725–1733". *Journal of Negro History* 31 (4): 444–69. doi:10.2307/2715217.
Hondius, Jodocus. 1606. *Septentrio America*. [Map.]
Hosack, William. 1876. *The Isle of Streams, or, The Jamaica Hermit, and Other Poems*. Edinburgh: Lorimer and Gillies.
Howell, James. 1659. *Paroimiographia: Proverbs, or, Old sayed savves & adages in English (or the Saxon toung), Italian, French, and Spanish [. . .] collected by J.H. Esqr*. London: Printed by J.G.

Hughes, the Rev. Griffith. 1750. *The Natural History of Barbados*. London: The author.

Huizinga. J. (1949) 1980. *Homo Ludens: A Study of the Play-Element in Culture*. London: Routledge and Kegan Paul.

Hulme, Peter, and Neil L. Whitehead, eds. 1992. *Wild Majesty: Encounters with Caribs from Columbus to the Present Day: An Anthology*. Oxford: Clarendon Press.

Hutson, J. Edward, ed. 2001. "A Briefe Discription of the Ilande of Barbados" [c. July 1650]. In *The English Civil War in Barbados 1650–1652: Eyewitness Accounts*, edited and annotated by J. Edward Hutson, 63–68. Bridgetown: Barbados National Trust.

Ionesco, Eugène. 1958. "A Reply to Kenneth Tynan: The Playwright's Role". *Observer* (London), 29 June, 14.

Isert, Paul Erdmann. 1793. *Voyages en Guinée et dans les iles Caraibes en Amerique* [. . .] *Tirés de sa correspondance avec ses amis. Traduit de l'allemand*. Paris: Maradan.

[St Isidore of Seville] Isidorus Hispalensis. Circa 630?. *Etymologiarum sive originum*, book 3, xv–xxiii: "De Musica".

James, C.L.R. 1963. *The Black Jacobins: Toussaint L'Ouverture and the San Domingo Revolution*. 2nd ed., rev. New York: Vintage Books.

Jobson, Richard. 1623. *The Golden Trade: or, A Discovery of the Riuer Gambra, and the Golden Trade of the Aethiopians*. London: N. Okes.

Jones, LeRoi [Amiri Baraka]. (1963) 2002. *Blues People: Negro Music in White America*. New York: HarperCollins (Perennial).

Joseph, E.L. (1838) 1970. *History of Trinidad*. Trinidad: H.J. Mills.

Kahn, Morton C. 1931. *Djuka: The Bush Negroes of Dutch Guiana*. New York: Viking Press.

Kaigh, Frederick. 1947. *Witchcraft and Magic of Africa*. London: Richard Lesley.

Kupperman, Karen Ordahl. 1995. "The Beehive as a Model for Colonial Design". In *America in European Consciousness 1493–1750*, edited by K.O. Kupperman, 272–92. Chapel Hill: University of North Carolina Press for the Institute of Early American History and Culture.

Labat, le R. Père Jean. 1722. *Nouveau voyage aux isles de l'Amerique*. Vol. 1. Paris: G. Cavelier.

———. 1724. *Nouveau voyage du Père Labat aux isles de l'Amerique*. Vols. 1 and 2. La Haye: Husson, Johnson, Gosse, Van Duren, Alberts, Le Vier.

———.1742. *Nouveau voyage aux isles de l'Amerique. Contenant l'histoire naturelle de ces pays, l'origine, les mœurs, la religion & le gouvernement des habitans anciens & modernes. Les guerres & les evenemens singuliers qui y sont arrivez pendant le séjour que l'auteur y a fait.* 8 vols. Paris: G. Cavelier.

———. 1931. *Voyages aux isles de l'Amérique (Antilles) 1693–1705; trente-deux illustrations d'après des documents de l'époque; avant-propos de A. t'Serstevens*. Vol. 2. Paris: Éditions Duchartre.

La Borde, Sieur de. 1674. *Relation de l'origine, moeurs, coustumes, religion, guerres et voyages des Caraibes.* No. 6 in *Recueil de divers voyages faits en Afrique et en l'Amerique: qui n'ont point esté encore publiez: contenant l'origine, les moeurs, les coûtumes & le commerce des habitans de ces deux parties du monde: avec des traites curieux touchant la Haute Ethyopie, le debordement du Nil, la mer Rouge, & le Prête-Jean: le tout enrichi de figures, & de cartes geographiques qui servent à l'intelligence es choses contenuë en ce volume.* Paris: Louis Billaine.

Lalla, B. 1981. "Quaco Sam: A Relic of Archaic Jamaican Speech". *Jamaica Journal* 45:20–29.

Lalla, Barbara, and Jean D'Costa. 1990. *Language in Exile: Three Hundred Years of Jamaican Creole.* Tuscaloosa: University of Alabama Press.

Lanaghan, Mrs. (or Flannigan). 1844. *Antigua and the Antiguans: A Full Account of the Colony and Its Inhabitants.* 2 vols. London: Saunders and Otley.

Larsen, Kay. 1928. *Dansk Vestindien 1666–1917.* København: C.A. Reitzel.

Las Casas, Fray Bartolomé de. 1957. *Historia de las Indias.* Biblioteca de Autores Españoles, vol. 95. Madrid: Ediciones Atlas.

———. 1986. *Historia de las Indias.* Edition, prologue, notes and chronology by André Saint-Lu. 3 vols. Caracas: Biblioteca Ayacucho.

———. 2011. "Contra Fernández de Oviedo: memoria, virtud, alegría, veracidad y animosidad de los indígenas americanos (1559)". "Selección de fragmentos de Bartolomé de Las Casas (1559)". *Historia de las Indias.* Madrid: Ginesta, 1875. Selección y resúmenes: David Pavón Cuéllar; transcripción: Karla Gabriela Cuadra Esparza; asesoría: Marcos Edgardo Díaz Béjar. In *Teoría y crítica de la psicología* 1, 27–32 (2011). http://www.teocripsi.com/2011/1casas2.pdf.

Le Breton, Adrien. (1702?) 1998. *Historic Account of Saint Vincent: The Indian Youroumayn, the Island of the Karaybes.* Mayreau: Mayreau Environmental Development Organization.

Ledru, André-Pierre. 1810. *Voyage aux îles de Ténériffe, la Trinité, Saint-Thomas, Sainte-Croix et Porto Ricco, exécuté par ordre du gouvernement français, depuis le 30 septembre 1796 jusquau 7 juin 1798, sous la direction du capitaine Baudin, pour faire des recherches et des collections relatives à l'histoire naturelle [. . .] Ouvrage accompagné de notes et d'additions, par M. Sonnini.* Vol. 2. Paris: A. Bertrand.

Lekis, Lisa. 1960. *Dancing Gods.* New York: Scarecrow Press.

Leslie, Charles. 1740. *A new history of Jamaica from the earliest accounts, to the taking of Porto Bello by Vice-Admiral Vernon. In thirteen letters from a gentleman to his friends.* 2nd ed. London: J. Hodges.

Levinson, Stephen C. 1979. "Activity Types and Language". *Linguistics* 17:365–99.

Lewis, Matthew G. (1834) 1969. *Journal of a West Indian Planter in Jamaica.* New York: Negro Universities Press.

Ligon, R. (1657) 1970. *A True and Exact History of the Island of Barbados.* Facsimile of the first edition. London: Frank Cass.

Lloyd, William. 1839. *Letters from the West Indies during a Visit in the Autumn of MDCCCXXXVI and the Spring of MDCCCXXXVII.* London: Darton and Harvey.

Long, Edward. 1774. *The History of Jamaica, or, General Survey of the Antient and Modern State of That Island: With Reflections on its Situation, Settlements, Inhabitants, Climate, Products, Commerce, Laws, and Government.* 3 vols. London: T. Lowndes.

Luffman, John. 1789. *A brief account of the Island of Antigua* [. . .] *Written in the years 1786, 1787, 1788.* London: T. Cadell.

Malagón Barceló, J. (1784) 1974. *Código Negro Carolino.* Santo Domingo, DR: Taller.

Malloch, Stephen and Colwyn Trevarthen, eds. 2009. *Communicative Musicality: Exploring the Basis of Human Companionship.* Oxford: Oxford University Press.

Mannix, Daniel P., and Malcolm Cowley. (1962) 1976. *Black Cargoes: A History of the Atlantic Slave Trade.* New York: Penguin.

Marat, Jean-Paul. 1789. *L'ami du peuple.* Issue 73, 21 December, 8.

Marees, Pieter de. (1602) 1987. *Description and Historical Account of the Gold Kingdom of Guinea (1602).* Translated from the Dutch and edited by Albert van Dantzig and Adam Jones. Oxford: Oxford University Press.

Marly; or a Planter's Life in Jamaica. 1828. Glasgow: Richard Griffin and Co.

Márquez, Gabriel García. 1982. "The Solitude of Latin America". Nobel Lecture. http://www.nobelprize.org/nobel_prizes/literature/laureates/1982/marquez-lecture.html.

Marsden, Peter. 1788. *An Account of the Island of Jamaica; with Reflections on the Treatment, Occupation, and Provisions of the Slaves. To Which Is Added a Description of the Animal and Vegetable Productions of the Island. By a Gentleman Lately Resident on a Plantation.* Newcastle: Printed for the author by S. Hodgson.

Marshall, W.K., ed. 1977. *The Colthurst Journal: Journal of a Special Magistrate in the Islands of Barbados and St. Vincent, July 1835–September 1838.* Millwood, NY: KTO Press.

Mathews, Samuel Augustus. 1793. *The Lying Hero; or an Answer to JB Moreton's "Manners and Customs in the West Indies".* St. Eustatius: E.L. Low.

———. 1822. *The Willshire Squeeze, to Which Are Added Specimens of the Negro Familiar Dialect and Proverbial Sayings with Songs.* Demerara.

Matthews, John. (1788) 1966. *A Voyage to the River Sierra-Leone, on the Coast of Africa; Containing an Account of the Trade and Productions of the Country, and of the Civil and Religious Customs and Manners of the People; in a Series of Letters to a Friend in England. By John Matthews,* [. . .] *With an Additional Letter on the Subject of the African Slave Trade.* London: Frank Cass.

Maurile de S. Michel, Fray. 1652. *Voyage des isles camercanes en l'Amerique qui font partie des Indes occidentales.* Le Mans: Hierôme Olivier.

Max-Radiguet, R. 1842. "Un bamboula à la Martinique. 1838". *France Maritime* 4:334–36.

M'Callum, Pierre. 1805. *Travels in Trinidad during the Months of February, March and April 1803 in a Series of Letters Addressed to a Member of the Imperial Parliament of Great Britain*. Liverpool: W. Jones.

Mellet, Jullien. (1824) 1913. *Viajes por el interior de la América meridional de Julian Mellet*. Translated from the second French edition of 1824. Santiago de Chile: Imprenta y encuadernación universitaria.

Mendoza, Plinio, and Gabriel García Márquez. 1982. *The Fragrance of Guava: Conversations with Gabriel García Márquez*. London: Faber and Faber.

Millington, Peter, and Caspar James. 2011. "Mummies and Masquerades: English and Caribbean Connections". Mummers Unconvention, Bath, 11 November.

Minshall, Peter. 2014. Interview by Vernon Ramesar. *One on One with Vernon Ramesar*. IETV. YouTube, https://www.youtube.com/watch?v=37mqAh009N8. 9 September.

Mintz, Sidney W. and Richard Price. 1992. *The Birth of African-American Culture: An Anthropological Perspective*. Boston: Beacon Press.

Moore, Thomas. 1861. *The Poetical Works of Thomas Moore. Complete in One Volume: Illustrated with Engravings from Drawings by Eminent Artists*. New York: Sheldon and Co.

More, Hannah. 1795. *The Sorrows of Yamba; or, the Negro Woman's Lamentation*. London: S. Hazard.

Moreau de Saint-Méry, M.L.E. 1796. *Danse*. Article extrait d'un ouvrage de M.L.E. Moreau de St-Mery Ayant pour titre: Répertoire des notions coloniales. Par ordre alphabétique. Philadelphia: The author.

———. (1797) 1958. *Description topographique, physique, civile, politique et historique de la partie française de l'isle Saint-Domingue. 1958. Nouvelle édition entièrement revue et complétée sur le manuscrit accompagnée de plans d'une carte hors-texte suivie d'un index des noms de personnes, par Blanche Maurel et Etienne Taillemite*. Paris: Société de l'histoire des colonies françaises et Librairie Larose.

Moreton, J.B. 1790. *Manners and Customs in the West India Islands. Containing various Particulars respecting the Soil, Cultivation, Produce, Trade, Officers, Inhabitants, &c., &c. With the Method of establishing and conducting a Sugar-Plantation; in which the Ill-Practices of Superintendents are pointed out. Also the Treatment of Slaves; and the Slave-Trade*. London: W. Richardson.

Morris, Robert. 1984. "Slave Society in Barbados". In *Emancipation: A Series of Lectures to Commemorate the 150th Anniversary of Emancipation*, vol. 1, edited by Alvin O. Thompson, 33–44. Cave Hill, Barbados: Department of History, University of the West Indies.

Native of the West Indies. 1783. *Poems, on Subjects, Arising in England, and the West Indies*. London: R. Faulder.

The Negro's Friend: Notes on Slavery, Made during a Recent Visit to Barbadoes. 1830. London.

Nicholl, John. 1607. *An Houre Glasse of Indian Newes* [. . .]. London: Nathaniell Butter.

Norvins, M. de. 1839. *Histoire de Napoléon*. Bruxelles: Société Typographique Belge.

Oexmelin, Alexandre-Olivier. 1686. *Histoire des Avanturiers qui se sont signalez dans les Indes, avec la vie, les moeurs, les coutumes des habitants de Saint-Domingue*. 2 vols. in one. Paris: Jacques Le Febvre.

———. 1774. *Histoire des Aventuriers flibustiers qui se sont signalés dans les Indes*. Vol. 1. Lyon: Benoit and Joseph Duplain.

Ogilby, John. 1671. *America, being the latest, and most accurate Description of the New World* [. . .] *collected from most authentick authors, augmented with later observations, and adorned with maps and sculptures*. London: Tho. Johnson.

Oldendorp, C.G.A. 1987. *History of the Mission of the Evangelical Brethren on the Caribbean islands of St. Thomas, St. Croix, and St. John*. English edition and translation by Arnold Highfield and Vladimir Barac. Ann Arbor: Karoma.

Oldmixon, John. 1708. *The British Empire in America, Containing the History of the Discovery, Settlement, Progress and Present State of All the British Colonies, on the Continent and Islands of America:* [. . .] *with* [. . .] *maps* [. . .] *by H. Moll*. 2 vols. London: John Nicholson.

Orderson, John. 1835. *The Fair Barbadian and Faithful Black; or, A Cure for the Gout: A Comedy in Three Acts*. Liverpool: Ross and Nightengale.

Ormond, R., and C. Blackett-Ord. 1987. *Franz Xaver Winterhalter and the Courts of Europe, 1830–70*. [Exhibition catalogue.] London: National Portrait Gallery.

Ortiz, Fernando. (1951) 1981. *Los bailes y el teatro de los negros en el folklore de Cuba*. La Habana, Cuba: Editorial Letras Cubanas.

O'Shaughnessy, Andrew Jackson. 2000. *An Empire Divided: The American Revolution and the British Caribbean*. Philadelphia: University of Pennsylvania Press.

Oviedo. See Fernández de Oviedo.

Pané, Fray Ramón. 1498. *Relación acerca de las antigüedades de los indios*.

———. 1999. *An Account of the Antiquities of the Indians: Chronicles of the New World Encounter*. Durham, NC: Duke University Press.

Parncutt, Richard, and Angelika Dorfer. 2011. "The Role of Music in the Integration of Cultural Minorities". In Deliège and Davidson 2011, 379–411.

Pascal, Blaise. 1958. *Pascal's Pensées*. Translated by W.F. Trotter; introduction by T.S. Eliot. New York: E.P. Dutton.

Patterson, Orlando. (1967) 1973. *The Sociology of Slavery: An Analysis of the Origins, Development and Structure of Negro Slave Society in Jamaica*. Kingston and London: Sangster's Book Stores/Granada.

———. 1982. *Slavery and Social Death: A Comparative Study*. Cambridge: Harvard University Press.

Pelleprat, Le Pere Pierre. 1655. *Relation des missions des pp. de la Compagnie de Jesus dans* les Isles, & dans la terre ferme de l'Amerique Meridionale. Divisee en deux parties: Avec une introduction à la langue des Galibis Sauvages de la terre ferme de l'Amerique. Paris: Sebastien Cramoisy and Gabriel Cramoisy.

Pernety, A. 1769. Journal historique d'un voyage fait aux îles Malouines en 1763 et 1764 pour les reconnoître et y former un établissement et de deux voyages au détroit de Magellan avec une relation sur les Patagons. 2 vols. Berlin: Etienne de Bourdeaux.

Peytraud, L.P. 1897. L'esclavage aux Antilles français avant 1789: d'après des documents inedits des Archives coloniales. Paris: Hachette.

Phillippo, James. 1843. *Jamaica: Its Past and Present State*. London: John Snow.

Phillips, T. 1732. *Journal of a Voyage Made in the Hannibal of London, Ann. 1693, 1694, from England, to Cape Monseradoe, in Africa; and Thence Along the Coast of Guiney to Whidaw, the Island of St. Thomas, and So Forward to Barbadoes: With a Cursory Account of the Country, the People, Their Manners, Forts, Trade, &c*. In *A Collection of Voyages and Travels, Consisting of Authentic Writers in our own Tongue, which have not before been collected in English, or have only been abridged in other Collections* [. . .], compiled by A. Churchill. Vol. 6. London: T. Osborne.

Picart, Bernard. 1735. *Cérémonies et coutumes religieuses des peoples idolâtres, représentées par des figures dessinées de la main de Bernard Picart: Avec une explication historique, & quelques dissertations curieuses. Qui contient les cérémonies des peoples des Indes occidentales*. Amsterdam: J.F. Bernard.

Pichardo y Tapia, Esteban. (1875) 1976. *Diccionario provincial casi-razonado de voces y frases cubanas*. Havana: Editorial de Ciencias Sociales.

Piersen, William D. 1976. "Puttin' Down Ole Massa: African Satire in the New World". *Research in African Literatures* 7 (2): 166–80.

Pinckard, George. 1806. *Notes on the West Indies*. Vol. 1. London: Longman, Hurst, Rees and Orme.

Plato. 2006. *The Republic*. Translated and with an introduction by R.E. Allen. New Haven: Yale University Press.

———. 2009. *The Laws*. Translated by Benjamin Jowett. http://www.classicallibrary.org/plato/dialogues/laws.

Poole, R. 1753. *The Beneficent Bee: Or, Traveller's Companion. Containing Each Day's Observation, in a Voyage from London, to Gibraltar, Barbadoes,* [. . .] *Containing a Summary Account of the Said Places,* [. . .]. London: E. Duncomb.

Poyer, John. 1808. *The History of Barbados, from the First Discovery of the Island, in the Year 1605, Till the Accession of Lord Seaforth, 1801*. London: J. Mawman.

Prévost d'Exiles, F. 1746. *Histoire générale des voyages*. Vol. 15. Paris: Didot.

Price, Hannibal. 1900. *De la réhabilitation de la race noire par la République d'Haïti*. Port-au-Prince: J. Verrollot.

Price, R., and S. Price, eds. 1992. *Stedman's Surinam: Life in Eighteenth-Century Slave Society*. Baltimore: Johns Hopkins University Press.

———. 1999. *Maroon Arts: Cultural Vitality in the African Diaspora*. Boston: Beacon.

Purchas, Samuel. (1625) 1905. *Hakluytus Posthumus or Purchas His Pilgrimes. Contayning a History of the World in Sea Voyages and Lande Travells by Englishmen and others.* Volume 6. Glasgow: James MacLehose and Sons.

Rabelais, François. 1890. *The Life of Gargantua and the Heroic Deeds of Pantagruel*. Translated from the French of Rabelais by Sir Thomas Urquhart; with an introduction by Henry Morley. 5th ed. London: George Routledge and Sons.

Ramsay, Rev. James. 1784. *An Essay on the Treatment and Conversion of African Slaves in the British Sugar Colonies*. London: J. Phillips.

———. 1788 *Objections to the Abolition of the Slave Trade*. London: J. Phillips.

Raynal, L'Abbé. 1777. *A Philosophical and Political History of the Settlements and Trade of the Europeans in the East and West Indies*. Translated from the French of the Abbé Raynal by J. Justamond. 3rd ed. Vol. 4. London: T. Cadell.

Renny, Robert. 1807. *An History of Jamaica: With Observations on the Climate, Scenery, Trade, Productions, Negroes, Slave Trade, Diseases of Europeans, Customs, Manners, and Dispositions of the Inhabitants* [. . .]. London: J. Cawthorn.

Resident. 1828. *Sketches and Recollections of the West Indies*. London: Smith, Elder.

Roget, Jacques Petitjean, ed. 1975. *Histoire de l'isle de Grenade en Amérique: 1649–1659*. Manuscript anonyme de 1659, vraisemblablement attribué à Benigne Bresson, présenté et annoté par Jacques Petitjean Roget. Texte établi par Élisabeth Crosnier. Montreal: Les Presses de l'Université de Montréal.

Rolph, Thomas. 1836. *A Brief Account, Together with Observations, Made during a Visit in the West Indies, and a Tour through the United States of America, in Parts of the Years 1832–3; Together with a Statistical Account of Upper Canada*. Dundas, Upper Canada: G.H. Hackstaff, printer.

Rosemain, Jacqueline. 1986. *La musique dans la société antillaise: 1635–1902, Martinique Guadeloupe*. Paris: Éditions L'Harmattan.

Rousseau, Jean-Jacques. 1755. *Discours sur l'origine et les fondemens de l'inégalité parmi les hommes*. Amsterdam: Marc Michel Rey.

Rugendas, J.M. 1827. *Voyage pittoresque dans le Brésil*. Paris: Engelmann.

Russell, Bertrand. 1930. *The Conquest of Happiness*. London: Allen and Unwin.

Sacks, Oliver. 2008. *Musicophilia: Tales of Music and the Brain*. Revised and expanded. New York: Vintage.

Saintard, Pierre. 1756. *Roman politique sur l'état present des affaires de l'Amerique*. Amsterdam and Paris: Duchesne.

Sartre, J.P. (1949) 1966. *What Is Literature?* Translated by Bernard Frechtman. New York: Washington Square Press.

Saunders, A.C. 1982. *A Social History of Black Slaves and Freedmen*. Cambridge: Cambridge University Press.

Scott, Michael. 1862. *Tom Cringle's Log*. New ed., illustrated. Edinburgh: William Blackwood and Sons.

Senior, Bernard M. 1835. *Jamaica, as It Was, as It Is, and as It May Be: Comprising Interesting Topics for Absent Proprietors, Merchants &c., and Valuable Hints to Persons Intending to Emigrate to the Island: Also an Authentic Narrative of the Negro Insurrection in 1831* [. . .]. *By a Retired Military Officer*. London: T. Hurst.

A Short Journey in the West Indies in Which Are Interspersed, Curious Anecdotes and Characters. 1790. 2 vols. London: Printed for the author, and sold by J. Murray, and J. Forbes.

Silva, Leonardo Dantas. 2001. *Carnaval do Recife*. Recife, Brazil: Fundação da Cultura da cidade do Recife.

Singleton, John. 1767. *A General Description of the West-Indian Islands, As far as Relates to the British, Dutch, and Danish Governments, from Barbados to Saint Croix. Attempted in Blank Verse*. Barbados: Esmand and Walker, for the author.

Skinner, Quentin. 2002. *Visions of Politics*. Vol. 3: *Hobbes and Civil Science*. Cambridge: Cambridge University Press.

Sloane, Hans, Sir. 1707. *A Voyage to the Islands Madera, Barbados, Nieves, S. Christophers and Jamaica, with the Natural History of the Herbs and Trees, Four-footed Beasts, Fishes, Birds, Insects, Reptiles, &c. Of the last of those Islands; To which is prefix'd an Introduction, Wherein is an Account of the Inhabitants, Air, Waters, Diseases, Trade, &c. of that Place, with some Relations concerning the Neighbouring Continent, and Islands of America* [. . .]. London: Printed by B.M. for the author.

Smith, Rev. William. 1745. *A Natural History of Nevis, and the Rest of the English Leeward Charibee Islands in America*. Cambridge: J. Bentham.

Smith, William, ed. 1870. *A Dictionary of Greek and Roman Antiquities*. 3rd American ed. New York: Harper and Brothers.

Souchu de Rennefort, Urbain. 1688. *Histoire des Indes orientales*. Paris: A. Seneuze.

Souza, Marina de Mello e. (2001) 2006. *Reis negros no Brasil escravista: Historia da festa de coroação de Rei Congo*. 1st repr. Belo Horizonte, Minas Gerais: Editora UFMG.

St Clair, Lieut. Col. Thomas S. 1834. *A Soldier's Recollections of the West Indies and America. With a Narrative of the Expedition to the Island of Walcheren*. London: Richard Bentley.

Stedman, John Gabriel. (1794) 1806. *Narrative of a Five Years' Expedition against the Revolted Negroes of Surinam, in Guiana, on the Wild Coast of South America from the Year 1772, to 1777*. Vol. 2. 2nd ed. London: J. Johnson.

Stewart, John. 1808. *An Account of Jamaica and Its Inhabitants. By a Gentleman Long Resident in the West Indies*. London: Longman, Hurst, Rees and Orme.

———. 1823. *A View of the Past and Present State of the Island of Jamaica; with Remarks on the Moral and Physical Condition of the Slaves, and on the Abolition of Slavery in the Colonies.* Edinburgh: Oliver and Boyd.

Stoichita, Victor, and Anna-Maria Coderch. 1999. *Goya: The Last Carnival.* London: Reaktion Books.

Storr, Anthony. 1992. *Music and the Mind.* New York: Ballantine.

Stravinsky, Igor. 1970. *Poetics of Music in Six Lessons.* English translation of *Poétique musicale sous forme de six leçons* (1942) by Arthur Knodel and Ingolf Dahl; preface by George Seferis. Cambridge, MA: Harvard University Press.

Strutt, Joseph. [1801] 1903. *The Sports and Pastimes of the People of England. A New Edition, Much Enlarged and Corrected by J.C. Cox.* London: Methuen.

Svalesen, Leif. 2000. *The Slave Ship* Fredensborg. Translated from Danish/Norwegian by Pat Shaw and Selena Winsnes. Kingston: Ian Randle.

Szwed, John F., and Roger D. Abrahams. 1976. "After the Myth: Studying Afro-American Cultural Patterns in the Plantation Literature". *Research in African Literatures* 7 (2): 211–32.

Tauzin-Castellanos, Isabelle. 2014. "De l'Aquitaine à l'Amérique au temps des indépendances: Représentation dans l'itinéraire de Jullien Mellet". In *Hommage à Geneviève Champeau*, edited by Christian Lagarde and Philippe Ravaté. In *HispanismeS*, no. 3: 136–50.

Tejeda, D. 2002. *La pasión danzaria: Música y baile en el Caribe a través del merengue y la bachata.* Santo Domingo, DR: Academia de Ciencias.

Thomas, Hugh. 1997. *The Slave Trade: The Story of the Atlantic Slave Trade 1440–1870.* London: Papermac.

Thompson, Donald. 1993. "The *Cronistas de Indias* Revisited: Historical Reports, Archeological Evidence, and Literary and Artistic Traces of Indigenous Music and Dance in the Greater Antilles at the Time of the *Conquista*". *Latin American Music Review* 14 (2): 181–201.

Thurston, Herbert. 1909. "Feast of Fools". In *The Catholic Encyclopedia*, 6:132–33. New York: Robert Appleton.

Tobin, James. 1785. *Cursory Remarks upon the Reverend Mr. Ramsay's Essay on the Treatment and Conversion of African Slaves in the Sugar Colonies.* London: G. and T. Wilkie.

Trevarthen, Colwyn. 1999. "Intersubjectivity". In *MIT Encyclopedia of the Cognitive Sciences*, edited by Robert A. Wilson and Frank Keil, 415–19. Cambridge, MA: MIT Press.

Tronchoy, Gautier du. 1709. *Journal de la campagne des isles de l'Amerique, qu'a fait Monsieur D***.* Troyes: Jacques Le Febvre.

Unger, Roberto Mangabeira. 2014. *The Religion of the Future.* Cambridge, MA: Harvard University Press.

Villault, Nicolas, sieur de Bellefond. 1670. *A Relation of the Coasts of Africk called Guinee; with a Description of the Countreys, Manners and Customs of the Inhabitants; of the productions of the Earth, and the Merchandise and Commodities it affords; with some Historical Observations upon the Coasts. Being Collected in a Voyage made by the Sieur Villault, Escuyer, Sieur de Bellefond, in the years 1666, and 1667. Written in French, and faithfully Englished*. London: John Starkey.

Waddell, Rev. Hope Masterton. 1863. *Twenty-Nine Years in the West Indies and Central Africa: A Review of Missionary Work and Adventure 1829–1858*. London: Nelson and Sons.

Walcott, Derek. 2007. "The Antilles: Fragments of Epic Memory". In *Music in Latin America and the Caribbean: An Encyclopedic History*. Vol. 2: *Performing the Caribbean Experience*, edited by Malena Kuss, 1–8. Austin: University of Texas Press.

Waller, John A. 1820. *A Voyage in the West Indies: Containing Various Observations Made during a Residence in Barbadoes, and Several of the Leeward Islands; with Some Notices and Illustrations Relative to the City of Paramarabo, in Surinam* [. . .]. London: Sir R. Phillips and Co.

Warner-Lewis, Maureen. 2003. *Central Africa in the Caribbean: Transcending Time, Transforming Cultures*. Kingston: University of the West Indies Press.

Watson, Karl. 1979. *The Civilized Island Barbados: A Social History 1750–1816*. Bridgetown: The author.

Weeks, John H. 1914. *Among the Primitive Bakongo; a Record of Thirty Years' Close Intercourse with the Bakongo and Other Tribes of Equatorial Africa, with a Description of Their Habits, Customs, & Religious Beliefs*. London: Seeley, Service.

Wells, H.G. (1920) 1951. *The Outline of History: Being a Plain History of Life and Mankind*. London: Cassell.

Wentworth, Trelawney. 1834. *The West India Sketch Book*. 2 vols. London: Whittacker.

Wilkinson, John Gardner. 1841. *A Second Series of the Manners and Customs of the Ancient Egyptians, Including Their Religion, Agriculture, &c. Derived from a Comparison of the Paintings, Sculptures, and Monuments Still Existing, with the Accounts of Ancient Authors*. Vol. 1. London: John Murray.

Williams, Cynric. 1826. *A Tour through the Island of Jamaica from the Western to the Eastern End in the Year 1823*. London: Hunt and Clarke.

Williams, James. 1837. *A Narrative of Events since the First of August, 1834*. London: John Haddon.

Wilson, Samuel. 1997. "The Legacy of the Indigenous People of the Caribbean". In *The Indigenous People of the Caribbean*, edited by Samuel Wilson, 206–13. Gainesville: University Press of Florida.

Wiredu, Kwasi. 1992. "Death and the Afterlife in African Culture". In *Person and Community: Ghanaian Philosophical Studies*, edited by Kwasi Wiredu and Kwame

Gyekye, 137–52. Cultural Heritage and Contemporary Change, ser. 2, vol. 1. Washington, DC: Council for Research in Values and Philosophy.

Wright, Philip, ed. 2002. *Lady Nugent's Journal of Her Residence in Jamaica from 1801 to 1805*. With a foreword by Verene A. Shepherd. Kingston: University of the West Indies Press.

Wright, Richardson. 1937. *Revels in Jamaica, 1682–1838*. New York: Dodd, Mead.

Young, Sir William. 1801. "A Tour through the Several Islands of Barbadoes, St. Vincent, Antigua, Tobago, and Grenada, in the Years 1791, and 1792". In Edwards 1801, 3:[241]–84.

Index

accommodation (cultural), 22, 332, 345, 346, 347
acculturation, 89, 194, 218, 257, 258, 259, 266, 269, 294, 296, 297, 308
acquiescence: as Anglican ethic, 2; as docility, 61; and dominance, 14, 15; as doubt, 18; and favouritism, 16; as helplessness, 20; in naming, 16; obsequiousness, 347, 348, 349; as self-preservation, 18, 324, 349; and singing, 276, 280
Actor-Boy, 206, 207, 346
actors, 16, 99, 100, 173, 206, 252, 294, 326
Adonia myth, 183, 184, 223
African essence, 315, 316; generalizations, 113, 140, 177, 194, 224, 305, 308, 309, 310, 315, 326, 327; homogeneity, 195, 227, 315
agitation of the body, 236, 237, 250, 252, 255, 341
alternative reality, 18, 19, 21, 24, 26, 29
ambivalence, 80, 186, 321
"antick" actions, 56, 69, 164, 225, 227, 239
antithetical figures, 96, 202, 205, 206, 223

appearance of happiness, 3, 5, 6, 8, 11, 12, 13, 14, 16, 321
archetypal view of culture, 184, 185
areito, 49–52, 62, 65, 115, 176, 269; aria, 63; dubious origin, 64
artificial enjoyment, 130
artification hypothesis, 24, 324
asceticism, 283, 333
assimilation, 346

ballet, 5, 44, 50, 64, 173, 239, 245, 325
balls: duration, 85; frequency, 86, 91, 94, 108; "grandy", "fancy", 103, 104, 132, 144, 148, 149, 243, 245, 257, 311; management, 89, 92, 329; mulatto, "dignity", 106, 108, 109, 149, 212, 340; official, high society, 83, 84, 85, 89, 90, 97, 109, 110, 170, 175, 273; other types, 86, 89, 97, 103, 106, 149, 255; significance, 83, 84, 85, 86, 89, 142, 149, 258, 283, 329, 330, 339, 350
beehive model (colony), 74, 75, 81, 274
belittlement, 28, 168, 269, 316
benefits of music and dance, 35, 41, 42, 130, 343, 344, 348
bias, 32, 137
bird masquerade, 55, 57–59, 61, 261

375

birds: blackbird, 3, 4, 5; bluebird, 3, 4; caged, 4, 263, 302; eagle, 302, 307; guiney, 264; hummingbird, 58; of prey, 59, 106; songbird, 4, 24, 263, 302, 307
Black Carib culture, 47, 71
boitio, 50, 115
bomba, 246
boucaniers, 66, 317, 318
bumping, 229, 230, 241, 244, 246
burial performances, 54, 55, 113, 157–68, 171, 172, 174, 236, 336, 337
"burying the carnival", 268

calenda: ban, 235; description, 229–34, 240, 242, 244, 246, 255, 256, 250, 261; influence, 238, 240, 338; sources, 231–34; South America, 232, 332
calypso, 11, 11n, 12, 13, 303
camaraderie, 93, 343
cannibal, 52, 58, 59, 67, 72, 316
carabela, 317
caramémo, 54, 62
carefree people, 10, 25, 30, 130, 134, 135, 137, 139, 283, 330, 351
caricature, 7, 81, 85, 103, 141, 142, 143, 144, 290, 291, 304, 308, 309, 321, 347
carnival: African attraction to 346; Catholic influence, 98, 222; crafts/trades, 179, 187,190; development, 12, 45, 97, 98, 182, 188, 220, 223, 346; discouraged, 334; economics, 1; European, 12, 43, 185, 187, 223; paganism, 178, 223; pre-Lenten, 97, 98; revolution, 223; significance of, 12, 20, 29, 30, 152; "tropical"/"negro", 181, 219, 220, 223, 319, 346; versions of, 182, 207, 219

carpe diem philosophy, 284, 353
celebrations, 61, 147, 156, 157, 178, 195, 201, 203, 294, 302, 322, 332; African, 156, 157, 191, 192, 194, 203; births, 53, 61, 84, 89, 97, 104, 147, 156, 157, 158, 162, 172, 178–79, 201, 240, 242; Christmas/year end, 96, 99, 103, 179, 180, 183, 202, 204, 215–16, 217, 231, 258, 324, 333; colonial, 84, 89, 97, 147; crop over, 103, 151–55, 156, 259, 339; death, 62, 160, 162; European, 20, 84; indigenous, 51, 55, 58, 65; marriage, 58, 61, 62, 156; May Day, 95, 186, 200, 207; pagan, 96, 223, 346; Three Kings' Day, 189, 190
chain gang, 311
Charity School girls, 198, 199
chica, 233, 234, 240, 254, 255, 256, 337, 338
children dancing, 87, 132, 133, 142, 235, 236, 260
church: attendance, 81–82, 343; and Congo kings, 188; control, 281, 328; criticism, 293; and dance, 43, 126, 332, 333, 345; and dressing up, 187; entertainment, 84, 152, 232–33; growth, 281–82; influence, 43, 81, 254, 292, 319, 332–33, 335; music, 81–83, 282, 343, 344, 345; and paganism, 43, 95–96, 98, 99, 165, 166, 178, 183, 190, 223, 333, 334, 341, 347; and plays, 80, 332; Protestants, 43, 139, 280, 283, 333, 334; school, 198; "societies", 222
climate and dance, 36, 37, 88, 89, 111–12, 255, 331, 332
colours in dress, 57, 58, 62, 79, 155, 179, 182, 201, 209, 210, 211, 212, 213, 214, 215
communicative musicality, 35, 36

communing wth the dead, 163, 165, 166, 337
competitiveness: in dance, 149, 175, 179, 224, 238, 241, 243, 261, 319, 326, 329, 339, 340; in singing, 149, 180, 273, 280
concerts, 83, 91–92, 93, 131, 204, 329
Congo culture, 113, 114, 164, 188, 190, 192, 193, 194, 195, 202, 203, 211, 219, 227, 232, 233, 246n, 255, 256, 260, 261, 278
contest s, 183, 211, 221, 255, 260, 321, 346
copying/plagiarism, 6, 115, 314, 324–25; *Authentic History*, 148, 238; Blasis, 255; French writers, 53, 63; Phillippo, 293; Renny, 270, 288, 289; Wentworth, 286
Coromantin/ee, 164, 167, 195, 237, 266
country vs town, 84, 94, 169, 215, 216, 217, 218
cowardice, 6, 28, 29, 30, 32, 306
creolizing, 81, 82
cricket, 20
crop over. *See* celebrations
crossing over, 102, 335, 336, 337
crossing the line ceremony, 101, 102,
curse of Ham, 17

dance: Ardra (Arada), 227, 229, 261; bamboula/baboula, 149, 240, 242, 246–49, 256, 259, 268; batuca, 226, 227; bèlè, 261; bolero, 245, 255, 256, 325; calenda (*see* calenda); coffee treat, 245; of death, 163, 165, 335; fandango, 233, 243, 251, 255, 256, 261; fertility, 185, 234; *filoux*, 230; gymnastic, 237, 241, 247, 249, 261; Joan-Johnny, 242–46, 247, 248, 256; Lancers quadrille, 90, 198, 259;

mating ritual, 261; myal, 163, 167–68, 341; pyrrhic, martial, 161, 236, 237, 250, 324, 325; ringed, 260, 261, 318, 319, 340; round/circle, 38, 56, 168, 224, 227, 260, 261; with soul, 59, 107, 224, 244; wriggle/writhe, 224, 238, 239, 241, 244, 245, 249, 252–53, 254
dancing: corruption, 254, 337; duration, 69–70, 128, 225, 343; in education, 87, 107, 297; and intellect, 133–34, 220, 256, 262, 315, 339, 341; itinerant women, 199; lascivious/obscene, 33, 170, 229, 231, 232, 234, 238, 239, 240, 244, 247, 254, 255, 334; nation, 157, 228; as a natural gift, 131–33, 344; obeah, 167; people, 308, 322; policy, 112, 125–27, 341; society strengthening, 41, 262, 324, 330
"dancing in the street", 39, 42, 178–223
"dancing the slaves", 117–25, 342
"dancing the treadmill", 323
debauchery, 75, 313
débauches, 52–57
depression, 41, 122, 343
deprivation (cognitive), 14, 18, 307, 308
derision, 258, 276, 288, 289, 299, 306, 320, 322
desensitization, 162–63, 335
dishonour, 3, 27, 28, 30, 72
disinformation, 315
disposition, 39, 342, 351
divide and rule policy, 15, 192, 344
divisiveness (singing/dancing), 276, 344–45
dolce farniente lifestyle, 68, 95, 98
dominance, 1, 2, 3, 10, 13, 15, 18, 19, 104, 177, 195, 291, 314, 320, 333, 347–49

drama, 83, 97, 99–101, 102, 104, 165, 168, 174, 184, 208, 246, 280, 296
dress colours: fondness for, 195–96. *See also* colours
dressing up, 59, 124, 155, 179, 185, 187, 195, 209, 210, 213, 222, 340
drunkenness, 53, 54, 56, 57, 59, 60, 61, 62, 63, 65, 66, 67, 166, 202, 203, 291
duplicity, 8, 321, 323

"education in the heels", 105–10
epic (national), 5, 13
Europeanization, 39–40, 42, 135, 136, 145, 164, 181, 283, 294, 301
exceptionalism, 288, 326, 327
excursions, 94, 95, 215, 216, 217, 329

family, 14, 18, 19, 85, 156, 157, 318, 319, 349
farce, 100, 101, 208
favouritism, 221, 321, 344
feasts: African, 189; Christian, 98, 178, 332; indigenous, 57, 63; Jewish, 151–53; "negro", 132, 158, 216; pagan, 96, 168, 231; rural, 93–95, 215, 329
festivals: Adonia, 183–85; African, 113, 267; Calends, 231; Carib, 48; carnival, 12, 178, 182, 223, 346; Congo, 190; crop-over, 152, 339; funeral, 160, 162, 163; Joan and John, 242; Loiza, 203; *maracatu*, 192; May Day, 200; "negro", 139, 149, 152, 216, 227, 266, 289, 294, 295, 296, 324; Our Lady of the Rosary, 191, 192; tourism, 348; Yam, 203, 331
festivity: crop time, 150, 151, 152, 279; venues, 34, 109, 148, 149, 244, 339, 340

flamboyance, 194, 196, 247, 248
French Revolution: influence of, 185–86
French Set-Girls, 210, 211, 247
frenzy, 65, 236, 237, 241, 340, 341, 343
friendly society, 345
friendship, 54, 61, 92, 123, 157, 158, 159, 162, 217, 265, 316, 318
frivolity, 1, 20, 25, 112, 161, 209, 287, 320, 329, 330, 350, 352
funerals: African, 115, 159; indigenous, 48–49, 54, 55, 56, 62, 114–15; "negro", 147, 157–63, 164, 166, 168, 173–74, 224, 236, 237, 241, 264, 267, 323, 331, 335, 336, 337, 344; other, 336
fusion of cultures, 80, 351

generational changes, 235, 258
"getting religion", 334
golden age of man, 311
gratification, 271, 329
green (colour) Irish, 79, 210
gregariousness, 318, 324, 345
griot, 115, 269
grotesque male character, 201–7, 346
guatiao, 316, 318, 351
guilds, 187

Haitian influence, 79, 80, 92, 185, 195, 198, 210, 211, 219, 333
happy slave image, 131, 134–46, 286, 301
headdress (indigenous), 57, 58
heritage, 73, 110, 204, 214, 227, 302, 319, 349
hero/heroic/heroism, 11, 28, 55, 206, 211, 266, 296, 298, 349
homeland, 111, 159, 160, 236, 306, 322, 336
honour: achievement, 4, 10, 27, 28,

32, 202, 215, 308, 312, 316, 320, 326, 346; competition, 321; death, 18, 28, 72, 92, 166, 304, 337, 348, 349; fighting, 1, 3, 11, 215; vs happiness, 3, 6, 8, 9–30; power, 265, 327
hostesses, 108, 109–10

images distortion, 122, 140, 309–15
imagination: artistic, 59, 213, 270; evolution, 38; happiness, 323, 324; perception, 21; in play, 26, 29, 163, 166, 177; popular, 353; of reality, 72, 115, 160, 309, 311; role, 29, 35, 353
improvement, 220, 321
independence, 15, 18, 20, 74, 100, 130, 185, 215, 324, 330, 348
indigenous image: cannibal, 52, 58, 59, 67, 72, 316; drunken, 53, 54, 57, 59, 60, 62, 63, 65, 66; noble savage, 60, 72, 311
influences on festivity: asceticism, 283, 333; Catholic Church, 98, 186, 187, 188, 192, 203, 222, 223, 332, 333, 334; indentured servants, 78, 80, 96, 170, 317; missionaries, 7, 70, 126, 127, 208, 220
interracial mixture, 108, 240, 345
inversion, 96, 153, 155, 158, 184, 185, 195, 205, 222, 223, 324

John Bull, 142, 143, 144, 145, 291, 321
John Connu, 201–7, 218, 222, 267, 346; house boat, 205; John Canoe, 205, 213; John Connú, 202; John Conny, 202; Joncanoe, 206, 217, 218; Jonkanoo, 104, 205, 206; Noah, 205
Johnny Newcome, 103, 104
journeys, 13, 202, 215, 216, 335, 336

king: black, 190, 191; mock, 168, 190
kokorioko, 201, 203, 204

landship, 214, 345
language games, 320
laws (anti-entertainment), 127, 129, 161, 341
legacy (indigenous), 68–73
liberated Africans, 5, 212

macaroni image, 76, 77
make-believe, 323, 324
march of intellect, 220, 334
Maroons, 15, 166, 167, 176, 329
masks, 3, 58, 97, 98, 126, 182, 186, 191, 201, 202, 203, 204, 205, 206, 207, 216, 217, 235, 321, 343, 346
masque, 97, 98, 333
masquerade, 55, 56, 57– 59, 61, 68, 96, 97, 185, 190, 204, 329
masquerade, 97, 99, 201–7, 216, 267
matelot, 317, 318
May Day. *See* celebrations
mentality: artists' intellect, 133, 134, 330; Christian, 302; *conquista*, 312; creole vs foreign, 81; frontier, 45, 83, 84, 86, 313; "negro", 135, 270; "no problem, man", 310, 351; Sisyphus, 319; warrior, 8, 58, 60, 65, 66, 72, 302, 349, 353
middle passage, 101, 102, 117, 119, 120, 121, 125, 200, 275, 283, 317, 320, 336
military pageantry, 214–15; uniforms, 84, 211, 212, 213, 214, 222
misrepresentation, 308, 313, 314
mobility/movement, 48, 61, 66, 215
morris dancing, 99, 200, 209
motion/rest (Plato), 31, 33, 314, 340, 342
mortality rate, 151, 157, 160, 162, 167, 172, 177, 241, 319

mummery/mumming, 20, 80, 99, 101, 169, 170, 184, 206, 207, 208, 209, 333
music: African, 5, 22, 113, 114, 115, 157, 163, 238, 265–69, 316, 323; Caribbean, 11, 12–13, 140, 316, 328, 340; Creole, 89, 107, 244; dance, 90, 247, 257; death/funeral, 161, 164, 165; in education, 31, 32, 87, 92; English, 77, 99, 279; ethnicity and, 131–34, 163, 281–82, 308, 310, 319, 323, 326, 335; European, 22, 78, 80, 283; happiness/joy, 8, 43, 312, 313, 319, 330, 344; indigenous, 49, 51, 52, 53, 55, 56, 58, 60, 70–71, 315, 331; innate, 34, 35, 36, 263; party, 180, 181, 198, 205; power in, 42, 43, 308; "proper"/formal, 83, 87, 91, 92, 93, 94, 294; reggae, 11, 11n, 12, 13; religious, 33, 34, 35; slave~white, 89, 106, 131, 135, 141, 237, 264, 300; Spanish, 80; variation in cultures, 34, 40, 43–45
musical people, 91, 330, 331

nannies, 87–88, 257
national character, 38, 39
natural ability, 131, 323, 328, 351; condition, 25, 33; difference, 23; disposition, 3, 39, 255, 342; dominance, 10; expression, 42, 133; generational transfer, 133, 235; gift, 131, 132, 323, 327, 344
"negro" diversions, 157, 175, 188
noble savage, 60, 72, 311

otherness (desire for), 104, 339
ouicou/vin (drunken party), 54, 62–63

pagan(ism), 43, 95, 96, 98, 99, 165, 166, 178, 183, 190, 223, 332, 333, 334, 341, 346
pantomime, 72, 101, 102, 173, 206, 329
parades: carnival, 222, 346; convoys/regiments, 182, 187; Corpus Christi, 193, 194; girls, 180, 197–200, 212, 213, 214, 217; John Connu, 202–7; liberated Africans, 212; organized labour, 187; race and class in, 218; royal court, 188–96; soldiers and sailors, 215; St Patrick's Day, 79, 210; Three Kings, 201
parody, 296
party: as activism, 185–87; African, 267; description, 171, 196–98, 200, 217; etymology, 179, 196–98; financial support, 220, 221; housewarming, 148, 171; indigenous, 54; maroon, 94, 95, 215, 216, 329; "negro", 169, 179–81, 295; racial divisions, 218–19; slave, 140; variety, 221; white, 85, 90
partner: dancing, 98, 103, 136, 142, 239, 243, 249, 259, 261; economic, 317
peer-group society, 284, 318, 319, 320, 334–35, 342, 344
personality (slave), 16–18
plagiarism. *See* copying
"play" (slave): usage, 168–75; concept, 175–77
play-day, 138, 174
playing mas, 12, 30, 97
playing the game, 316, 321
prejudice, 42, 59, 78, 313
propaganda (abolition), 101, 142, 216, 293, 309
punishment, 15, 19, 122, 289, 309, 311, 323, 352

quality balls. *See* balls, mulatto

rejoicing, 61, 62, 64, 147, 152, 156, 157, 159, 160, 161, 162
religion of the future, 29
reparation, 134, 142, 145, 291, 311
responsibility for self, 348, 350
retaliation, 275, 321
revels/revelry, 53, 54, 96, 170, 179, 313, 333
revolutionary spirit, 185–86, 223, 291, 304, 331,
rhythm: aesthetic formation, 31; African, 315, 316; animal pleasure, 23; character, 310; community building, 41, 324, 345; human life, 25; indigenous, 59; music, 44, 238, 301; musicality, 35; "negro", 131, 309; slave dance, 225, 226, 250; songs, 272, 300; work, 274, 275, 323, 351
ridicule, 2, 8, 143, 258, 288, 289, 291, 347
rites, 48, 98, 156, 158, 160, 162, 163, 167, 185, 196, 201, 234, 335
ritual, 1, 20, 23, 43, 51, 58, 61, 99, 101, 102, 156, 162, 168, 185, 198, 199, 203, 227, 261, 280, 331, 333, 334, 335, 337, 341
rivalry, 15, 179, 183, 210, 211, 212, 214, 221, 222, 296, 345

sanctity, 147, 178, 225
sartorial elegance, 196, 199, 201, 205, 213
satire, 7–8, 103, 140, 143, 145, 259, 276, 288–91, 305, 309, 323, 345, 347
Saturnalia, 95–96, 153, 185, 204, 205, 324, 345
scare tactics, 311
scars of music and dancing, 323

scoffing matches, 321–22
seasonal changes, 3, 98, 183, 184, 332
seasoning process, 125, 265, 345
selection process, 83, 91, 124, 181, 197, 198, 199, 218, 267, 269, 273, 319, 320, 321, 339, 344
self-preservation. *See* acquiescence
serenade, 83, 92–93, 329
sets/set girls, 90, 92, 93, 178, 196–200, 201, 202, 206, 210, 211, 212, 213, 214, 216, 217, 218, 219, 244, 247, 267, 273, 294, 345
sex, 16, 33, 44, 51, 58, 69, 83, 102, 103, 104, 105, 107, 108, 109, 170, 199, 220, 234, 236, 297, 303, 306, 334, 338, 347
sexuality, 57, 225, 230, 238, 241, 261, 303, 329, 338
shipmate/*batimens*, 117, 148, 317–18, 320, 322, 336, 345
singing: as acquiescence, 2, 276, 349; African vs creole, 264–69; as art, 33, 44, 51, 77, 273, 275, 277, 278, 280, 303, 307, 325; call-and-response, 69, 261, 278, 279, 280; choral, 50, 136, 217, 267, 275, 276, 277, 278, 286, 292, 295, 297, 301, 302; church, 281–82, 343, 344, 345; in formal schooling, 281, 297, 323; loudness, 122, 264, 265, 267, 282, 283, 306; as natural, 131–34, 327, 345; in religious education, 280–83; while working, 75, 132, 151, 272, 274, 275, 278, 279, 281, 286, 344, 351
"singing race", 132, 263, 302, 322, 327, 342
"singing the slaves", 117, 121, 122, 274
slave: behind the door, 104; coronations, 168, 190, 194–95; outside looking in, 258

slave songs: blues/melancholy, 3, 13, 267, 283–87, 305, 323–24; genuine, 285, 293, 298, 299, 300, 301; impromptu, 177, 269, 270; improvisation, 177, 269–71, 277, 353; liberation, 291–93; repertoire expansion, 271, 294–97; social commentary, 277, 288, 289, 302; structural simplicity, 271–73, 289, 301, 303; work, 264, 272, 274, 275, 276, 277, 278, 279, 280, 286; yo-yo, 123, 265
snobbery in classification, 32
social skills: and play, 23; slaves, 262; whites, 329
societies (St Lucia), 182, 183, 185, 193, 211, 214, 222
soundness (for sale), 122, 123, 124, 319, 322, 342, 344
spiritual: development, 19; medicine, 342; renewal, 184; transformation, 29
spirituality, 13, 177, 184, 280, 332, 337
stamina, 225, 227, 322
stick fighting/*kalenda*, 260
storytelling, 44, 139, 264, 282, 286, 287, 300, 314, 324
sublimation, 337
suicide, 28, 72, 321, 344, 346, 349, 350, 353

tea meetings/soirées, 282–83
theatre, 5, 99, 100, 175, 190, 279, 332, 333, 335, 353

therapy (music and dance), 42, 85, 117, 343
tourism, 1, 11, 12, 79, 309, 346, 348, 352
tradition/traditional culture: African, 19, 147, 153, 156, 157, 158, 161, 166, 189, 190, 192, 203, 218, 223, 224, 228, 257, 258, 269, 288, 331, 335, 348; British, 77, 79, 153, 198, 206, 207, 209, 332–33; Christian, 17, 98, 155, 192, 222, 232, 319; European, 42, 50, 75, 79, 95, 96, 99, 104, 136, 153, 168, 183, 186, 190, 200, 207, 301; French, 70; indigenous, 60, 64, 115, 269
transition outdoor to indoor, 103, 104, 149, 154, 174, 199, 259, 283, 340

uniformity in dress, 180, 199, 212, 213

Victorian morality, 40, 334
vin. See *ouicou*
virtuosity, 5, 324, 326

wake, 79, 158, 161, 164, 171, 173, 174
water jumps, 336
wealth, 13, 37, 68, 75, 77, 101, 102, 176, 221, 313
well-being, 13, 102, 149, 151, 275, 309, 320, 345, 347, 351, 353
winty-play, 166–67, 176

Yam Custom/festival, 151, 153, 154, 203, 331

www.ingramcontent.com/pod-product-compliance
Lightning Source LLC
Chambersburg PA
CBHW021815300426
44114CB00009BA/189